BY THE AUTO EDITORS OF CONSUMER GUIDE®

Ford
1903 to 1984

DAVID L. LEWIS
MIKE McCARVILLE
LORIN SORENSEN

BEEKMAN HOUSE
NEW YORK

Louis Weber, President
Publications International, Ltd.
3841 West Oakton Street
Skokie, Illinois 60076

Permission is never granted for commercial purposes.

Library of Congress Catalog Card Number: 83-62121

ISBN: 0-517-41443-0

This edition published by:
Beekman House
A Division of Crown Publishers, Inc.
One Park Avenue
New York, N.Y. 10016
By arrangement with Publications International, Ltd.

Manufactured in the United States of America
10 9 8 7 6 5 4 3 2 1

Principal Authors
David L. Lewis
Mike McCarville
Chris Poole
Lorin Sorensen

Photo Credits
William L. Bailey
Ford Archives, Henry Ford Museum
Ford Motor Company Photomedia Department
David Gooley
Bud Juneau
Richard M. Langworth
David L. Lewis
Doug Mitchel
Lorin Sorensen
Nicky Wright

Acknowledgements and Bibliographic Notes
The authors and editors acknowledge with thanks the many
individuals and organizations whose timely and generous
contributions helped to make this book possible.

Portions of the commentary on model years 1930 to 1969
are excerpted from the following titles previously issued by
CONSUMER GUIDE® Publications: *Cars of the '30s, Great
Cars from Ford, Mustang: The Original Ponycar,* and
Prototype Cars: Cars That Never Were (principal author
Richard M. Langworth) and *Muscle Cars* (principal author
Phil Hall).

Major reference sources include: *Illustrated History of Ford
1903-1970* by George H. Dammann, *Fearsome Fords 1959-1973*
by Phil Hall, *Personal-Luxury: The Thunderbird Story* by
Richard M. Langworth, and *Ford in the Thirties* by Paul R.
Woudenberg. Production figures cited are drawn from
CONSUMER GUIDE® Publications' *The Encyclopedia of
American Cars 1940-1970* and from *The Production Figure
Book for U.S. Cars* by Jerry Heasley.

Contents

Introduction

Ford's founder: colorful, controversial—and a genuine folk hero

Henry Ford, circa 1910   courtesy Ford Archives, Ford Museum

Henry Ford, the founder of Ford Motor Company and the driving force behind the firm and its products for more than four decades, made an extraordinary impact on the American scene. Several of his most notable accomplishments—the Model T, institution of mass-production methods, and his wage-price practices—revolutionized industry and society as a whole not just in America, but around the world.

A true folk hero, Ford was an appealing figure to millions of his fellow citizens. He was viewed as one who succeeded through his own creativeness and hard work, and by supplying a product to meet the public's desires rather than manipulating money or people. He also was admired, despite his great wealth, for having retained the common touch. Asked on his 50th birthday to cite the greatest handicap of the rich, he replied, "For me, it was when Mrs. Ford stopped cooking." Regarded as an industrial superman and widely believed to typify American civilization and genius, he nevertheless reminded many people of an earlier, simpler time.

Ford was a late starter: for him life began at 40. Born in 1863, he was unknown outside Detroit until 1901, when his racing exploits put his name on the sports pages. He made two false starts as an auto manufacturer before founding the Ford Motor Company in 1903. Within a decade he had become fabulously wealthy and the auto industry's dominant figure. In the process, he also gained a measure of national prominence. In 1914, at age 51, he became an overnight international celebrity by more than doubling the wages of most of his workers. Ford's prime extended into his late 60s, and perhaps would have lasted longer had it not been for the Great Depression. Even so, he remained vigorous, and continued to guide and personify his company well into his 70s.

Controversial, paradoxical and always colorful, Henry Ford was an enigma, endlessly fascinating. An idealistic pioneer in some respects, he was a cynical reactionary in others. He had a selfish, mean, even cruel streak, yet he was often generous, kindly, and compassionate. He was ignorant, narrow-minded, and stubborn, yet at times he displayed remarkable insight, vision, open-mindedness, and flexibility. His mercurial, chameleon-like personality baffled his associates. "History," he once proclaimed, "is more or less bunk." He then proceeded to build Greenfield Village, a depository of Americana. He constructed the world's biggest factory, yet found delight in building hydroelectric plants that employed as few as 11 workers. He did not believe in organized charity, yet gave millions to good works. The list can go on and on.

How, one must ask, could a man like this rise to such greatness? Part of the answer is that Ford possessed several outstanding qualities. He had native intelligence and common sense (even though the latter occasionally failed him), an intuitive mind that leaped beyond the present, a special engineering talent that combined creativity with practicality, a remarkable memory, a missionary's zeal, and a lifelong capacity for hard work (especially thinking, which he termed "the hardest work there is"). He shunned the conventional vices. He also had, or made, his share of good luck. His entry into automaking and the introduction of his Model T were both perfectly timed. He was teamed, by accident, with James Couzens, who contributed enormously to Ford Motor Company's early success.

His personal life also played a part. Ford married a woman who understood and complemented him well. Clara Bryant, like Henry, was born on a farm in the Dearborn area. Three years younger than her husband, she was convinced from the time they were wed, in 1888, that her husband would accomplish great things. Ford called her "The Believer." Clara encouraged and stood by her husband for a remarkable 59 years.

Henry and Clara had but one son, Edsel, born in 1893.

Edsel grew up with the Ford company and, although named president of the firm in 1918, would always remain in his father's shadow. Competent and respected, he gradually gained responsibility for styling, sales, and advertising—but never for labor relations, engineering, or manufacturing. Edsel and his wife Eleanor Clay (born in 1896 into a socially prominent Detroit family) had four children between 1917 and 1925: Henry II, Benson, Josephine, and William Clay. Henry II administered the company from 1945 until his retirement as chairman in 1980. Benson served as vice-president and general manager of Lincoln-Mercury Division in 1948-55 and as chairman of Ford's Dealer Policy Board from 1956 until his death in 1978. William Clay Ford is currently the company's vice-chairman.

Fourth-generation Fords (including Edsel II, son of Henry II, and William Clay's son, William Clay Jr.) are now rising within the company. However, it's unclear whether another family member will ever rise to run the company. The Ford family still maintains control of the firm, holding 40 percent of the voting shares, and can install one of its own at will. But the stakes are too high to promote anyone but a highly qualified person to the post

courtesy Ford Archives, Ford Museum

Henry and Quadricycle, 1899

Introduction

of president or chairman. Henry II has said many times that family members will have to earn higher positions like anyone else.

As for Henry Ford Senior, he left a magnificent legacy. Idolized by many Americans during his lifetime, he remains a legendary figure to this day. Millions drive vehicles bearing his name; additional millions see the name "Ford" daily on cars and trucks and in advertisements. The company invariably invokes his memory during anniversaries and milestone celebrations despite the mutterings of a few executives that "ancient history and Model T talk don't sell cars." But the company can scarcely do otherwise, so closely intertwined is its history with Ford's life.

Among the more tangible reminders of the Ford legacy are an estimated 300,000 surviving Model Ts, much larger numbers of Model As and early Ford V-8 models, and lesser numbers of Mercurys, Lincolns, Lincoln-Zephyrs and Continentals, all produced during the auto magnate's lifetime. Many of these cars have been viewed in museums by millions of people; many others are displayed in parades and tours and at old-car meets. Most of these carefully preserved vehicles, whether owned by individuals or museums, seem likely to outlast the massive plants in which they were built.

As the years pass and our vision of the man blurs somewhat, it is likely Henry Ford will be best remembered for his singular contribution to the industrial revolution. By promoting high-volume production, low prices, and universal consumption, he became the key figure in a process more far-reaching than putting a car in every garage. He and his Model T, and the mass production methods by which it was built, actually helped remold the world.

Of his company, Ford said to Edsel one day, "Well, we'll build this as well as we know how, and if we don't use it, somebody will. Anything that is good enough will be used." Because of its founder, the Ford Motor Company today has as rich and valuable a heritage as any commercial organization on earth, perhaps richer than any other. Henry Ford obviously built well.

Henry and Clara out for a spin in the Quadricycle, circa 1920

1896-1902

Quadricycles and early racing success launch Henry Ford as an automaker

Henry's first car, photographed prior to restoration in the '50s

In the winter of 1895-96, a hopeful 32-year-old inventor named Henry Ford struggled to build his first car. On June 4, 1896, he drove his "quadricycle," as he called it, through the streets of Detroit. This initial run of the little vehicle went unreported in the local newspapers, Ford having neither publicly announced a demonstration nor made a photograph or description of his car available to any publication.

Ford sold his first car, then turned to building a second. The work went slowly, and it was carried on pretty much anonymously. The first reference to Henry Ford in an automotive context appeared in the November 1898 edition of *Horseless Age* under the heading "Minor Mention":

"Henry Ford, of Detroit, Mich., chief engineer of the Edison Electric Light Co. of that city, has built a number of gasoline vehicles which are said to have been successfully operated. He is reported to be financially supported by several prominent men of the city, who intend to manufacture the Ford vehicle. From Mr. Ford himself no information can be gleaned regarding his vehicles or his plans for their manufacture."

Ford's second car (the *Horseless Age* item had over-

stated the number built) was working in the summer of 1899, and led to his first press interview and an accompanying photo feature in the July 29th edition of the Detroit *Journal.* A week later, largely on the strength of a success-

The working end of Henry Ford's 1896 Quadricycle

The restored Quadricycle as displayed today at Greenfield Village

courtesy Ford Archives, Ford Museum

ful demonstration given by Ford to a wealthy Detroit lumberman, the Detroit Automobile Company was organized. Ford was given a small share of stock in the concern and was named its superintendent.

In early February 1900, Ford again demonstrated his

A dapper young Henry poses with Quadricycle, circa 1898

car's capabilities, this time to a reporter for the Detroit *News-Tribune*. Normally shy with strangers, Ford was at home behind the tiller, and he proved as loquacious as a snake-oil salesman. The rollicking three-column story that followed—headlined "Swifter Than A Race-Horse It Flew Over The Ice Streets"—provides the first inkling that Ford would one day have an easy way with reporters.

Whatever their virtues, the cars produced by the Detroit Automobile Company did not sell. Apparently, Ford wanted to improve the model, but the company's stockholders vetoed the suggestion. The firm slowly ground to a halt in late 1900.

Ford and his assistants spent the spring and summer of 1901 building a race car. By fall, a trim, light, 26-horse-power machine was ready. Its first test came at the Grosse Pointe race track, near Detroit, on October 10th. Several of the nation's outstanding drivers, including Alexander Winton, were on hand. Ford's machine was entered in the 10-mile sweepstakes event, in which Winton was heavily favored. The champion's sales manager, Charles B. Shanks, was so confident of his employer's victory that he had picked as the prize a beautiful punch bowl, which he thought would look good in the bay window of the Winton dining room.

Winton and Ford were the only starters in the main

event. (A third competitor, William N. Murray, Pittsburgh millionaire and owner of one of the fastest cars in the country, withdrew because of mechanical difficulties.) Winton was on the inside, and his deftness in rounding curves enabled him to open up a ⅕-mile lead at the three-mile mark (Ford had to shut off power and run wide on each curve). Midway through the race, Ford picked up lost ground on the straightaways, and by the sixth lap had improved his position perceptibly. As the crowd urged Ford on, Winton began to have trouble with over-heated bearings. Shanks, riding with him, drenched the bearings with oil, but to no avail. Ford shot ahead on the eighth lap and swept across the finish line well ahead of the faltering champion. His average speed: 43.5 miles per hour.

This victory brought Henry Ford national attention, which in turn provided the impetus for formation of a new company. A number of prominent Detroiters, including several former stockholders of the Detroit Automobile Company, had seen the triumph and were fired by the commercial possibilities of the Ford machine. Accordingly, they organized the Henry Ford Company on November 30, 1901, the name itself a tribute to Ford's newly won reputation. Ford was given a one-sixth share in the new firm and the post of chief engineer. But Ford's continued preoccupation with racing quickly produced friction between him and the other stockholders. He left after only three months, taking with him a $900 settlement and the uncompleted drawings for a new racing car. The company agreed to discontinue the use of his name.

By early May 1902, Ford had joined forces with Tom Cooper, a former bicycle champion who also had racing fever. With Cooper's money and Ford's know-how, the two men were able to build two 80-horsepower monsters, dubbed "Arrow" and "999," the latter named after a record-breaking New York Central train. "There was only

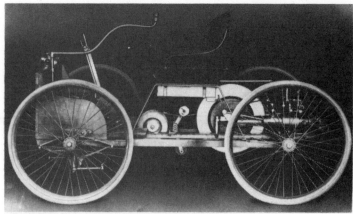

The 1896 Quadricycle: an elegantly simple machine

Henry Ford's second car was this 1898 four-wheeler

one seat," Ford would recall later. "One life to a car was enough. I tried out the cars. Cooper tried out the cars. We let them out at full speed...Going over Niagara Falls would have been but a pastime after a ride in one of them." Neither Ford nor Cooper had the nerve to drive

Daredevil driver Barney Oldfield takes the helm of "999" in 1902

the cars in competition. Cooper, however, said that he knew a man "who lived on speed, that nothing could go too fast for him." A wire to Salt Lake City secured the services of one Barney Oldfield, then a professional bicycle rider. Oldfield had never driven a car, but said he would try anything once. He learned quickly, and proved fearless.

Oldfield was primed for the five-mile Manufacturers' Challenge Cup, which was held at the Grosse Pointe track on October 25, 1902. Four drivers started, Winton and Shanks among them. Oldfield opened up the "999" immediately, was never headed, and defeated runner-up Shanks by a lap. The time was 5 minutes, 28 seconds—not quite a mile-a-minute record he had said he would aim for a year earlier, but an American record nevertheless. Once again, Ford's name resounded in the press, and Oldfield was launched on his career as one of America's greatest race

drivers. It also marked the end of Ford's preoccupation with racing. For purposes of advertising he would set a world's speed record two years later and his cars would race until 1912. But with his reputation firmly established, he was now able to turn to his life's work, "putting a 'family horse'" on the market.

Meantime, on August 20, 1902, Ford and Alexander Y. Malcomson, a Detroit coal dealer, signed an agreement to develop a commerical automobile. In November they carried their partnership a step further by organizing The Ford & Malcomson Company, Ltd., and offering shares for sale. By the following June, 10 investors had joined them, and on June 16, 1903 the Ford Motor Company was incorporated with a paid-in capital of $28,000. Henry Ford, who contributed his patents, his engine, and his knowledge to the new enterprise, was awarded a 25.5 percent interest.

1903

A fledgling Ford company presents its first car, while Henry goes to court

---

The first production Ford, the 1903 Model A (right) and Henry Leland's first Cadillac, which bowed that year

Ford Motor Company was launched with a minimum of fanfare. It made no apparent attempt to win publicity for itself or the car it was putting on the market, the Model A. Detroit's three daily newspapers were unaware of the firm's incorporation until three days after the event, and even then the news was buried in brief stories on their back pages. *Horseless Age* devoted a few lines to a rumor that the "Ford Automobile Company will build a factory at Pontiac." *Motor Age* told its readers—in one paragraph—that the company would place a "Fordmobile" on the market. *Cycle and Automobile Trade Journal*

ran a longer, more factual story since, by coincidence, its June issue featured the automotive industry in Detroit. *Automobile* and *Automobile Topics* ignored the new firm completely.

Of course, even if the fledgling concern had tried to garner press notice it's doubtful it would have received much. Ford was but one of 15 Michigan companies and one of 88 firms in the nation introducing automobiles in 1903, and neither the amount of its capitalization nor its prospects for success were particularly noteworthy.

The first production Ford car, the Model A, had the

Detachable rear tonneau made the 1903 Model A runabout into a four-seater.

The 1903 Model A pauses in front of the Greenfield Village general store.

great merits of simplicity, lightness, and efficiency. Its principal innovation was a two-cylinder opposed engine that developed eight horsepower and, on good roads, could produce speeds up to 30 mph. Wheelbase of the little runabout measured just 72 inches. As in most other horseless carriages of the period, the steering wheel was on the right. The driver opened no door, but simply slid into his seat, his whole body in full view. The car had no running boards and stood high above the street. The passenger thus had to contend with a small, sharp, sometimes slippery carriage step. The transmission, then often called the "change-gear," was of the planetary type, with two speeds forward and one reverse. Both ignition and throttle were adjusted by hand, the former getting its spark from two sets of six dry-cell batteries. The tonneau or back seat attachment was slipped on and off from the rear. The complete car weighed only 1250 pounds, in line with Henry Ford's insistence that weight had no relation to strength. "The car that I designed was lighter than any car that had yet been made," he later declared. "It would have been lighter had I known how to make it so."

"This new, light touring car fills the demand for an automobile between a runabout and a heavy touring car,"

declared one of the early advertisements. "It is positively the most perfect machine on the market, having overcome all drawbacks such as smell, noise, jolt, etc. common to all other makes of auto carriages." Such boasts notwithstanding, a great many faults had to be eliminated. Radiators, for example, were so inadequate that the engine got hot enough to boil its cooling water even when the car was run in high gear on a level road. The first carburetors were inefficient, and there were brake problems. The splash lubrication system needed excessive amounts of oil, the circulating pump was inefficient, and the spark plugs became dirty because oil leaked past the piston rings. Transmissions provoked complaint because their bands slipped. But every early auto manufacturer had such difficulties. Ford tinkered and replaced, and after six months the Model A was running smoothly.

The soon-to-be famous Ford script was used as the new company's symbol right from the start. It was provided by one of Henry Ford's first associates, C.H. Wills, who would later build the Wills St. Claire car. As a boy of 15 or 16, Wills had earned some money by making calling cards, which he lettered in flowing script. When the company first grappled with advertising, nobody was satis-

Rear passengers entered through "back door" on tonneau of the 1903 Model A.

With its two-cylinder opposed engine, the 1903 Model A could run up to 30 mph.

fied with the appearance of the name Ford. Wills rummaged an attic for his old printing outfit and wrote out F-O-R-D in its now-familiar style. The design was immediately accepted and endured until the post-World War II era, when it was replaced by block letters. In the 1960s, the flowing script was revived, framed in an oval against a blue background, and is in worldwide use today.

From the outset Ford Motor Company could be distinguished from most of the other new automakers of 1903—and, indeed, from many of the established companies in the industry—in that it made money. It netted a total of $36,957 within its first 3½ months, and paid a 10 percent dividend on November 21. Sales were quite respectable: 1708 units for the calendar year. The flow of dividends would continue unabated for the next 23 years and at a phenomenal rate in most of them. In 1903, however, profits were overshadowed by legal entanglements. Ford was the target of litigation, the celebrated Selden case, the outcome of which would affect the pocketbook of everyone who made, sold, or bought an automobile in America.

The Selden suit was filed in 1903 by George B. Selden, a Rochester, New York, attorney, and the Electric Vehicle Company. Selden had obtained a patent for a "road carriage," covering all gasoline-powered vehicles designed since 1879 and manufactured, sold, or used in the United States in the 17-year period ending in 1912. In 1899, Selden had assigned the patent to a firm that became the

Electric Vehicle Company and, by March 1903, most auto companies had been intimidated into acknowledging the validity of the patent. By that summer, 26 firms had formed the Association of Licensed Automobile Manufacturers and struck a deal with the patentholders, agreeing to pay them a royalty of 1.25 percent of the price of each car sold. The Association was given the privilege of selecting the manufacturers to be licensed under the patent

The 1903 Model A with tonneau

15

A signature known round the world

and those to be sued. The latter, presumably, were to be put out of business.

In February and again during the summer of 1903, Henry Ford and his associates approached the acting president of the ALAM about obtaining a license for their fledgling company. They were rebuffed, the ALAM executive expressing a lack of confidence in Ford's ability to meet the Association's manufacturing standards and to qualify as a creditable member of the auto industry. Undeterred, Ford continued to produce and sell cars. Soon, the ALAM warned the company that it and its dealers and customers were subject to prosecution for patent infringement. Ford, in turn, promised his buyers protection against suits. "Our Mr. Ford made the first Gasoline Automobile in Detroit and the third in the United States," the firm's advertising inaccurately proclaimed. "Our Mr. Ford also built the famous '999' Gasoline Automobile, which was driven by Barney Oldfield in New York on July 25, 1903, a mile in 55⅘ seconds, on a circular track, which is the world's record. Mr. Ford, driving his own machine, beat Mr. Winton at Grosse Pointe track in 1901. We have always been winners."

Not surprisingly, the patentholders sued Ford, and by 1907 all the evidence had been submitted to the court. At that point, both sides began an all-out effort to curry public favor. The fireworks centered around the main exhibits presented during the trial. The Seldenites had constructed a motor buggy to demonstrate that a car built in accordance with the patent's specifications would run. Ford insisted the Selden buggy would start only when facing downhill, and demonstrated a machine with an engine resembling one patented by an Englishman in 1869 to refute Selden's claim to originality. Ford also claimed its car traveled four times as far and as fast as the Selden machine, and daringly offered to race a Selden car over 50 miles—giving it a 45-mile head start.

Finally, in 1909, the federal district court in New York ruled in favor of Selden. Henry Ford appealed. "The patent," said the automaker, was "a freak among alleged inventions," and he offered a bond to each buyer, backed by the $12 million assets of the company and its bonding company. To the Detroit *Free Press*, which echoed the sentiments of many of its readers, Ford's stand was heroic. "There's a man for you, a man of backbone," declared an editorial entitled, "Ford the Fighter." "Of the case behind him, the lawyers were more able to talk, but as a human figure he presents a spectacle to win the applause of all men with red blood; for this world dearly loves the fighting man, and needs him, too, if we are to go forward."

The appellate court's decision was handed down on January 9, 1911. This time the victory went to Ford, and it was total. Dozens of telegrams and letters poured into the Ford offices, many from opponents as well as from friends. Every automobile man in the country had the name "Ford" on his lips. For the first time in his life, Henry Ford was front-page news in Detroit and in the trade press. He was lauded on all sides as a giant-killer, as a symbol of revolt against monopoly, and as a magnificent individualist. The victory was of tremendous advertising value to the firm and its then-current Model T. As Ford himself later said, "no one factor publicized the company and its products as effectively as the company's role in liberating an industry."

1904

Putting new speed records on ice, and rules for early Ford dealers

Ford Motor Company entered the 1904-05 selling season—that is, the year beginning in autumn and running through the ensuing spring and summer—with three new models. The Model A gave way to the improved 1250-pound Model C runabout selling at $800 ($900 with tonneau). A new touring car, the 1400-pound Model F, was priced at $1000. Both had Ford's original, but now revised, two-cylinder opposed engine. In an effort to reach wealthy people, the company also introduced a heavier, faster four-cylinder touring car, the Model B, at $2000.

The firm was moving away from, not toward, the $500 car Henry Ford wanted to sell, and this disturbed him. But all these new cars were better than the original Model A. The Model C had 10 horsepower, the Model F had 12, both through greater bore and stroke. They had wheelbases 6 and 12 inches longer, respectively, than the A's;

1903 Model C

The FORD
A Colossus in Strength

Like the **Colossus of Rhodes**, one of the seven wonders of the world, the FORD MOTOR CAR stands today the marvel of the automobile industry.

The FORD is the Colossus of its class in strength, construction and value, and is the greatest thing in the motor world today.

Mr. Henry Ford has spent the best years of his life in perfecting this car. The FORD has sounded the death knell of the Trust with its attempt to make a monopoly of the motor car industry and to charge exhorbitant prices for inferior cars.

Price with Tonneau $900.00
As a Runabout $800.00

The lowest price tonneau car with a double opposed motor sold by the Trust is $1500.00. The Ford saves you $600.00.

We agree to assume all responsibility in any action the *Trust* may take regarding alleged infringement of the Selden Patent to prevent you from buying the FORD—*"The Car of Satisfaction."* Write for illustrated catalogue and name of our nearest agent.

The Ford Motor Co., Detroit, Mich.

Ford ad from Leslie's Weekly, *March 1904. Note references to Henry's battle with the Selden patentholders.*

courtesy Ford Archives, Ford Museum

Henry and son Edsel in a Model F, circa 1905

courtesy Ford Archives, Ford Museum

Henry and "Arrow" on the ice at Lake St. Clair, 1904

and they were more attractively painted. The Model B, with 24 horsepower, could be pushed to a speed of 40 mph. It boasted storage batteries instead of dry cells, a 15-gallon fuel tank, and a weight of 1700 pounds. Of the three newcomers the Model C and Model F did well; demand for the Model B was weaker. Production totals in both 1904 and 1905 lagged behind the new company's first-year pace. Ford built 1695 and 1599 units, respectively.

Ford vehicles were first exhibited at auto shows in New York, Chicago, and five lesser cities in early 1904. From 1905 to 1910 the company exhibited under the auspices of a small group of manufacturers not licensed under the Selden patent. After winning the Selden case in 1911, Henry Ford refused to exhibit in New York City under the aegis of successor associations, a policy he maintained all the way through 1940. The company did participate in trade association auto shows outside New York in 1911-12, then began introducing its new models at private showings in New York and other key cities.

Numerous nonautomotive shows and expositions also attracted the company during its early years. Three cars were displayed in 1904 at the Louisiana Purchase Exposition in St. Louis, and cutaway chassis and engines operated by electricity were featured at industrial shows several years later. Henry Ford's personal interest in rural life was reflected in an exhibition of Model Ts at the New York Land Show (for farmers) in 1911-12.

The Ford company, before establishing branches and dealerships throughout the country, sent out "missionary mechanics" to aid and appease complaining customers. Later, under the watchful eye of sales manager Norval Hawkins, dealers had to provide top-notch service facilities in order to obtain and retain their franchises. Clean, neat places of business, pleasing show windows, and attractive cars for demonstrations were required. Branch roadmen took photographs of dealerships, inside and out, to satisfy the home office that its conditions were being

met. Snapshots were taken of managers and salesmen to ensure their correct and businesslike appearance. Roadmen also kept a constant watch over their franchisees' financial condition and their standing in the community, comparing them with dealers handling other makes.

Early Ford agents were instructed to keep their garages and stockrooms separate from sales and display areas so that prospective consumers would not be able to see cars being ripped apart for repairs—or hear owner complaints.

Chains could not be advertised or sold in dealerships for fear this would suggest the possibility of breakdowns, and at least one branch ordered that malfunctioning cars be towed in only after nightfall, so as to reduce the impact of this "very bad advertisement." Nobody, including customers and visitors, was permitted to smoke in a Ford dealership. Tipping was not tolerated, and acceptance of a gratuity brought instant dismissal. Fresh, clean signs—not faded or soiled ones that "invite breaking of rules"—had to be posted prominently throughout the premises. Strong efforts were made to induce dealers to buy standardized Ford letterheads and outdoor and window signs. Hawkins and James Couzens frequently lectured factory, branch, and dealer personnel to be on their best business behavior at all times, to answer letters promptly, and to "see callers right off."

This concern with customer relations was well founded. Within less than a decade of its incorporation, Ford had grown a vast dealer network, which meant more of its personnel had contact with the public than those of any other automobile or manufacturing company. In fact, Ford probably had more sales outlets (some 7000) and personnel than the rest of the automobile industry combined.

In January 1904, Henry Ford returned to racing to promote the Model B. As a spectacular stroke was needed to give the new car nationwide publicity, Ford announced he would break the world's record for the timed mile with an engine practically identical to the production version. The test was to be made on the cinder-covered ice of Lake St. Clair, northeast of Detroit. On January 9, Ford unofficially ran the distance in 36 seconds, 10 full seconds under the world's record. On January 12, with official timers on hand, he repeated the run in 39⅖ths seconds (91.37 mph). It was, said the Detroit *Tribune*, "the wildest ride in the history of automobiling... Humped over his steering wheel, the tremendous speed throwing the machine in zigzag fashion across the 15-foot roadway, Ford was taking chances that no man, not even that specialist in averted suicide, Barney Oldfield, had dared to tempt."

Ford was very much aware of the dangers, but, as he wrote later, having come this far, there seemed no way out. "The ice seemed smooth enough, so smooth that if I had called off the trial we should have secured an immense amount of the wrong kind of advertising, but instead of being smooth, that ice was seamed with fissures which I knew were going to mean trouble the moment I got up speed. But there was nothing to do but go through with the trial, and I let the old 'Arrow' out. At every fissure the car leaped into the air. I never knew how it was coming down. When I wasn't in the air, I was skidding, but somehow I stayed top side up and on the course, making a record that went all over the world."

Automobile people everywhere were astounded by Ford's performance, regarded as "so sensational that even the most enthusiastic supporters of American speed machines admitted that they would like to see further proof before accepting the figures." Under the headline "Ford's Mile Raises the Dander of the Track Champion," the Detroit *Tribune* pictured Barney Oldfield as green with envy. Dominique Lamberjack, the French champion, flatly stated that the time was an impossibility. A Detroit newspaper, after thoroughly considering the question, decided that it was unlikely that any car would ever travel a faster mile. Eastern officials of the American Automobile Association discounted wire reports, and insisted on seeing affidavits signed by the six timers and two surveyors before admitting the record was even possible. The group's chairman also said that if the time were authentic, it would be put in a special "made on ice" category, a view that incurred the wrath of Detroit newspapers.

On January 20, 1904, Ford's record was made official. Seven days later, William K. Vanderbilt, on the sands of Ormond Beach, Fla., eclipsed it with a run of 39 seconds flat.

The Model B profited only a little from Ford's daring and the ensuing controversy. The press persisted in calling the rebuilt Arrow the 999, even though Ford personally visited the sports desk of each Detroit newspaper to see that the Model B received its full due.

Ford apparently didn't race again in 1904. The following year, however, he attempted to regain the mile speed record on the beach at Cape May, New Jersey, in a new racer, but he could not break 41 seconds. The car was rebuilt, and Ford announced in 1906 that it would do the mile in 30 seconds (120 mph). Despite this claim, it failed to break 40 seconds in exhibitions at Ormond Beach.

Meanwhile, the company's racers were achieving success on midwestern and eastern tracks. The firm entered the lists in 1904, and that year a daring mechanic, Frank Kulick, set light-car records that stood for more than half a dozen years for one, three, four, and five miles. Between 1904 and 1907, Ford racers proved themselves almost invincible in their class, and frequently won contests with larger vehicles in open competition. Probably the most publicized victory was a 24-hour speed-endurance contest won by Kulick and a co-driver over eight other cars at the Michigan State Fairgrounds in mid-1907. Ford ads called the race "the swiftest, maddest driving ever witnessed" and claimed world's records for distances covered in one,

The record-setting "Arrow" racing car as seen today at the Henry Ford Museum

courtesy Ford Archives, Ford Museum

eight, and 24 hours. The company also promoted races among its test drivers and customers on a private track in Highland Park, Michigan, in 1907. Contests were held on alternate Saturdays, and proved popular drawing cards for Detroit-area motorists.

Although racing enjoyed wide popularity in most years before World War I, it came in for considerable criticism between 1905 and 1907. Accidents had become commonplace, and six drivers were killed in 1907 events. Henry Ford and his company had abandoned racing by fall, the founder for good, the firm for almost two years. Kulick, in testing a new racer, went off the Michigan State Fair track at full speed, narrowly escaping death. Shaken by the accident, Henry Ford declared that until the industry could agree on limiting the speed and power of racing vehicles, he and his company would forego the sport. He suggested that maximum cylinder displacement be restricted to 250 cubic inches as a way to permit engineers to show the superiority of their designs and to bring about sane racing. The suggestion fell on deaf ears, however. Machines with engines of up to 600 cid continued to ply American tracks and, with the exception of Barney Oldfield and the Locomobile and Thomas companies, most of the leading drivers and sponsors continued to race.

Ford apparently had another reason to quit racing: his cars had virtually run out of competition in their low-price, lightweight category. In explaining the move, the *Ford Times* could grumble with considerable justification, "After we had beaten all the one and two-lungers and other low-priced cars, what good would the victory do us?"

Nonetheless, Ford's decision was sharply criticized by dealers, who had come to rely heavily on the racing prowess of the Ford car in their advertising. Since 1904, many dealers had entered contests themselves. Now they felt the need to intensify their efforts in order to keep pace with the competition. The *Ford Times*, fully aware of racing's promotional value, sympathetically chronicled all Ford victories so that dealers could list them in their ads. The publication also devoted considerable attention to Ford's racing triumphs in Europe, where branches were not bound by the policy.

1905

A sign of success: moving to a larger plant, birthplace of the Model T

The Ford model trio continued basically unchanged in 1905. However, production was shifted from the original plant on Mack Avenue, a converted wagon shop, to a new factory on Piquette Avenue 10 times larger. The main building (a power plant, paint shop, and testing house stood near it) occupied a site 402 by 56 feet, and stood three stories tall. This plant served as Ford's principal manufacturing facility until superceded by the Highland Park factory in 1910.

The Piquette plant not only produced a variety of pre-T Fords, it was also the place where the Model T was conceived and first built. Ironically, a Michigan Historical Commission marker designates the Highland Park factory as "The Home of the Model T," while the older plant remains unmarked. The Piquette plant, later used for E-M-F and Studebaker production, still stands.

The Mack plant, destroyed decades ago by fire, was located in what is now the heart of Detroit's black community. A scaled-down reproduction of it, ordered by Henry Ford, stands in Dearborn's outdoor historical museum, Greenfield Village. Another, mobile replica was built by Metro Detroit Ford Dealers for the company's 75th anniversary in 1978, and appeared in many parades. No historical marker designates the site of the Mack plant.

1906-07

Henry takes over, while more and more Americans "watch the Fords go by"

The four-cylinder Model N, progenitor of the Model T, was introduced for the 1906-07 selling season. It was a much better design than its predecessors. It was, in fact, one of the best-designed cars yet seen in the United States. A compact, 1050-pound vehicle powered by a 15-horsepower four-cylinder engine, it could go 45 mph and deliver up to 20 miles per gallon. And the price was right: $600. If still reminiscent of the buggy in the lines of its folding top and two-passenger body, the Model N was nevertheless trim and dashing. The engine was placed in front under a nickeled hood. Two handsome nickeled lamps adorned the radiator, and there were two more on the dashboard. Wheels were nestled under short mudguards, and the short fenders were brightly polished. Comparing favorably in appearance with the smarter models of its day, the N offered remarkable value for the money.

The N was greeted with a burst of enthusiasm, reflected in a prodigious jump in sales. From just under 1600 cars the previous year, Ford's calendar 1906 output soared more than five-fold to 8729. "This car," declared the *Cycle and Automobile Trade Journal*, "is distinctly the most important mechanical traction event of 1906."

Beside the N, Ford introduced two other new light models during this period: the slightly costlier Model R— "a car of more pretentious appearance," as the company put it—and the model S, a further refinement. Both were better-looking than the N, and had slight differences—a footboard instead of a small carriage step and a mechanical oiler instead of a force-feed oiler. The Model S also had a single-seat tonneau at the rear. The N, R, and S all disappeared from Ford showrooms as the first of the Model Ts arrived. The S was the last pre-T model and conse-

The 1906-07 Model R as it appeared when new

A restored example of the 1906-07 Model R

Models R and S in the finishing yard at Ford's Piquette Avenue plant

quently the last Ford with right-hand drive.

Meantime, Ford introduced the six-cylinder Model K, a slightly improved replacement for the Model B, weighing a ton and priced at $2800. The very idea behind the K divided Henry Ford and his chief partner. Alexander Malcomson was a strong advocate of high-priced luxury cars, while Henry wanted a $500 product for the masses.

This plus Malcomson's sizable investment in a rival auto company led to a split. In July 1906, Ford bought Malcomson's quarter-interest in the Ford company, and also became president, succeeding banker John S. Gray, who died that month.

Ford and James Couzens also bought out three other shareholders in 1906-07, by which time Ford owned 58.5

21

Henry and guests in the big Model K in front of a Ford showroom

courtesy Ford Archives, Ford Museum

percent of the company, Couzens 11 percent. Henceforth, Ford could, if he wished, have the last word on every matter concerning what was now definitely his company.

The 1906 model lineup stayed essentially the same into 1907, but throughout the year Ford struggled unsuccessfully to sell the big Model K. Company policy seemed to force the car on the market. For example, applications for new Ford franchises were not accepted unless an applicant agreed to order at least one Model K, and discounts of up to 20 percent were allowed. The firm also tried to insist that agents accept one K for every 10 Ns. But all this was to no avail: the car simply didn't sell. At year's end,

those that remained had to be cleared at $1800, a $1000 chop off the original list price. Despite this, Ford's total calendar year output took a vertical leap—to 14,887 cars. This was remarkable for a new auto company not even five years old.

One of Ford's most famous and enduring slogans, "Watch the Fords Go By," emerged in 1907, and was used from time to time in company advertising through the early 1940s. It originated with either advertising manager E. LeRoy Pelletier or traffic manager W.S. Hogue. *Ford Times*, after Pelletier's departure, credited the phrase to Hogue, who was said to have shouted it at a

One of the earliest uses of the famous slogan on the banner was this publicity photo featuring a lineup of Model Rs.

1906-07 Model K runabout with "mother-in-law" seat

1906-07 Model K touring with unusual sidemount spare

race in which Fords were whizzing by the competition.

These words were a familiar sight on many of the "all-Ford" trains that puffed out of Detroit to all parts of the country. They were also seen on a mammoth electric sign erected atop Detroit's Temple Theater in 1908. Though other Ford slogans and the company's "winged pyramid" trademark pushed it aside within a few years, "Watch the Fords" became one of the two best-known automobile slogans of all time (Packard's "Ask the Man Who Owns One" is the other).

Numerous "takeoffs" on this phrase have also appeared over the years. J.T. Flynn wrote an article entitled "Watch the Ford Myths Go By" for *New Republic* in 1937. Al Pearce, appearing for Ford on radio the same year, called his show "Watch the Fun Go By." A Ford-sponsored radio newscast during the World War II years was entitled "Watch the World Go By." A 1940 cartoon showing Henry and Edsel Ford whizzing by labor leader John L. Lewis was captioned "Watch the Fords Go By." So was a 1944 editorial that equated Henry Ford's 1942 and 1944 predictions that the war would end in a few months with his 1931 statement that "prosperity is here, but only a few realize it." *Broadcasting-Television* magazine ran a 1949 article titled "Watch the UN Go By!" concerning the company's sponsorship of United Nations telecasts. The slogan also inspired the headline over a 1963 *Newsweek* story on Henry Ford II's luxurious new yacht, and found expression in the form of "Watch the Fords Go Back" for a 1972 *Business Week* magazine article on Ford's recall of faulty cars.

Note the long six-cylinder engine in the 1906-07 Model K chassis. Model was officially designated the 6-40.

1908-09

The car that will change the nation appears: Henry's immortal Tin Lizzie

The 1908-09 Model T roadster with the extra-cost removable rear seat

Although a latecomer to the automotive field compared to many of its principal competitors, Ford Motor Company had produced eight models—A, B, C, F, K, N, R, and S—by 1908. The new firm had also firmly carved a niche for itself in the industry. In the fiscal year ending July 31, 1908, the company sold 6398 cars. In the 15 months ending December 31st of that year, it netted over $1.1 million. In sales, Ford was among the industry's "Big Four," and was perhaps four rungs from the top of the profit ladder.

As the company introduced its ninth model, competition was still formidable and the dark cloud of the Selden suit hung ominously on the horizon. But with the Model T, Ford abruptly left the pack. The company would dominate U.S. car sales for the next 18 years, and would account for more than half the industry's total output in 1918-19 and in 1921-25. Profits soared accordingly and in 1911-15, 1918, and again in 1921, Ford earned more than the rest of the industry combined.

On March 18, 1908, advance catalogs describing the Model T were sent to Ford dealers throughout the nation. They evoked an immediate and enthusiastic response. "We must say it is almost too good to be true," a Detroit dealer wrote to headquarters, "and we have rubbed our eyes several times to make sure we were not dreaming." Averred a Pennsylvania agent: "It is without doubt the greatest creation in automobiles ever placed before a people, and it means that this circular alone will flood your factory with orders." Several dealers told the company they were hiding the information, because they feared it would be impossible to sell older models on hand if word of the Model T got out. "We have carefully hidden the sheets away and locked the drawer, throwing the key down the cold-air shaft," declared an Illinois agent.

The 1200-pound Model T was introduced on October 1, 1908, and is thus technically a 1909 model in line with the auto industry's practice of dating cars by their model or style year rather than actual year of manufacture. The

T's essential note was utility, not beauty, yet its very homeliness had an appealing honesty. Its compact body, set on a wheelbase of 100 inches, stood high off the road, yet the car's sheer ungainliness somehow gave the impression of a lithe toughness. And the inline four-cylinder 20-horsepower engine, ample fuel tank capacity (10 gallons for the touring model), and the stout wheels and springs all suggested the Model T had an ability to travel far and wide and with utter reliability.

Because it may be unfamiliar to those too young to remember it first hand, let's briefly describe the car that once was as common as goggles and duster coats on the rugged, rutted roads of early 20th Century America. The Model T used a side-valve, three-main-bearing, engine with the cylinders cast *en bloc*. Displacement was 176.7 cubic inches, and compression ratio was 4.5:1. "It will run," as one contemporary wag put it, "on almost anything from gasoline to a good grade of kerosene." That's maybe a shade optimistic, but octane level certainly didn't matter to a Tin Lizzie. Lubrication was accomplished with a combination of gravity and splash systems. Cooling was by means of the thermosyphon system (except on the first 2500 cars, which had water pumps). The sturdy chassis featured a beam axle and transverse leaf spring at the front—and the very same arrangement at the rear. Mr. Ford saw no need for a different suspension layout or geometry at each end of his "Universal Car." Initial body styles comprised the open touring car, a two-door landaulet with fabric rear roof section, a two-seat roadster, and a more formal sedan-like model called the town car.

The key to making the thing move was Ford's patented planetary transmission, built in unit with the engine. The tail end of the transmission housing had a ball and socket joint that received the ball front of the driveshaft and took the driving thrust (along with radius rods) from the rear wheel bearings. On all except the earliest cars built the transmission was controlled with what one writer termed "the three most famous pedals in the world." These were marked "C," "R," and "B"—presumably to prevent novice drivers from forgetting. Pedal "C" (clutch) worked a band, located inside the transmission, that engaged one of the two forward speeds. Pedal "R" (reverse) was connected to a similar reverse band. Pedal "B" (brake) operated a brake band that simply stopped the driveshaft from rotating, which brought the car to a halt. The gas tank was housed under the front seat.

The Model T had several attention-getting innovations. The steering apparatus was on the left, a feature with far-reaching consequences because of the Model T's ultimately huge production volume. Within a few years, every other manufacturer in the United States had followed suit. The three-point engine mounting, as yet a novel idea, was especially important in an era of bad roads. It avoided the distortion of the engine base common with two-point mounting, and was soon adopted by other manufacturers. The detachable cylinder head was also a valuable innovation. Many automakers ridiculed it, asserting that it was impossible to cast a separate cylinder head that would not leak. But within a half-dozen years they were following Ford's example. The arc springs, while affording no luxurious ride cushion, freed the entire body and chassis from the racking torsional stress then common in most cars. The T's improved version of the Ford planetary transmission got away from heavy stick clutches and stripped gears in a period when countless Americans did not know how to shift gears and the metal in transmissions was soft. The simple, ingenious magneto replaced the dry cells of early cars. Built into the engine, it supplied current for ignition and lamps. "Every time the flywheel revolves," stated the company, "you get a series of sparks." The magneto required few subsequent modifications. Sturdy vanadium steel, borrowed from the N, R, and S, was used in crankshafts, axles, gears, and springs. These features, plus the fact that the new car was to sell for only $825 and up, gave Ford considerable justification for claiming, "No car under $2,000 offers more, and no car over $2,000 offers more except in trimmings." In the T, the company had an Aladdin's lamp that only needed to be rubbed vigorously to produce a long career of industrial growth, fame, and prosperity.

Still, early Model Ts had many faults. One weak point was the rear axle bearings, initially made of babbitt metal. Continued pounding on bad roads elongated them, and they consequently required frequent replacement. Roller bearings were substituted by 1910. Transmission bands gave constant trouble, for their linings easily burned out until a better material was employed. Owners complained that front and rear wheels were of different sizes, which necessitated carrying double sets of tires and tubes. The rear seat of the touring car was too narrow at first. Riveting improvements were needed and made. Cranking the Model T, especially in cold weather, was a source of innumerable broken arms and endless profanity. The company suggested that owners with cold garages attach an electric light to a long cord and keep it burning under the hood to keep the engine warm.

Owners also quickly learned that no two cars were quite alike. Mastery of any one involved a high degree of cour-

The Model T's driving controls: not as easy as A-B-C

courtesy Ford Archives, Ford Museum

The Fabulous Flivver, the 1908-09 Model T touring

age, skill, intuition, and luck. With all of its superior dependability and simplicity, the T was devastatingly eccentric. It had more character than any other car ever known to man. To buy one was to embark on a great adventure.

So was driving one. After checking fuel level (by peering into the tank), the driver fired up with a few healthy cranks on the starter handle. (An electric starter became an option in 1919.) Once the engine was chugging, it was time to adjust the spark by means of a lever on the left side of the steering column. Dyed-in-the-wool T-drivers took pride in knowing precisely where to set the spark and throttle levers before starting and how to adjust the choke just so. "We all had to know the hand-cranking procedure, with the choke wire by the radiator," remembers longtime T-driver Robert Bateman. "Your left toes knew the pressure and angle to hold it in neutral while you released the handbrake-cum-clutch-neutralizer. The idea was to shove in the pedal to get to low speed as fast as possible, because a slow application wore out the bands. When you judged the speed sufficient for the load and grade you eased back into high, controlling the gas lever at the same time."

Bateman makes it sound easy. The complete Model T shifting drill is extremely complicated for the first-time driver. A newcomer, who may not appreciate that Lizzie isn't just another car, will invariably push the right pedal to accelerate and the left to declutch—with predictable results. It usually took at least a year of practice, John Keats once wrote, before the Model T pilot "could get into high without bounding down the road looking like a frog with St. Vitus' dance and sounding like a canning factory with something wrong with it."

Braking in a Model T is also an interesting exercise, which new drivers attempt only because...well, a T is so unbreakable (no pun intended). If it does hit anything, chances are it will just bounce off. To stop, you would ostensibly stomp on the "B" pedal, but this rarely does more than slow the pace a little. The aforementioned left handbrake/declutch lever is usually needed, and it doesn't hurt to jab the "R" pedal on occasion, either.

The seating position in any Tin Lizzie is towering. The commanding view allows you to look *down* on the car's hood from a perch that is level with the roofs of most cars built after 1955 or so. Roadholding, given the rudimentary suspension, is quite good. A Model T really isn't fast enough (only 35-40 mph tops) to put it to a severe test, which it would undoubtedly fail in a hurry. Steering, with four turns lock-to-lock, is fairly fast even by modern standards. The only steering reduction is a planetary gearset under the steering wheel. The lower end of the steering shaft has a bolt-on lever that pushes or pulls a rod working on the tie rod, located between the spindle arms.

Hills present a special challenge. Usually the Model T

driver would approach one either flat out (by getting a running start) or—to make it to the top of steeper grades—in reverse. There were two reasons for this. First, reverse was geared higher (4:1) than low (3:1). Second, the gravity-feed gas tank was placed higher than the carburetor. Unless the tank was full, the car would stall going forward up a grade of one-in-five or steeper. And there was a reason for that. The gravity/splash lube system was not fully effective at such angles. Ford had placed the gas tank so as to eliminate the chance of oil starvation on steep grades!

The T's introductory publicity was perhaps the most energetic yet seen from an American manufacturer. News releases, photographs, and sketches were sent to the press on an unprecedented scale, and the response proved commensurate with the effort. *Horseless Age* and *Motor Age* magazines each published eight photos or diagrams of the car, along with highly complimentary stories. *Mo-*

tor World ran four large pictures, and called the T "a credit to the genius of Henry Ford." A record amount of literature went to dealers, who sent back a torrent of orders by mail, telegraph, telephone, and personal visits. Branch managers, called to Detroit in September, demanded 15,000 cars for their requirements alone. Immediately thereafter, ads appeared in trade journals prompting a flow of urgent orders from general dealers. Ads were also placed in the national weekly magazines. "If we were flattered by the reception the trade tendered the T," stated the company's employee/dealer magazine, *Ford Times,* "and surely no announcement ever received so glorious an acknowledgement....much more were we elated by the response from the consumer. The 'ad' [in the national magazines] appeared on Friday; Saturday's mail brought nearly 1,000 inquiries. Monday's response swamped our mail clerks and by Tuesday night the office was well nigh inundated. There isn't a state in the Union

Early 1909 Model T ad stresses low price, high value

that has not registered its approval of the Model T and the Ford Policy." Branches and local agencies also beat the drums as never before, buying unusually large amounts of newspaper space to advertise the new Ford.

Once loosed, the cascade of orders continued unchecked. By winter of 1908 demand was running so far ahead of production that the company could insist that it would supply Ts only to those dealers who had sold off all their old models on hand. Such "rationing" was unheard of in the automobile business. By May 1, 1909, sales were so far ahead of production that the company had to stop taking orders for nine weeks. The grand total rose from

10,202 units in the "transition" 1908 calendar year to a very healthy 17,771 for all of 1909.

Model T sales literally skyrocketed for a decade, some years showing more than a 100-percent increase over the year before. America's involvement in Word War I broke the upward spiral from 1917 to 1919. But then came the T's heyday: six years in which domestic sales passed the one-million mark, and one in which they topped two million.

The T's sturdy dependabilty, plus the urging of a thousand dealers and a host of enthusiasts, induced Henry Ford to approve an official factory entry for a New York-

Frank Kulick at the wheel of Ford No. 1, which competed in the 1909 New York-to-Seattle transcontinental road race

Ford No.2 won New York-to-Seattle race, was later disqualified

to-Seattle race in the spring of 1909. Robert Guggenheim, the mining magnate, had arranged the cross-country run to promote the Alaska-Yukon-Pacific Exposition. He imposed rigid requirements on the competitors. Cars had to check in at 30 points; they could obtain new parts only in Chicago and Cheyenne, Wyoming; and they were forbidden to travel on railroad tracks.

There were 14 vehicles entered, but only five—two Model Ts, an Acme, a Shawmut, and an Italia—responded to the starting gun. Both Fords reached St. Louis some two hours ahead of the nearest rival, and remained together until reaching Idaho. Then Ford No. 1, driven by Frank Kulick and advertising manager H.B. Harper, forged ahead with a nine-hour lead. However, because of misdirections they got lost twice and fell a day and a half behind. In the meantime, Ford No. 2 headed straight for Seattle, arriving at the exposition amid the cheers of 200,000 people. The trip had taken 22 days and 55 minutes. The Shawmut arrived 17 hours later, followed several hours later by Ford No. 1. The Acme reached Seattle a week later; the Italia had been withdrawn at Cheyenne.

The race was widely reported, and Ford lost little time in capitalizing on the high public interest in it. Harper's booklet, *The Story of the Race,* was distributed to dealers by the tens of thousands. A large-scale newspaper and magazine advertising campaign trumpeted the achievement, and flailed the many manufacturers who had refused to enter the contest. The winning car was displayed at hundreds of dealerships during a 6000-mile swing from Seattle to Los Angeles to New York, reaching the latter city in time to be exhibited at the Hudson-Fulton celebration.

But the boom of Ford's victory drums was soon silenced. Five months after the race, the judges discovered that the crewmen of Ford No. 2 had violated the rules by changing the engine during the run. First prize was thus awarded to the Shawmut. At this stage, Ford may have felt it had lost only a moral victory; the propaganda hay had been lofted long before.

A historical footnote: Ford "reenacted" the race for publicity purposes in 1959. A 1909 Ford stopped in 85 cities along the original route, and was seen by tens of thousands of people. William Clay Ford, a company vice-president and youngest grandson of Henry Ford, greeted

Frank Kulick in transcontinental race reenactment, 1959

Kulick as he appeared at the start of the 1909 race

the car and escorting vehicles at the future site of the 1962 Seattle World's Fair. According to the company's northeast regional office, which had major responsibility for it, the promotion was "the most important and successful program carried out by this office in recent years." Interestingly, none of Ford's press releases, nor a film of the expedition released in 1962, mentioned the disqualification of the original Model T "winner."

En route to Seattle, the two Model T entrants contend with the muck and mire of Goodland, Kansas, on June 11th.

1910

Its future assured, Ford becomes "the wonder of the automotive world"

1910 Model T runabout with optional rear seat

The 1910 Model T was virtually unchanged from the 1908-09 version. The exception was introduction of a new body style, the racy Torpedo roadster. Its long steering column and windshield were set at a rakish angle to suggest speed. The Torpedo was relatively fast—at least quicker than any other production Model T. Public acceptance of all Fords was seen in another sharp jump in calendar year output: 32,053 cars left the factory, a gain of nearly 50 percent.

Throughout its life, the Model T was known almost as much for the plant in which it was built as for its qualities as a car. This was Ford's mammoth factory in Highland Park, Michigan, then a community of 4120, surrounded by the city of Detroit. Designed by Detroiter Albert Kahn, America's greatest industrial architect, it was the world's largest auto factory and Michigan's largest building under one roof. It was also the most aesthetically pleasing factory of its day in architecture, cleanliness, and arrangement. Measuring 865 feet long by 75 feet wide, the four-story building had more than 50,000 square feet of glass, which led some to call it the "Crystal Palace." The company's publicity staff spared little effort in touting Highland Park as "the wonder of the automobile world," the "largest single manufacturing institution in the world," and that it maintained the "largest machine shop in the world." A photograph showing some 12,000 of the 16,000 employees in front of the factory was run by many newspapers, accompanied by stories stating the picture was the "largest specially posed photo ever taken, and [is] far and away the most expensive, considering the employees' time and loss of production."

As time went on, the plant's size (the entire complex including a foundry covered 60 acres by 1913) evoked less interest than its production feats. To the Boston News

Most people think of the ubiquitous touring (1910 shown) when they think of the immortal Tin Lizzie.

Bureau, Ford's 1912 output (over 78,000) was "remarkable" and in 1913 (over 168,000) it was "simply phenomenal." Executives of other car companies, realizing that size alone could not account for such prodigious numbers, hastened to Highland Park to examine the techniques that made it all possible. They were generous in their praise. Karl Neumaier, general manager of Germany's famed Benz Company, told the press, "The Ford plant is the most remarkable in the world; it is the very best in equipment and method." Louis Renault, head of the French automobile firm bearing his name, declared that the plant was "the best organized in the country" and that he was "very much impressed by the ingenuity displayed in the manufacturing of cars."

The advent of mass production that began with the Model T is generally regarded as the greatest achievement associated with Henry Ford and his company. It certainly received a tremendous amount of public notice beginning in 1914. For much of the world, Henry Ford became the symbol of the process and its rewards. As such, he was something of a messiah to those impressed by bigness, vast quantities of goods, and the higher standard of living mass production made possible. Conversely, he was a devil to those who deplored the "triumph" of machine over man and who found no solace in huge industrial operations and product uniformity. Ironically, even many of these people drove Model Ts.

Engineering societies, business organizations, and dealer groups began visiting Highland Park as early as 1910 to see the "magic methods" about which they had read or heard. Two years later, *Ford Times* reported that "the reception business is being systematized and soon

1910 Model T touring. Note configuration of the folded top.

will be able to handle four or five crowds a day." A 24- to 30-man guide corps was organized, and a concerted effort was made to encourage plant visits. The promotional efforts were evidently successful, the *Christian Science Monitor* reporting that "the competent corps of guides" had escorted "thousands of persons" through the plant in 1912. By early spring of 1914 an average of 150 guests were touring the factory each day. By this time the company's newly organized Motion Picture Department—which in 1913 featured the plant in a nationally distributed newsreel, believed to be the first ever made in an industrial plant—was filming visiting celebrities to provide exclusive material for its newsreel, the "Ford Animated Weekly."

Early Model Ts were admirably suited for traveling the rough and rutted roads of rural America.

A 1910 Model T makes a run at a not-so-steep grade.

matter of fact, was supremely confident that Kulick, "The Pride of the Company," could defeat anyone. When rain postponed an exhibition between Barney Oldfield, who had a specially built, 200-horsepower Benz, and Kulick, *Ford Times* was keenly disappointed: "...such is fate, and the honors that would have come to Ford were postponed for another meeting."

1911

Lizzie flirts with High Society and shows its competitive mettle.

After the announcement of the five-dollar-a-day wage in early 1914, the plant became "a national landmark and a new Niagara Falls," a place to be seen by every visitor to Detroit. William Howard Taft thought the place "wonderful, wonderful," and Roger W. Babson, president of the Babson Statistical Organization, said his visit was as a pilgrimage to a shrine. His view was shared by William Bausch, head of Bausch & Lomb Company, who, with 19 business friends, traveled the 320 miles to Michigan just to see the Ford factory. During 1915, approximately 100,000 persons visited Highland Park, and this figure more than doubled two years later. The plant—and Model T manufacturing—thus became a major Midwest tourist attraction.

Following its return to racing in 1909, Ford resumed full-scale competition the following summer. Dealers were delighted, and within a few months many were reporting that the move was greatly stimulating sales. Frank Kulick was again a consistent winner, *Motor Age* magazine ranking him as one of America's top drivers during 1910-11. Two other pilots helped the Ford cause. R.P. Rice, manager of the Seattle branch, dominated Northwest tracks and held the Seattle-to-Portland road race record from 1910 to 1912. E. Roger Stearns, a Los Angeles dealer, was California's top driver in 1910, ousting Barney Oldfield (who by then had also resumed racing) and other leading professionals that year.

The Model T was handicapped in competition by its low price and low power-to-weight ratio. In order to compete with the heavier, higher-powered cars whose defeat would count for something, the 950-pound Ford would have been required in certain meets to carry several hundred pounds of dead weight and to be hundreds of dollars more expensive. On principle, Henry Ford refused to bow to such demands just to meet classification requirements, for he regarded the T's lightness and low cost as its chief attributes. In a contest open to it, the little 20-horsepower stock chassis proved a match for the heaviest, most powerful vehicles in the land. The company, as a

The year 1911 saw the first use of sheetmetal in Model T bodies. Up to this time, most bodies had been made entirely of wood, though aluminum had been used for some in 1909. This year's cars changed from all-wood construction to sheetmetal over wood framing. All 1911 models received new metal runningboards stamped with "Ford" script, and steering wheel diameter grew to 15 inches, presumably for better leverage and less steering effort. There were also several minor mechanical changes.

Prices began on what would turn out to be a long downward spiral. The touring was cut from $950 to $780, the roadster dropped from $900 to just $680, and even the town car, the most expensive offering, took a price tumble, from $1200 to $960. These reductions had a predictable effect on sales, which were more than double the 1910 total. Calendar year output climbed to 69,762 units, setting another record for the third year in a row.

In the Model T's early years—through 1914—Ford made a curious and vain effort to establish its indomitable little rattletrap as something of a prestige item. Press releases boasted of English aristocrats who owned Fords, and stories appeared around the country under such headlines as "'Swells' Own Fords." *Ford Times* pointed out that two Russian grand dukes and 19 princes owned them and that President Wilson had bought one for use at his summer home. Company publicists arranged for

1911 Model T "Torpedo" runabout

This Model T did well in the famed Glidden Tour of 1911.

1911 Model T touring towers over modern-day cars.

show business celebrities like Eddie Foy, Billie Burke, and Henrietta Crossman to be photographed in Model Ts as testimonials. Similarly, dealers were asked to furnish pictures of well-known customers and their cars against backgrounds of "fine-looking residences."

But in the long run the campaign was doomed. Henry Ford was hardly selling an automobile for the elite. "I will build a motor car for the great multitude," he stated early in his career, "...constructed of the best materials, by the best men to be hired, after the simplest designs that modern engineering can devise...so low in price that no man making a good salary will be unable to own one and enjoy with his family the blessing of hours of pleasure in God's great open spaces." In view of the times and the embryonic auto market, Henry could not have conceived a more intelligent marketing approach, nor could he have a more appealing message for consumers. The Model T, of course, was the embodiment of Ford's vision. It was designed primarily for farm and family use. Utility, not stylish beauty, was its hallmark. Besides, the T's inexpensiveness—and it would be even less expensive as time went on—subverted the company's efforts to sell the car on the basis of snob appeal.

If the Model T was not a prestige car, it was a hillclimber par excellence. Certainly, on a pound-for-pound basis, there is considerable evidence to support the *Ford Times* contention that it was "the greatest hill climber ever built." The car had no real rivals in the low-price class, and carried off honors time and time again in climbs against the most expensive and powerful of automobiles.

During what we might call the hillclimbing era of the automobile's early years, virtually every navigable summit in the country was scaled, some with monotonous frequency. A victory in one of the more important climbs definitely boosted a car's prestige. Ford consequently focused on the "name" contests, especially the event in Algonquin, Illinois, where it scored notable victories from 1910 to 1912. Meantime, dealers and owners carried the Ford banner in innumerable minor events.

Some dealers were so eager to demonstrate the Model T's capabilities that they advertised for competition. A typical notice was posted by a Columbia, South Carolina, agent: "CHALLENGE—Regardless of price, and including Steamers, July 5th, '09, The Ford Model T cleaned up every automobile sold in Columbia in a Hill Climb. If you want to make a little more sport for Labor Day, the Ford is ready." Between contests, many dealers drove their Fords up and down a variety of near-perpendicular surfaces. A Model T climbed Ben Nevis, Britain's highest mountain, in 1911, receiving widespread publicity in Great Britain and the United States. Before thousands of spectators, the company's Nashville dealer drove his car up the 66 steps of the Tennessee capitol building. The Duluth agent covered a $100 bet by climbing up three flights of courthouse steps in a Model T, and a Los Angeles dealer used dynamite to blast his way in and out of the Grand Canyon.

The Ford company never quite worked up the enthusiasm for reliability-endurance runs that it had for racing and hillclimbs. Perhaps it regarded the former as being too tame. "Endurance runs," complained *Ford Times*, "are that only in name; in actuality they are joy rides that accomplish nothing except a holiday for the contestants and advertising orders for the newspapers." The publication also complained that many of the contestants who finished with perfect scores had cheated, and suggested that each car should be equipped "with a moving picture machine and a talking machine to see what the driver and observer are up to." All this aside, during 1907-12 the company, some of its branches, and many of its dealers participated in hundreds of contests. Fords were frequent winners in their class and occasionally showed up well in the sweepstakes competition of important tours. A Model T finished second in the 1910 Munsey Tour, and a team of three Fords ranked fourth, ahead of Cadillac, Marathon, and Flanders, in the prestigious Glidden Tour of 1911. Perhaps the T's greatest victory came in Russia, where it was the only car out of 45 European and two American entries to earn a perfect score in a 1954-mile test con-

This near-stock Model T finished second in the 1910 Munsey Tour, another demonstration of Lizzie's stamina.

ducted by the Imperial War Department. Czar Nicholas II personally inspected the winning T and recommended Fords for the Russian army.

Ford dealers often conducted special endurance tests and stunts to show that their cars could withstand the roughest kind of treatment. A dealer in Rochester, New

A typical family outing Model T-style, circa 1911

York, annually sponsored January tours over hundreds of miles of snow-covered roads. Other dealers loaded Model Ts with a dozen or so persons for a "parade" down Main Street. This stunt reached its climax in 1911 when a flivver carrying 34 boys, who weighed a combined 3492 pounds, was driven around Payne, Ohio.

A Wichita dealer started a craze by introducing auto-polo, played with two Model T chassis as field cars and two touring cars as goal-tenders. "Endurance runs, speed races, hill climbs and all other contests are mere parlor games in comparison," the enthusiastic agent assured the company. The Wichita team staged exhibitions all over the country, concluding with a match in Madison Square Garden.

Meanwhile, Ford and its ace driver, Frank Kulick, bowed out of track racing at the Michigan State Fair in September, 1911. In an exhibition mile, Kulick defeated some of racing's biggest names and broke the track record in the process. Immediately after the race, a delighted Henry Ford pressed a $1000 bill into his hand.

The victory marked Kulick's last appearance on a race track. However, he figured in two more events before his retirement. In January, 1912, he drove the second 999 over the measured mile in 33⅖ths seconds on the ice of

Lake St. Clair, the fastest anyone had run on ice since Henry Ford's 1904 effort. During the summer of 1912, he made "the automobile world stand aghast" as he won the celebrated Algonquin Hill Climb in record-breaking time. His performance so embarrassed big-car manufacturers that in 1913 none would enter the contest unless Kulick and his machine were barred. But a boycott was avoided when it was announced that Kulick and the Ford company were finished with competition.

Ford did not sponsor a racing entry again until 1935. Its dealers, with a few exceptions, also abandoned racing between 1912 and the mid-1930s. Private owners and auto accessory firms, however, entered Model Ts in hundreds of races in the 'teens and '20s. During this period, Model Ts—particularly the so-called Fronty-Fords equipped with the powerful Frontenac cylinder head—dominated the country's small-town dirt tracks. In 1923, three Fronty-Fords qualified for America's premier race, the Indianapolis 500 Memorial Day classic. To the delight of race referee Henry Ford and to the surprise of the racing fraternity, each of the Ts was still running at the finish. The fastest of them, averaging 82.58 mph, captured fifth, an exceptional showing for an inexpensive modified stock car. After the introduction of the Model A in 1927, the machine-gun blast of the racing Fords was heard less often, although Ts continued to compete on dirt tracks into the 1930s.

The promotional value of hillclimbs and reliablity runs underwent a slow decline between 1910 and 1913, then rapidly fell off as most all cars became powerful enough to whisk up almost any hill and easily cover routes between distant points. Economy runs, although they survived much longer, were never as popular as other

The 1911 Model T coupe, truly a "phone booth on wheels"

contests during the early years, and Fords were entered in only a handful of them. Winning performances in these were based on a fuel-to-weight ratio, which the company regarded as unfair for its light, economical car. Ford's recommendation that weight should be a criterion in economy runs elicited no response among contest sponsors.

Ford's successful participation in racing and the more practical forms of competition convinced many motorists that the Model T was spirited, dependable, and economical to operate. It did much to propel the Tin Lizzie to its commanding sales leadership.

Ford's ace factory driver Frank Kulick takes the wheel of a Model T at the 1911 Elgin (Illinois) Road Race.

1912

Lower prices, more doors, and buyer surveys keep Ford forging ahead.

The 1912 "Fore Door" touring with Henry Ford at the wheel

The most notable change in the 1912 Model T was availability of what we'd now call an option. In this case it was separate front doors for the ubiquitous touring, thus changing its name to "Fore-Door." After a brief life, the Torpedo Runabout was discontinued. New to the line was a Commercial Runabout featuring a flat rear deck for hauling cargo, something like that of a modern pickup truck, and equipped with a detachable "mother-in-law" bucket seat. In this final year before the advent of the mass-production assembly line at Highland Park, output rose again. The total for the calendar year was 78,440.

By this time, Henry Ford was convinced that price cuts were by far the most important element in merchandising the Model T. He often said that he gained 1000 new customers for every dollar he cut the price, and justified his practice by relating T prices to mounting sales figures. In spite of prodigious production increases the company could scarcely meet demand.

Ford's price cuts were generously reported in newspapers and magazines. Wire services, which rarely carried automotive news, flashed stories highly favorable to Ford following the 1912 and 1913 reductions. *Harper's Weekly*, after weighing the contribution of these to the T's success, agreed that Ford "has thought out the best adver-

This 1912 Model T runabout bristles with accessories, including luggage box and auxiliary gas lamps.

Ford Model T Town Car
6-Passenger 4-Cylinder 20 Horsepower
Car. Price $800 includes a speedometer,
two 6-inch gas lamps, generator, three
oil lamps, horn and tools, including
jack—f.o.b. Detroit. No Ford Cars sold
unequipped

Model T Town Car (1912 shown) was popular for taxi service.

A 1912 touring adapted for rail inspection duty in Indiana

tisement, and made the deepest, most sensational appeal to human nature he could have made."

Along with the price cuts, Model T advertising in 1912-16 emphasized the Ford company's "'winged pyramid" trademark. This was described by advertising manager Glen Buck as "a happy combination of two of the oldest Egyptian symbols—the pyramid symbolizing strength and stability—the scarab wings symbolizing lightness and grace." The symbol literally permeated the Ford organization for several years. "Here is the new sun of the Ford advertising system," rhapsodized Buck in one of many articles extolling the trademark. "It shall be the 'blazing flag' around which the Ford forces shall rally."

More than half the space in some Ford ads was devoted to reproductions of the new emblem. Dealers were ordered to have it painted on their sales windows and were

Without windshield, this 1912 Model T runabout looks almost racy. Note auxiliary bumper bar at the front.

1912 Model T runabout, part of the Ford Museum collection

A 1912 Model T runabout, ready for winter with snow chains

strongly urged to use trademarked letterheads. After October 1912, number plates on all Model Ts bore the emblem. Within a year of its introduction, the trademark was "widely established all over the world," according to one latter-day expert, and was of "enormous value" to the company. It was used consistently until late 1916 when, for some reason, the firm's Operating Committee questioned whether it should be continued. The question was referred to Henry Ford who, according to secretary Ernest G. Liebold, abolished the symbol after being told that "scarab" is another name for dung beetle."

The Model T was the only car built before World War II that was subjected to market research. Ford first surveyed public opinion in early 1912, when 1000 Model T owners (a sample of 1 percent) were asked, "Just what reason or reasons were foremost in your choice of a Ford car?" Twelve respondents indicated that low price was the primary reason, 39 pointed to the sound ignition system, 108 referred to the low maintenance cost, and 842 reported that they had made the purchase on the recommendation of other owners. The same question was

asked in a poll of 2000 owners in the fall, but the results have been lost.

The company soon abandoned its pioneering work in market research, ironic in view of what would happen much later with the development of the Edsel. The statement, "The public can have any color it wants so long as it's black," if not actually made by Henry Ford, at least expressed his attitude regarding customer opinion during the years when the Model T dominated the market. Ford was ultimately compelled to answer demand for more colorful, more stylish cars in the mid-1920s, but the firm would not resume its public opinion research until the late 1940s.

1913

Cheaper by the millions: Henry begins a new kind of industrial revolution.

The 1913 Model Ts were the last available in a choice colors. Not until 1926 would Ford offer an alternative to black. Once again, Lizzie showed almost no change. One difference again concerned the touring car, which now came equipped without a separate tonneau. It also sported front doors instead of the previous cut-outs, but appearances were deceiving. The driver's "door" was actually fixed, embossed in such a way as to make it look like it opened. The reason for this was the outboard handbrake, which hindered access on that side.

In August of this year the first mass-production automobile assembly line began experimental operation at Ford's Highland Park factory. As an event in industrial history it would have tremendous significance. It would not only make Henry Ford the "father" of the automobile industry as we know it today, it would also change the face and pace of the nation. The Model T was the first car built by the thousands, not one at a time, on a moving assembly line with sequentially placed work stations. It was one of the earliest cars to employ the principle of interchangeable parts that had been successfully employed in Henry Leland's Cadillac. All these factors, not to mention its simple design, enabled the Model T to be sold at very low prices well within the reach of a vast number of Americans who had never been able to afford a car before. And that, of course, is the main reason why it and all automobiles became so universal.

Small-scale assembly line methods and standardized parts were in use well before this time, both at Ford and elsewhere. The idea of a moving production line was probably first conceived by Ransom Eli Olds, whose cars were once the number-one sellers in the country. But it was Henry Ford who perfected the idea. Toward the end of their life the Ford Models N and S had been built by means of a "sequential floor plan" in which machines and manpower were strategically located to "add" to each car

1913 Ts were the last "colorful" Lizzies until 1926.

Partial front seat windows were new on the 1913 Town Car.

as it proceeded on its orderly way through the Piquette Avenue factory. As author Beverly Rae Kimes has noted: "A hundred cars a day could be easily built that way. But Henry Ford was thinking bigger. What was needed to build thousands was *movement*, continuous and carefully timed movement throughout the production procedure... It was not until the move to the newer and larger Highland Park plant in 1910 that the idea could be given full attention and the awkward beginnings made." Henry Ford later attributed the idea to foreman William C. Klann, who was inspired by "the overhead trolley that the Chicago meat packers used in dressing beef."

At first, parts were moved around the factory on conveyors. Ultimately, the notion was expanded to having not only assemblies but also partially completed cars move slowly past workers. The assembly process was refined through several stages, and by October 1913 it had yielded staggering results: Ford's assembly time had been cut in half. It would soon be halved again. Thus, from 78,440 cars in 1912, output zoomed to 168,220 in 1913, then shot past the half-million mark just three years later. Through mass production, Ford factories built more than 15 million Model Ts between 1907 and

1927. It was a single-model record that would stand until the 1960s, when it was surpassed by another car of universal popularity, the Volkswagen Beetle.

In 1913-14 some people thought what was termed the cycle car, a miniature runabout seating two people, might make a dent in Model T sales. Henry decided something should be done about that. Accordingly, he built a smaller version of the Model T, neat and streamlined. His son Edsel showed much interest in its construction. When it was completed, Henry said to him: "Now you take it down and park it in front of the Pontchartrain Hotel." Edsel obeyed. A curious throng gathered, saw the name "Ford", and concluded Henry was about to bring out a cycle car. That ended the cycle-car threat.

In 1913, as in other years, Model T promotion was closely tied to current events. For example, when trouble with Mexico was anticipated that year, Ford publicists recommended that every American battleship be equipped with Model Ts to enable the Marines "to charge on Mexico City from Vera Cruz in record time." The idea was hailed in metropolitan papers all over the country. Model Ts actually participated in a Mexican border skirmish in 1917, the episode inspiring a juvenile novel,

Fishing by Model T on a lazy afternoon in 1913

A 1913 Model T commercial runabout, down on the farm

A 1913 runabout with special pickup box for dealer service

Charge of the Model Ts. Ford's board of directors also appointed one of its members to arrange for a Ford to be the first automobile to pass through the Panama Canal. The mission must have been unsuccessful, for the company never published an account of any such milestone.

The Model T had more slang names than any other car ever built. Of course, it is best known today as the Tin Lizzie or flivver. But over the years it has had at least 48 other nicknames, each of which enjoyed brief popularity. Here's a rundown: T-bone, Detroit Disaster, Michigan Mistake, Flapper Flivver, Chicken Coup, Bone Crusher, Bouncing Betty, Cattle Hack, Fresh Air Taxi, Galloping Snail, Prince of Snails, Graf Zep's Uncle, Henry's first go-car, Lazy Lulu, Leaping Lena, My Lizzie of the Valley, Navigatin' Nancy, Noah's Ark, Old Faithful, Passion Pot, Puddle Jumper, Road Louse Exterminator, Rough Rider, Satan's Nightmare, Silly Symphony, Spirit of Bumps, Spirit of Detroit, Spirit of Jolts, Spirit of St. Vitus, Madame Elizabeth, Henrietta Elizabeth Van Flivver, Henry VII (capacity four gals), Gilda Gray—shimmy expert, September Morn, Toonerville Trolley, A-Cute Digestion, Little Asphalt Annie, Little Bo-Creep, Rolls Rough, Tacks Collector, United Parts of America, Baby Lincoln, Lincoln's Baby, Lincoln's Relation, and the Missing Link in Lincoln.

1914

It's $5 a day for workers, "any color as long as it's black" for buyers.

Beginning with the 1914s the Model T would be sold in only one color—black—for the next dozen years. The main reason for this was the particular kind of black enamel favored by Henry Ford: it dried more quickly than other paints and thus helped speed up production.

So, fashion notwithstanding, it was "any color you like, as long as it's black." Calendar year output forged ahead, setting another all-time record at over 308,000 units. That was about 100,000 more than were built by the rest of the American industry combined.

The 1914s would also be the last Ts to carry the acetylene gas lamps, cherrywood dashboard, and straight rear fenders of the 1909 original. A minor styling change this year brought rounded bottom corners on the doors, which enabled Lizzie to shed a little of her "antique" look. The Model T's base price now stood at $490, and it would drop another $50 the following year.

As Henry Ford and James Couzens became rich, paid higher salaries and bonuses to executives, and gave the public ever cheaper Model Ts, they began to ask themselves, "What of our workers?" Their answer was the celebrated "five-dollar workday," introduced on January 12, 1914. Besides the new basic wage, length of the work day was reduced from the usual 10 to eight hours, and a third shift was added at Highland Park to make up the difference. This announcement, made in the midst of a mild worldwide depression, was immediately flashed to every corner of the globe. Forty years later, the London *Economist* called the move "the most dramatic event in the history of wages." In 1959 the distinguished French intellectual, Father R.L. Bruckberger, went further: "I consider that what Henry Ford accomplished in 1914 contributed far more to the emancipation of workers than the October Revolution of 1917...He took the worker out of the class of the 'wage-earning proletariat' to which Ricardo and Marx had relegated him and...made every worker a potential customer."

Although Ford and Couzens regarded the five-dollar daily wage as "the greatest revolution in the matter of rewards for...workers ever known" and were aware that the plan would be of great advertising value, they vastly underestimated the scheme's immediate worldwide impact. The announcement was easily the biggest news story ever to come from Detroit up to that time. The statement was issued in mid-morning. By noon, cables and telegrams from wire services and newspapers were pouring into Detroit from all over the globe. By the following morning, every daily paper in the country and thousands more abroad had carried the story. Over seven days the New York City press alone devoted 52 columns—most of it front-page space—to the profit-sharing plan and to Ford.

Many newspapers hailed the five-dollar day as an economic second coming. The Cleveland *Plain Dealer* editorialized that the announcement "shot like a blinding rocket through the dark clouds of the present industrial depression." The New York *Sun* described it as "a bolt out of the blue sky flashing its way across the continent and far beyond." The New York *Herald* called it "an epoch in the world's industrial history." Some papers were so impressed that they made a special point of publicizing the Model T. The East Boston *Free Press* suggested that, "When you see his [Ford's] modest little car running by, take your hat off." The Cleveland *News* ran a large photo of a Model T touring car under the headline, "The Car Humanitarian Henry Ford's Making."

Sporting new electric headlamps, this late 1914 Model T touring also wears the 1915-style hood and rear fenders.

courtesy Ford Archives, Ford Museum

This "ocean of publicity" made Ford the best-known manufacturer in the world by mid-1914. One newspaper even predicted that Henry Ford would become "one of the best-known men that America has ever produced," and that his name would "be famous until the sun takes its first chill." Ford himself enjoyed the headlines. In fact, he quickly developed a strong, lifelong appetite for publicity, much of which would help sell Model Ts and, later, Model As and V-8s.

Also in 1914, the Model T figured in one of the most striking sales promotion events in business history. This was Ford's offer of July 3rd to rebate $40 to $60 to each flivver customer should sales exceed 300,000 units during the following year. Coupled with this offer was a $60 price cut on each Model T and a promise not to cut prices again until August 1, 1915.

Unfortunately, the proposed refund was announced at one of the least propitious times imaginable: the start of World War I. Metropolitan newspapers, particularly on the eastern seaboard, relegated the offer to back pages, while their front pages screamed about the outbreak of hostilities in Serbia and the Kaiser's ultimatum to Russia. The New York *Times*, in an editorial entitled "Well Devised But Ill Timed," apologized for putting the rebate news on page five, conceding that it deserved as much publicity as Ford's widely heralded five-dollar day.

Nevertheless, the announcement did appear in virtually every newspaper in the nation, and in the smaller dailies and country weeklies it received rave notices. The reaction was exactly what sales manager Norval Hawkins had anticipated when he proposed the idea to Henry Ford, and in many communities during the rebate year the best Model T salesmen were people who had bought Fords after August, 1914.

As promised, the company announced sales figures on August 1, 1915. It sold exactly 308,213 automobiles the previous year, and accordingly set the amount to be refunded to each buyer at $40, about 9 percent of the average purchase price. "Profitsharing" checks totaling nearly $15.5 million were duly mailed to most every American hamlet, town, and city during the next few months. Many newspapers, acknowledging that the rebate offer "was a game in which Ford had everything to win and nothing to lose," (except the refunds) congratulated the company on its "sales-promotion genius" and its customers on their good fortune in climbing aboard the "rebate wagon." The checks, later called "the most virile crop of goodwill seeds ever planted," naturally made hundreds of thousands of friends for the Model T, Henry Ford, and Ford Motor Company.

On the eve of World War I, the Model T was selling at an annual rate of 250,000 and had attained a worldwide

Sleeker "turtleback" rear body was a new feature of the 1914 Model T runabout. Car's price now stood at $440.

reputation enjoyed by no other car. "While the Constitution may follow the flag, or the flag the Constitution, all depending on the viewpoint with reference to the foreign policy of the United States," reported the Indianapolis *Star*, "the Ford Motor Company has beaten out both the flag and the Constitution in carrying civilization into the wild places of the world." Here are a few examples. Twenty Model Ts were used in the construction of the Amur River Railroad in Siberia. Thirty Indian princes rode in Model Ts, interspersed with elephants, camels, and horses, at the Delhi coronation of King George V. A Model T was delivered to the Tasha Lama of Urga, after a 700-mile trip across the Gobi desert. A T won the Johannesburg-Bereeniging race in South Africa. French troops used Ts in pursuit of brigands in Morocco. By mid-1914, more than 550,000 Model Ts were on the roads of the world, traveling 10 million miles daily. "A car that is seen as often as the Ford must be right," the *Ford Times* declared with some justification, "or its very presence would kill it."

The vehicle's prodigious numbers were, in fact, an advertising asset. Every car bore the name "Ford" in bold script on the radiator and, apart from that, the distinctive design of the Model T made it recognizable a half-mile away. In a day when every automobile purchase and virtually all out-of-town trips were reported in the "personals" section of small-town newspapers, Fords naturally were mentioned thousands of times. "W.H. Judd is now riding around in a new Ford car, which he recently purchased. These are a very neat little car..." "Our genial and efficient mail carrier now delivers the mail on his route in a stylish and comfortable runabout of the Ford make whenever the conditions of the roads will permit." "R.E. Rice is sporting a fine Ford runabout which he purchased from Agent Fred Scott of Coalton." "Mr. and Mrs. John Inglebrecht and children, of near Jefferson City, drove over to Eldon Saturday in their Ford to visit Mr. and Mrs. R.J. Rush." Sometimes the publicity backfired: the Elgin (Illinois) *Courier* reported that "The funeral of William Kiel, who was killed last Friday from being tipped in the Ford automobile, which he and Joy Seyle were driving, was held Sunday."

The Model T inspired more than 60 melodic tributes. Of these, "The Little Ford Rambled Right Along," written in 1914, was perhaps the most popular. Many of the tunes attempted to capitalize on Model T jokes. Typical of such titles were "I Didn't Raise my Ford to be a Jitney," "It's a Rambling Flivver," and "Let's Take a Ride on the Jitney Bus." Others had a more romantic flavor. "The Packard and the Ford" suggested that Mr. Packard and Miss Flivverette marry and give birth to a Buick, and "The Scandal of Little Lizzie Ford" depicted a demure T garaged with a rakish, low-slung sports car. "On the Old Back Seat of the Henry Ford" promised that the moon would smile on couples spooning in flivvers.

The Model T even formed the theme for a fantasy, "Flivver Ten Million," which "created a furore" when performed by the Boston Symphony Orchestra and at-

Coupelet was a new Model T body style offering for 1915.

Boston Symphony, protested against some of the honks, rattles, squeaks, and crashes in the score, but Converse insisted they were essential. The composer's judgment was upheld by favorable reviews in the Boston *Transcript* and the New York *Times*.

The last Model T songs were suggested by the car's demise in 1927. "Henry's Made a Lady Out of Lizzie," which alluded to the new Model A, of course, and "Poor Lizzie, What'll Become of You Now?" were typical of the nostalgic compositions.

1915

Missing the milestone million; showing how it's done in San Francisco.

tracted a record crowd at New York's City College Stadium when played by the New York Philharmonic. Written by T.S. Converse, a professor of music at Harvard, the 14-minute "joyous epic" described the assembling of the 10-millionth Model T (announced by a motor horn, full blast) and followed its wandering across the country. After a necking party and a joy ride (interrupted by a collision), "'Phoenix Americanus,'" according to the program note, "righted and shaken, proceeds on his way with redoubled energy, typical of the indomitable spirit of America." At first, Serge Koussevitzky, conductor of the

Two new body types were added to the Model T stable for 1915. One was the Center-Door Sedan, a high, upright closed model with full-length bodywork, three windows per side, and a pair of doors located slightly behind the center point of the wheelbase. The other newcomer was the Coupelet, a two-seat convertible replacing the Coupe. The previous bulb horn and acetylene gas headlamps were replaced on all models by a hand-operated Klaxon horn and brass electric headlamps powered by the magneto. Also, the former straight-topped

New 1915 Center-Door Sedan proved more popular than Coupelet.   *Distinctive rear side lamps were used this year only.*

Model T prices continued to fall. 1915 runabout cost $390.

The 1915 Center-Door Sedan, priced at $740 fully equipped

rear fenders were now curved, though front fenders remained as before and, without exception, were lipped. Hood louvers and an unbraced windshield also appeared for the first time, and wire wheels were offered as an accessory. Base price for the most popular model, the touring, stood at a sensationally low $440. Production passed the milestone half-million mark for the calendar year.

Production of the one-millionth Ford, which rolled off an assembly line in September, went unnoticed, much to Ford Motor Company's chagrin. It was really the firm's fault. "With twenty-five assembly plants...and with a big factory in Detroit assembling so many Ford cars a day," *Ford Times* lamented, "we passed the million mark without knowing it."

The milestone car was presented by Henry Ford to one of his favorite dealers, Stanley Roberts of Toledo, who had requested the vehicle. Roberts displayed and raced the car at numerous northwestern Ohio county fairs; it was later wrecked with his brother at the wheel. A 1983 search for the vehicle, or old-timers' recollections of it, conducted in cooperation with the Toledo *Blade*, turned up nothing.

A highlight of Model T promotion this year was a striking demonstration of automobile production at San Francisco's Panama-Pacific Exposition. From 18 to 25 cars were built during the three hours each day the model assembly line was in operation. Easily the most popular industrial demonstration at the fair, the exhibit received

courtesy Ford Archives, Ford Museum

The miniature Model T assembly line (above) and a day's output at the 1915 Panama-Pacific Exposition

nationwide publicity and was seen by huge crowds. In recognition of its contribution to the exposition's success, it was awarded a special gold medal by the fair's management.

1916

Ford jokes sweep the nation and Flivver fables abound.

Big changes were in store for the Model T, but most of them would have to wait until the middle of calendar year 1916. The initial '16s sold were the last Model Ts with the dinky brass radiator, of which only 800 were made. The brass headlamps and horn—the "brassies" so highly prized by T enthusiasts today—were phased out in favor of pressed-steel equivalents, painted black, of course. The small boxlike hood remained, but was now fashioned of steel instead of aluminum. No new body styles appeared. The 56-inch tread width was standardized in all parts of the country. Previously, cars sold in the South were made with a wider 60-inch tread to match the width of ruts in rural roads in that part of the country.

If the Tin Lizzie's looks seemed to remain nearly constant, so too did Henry Ford's practice of cutting prices nearly every year. In August he ordered another round of reductions. This time, the touring model was lowered by $80 to $360 and the little runabout went from $390 to an unbelievable $345. The Center-Door sedan dropped by $95 to $545. Another Ford constant, rising production, continued unabated, hitting a new high of nearly 735,000 units for the calendar year.

The 1914-20 period was the heyday of the "Ford joke" precursor of Jeep and Volkswagen Beetle jokes of a later era. In these years, Ford jokes were as much a part of everyday conversation as shoptalk and office gossip, sports talk or interest in the weather, and were as likely to be heard over a glass of tea at a church social as over a glass of beer at the corner saloon. To vaudeville monologists they were the staff of life, to toastmasters a rock of refuge in time of need. Salesmen opened solicitations with them, clergymen punctuated sermons with them, and physicians carried them as part of their pharmacopeia of cheer. For half a dozen years, Ford jokes were as universal and innumerable as America's time-honored jokes about mothers-in-law, Pat and Mike, and the farmer's daughter. Not surprisingly, scores of Ford joke books, some of which sold in the tens of thousands, appeared in these years. Most of them were cheap paperbacks hawked for five, 10, or 15 cents. Some of them, however, featured contributions by the nation's leading humorists and cartoonists, including Ring Lardner, Irvin S. Cobb, Bud Fisher, Chic Jackson, and H.T. Webster.

It's impossible to determine the exact origins of the Ford joke. It may have been an offspring of the "auto-mobile joke," which was a stock-in-trade of vaudeville performers after 1902. The Essex, the Saxon, and even the high-priced Pierce-Arrow were among the targets during the automobile's early years. One gag that always brought a laugh at the Franklin's expense was the description of a bucktoothed girl: "She wouldn't be so bad-looking only she's got Franklin teeth—they're 'air-cooled.'"

Another view, shared by advertising manager Charles A. Brownell, was that the Ford jokes were started by competitors in the early days of the company. "It's not a car," rival salesmen allegedly told potential buyers, "it's just a Ford." Some of the company's 1907 advertising supports this opinion: "The Ford 4-cylinder ($600) runabout owes half its unparalleled popularity to the misrepresentation of jealous rivals." Another ad stated: "Had you ever noticed that it is a weakness inherent in disciples to disparage their leader? Some makers affect to discount the achievements of FORD." Vanadium steel was criticized by many manufacturers who, until the alloy was adopted as armor plating on American warships, predicated that Ford's "flimsy contraption" would soon fall apart. Some rivals carried on an organized "mud-slinging propaganda campaign" against the Model T. "The best wits were hired to write the material," noted the Ft. Atkinson (Wisconsin) *Union*, "and many were the editors who were caught by it. It came in a blank envelope, apparently from nowhere, and usually had concealed somewhere a thrust at the 'Tin Lizzie,' coupled with a cute story."

Some believed a source of the quips and gibes was the self-consciousness of Ford owners. Out of the desire to forestall or avert criticism, they resorted to "the psychology of the defense mechanism." By joking about the car's small size, its low price, and so on, the Ford owner "could laugh off any joshing the owner of a bigger and higher-priced car might be disposed to give him."

Certainly the Model T, because of its very cheapness, versatility, and toughness, must have encouraged many jokes. Almost everyone knew that more than half of the pieces that made up the Ford engine sold for a dime or less. News stories frequently told of a stationary Model T providing power for motors that did everything from running newspaper presses to pumping water. The car's toughness was also widely discussed. A Texan had to abandon his T to escape Mexican bandits, who hacked and burned the car until it was a wreck. However, the owner returned and was able to drive the T away. Another Ford, although buried for six years in the muck of a California riverbed, still had gas in its tank and ran "as good as new" after starting wires were installed. Still another true story concerned the Ford whose engine had been removed to pump water and whose body was drawn by a burro. The moral, as the press was quick to point out, was: "You may dissect a Ford, but you cannot kill it."

Such stories made the public feel anything was possible for a Model T—hence the countless jokes which, though bordering on the ridiculous, had a trace of plausibility about them. No doubt many of those who invented or repeated them fully shared the opinion expressed by crusader Ida Tarbell in 1915: "I have never in all the world... seen so much to cause me to laugh and weep, to wonder and rejoice, as I have at the Ford."

Many accessory manufacturers generated additional jokes by their advertising. While Ford company ads proclaimed the Model T to be as flawless as any car ever made, gadget and parts makers catering to T owners spent huge sums to convince the public that their wares made for a much better-performing, easier-riding, more powerful, more economical car. Ford owners were told that their cars drove like trucks and that a certain kind of shock absorber would make them ride like Pullmans. They were assured that by buying a $2.50 crankcase support they could actually save $20 for otherwise the crankcase would surely break and entail a $22.50 repair bill. The difficulty of starting a Model T was emphasized in ads suggesting that old-fashioned blow torches should be replaced by special firetraps built into the intake manifold. Finally, every potential rattle in the Model T could be countered by "anti-rattler" devices claimed to silence offending parts. (Of course, like the factory parts, the anti-rattlers eventually worked loose too, adding to the clatter.) It's doubtful any consumer product in history ever had its real and imaginary shortcomings so thoroughly exposed as the Model T. That such publicity should inspire and add fuel to the Ford joke craze is hardly surprising.

Ford jokes followed several patterns. Perhaps the most numerous were those concerning the Model T's diminutive size. Postmen were reportedly upset over the rumor that Ts were to be delivered by mail. A garbage collector complained of the difficulty of sorting dead cats, broken bottles, and Fords. A patron who asked for tires for his T at a large department store complained of being directed to the "Rubber Band Department." The Model T's loose-joined qualities inspired innumerable "rattle and shake" jokes. Henry Ford was reputedly a better evangelist than Billy Sunday because he had shaked hell out of more people than Sunday ever saw. A Ford owner, asked if his car always made a racket, innocently replied, "Oh no, only when it's running."

The general belief that Fords were made entirely of tin provided the theme for the "Tin Lizzie" jokes. Question: "What time is it when one Ford follows another? Answer: Tin after tin." The Ford company planned to produce cars without doors, but would furnish can openers. A man hitched his dog to his balky flivver, then was arrested for tying a tin can to a dog. A farmer, knowing that the Ford company needed lots of tin, shipped a battered tin roof to Detroit, and later received a letter stating, "While your car was an exceptionally bad wreck, we shall be able to complete repairs and return it by the first of the week."

Another joke theme involved the T's social inferiority. Question: "Why is a Ford like a bathtub? Answer: Because you hate to be seen in one." A Ford reportedly ran over a chicken, which got up saying, "cheep, cheep, cheep." Henry Ford, when offered $1.50 after repairing a farmer's stalled car, refused, saying he had all the money he wanted. "You're a liar," retorted the farmer, "because if you had plenty of money you'd take some of it and buy yourself an 'automobile!'"

Counterbalancing the jokes that ridiculed the Model T

were those that testified to its sturdy dependability. A man wanted to have his Ford buried with him, for it had always gotten him out of every hole he had ever been in. Owners of Cadillacs, Pierce-Arrows, and Packards carried Fords in their tool boxes to pull the big cars out of the mire when they bogged down. A Ford was like a motion to adjourn—because it was always in order. A Model T left the assembly plant without an engine but ran for a month anyway—on its reputation.

Other jokes—inspired by Dearborn's mass-production techniques, five-dollar workday, fifty-dollar rebate, and other departures from convention—complimented the company. In order to avoid fire risks, according to one story, Ford was shipping Model Ts in asbestos crates, because the cars came off the line so fast their metal was smoking. Although two flies could "manufacture" 48,876,552,154 new flies in six months, they didn't have anything on two Ford factories. A worker on the Ford assembly line dropped his wrench, and before he could pick it up, 20 Model Ts had passed by. The company planned to retail its cars at grocery stores and would paint them yellow, rather than black, so that they could be hung outside and sold in bunches like bananas.

Most Ford owners enjoyed hearing these gags, and were among the more inveterate spinners of them. Even if some of the puns rubbed them the wrong way, "they could," as one of the joke books pointed out, "always pat their pocketbook, let in the clutch, and ride serenely on their way, proud of their possession and confident of their good judgment."

However, there were Ford owners who never quite got used to the incessant teasing. In 1920 a long-suffering Englishman, in a widely reprinted letter to a British motor publication, expressed the anguish that this dissident minority had experienced over the years: "In our opinion it is quite time that we Fordists should strongly protest against the jokes and insults which have been hurled at us. For years we have been the stock joke of the vermillion proboscis tinted 'comedian'; sneered at by the nut whose sole ambition in life soared to the height of his socks matching his coachwork, and the glossiness of his hair equaling a seal emerging from the water; held in contempt by the chauffeur of a big "six," doubtless because a Ford has passed him on the hill; treated with brusqueness by many a garage man—such has been the experience of most of us.

"I took delivery of my earliest Ford ten years ago and at the first garage at which I stopped I was strongly advised to have fitted a tray under the chassis. Innocently I asked the reason. "So that it will pick up the nuts," came the reply. I have lost count of the number of times people have told me that they would not be found dead on a Ford.

"But what angers me most is when we are classed as a God-forsaken, poverty-stricken lot. 'He has to put up with a Ford because he cannot spring enough to buy a car.' That is what I frequently hear. Could anything be more insulting? Could anything be more remote from the truth?

"Many a Fordist could buy up a majority of these revilers; many a Fordist is their intellectual superior; many

Adapting a Model T to power farm machinery was just what Henry Ford had in mind for his car, and many people did it.

courtesy Ford Archives, Ford Museum

a Fordist possesses more gentleness and character. Therefore, should these lines reach the eye of a Ford scoffer, I will tell him plainly that he is a snob. And a snob of the worst order."

Advertising men were asked constantly whether the Ford joke helped or hindered Model T sales. Until the early 1920s most of them agreed that "every knock was a boost" and that the jibes unquestionably made the car all the more popular. When asked to place a value on the company's stock as of 1913, a New York investment banker testified in 1927 that the jokes were "an important asset" of the firm and that any manufacturer, if he had a sense of humor, would have welcomed them. Many newspaper editorials echoed this view.

Henry Ford himself was delighted with the jokes and, according to his advertising manager, told more of them than anyone in the country (his favorite was the one about the man who wanted to be buried with his T). Some publications, knowing he had a fresh joke for every reporter who came into view, even credited Ford with concocting the best of them during his leisure moments. Toastmasters invariably bantered the Model T at banquets at which Ford was a guest, and no one enjoyed the witticisms more than than the head man himself. He did not, however, as rumor often had it, subsidize publication of Ford joke books, although he often made a considerable show of buying them. "The jokes about my car sure help to popularize it," Henry once remarked. "I hope they never end."

But all good things must come to an end, even bad jokes. After the early 1920s, Chevrolet, Dodge, Hudson-Essex, and Willys-Overland all moved rapidly to the fore. The Model T had become an anachronism by then, and the Ford joke boomeranged too often to be considered an asset any longer. Now, Ford owners realized their critics were in dead earnest, and fewer of them could laugh off the barbs. The nationwide Keith-Albee vaudeville organization, perhaps the country's leading arbiter of street-corner humor, issued a mandate that Ford jokes be banned from the stage because they weren't funny anymore. Advertising experts also sensed the change, and suggested that Ford ought "to give the T prestige and to take the joke out of the car." A number of Ford executives, including Edsel Ford, agreed. In 1923, after a lapse of several years, the company resumed Motel T advertising on a massive scale, aggressively promoting the car as "a quality product" with "a high social standing." For practical purposes, then, the Ford joke died with the Model T. The Model A, introduced in December 1927, was too highly regarded to lend itself to humor. "With her," observed the New York *Sun*, "he who goes to josh remains to praise."

The Ford joke lingered on for many years, however. In 1953, an owner of a 1909 Model T was fined for speeding. His widely reported courtroom comment was in keeping with the best Tin Lizzie tradition: "It was only hitting on three. If it had been hitting on all four I doubt if you would have caught me."

1917

Lizzie gets a facelift while Ford axes ads as "economic waste."

Changes in the 1917 Model T were striking. The New York *World* in running a photo of the much-modified new model was compelled to assure readers, "Yes, it's a Ford." It seemed almost like a new Lizzie—comelier and sturdier—and it generated considerable excitement. In Chicago, a stampeding crowd broke down the window of the showroom where the car had been put on display.

The hood was now almost streamlined. The radiator, necessarily recast, was larger and had a more pleasing shape. It also had a separate shell made of pressed steel that gave it greater strength than the old one-piece construction, simplified repair, and enhanced cooling capacity. Set higher, the radiator blended nicely into the rounded hood, which in turn swept more gracefully back to the cowl. Crowned, curved fenders were the—dare we say it?—crowning touch. Brass trim had given way to black enamel or, for radiator and hubcaps, shining nickel plate. Early Model Ts were easily spotted by their squarish hoods and brass radiator caps, and had become as

much a part of every day Americana as baseburner stoves and kerosene lamps. Now, the Ford owner need scarcely blush as he passed other cars. "This comparatively tremendous advance in styling," as historian Leslie R. Henry would later write, "served to set the pattern for most of the succeeding decade."

The more stylish '17s caused something of a business blight among those companies that up to this time had done well selling crowned fenders, V-shaped radiators, and other embellishments to style-sensitive Model T owners. "More Class for Your Ford," advertised one such firm. "Make It Look Like a $1000 Car." Dealers were delighted, and the trade value of older models significantly declined.

In early 1917, Ford Motor Company halted paid Model T advertising, and bought not a line of space (not counting tractors and Lincoln cars) until 1923. This move was in line with a policy established in 1910 where advertising expenditures (or the lack thereof) were prorated according

Compared to earlier years, changes to the Model T for 1917, such as this runabout, were almost revolutionary.

to the number of orders in hand. Thus, in February, advertising manager Charles A. Brownell wrote to branch managers: "Today, we have instructed our advertising agency to wire immediate discontinuance of all Ford advertising. This is done because we are now from 40,000 to 50,000 cars behind orders, and it is simply a waste to continue advertising when production is behind." Similar messages went to the branch managers the following May and November. Almost all national magazines were dropped from the schedule after 1914, and motoring magazines were omitted starting in 1916. That year, the company spent only $6000 on paid advertising, virtually all of it for tiny newspaper ads.

Henry Ford's attitude toward paid advertising explained his firm's policy; he felt most of it was unnecessary. He conceded that advertising was "absolutely essential to introduce good, useful things," but argued that it was "an economic waste" for products already on the market. "If you really have a good thing," he often pointed out, "it will advertise itself."

Ford also liked to say that "our best advertising is free advertising" and that he would rather have a news story on the front page than have to pay for space. Ad executives were at a loss to refute him on this point for, as *Printers' Ink* lamented in 1926, the auto magnate had for years found it "a simple matter to break into the front pages of newspapers almost at will." The magazine, whose view was naturally not a detached one, believed that such publicity was largely worthless, for it "does not tell the full story of the Ford car to buyers" or "firmly fix it in the consciousness of the buying public." Others, however, were convinced that the Model T profited from the industrialist's activities and, indeed, owed a considerable portion of its success to the fact that the name "Ford" was constantly appearing in headlines.

The chief reason the company could afford to forego advertising for six years was continued strong demand for the Model T. The flivver enjoyed a seller's market even before America entered World War I, and production cutbacks during the conflict contributed to a shortage well into 1920. Sales fell off alarmingly during the winter of 1920-21, but bounced back so vigorously in the spring of 1921 that the company had to strain its capacity for two years in order to meet the huge demand. This situation embarrassed advertising types, "some of whom," said *Printers' Ink*, "would have felt inclined to chip in if Ford had passed the hat, just to get away from the task of trying to answer reactionaries who pointed to Ford's nonadvertising success."

The fact was, however, that although Ford Motor Company itself did not advertise, its dealers did. Indeed, the irascible Henry Ford, despite his claim that advertising was "an economic waste," actually required dealers to run ads under terms of their contracts. For many years, dealers handled their advertising individually but, in late 1916 at the company's suggestion, outlets in larger cities began "clubbing together." Full-page ads listing dealers' names appeared in metropolitan dailies, with cost shared according to the number of cars sold by each agent. A number of dealers balked at this policy, claiming that Ford was using them "to pay its bills." Others, because

they thought the investment was sensible as well as necessary, went along without objection. From 1917 to 1923, Ford dealers bought space at the annual rate of $3 million, a figure which, in the company's view, placed Ford among the nation's largest advertisers. Strictly speaking, the company spent only a few thousand dollars a year on materials for dealers who would use them.

Ordinarily, Ford Motor Company didn't concern itself with a dealer's choice of media or copy appeals. However the company did insist that its trademark signature, the famous Ford script, in use continuously from 1903, appear in all local advertising. Also, the parent firm strongly reprimanded dealers who resorted to unfair practices. Referring to an ad that showed a broken down competitive car over the caption, "Sell it and buy a Ford," Brownell angrily told branch managers, "This is an unwholesome type of advertising which has long since been taboo, and we certainly feel that Ford dealers have enough good things to say about our cars without knocking the other fellow."

1918

The "Fighting Pacifist" hurls his industrial might; Lizzie goes to war.

Again for 1918, Ford made no design changes in the Model T. The Town Car, despite having achieved popularity as a taxi, was phased out. So was the Coupelet. Americans, it seemed, were not yet ready for this concept, which might be considered an ancestor of the modern targa top. Total output for the calendar year dropped by nearly 200,000 units to some 436,000 cars, reflecting wartime production cutbacks.

World War I would end late in the year, and the T was cited for "gallantry in action" in a number of battlefield dispatches. Ten machine gun-laden Lizzies were used to drive Germans from an entrenched position on the

1918 Model T "high body" coupe

A collection of Model T cars and Model TT trucks as seen at a contemporary auto show

The ups and downs of driving a Model T are graphically illustrated by this 1918 Center-Door Sedan.

A wartime medical field drill conducted with a Model TT ambulance in front of the Ford factory in Highland Park

Dependable workhorse: the 1918 Model TT stake-body truck

The 1918 Model TT ambulance saw action late in World War I.

courtesy Ford Archives, Ford Museum

Marne, and the sturdy little car was the only vehicle that could get through to wounded men during the first days of fighting in the Argonne Forest. "Without a doubt the best car for the advance [ambulance] work is the Ford car," ran a 1918 medical report recently published in *Antique Automobile*. "It is small, light, easy to run, easy to maintain, simply constructed, economical in the con-sumption of gas, does not take much road space, and can be handled by one man when necessary...I am firmly convinced that the Ford ambulance...can operate in any place where troops go...in no case have I known where a Ford was blocked for more than a few minutes. On account of this fact, should the car accidently run into a hole, it may be literally lifted out."

Ford supplied these Model TT trucks for the German army's East Africa campaign in 1918.

courtesy Ford Archives, Ford Museum

Ford Model T Delivery Car

Tougher than
an army mule
and cheaper than
a team of horses.

THE FIGHTING PACIFIST

And he makes Americans out of foreigners yet.

HENRY FORD IS THE MOST POWERFUL
INDIVIDUAL ENEMY THE KAISER HAS.
— LONDON ILLUSTRATED NEWS

A trio of Model T chassis gets the once-over before heading for the front—with some help from local citizens.

1918 Model TT Special Delivery as supplied to U.S. Army

In Africa, the T saved a detachment of British soldiers from starvation by providing motive power for flatboats. General Edmund Allenby attributed the success of the Palestine campaign to "Egyptian laborers, camels, and Ford cars." According to newscaster Lowell Thomas, then lecturing on the Middle Eastern campaign, Allenby rode in a Rolls-Royce, but always had a Ford on hand as a kind of insurance.

"Hunka Tin," a parody on Rudyard Kipling's "Gunga Din," brought down vaudeville houses after its publication in the *American Field Service Bulletin*, and was used in Ford dealers' advertising all over the country. Cited by *Printers' Ink* as the most effective product advertising to emerge from the war, the poem concluded with a rattling stanza fully worthy of its subject:

> Yes, Tin, Tin, Tin,
> You exasperating puzzle, Hunka Tin,
> I've abused you and I've flayed you,
> But, by Henry Ford who made you,
> You are better than a Packard, Hunka Tin.

1919

Henry Ford turns actor, fools stockholders into selling out.

Though Model T styling remained unchanged for 1919, the year introduced an electric self-starter and demountable rims as new optional equipment items. Initially available on closed cars only, they were extended to all models by June.

The task of cranking the Model T by hand had always been especially troublesome, as related by an old-time auto writer, Murray Fahnestock, in 1924: "Mr. Smith...climbs in by the right-hand door (for there is no left-hand door by the front seat), sets the spark and throttle levers in a position like that of the hands of a clock at ten minutes to three. Then...he gets out to crank. Seizing the crank in his right hand (carefully, for a friend of his once broke his arm cranking), he slips his left forefinger through a loop of wire that controls the choke. He pulls at the loop of wire, he revolves the crank mightily, and as the engine at last roars, he leaps to the trembling running board, leans in, and moves the spark and throttle to twenty-five minutes of two. Perhaps he reaches the throttle before the engine falters into silence, but if it is a cold morning perhaps he does not. In that case, back to the crank again and the loop of wire."

This year also marked the only time during the Model T's long production run that Henry Ford talked of building another car. He did so to soften up his fellow stockholders before buying them out. The automaker loathed stockholders, equating them with drones and parasites—people who "gave nothing but money to an enterprise." He decided they had to go. On December 30, 1918, the magnate took the first step. He submitted his resignation, effective the following day, as president of Ford Motor Company "to devote my time to building up other organizations with which I am connected." His son Edsel was elected president; Henry retained his seat on the board.

Vacationing in California, Ford next told a reporter that it was his intention to build a new and better car that would undersell the Model T (by now, selling at an average $466) by $100 to $200. The new vehicle was to be built and marketed by a concern other than Ford Motor Company. The old company? "Why, I don't know exactly what will become of that," he said vaguely. The story was page-one news across the country. "The new car is well advanced, for I have been working on it while resting in California," said Ford later. Speculation mounted as to what he would do next. One of the wire services reported that Harvey Firestone would be his partner in a $200 million venture. *Printers' Ink* speculated the new car would be called the "Flivv Junior," while the Washington *Herald* was sure it would be named "Flivverette."

Within two weeks the loose comment had gotten out of hand, and many Ford dealers began to panic. Edsel was forced to write them a soothing letter. "A new car may be manufactured, but...[it] could not possibly be designed, tested out, manufactured and marketed in quantities under two or three years' time." He admonished dealers to stop worrying about the new car and to get busy selling Model Ts.

Company stockholders were also worried—concerned that Henry would actually carry out his threat and thereby depress the value of their holdings. They were thus softened up for the calls made by financial agents acting secretly in Henry's behalf. The buyout, completed by July 1919, cost Ford $105 million, $60 million of which he borrowed, though he knew the price was reasonable. When his stock-purchasing emissaries told him they had completed their mission, he reportedly "danced a jig all

Roadster Pickup like this 1919 example was part of the standard Model T line. Boxes were by various suppliers.

around the room." Ford immediately abandoned plans—assuming he ever really had any—for a Model T rival. Thus the curtain closed on the most adroit financial performance of his entire career.

But coming up with the money would not be easy. Because of curtailed civilian production during World War I, Henry anticipated unprecedented demand and high prosperity for his firm in the postwar era. The Ford company, which had sold from one-third to one-half of America's cars up to the end of the war, built a record-breaking 750,000 units (40 percent of national production) in model year 1919. Unfortunately, a postwar economic slump set in beginning in mid-1920 and auto sales, including Ford's, began falling. Now it was Henry who was concerned. He needed $25 million by April 1921 to pay off his 1919 loan; he also owed from $18 to $30 million in taxes, and he was determined to pay $7 million in employee bonuses in January 1921. Yet in the summer of 1920, he had just $20 million in cash to meet all his obligations.

To maintain production and income, Ford decided to rely on a familiar ploy: reduce prices so drastically as to shake up the industry and startle the nation. Over the objections of key executives, he instituted more price cuts on September 21, 1920, ranging from $105 to $180 on his five models, which had been priced from $525 to $975. The reductions, averaging $148, were, in percentage terms, the largest in industry history. Again, a Ford announcement was front-page news. Not untypically, the Sidney (Delaware) *Record's* three-deck headline read, "Henry Fires a Bomb," "Just Like Him," "The Ford Is The Thing and Everybody Can Afford to Buy a Ford." Several papers suggested that the industrialist—since he alone had demonstrated the courage and ability to give people relief from inflation—should be made "general manager" of the nation.

The rest of the auto industry was incensed over the move. Representatives from several firms—including General Motors, Dodge, Maxwell-Chalmers, Hupp, Hudson, Essex and Paige—met in Detroit and solemnly announced that prices should not be lowered, because buyers would then expect further reductions and all buying would cease. Such statements only made Henry's halo glow all the brighter. Though reluctant, a number of rivals led by Franklin, Studebaker, and Willys-Overland found it expedient to follow Ford's lead. By October 9, some 23 automakers had lowered prices, 28 had not.

For a time it appeared that Ford's pricing strategy might succeed, as more than 100,000 Model Ts were sold in October. In November, however, sales were off approximately 10 percent, and in December they sank to less than 50 percent of the November figure. As the recession wore on, Ford produced 78,000 Model Ts—some 35,000 more than dealers could sell—during the first 24 days of December, then closed its plants "for inventory," promising to reopen the following January 5. But the hiatus actually extended to February 1. Meanwhile, rumors that Ford was in financial straits spread throughout the country. Many people were genuinely alarmed at the automaker's plight, and Model T owners "rallied like bees" to a suggestion by the chief of the Columbus, Ohio, Western Union bureau that each lend $100 to Henry to tide him over.

Ford declined all such offers, recalled workers, and in February assembled 35,000 Model Ts from stocks on hand. These cars, along with 30,000 unconsigned vehicles produced in late 1920, were immediately shipped to dealers. As was then industry practice, dealers had to pay for the cars upon arrival or forfeit their franchises. In most instances they went to their bankers, got the money they needed, and watched demand gradually use up the excess supply. Instead of borrowing money himself, Ford had, in effect, forced dealers to borrow for him. Fortunately for all concerned the recession ended and, by the spring and summer of 1921, Model Ts were being built and sold at a record-breaking rate. Henry had outwitted Wall Street and paid his way out of trouble. His stature as a folk hero had reached new heights.

1920

America's most diversified industrial empire gets into the movie business.

No entry/exit problems in the 1920 Model T coupe!

Model T styling stayed the same as the Roaring '20s opened. A minor change was the switch from wooden to composition steering wheels, which were also enlarged from 15- to 16-inch diameter. Calendar year production fell sharply from its 1919 level, from about 820,000 to 419,517.

Throughout the 1920s, Ford dealers made considerable use of sales promotion films. A sales representative reported that in Pound, Wisconsin, a village of 400, more than 2000 people flocked in from the surrounding area to view films at the Ford dealership every Wednesday night. In Bridgeboro, N.J., an agent showed the movies in a nearby grove to an eager audience of 1800-2000 farmers every week. Many branches and dealers kept specially

A typical publicity photo for the 1920 Model T line. This one shows a sedate twosome in their new runabout.

It seemed somebody always had a new use for a T in the '20s. A good example is this half-track converted from a coupe.

equipped Model Ts and projectionists on the road. "We've given more than 40 shows with an average of 200 to 250 on hand," reported the dealer at Silsbee, Texas, "and are creating goodwill by the bushel." The Ford films were the first motion pictures many people had ever seen, a number of dealers reported. Besides dealer showrooms, the films sometimes were shown in prospective buyers' homes and—in many small towns—on the side of a billboard or building. All these were, of course, silent movies—"talkies" were still a few years away.

From 1920 on, Henry Ford did far more than run the "Model T Company." Indeed, he developed America's first vertically integrated, highly diversified industrial empire. His company mined coal, iron ore, and lead; owned timber lands, sawmills, dry kilns, a wood distillation plant, a rubber plantation, and a series of "village industries"; operated a railroad, blast furnaces, coke ovens, foundries, steel mills, and lake and ocean fleets; produced

Another, more elaborate snow vehicle, based on the runabout

And here's a "church" that drives to you, not vice-versa!

glass, artificial leather, textiles, gauges, paper, and cement; built airplanes; farmed 10,000 acres; and made Fordson tractors and Lincolns in addition to Model Ts. The company also prospected for oil, bought dolomite lands with the production of magnesium in mind, took steps to produce abrasives, bought acreage in the Florida Everglades with the intention of planting rubber trees, and experimented with the development of power by burning coal at the mine and making charcoal iron. These various activities received wide attention during the 1920s, and contributed importantly to the popular belief that Henry Ford had a daring and highly original mind, virtually unique technical skills, and a never-ending desire to serve mankind.

1921

Small-town America celebrates Ford Days; Henry unwisely attacks Jews.

Though the Model T itself didn't change for 1921, its production figures did, which must have been a relief to Ford accountants. From the depressed level of 1920, calendar year output more than doubled to nearly 904,000, a new record.

This was the year that saw the emergence of Ford Days in hundreds of small communities throughout the country. Town merchants, at the instigation of the local Ford dealer, would set aside a day and invite every Model T owner or driver in the surrounding area to come in. Businesses offered them special bargains, and a carnival atmosphere prevailed as Main Street was taken over for parades, band concerts, vaudeville performances, dancing, queen crownings, and Model T and athletic contests. Prizes were awarded to contest winners and to owners of the cars carrying the biggest load of produce, the most eggs, the most children, the five prettiest girls, and so on. Model T owners turned out by the thousands for Ford Days, and virtually took over some towns inasmuch as drivers of other cars were usually fined if their vehicles appeared on the streets.

Ford Days continued until 1931. Model Ts, even after production ceased, continued to make up a large proportion of the participants.

The Model T became the first American car to be boycotted by a consumer group. The boycott, by Jews, was in reaction to a notorious, 91-week anti-Semitic campaign launched in 1920 by Henry Ford's weekly magazine, the *Dearborn Independent*. Ford, whose anti-Semitism stemmed more from ignorance than deep-seated bigotry or malice, believed that Jews wanted to gain control of the nation's finances, commerce, and politics at the expense of Christians, and thought he was performing a great service by exposing this. Jews thought otherwise, of course and, although no Jewish organizations or groups declared a formal boycott of the Model T, many

Jewish firms and individuals stopped buying Fords nonetheless. So did some other firms doing business with Jewish concerns and dependent on their goodwill. Jews in Hartford, Connecticut, in staging a 400-car parade in honor of Dr. Chaim Weizmann and Albert Einstein, ordered "Positively no Ford machines in line."

Ford's branch managers and dealers, particularly those in cities with large Jewish populations, complained bitterly about the sales resistance and economic pressure prompted by the *Independent's* campaign. The manager of the second-ranking dealership in the New York branch even went so far as to suggest that if Ford put the money spent on the anti-Semitic articles into making better cars, everybody would be happier. Some dealers were threatened with eviction by Jewish landlords, but got little sympathy from Ford's personal secretary. In reply to a Minnesota dealer urging the articles be stopped, he suggested that dealers should own their own buildings so as not to be vulnerable to such pressure. Ford himself was similarly unmoved. His stock answer was, "If they want our product, they'll buy it."

It's difficult to determine the number of Model T sales lost to this boycott. There was a sharp drop in sales during the last half of 1920, but this was due to a general economic decline that affected the entire industry. Then, as the economy improved, Ford sales reached new highs in 1921-23. Unquestionably, some Jews condemned Ford's actions but still bought his products. As Will Rogers pointed out, the boycott "may not be a complete success yet—but it will be as soon as someone learns how to make a cheaper car." At this point the Model T was definitely a better buy than any competitor. However, it wasn't in the mid-'20s, and Henry would learn he could no longer be complacent about boycotts when he launched a second anti-Semitic campaign.

As impulsively as he had begun it, Ford ordered the series of articles discontinued in January, 1922. The reasons are not altogether clear. One possibility is that his New York manager finally convinced him of the difficulty of selling Model Ts in areas with large Jewish populations.

The Center-Door Sedan was still listed in the 1921 catalog.

The 1921 edition of the evergreen Model T touring. Note neat "boot" to partly conceal the folded top.

courtesy Ford Archives, Ford Museum

Another is that Ford was swayed by William Fox, president of Fox Film Corporation, who threatened to show choice footage of Model T accidents in his newsreels if Ford persisted in attacking the character of Jewish film executives and their motion pictures. In any event, Henry called off the campaign, although in so doing he retracted nothing and, indeed, later boasted that his articles had opened the minds of Americans to possible evils.

In 1924, the *Independent* launched its second series of anti-Semitic articles under the general title, "Jewish Exploitation of Farmer Organizations." Ford thought that a Jewish group was trying to obtain control of American wheat farming. One of those he attacked, Aaron Sapiro, a prominent Chicago attorney, filed a million-dollar suit against Henry Ford (not the *Independent)* for defamation of character. Ford settled out of court in July 1927, and published both a personal apology to Sapiro and a formal retraction of all his past attacks on Jewish people. His motives for issuing the apology were complex. An important factor undoubtedly was the critical changeover from Model T to Model A production at a time when much of the sales force was complaining that Jewish hostility hurt business.

After this, many Jews resumed buying Ford products. But they were alienated again in 1938 when Ford, on his 75th birthday, accepted the Grand Cross of the Supreme Order of the German Eagle, the highest honor Hitler's Third Reich could bestow on a foreigner. An accompanying citation observed the medal was given to recognize Ford as a pioneer of motor cars for the masses. But his acceptance of the award along with other anti-Semitic and pro-Nazi accusations against him led to an active and effective boycott of Ford products in the years just before World War II by Jews and other Americans unsympathetic to his views. The resulting sales slump was particularly acute in the company's eastern sales region, which had the largest Jewish population in the country. Region manager W.K. Edmunds wrote in 1944: "Mr. Edsel Ford understood this situation thoroughly, and just prior to the time we discontinued making automobiles, he had alloted us a special fund (approximately $50,000) to be used for sales promotion and advertising in this area to improve our sales and counteract the existent antagonism." A company-conducted investigation also revealed that in Hollywood, "Jewish interests...agreed to ban all Ford units from their studio lots and forbade employees and stars to buy Ford products." The report added, "A few stars are in a position to disregard the order, but many sales are being lost."

To this day, many older Jews have not forgotten, and many have not forgiven, Henry Ford. A dwindling number of elderly Jews still will not buy a Ford vehicle and are critical of those who do. Since the late '40s, however, almost all Jews have been gratified by the friendliness of the Ford family and company toward the Jewish community. "The new generation of Fords," declared an influential Jewish editor in 1970, "looks back at the era of their grandfather with a sense of deep regret, rejecting whatever smacked of prejudice and of anti-Semitism."

1922

Got something to say? Why not paint it on your Flivver?

Henry Ford (left) and Henry M. Leland in 1922

The trusty T was again unchanged for 1922. The so-called Center Door Sedan with its distinctive oval rear window was discontinued. The doors' position made entry/exit awkward, and the car was considered top-heavy, slow, and expensive.

The T's most highly publicized hillclimb victory occurred this year, when a flivver triumphed in the fourth annual world's championship contest held on Pike's Peak near Colorado Springs, Colorado. The win had rags-to-riches overtones worthy of the T. Owner and driver of the winning car was a 21-year-old small-town Nebraskan, Noel E. Bullock, who had driven up the mountain only once before the race. The car itself, named "Old Liz," was unpainted and hoodless, and had been "home brewed" by

the youth in a blacksmith's shop in 1918. The Ford entry had been publicly ridiculed before the run by several drivers who called it a "tin can" and a "cross between a kiddie-car and a pushmobile." Yet this T flashed to the top, besting the elite drivers of road racing and many of the highest-priced makes in America. Bullock planned to race up Pike's Peak again in 1923. But he was blacklisted nine days before the event for participating in a nonsanctioned dirt-track race in South Dakota. No other Model T ever won on the mountain.

Henry chats with a bevy of beauties in a well-loaded Lizzie. Writing on hood reads "Stop and Reconsider."

During the early and mid-1920s the "Lizzie Label" craze, humorous comments painted on flivvers, was at its height. The Label flourished particularly in land-grant college communities where small-town smart alecks and country clowns had an abundance of dilapidated Model Ts for "canvases." The exact origin of the Lizzie Labels is obscure. But a contemporary professor believes that they were greatly popularized by *Judge*, a widely quoted satirical weekly, which gave this peculiar folk art the dignity of humorous literature by paying five dollars each for the best of them.

Like the Ford jokes, Lizzie Labels had certain discernible patterns. Many of them borrowed quotations, such as "Abandon home, all ye who enter in" and "I do not choose to run." Others were familiar contemporary sayings, such as "Barnum was right," and "Our booz 'em friend." Another group parodied advertising slogans and the titles of songs, plays, and movies. Some were in the form of notices, like "Quiet please, violent ward" (on hood) or "Night calls by appointment only." Another theme was the wisecrack: "Follow us, farmer, for haywire"; "You may pass me, big boy, but I'm paid for"; "Heck of the Resperus." Sex was perhaps the most prevalent theme: "Girls, watch your step-ins" and "For fastidious flappers" are examples.

This year, for the first time, Ford supplemented Model T production, albeit on a much smaller scale, with another car, the Lincoln. The Lincoln Motor Company had been organized in 1917 by Cadillac founder Henry M. Leland and his son Wilfred to produce Liberty aircraft engines for the war effort. The firm then turned to automobile manufacturing. Unfortunately, its car didn't reach the market until September 1920, when auto sales had begun to sink from prewar levels. The Lelands' car, selling in the $5000-$6000 range, was thus handicapped from the outset. Furthermore, though it was mechanically one of the soundest cars made in America, it lacked style. Sales totaled only 752 units in 1920, and the firm proved unable to produce and sell profitably during 1921. Later in the year, the company faced bankruptcy.

Henry Ford stepped into the breach, buying Lincoln at the receiver's sale in February 1922. The Lelands had the impression they could continue to run the plant, but Ford's people soon forced them to resign. The Lelands feared that the Ford organization might lower the high standards that they had set, but this proved groundless. The Lincoln's mechanical excellence was maintained and its styling—which was now Edsel Ford's responsibility—was considerably improved. Edsel also enlisted the services of the great coachbuilding houses of the day—Judkins, Brunn, Le Baron, Willoughby, Dietrich, and Locke. Prices for standard-body models, styled by Brunn, were cut to between $3300 and $4900. Custom-body examples ran from $4600 to $7200.

Ford Motor Company immediately began a publicity and advertising campaign to promote Lincoln as a car of the highest quality. At auto shows and in hotel lobbys, Lincoln exhibits (frequently called the Lincoln Salon Petite) strove to create an aura of snob appeal. "Guests," many of whom had been sent engraved invitations, were greeted by "doormen and other attendants appropriately uniformed and carefully schooled in the proprieties." They were then escorted to the display, "a picture of exquisite appointments, floral decorations, and perfumed fountains, further enhanced through artistic lighting effects." "Charmingly costumed" pages and tuxedo-clad salesmen, each of whom wore a white carnation, were on hand to serve the guests, while liveried drivers waited outside to demonstrate the "chauffeur-driven equipage."

During 1923-24, Ford spent more than $400,000 on Lincoln advertising. Much of that went to 10 "class" magazines such as *Vogue, Vanity Fair, Town & Country, Spur,* and *Motor Life.* Aside from print advertising, Lincoln's leading sales-promotion medium was a monthly motoring magazine simply called *Lincoln.* Introduced in December 1922, it was designed to appeal to "people of taste and culture," and contained little of the "hard sell" copy that had been a feature of *Ford Times.* The periodical was sent to Lincoln owners and prospective buyers, as well as to "many of the finest clubs" in the country. Circulation stood at 70,000 in 1924.

Lincoln was not an outstanding sales success in its early years as a Ford Motor Company product. An average of some 7000 cars were retailed annually between 1922 and 1930. Packard and Cadillac, competing at the same price level, outsold Lincoln more than three to one, while Pierce-Arrow, priced considerably higher, marketed almost as many units as Ford's luxury entry.

1923

A thoroughly modern Lizzie may not be modern enough in the Roaring '20s.

The first major appearance alterations to the Model T in nearly five years were introduced for the 1923 models. The most obvious were bodies set lower on their chassis and higher radiators. Two new closed body styles were offered, two- and four-door sedans. The latter was predictably marketed as the "Fordor," a play on the name Ford; the former was called "Tudor" for consistency, though the spelling had nothing to do with England.

Both of the new sedans and the familiar Coupe featured a large, rectangular rear window, thus improving visibility astern. Rotary window regulators, a cowl ventilator, and square fuel tanks were adopted across the board. The Coupe's rear compartment was now formed integrally with the rest of the body. The Runabout retained its detachable rear compartment that permitted it to be easily converted into a "pickup delivery." Open cars had new tops that could be erected or folded by one person, and their windshields were set at a more jaunty angle, with the upper section pivoted at the top of the frame.

Though production would set another record this year—over 1.8 million units—the Model T was looking decidedly old-fashioned by now, and becoming more so all the time. This may be the reason Ford resumed heavy ad-

Ford Touring Car
$295

F. O. B. DETROIT
Starter and Demountable Rims $85 Extra

OF all the times of the year when you need a Ford car, that time is NOW!

Wherever you live—in town or country—owning a Ford car helps you to get the most out of life.

Every day without a Ford means lost hours of healthy motoring pleasure.

The Ford gives you unlimited chance to get away into new surroundings every day—a picnic supper or a cool spin in the evening to enjoy the countryside or a visit with friends.

These advantages make for greater enjoyment of life—bring you rest and relaxation at a cost so low that it will surprise you.

By stimulating good health and efficiency, owning a Ford increases your earning power.

Buy your Ford now or start weekly payments on it.

courtesy Ford Archives, Ford Museum

Ford resumed corporate car advertising in 1923 after a six-year hiatus. Prices got the major emphasis.

Ford
RUNABOUT ~
$265 ~

f. o. b. Detroit

[Demountable Rims and Starter $85 extra.]

FOR summer trips—a long tour or a short spin—a Ford car gives the most pleasure and convenience at the lowest cost.

Tuck your bundles into the spacious rear compartment. Take the family along with every assurance that your Ford will prove dependable for driving on any road in town or country.

Ford driving is safe driving. Ford quality and careful manufacture contribute to the dependable, safe driving of Ford cars.

Ford driving is economical driving. No other car requires such a small outlay to buy, costs so little to maintain.

Owning a Ford gives you freedom from the hardships of summer weather—gets you out and away into new surroundings at a moment's notice any time.

Be independent of distance. Let us show you how much a Ford will mean to you and your family this Summer and Fall.

FREE AND INDEPENDENT
with a Ford car

courtesy Ford Archives, Ford Museum

The lure of the great outdoors has been a consistent Ford ad theme. Shown is a 1924 ad for the Model T runabout.

Priced at about $390 in 1923, the Model T touring was still enormously popular even after 15 years on the market.

vertising of the Model T beginning this year. During the previous six years the company had bought no ad space at all, leaving individual dealers to carry the ball instead. But this left much to be desired in that sales pitches were neither uniform nor consistently seen in all parts of the country. The result was that in August 1923, following a conference with branch managers, Edsel Ford announced the reestablishment of an advertising department in Dearborn.

Ford was one of the nation's biggest ad buyers in the mid-1920s, spending nearly $15 million between September 1923 and October 1926. About eight percent of the total budget was scheduled for women's and "prestige" magazines, as the advertising staff sought to imbue the Tin Lizzie with "an atmosphere of 'Pride of Ownership'....of class and quality." As with prewar attempts to establish the Model T as a prestige item, this aspect of the campaign met with little success. In fact, by this time a Ford probably evoked less pride of ownership among women and prestige-conscious men than any car on the market.

Henry Ford's basic dislike of advertising again surfaced in June 1926, when he told his dealers to fend for themselves once more. From mid-1926 until the Model A's introduction in late 1927, the company bought virtually no advertising space. Dealers in many metropolitan areas again banded together, retained advertising agencies, and resumed campaigns on a city-wide basis.

1924

Lizzie turns Sweet Sixteen and the 10-Millionth T tours the country.

Lizzie was Sweet Sixteen in 1924, and still going strong. On June 15th that year the 10-millionth Model T left the assembly line at Highland Park. The milestone flivver led parades through most towns and cities along the Lincoln Highway (New York to San Francisco) and along Route 66 (Chicago to Los Angeles). Several million people are estimated to have seen the vehicle, which was "greeted" by governors and mayors at each stop along the route. The tour was documented in a film entitled "Fording the Lincoln Highway," which was widely exhibited in the mid-'20s.

The 11-millionth Ford was presented to the Prince of Wales during his visit to Highland Park in October of this year. Afterward, the Prince spent time at Fair Lane, the Ford family estate in Dearborn. A photo taken there of Henry, posed with son Edsel and the Prince, served as a model for a life-size statue of the automaker that was installed in front of Dearborn's Henry Ford Centennial Library in 1974. Stated sculptor Marshall Fredericks: "This

Henry with the first and 10-millionth cars to bear his name, photographed at Ford's Fair Lane estate in 1924.

The 1924 Model T coupe was priced at $525.

Ex-racer Frank Kulick begins the "Lincoln Highway" trip.

"Cotton Beverly," a special Model T "Depot Hack" of 1924

1924 Model TT "side screen delivery" truck

pose, the thoughtful look, represents him in the best way. I like to see him thinking.''

Though there were no physical changes in the evergreen T for 1924, Henry was sharpening his pencil for another price reduction, announced in December. The figures were astonishing: an unheard of $260 for the runabout and a mere $290 for the touring, both all-time lows. Despite such bargain-basement rates, Ford made an average of $50 per car and netted a $100 million total profit for 1923-24.

Meanwhile, the competition was preparing to put an end to the Model T's incredible market domination. General Motors, reorganized after the 1920 recession by Pierre duPont and Alfred Sloan, was readying a Chevrolet only slightly more costly than the Ford and yet far more modern and better-looking. It would take some time to halt the Model T juggernaut, but it's interesting to note that 1923 would be the peak year for Ford sales. From 1925 on, the trend would be inexorably downward.

1925

Balloon tires are nice, but how 'bout a proper transmission, Mr. Ford?

For 1925, the T received a facelift. This included larger fenders and newly optional nickel-plated radiator shell. Balloon tires were offered as a new accessory at $25 apiece and, when so fitted, made this year's Tin Lizzie look almost modern. Another new extra was a factory-installed, hand-operated windshield wiper. The price cuts instituted in late 1924 remained in force. The most expensive model in the line was the Fordor sedan at $680. Next came the Tudor priced at $580, followed by the Coupe at

U.S. car prices reached an all-time low with the 1925 Model T runabout—an astounding $260 f.o.b. list.

courtesy Ford Archives, Ford Museum

Company ad clearly shows 1925's ultra-low Model T prices.

Another 1925 ad stresses affordability, driving safety.

The 1925 Model T runabout, with optional balloon tires

$520. The two open cars, Runabout and Touring, remained at $260 and $290, respectively.

By this time the sliding-gear selective transmission, usually with three speeds forward, was coming into more general use. Ford dealers, finding the Model T's planetary transmission increasingly difficult to sell, clamored for a change. So did many T owners. But Ford clung to the old gearbox like a kid with a well-used toy. In fact, he seemed to have something of a prejudice against sliding-gear transmissions. In 1910, a Ford test driver crashed into a telephone pole with a vehicle equipped with one of the new gearboxes, and there was a chance the transmission was partly to blame. "Mr. Ford was tickled to death," recalled an associate. "He was glad it was smashed up, and he never had anything to do with it (the sliding-gear transmission) until we came to the Model A."

1926

"You can paint up a barn, but it will still be a barn and not a parlor."

For the first time in more than a decade, closed versions of the Model T were offered in a choice of colors as well as black. This followed development of new lacquer paints that dried fast enough to match the line rate at Highland Park. Also for 1926, chassis were lowered on all models, and fuel tanks were relocated to the cowl area except for Fordor sedans. The nickel-plated radiator shell was made standard equipment on closed cars, and was optional for the Touring and Runabout. Inside, steering wheel diameter was enlarged once more, to 17 inches. Wire wheels were a new accessory, and complemented the balloon tires introduced the previous year. Finally, open cars were at last equipped with an opening left front door; no more sliding in from the passenger's side or hopping over the driver's-side gunwale.

1926

When finished in one of the new hues—named gunmetal blue, highland green, phoenix brown, and fawn gray—the faithful Tin Lizzie reminded one of a prim but made-up spinster out on a fling. But colors and minor alterations made no difference: the Model T was on its last legs. In 1921-26, Ford accounted for more than half the cars and trucks sold in the United States. The firm's best sales year before 1955 was 1923, when more than 2 million Model Ts were sold. But by then, the car was rapidly becoming obsolete next to its competitors.

The T's greatest competitive assets—low price and a reputation for utility and sturdiness—had served it well in an era of poor roads and equally unsophisticated yet higher-priced rivals. But during the mid-1920s, as hard-surfaced highways fanned across the nation and mechanically sound cars became more commonplace, these selling points began to pale. Furthermore, although Ford had cut prices $100 between 1922 and 1926, Chevrolet had slashed prices $140, Overland $300, Maxwell $490, and Dodge $890 during the same period.

More important, public tastes were changing. Increased affluence and new values made many car buyers—especially women, who had come to have more influence in car sales—increasingly style-conscious and interested in more comfort and conveniences. Many men insisted on the latest mechanical innovations and additional speed and power. The Model T had little style. Convenience features and mechanical refinements if they could be had at all, cost extra.

All dressed up but nowhere to go: the 1926 Model T touring

A number of manufacturers, sensing the shift in attitudes, rose to the challenge with extensive consumer research programs. General Motors surveyed hundreds of thousands of motorists to find out what they liked and didn't like about their cars, then skillfully designed and effectively promoted its new models accordingly. Noting Ford's inactivity in this area, one magazine correctly opined: "It is difficult to imagine Henry Ford asking one motorist for advice, let alone taking it." Ford, perhaps the only automaker to conduct formal market studies before World War I and once so attuned to the public's needs, stubbornly ignored the winds of change.

This 1926 Model T touring wears accessory side curtains, balloon tires, wire-spoke wheels, full top boot.

Showing roomy interior of Tudor Sedan. Both front seats tilt forward permitting easy access through either door. Driver's seat adjustable for comfortable driving.

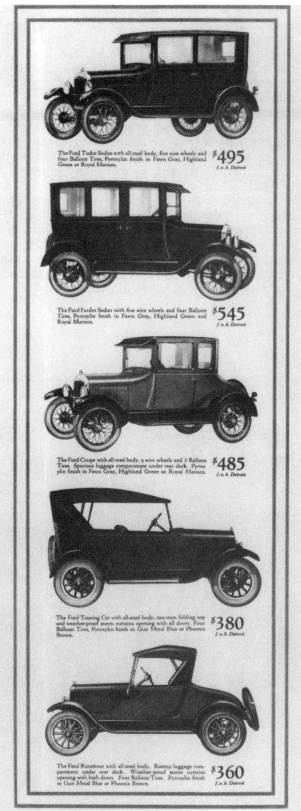

The Ford Tudor Sedan with all-steel body, five wire wheels and four Balloon Tires. Pyroxylin finish in Fawn Gray, Highland Green or Royal Maroon.
$495
f. o. b. Detroit

The Ford Fordor Sedan with five wire wheels and four Balloon Tires. Pyroxylin finish in Fawn Gray, Highland Green and Royal Maroon.
$545
f. o. b. Detroit

The Ford Coupe with all-steel body, 5 wire wheels and 4 Balloon Tires. Spacious luggage compartment under rear deck. Pyroxylin finish in Fawn Gray, Highland Green or Royal Maroon.
$485
f. o. b. Detroit

The Ford Touring Car with all-steel body, one-man folding top and weather-proof storm curtains opening with all doors. Four Balloon Tires. Pyroxylin finish in Gun Metal Blue or Phoenix Brown.
$380
f. o. b. Detroit

The Ford Runabout with all-steel body. Roomy luggage compartment under rear deck. Weather-proof storm curtains opening with both doors. Four Balloon Tires. Pyroxylin finish in Gun Metal Blue or Phoenix Brown.
$360
f. o. b. Detroit

Meeting every modern need of
TRANSPORTATION

Unless you have inspected and driven a Ford car recently built, you will be amazed at the many features which make Ford ownership so desirable.

Closed car interiors are roomy with every provision made for comfort and convenience. Seats are set at the proper angle for relaxation, deeply cushioned and with plenty of leg room for both front and rear seat occupants. Upholstery and trim have been selected for beauty and durability, and harmonize with body colors, which may be had in optional shades of Pyroxylin finish.

Both without and within there are refinements and features in the all-steel bodies that must be seen to be properly appreciated.

Furthermore, you are not familiar with Ford performance and operating economy unless you have driven a Ford car manufactured within the last few months. Many improvements have been effected including a new carburetor vaporizer, which makes the Ford engine smoother, quieter, and more powerful at all speeds—with greatly increased gasoline mileage.

We urge you to go to the Ford dealer whose name appears on this folder, and let him show you what Ford value means today.

Ford Motor Company
DETROIT, MICH.

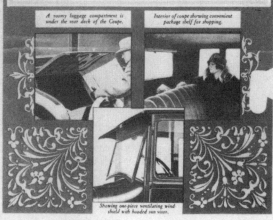

A roomy luggage compartment is under the rear deck of the Coupe.

Interior of coupe showing convenient package shelf for shopping.

Showing one-piece ventilating wind shield with hooded sun visors.

New Colors — Increased Mileage — Better Motor Operation

1927

But even Ford couldn't ignore the sales figures. From 1924 to 1925 unit sales dropped from 1,870,000 to 1,675,000 while Chevrolet advanced from 280,000 to 470,000. In response, Henry cut prices twice in 1926. But for the first time in Model T history these trumps failed to boost sales. Ford's 1926 deliveries were almost 400,000 units below the 1925 figure. Meanwhile, Chevrolet gained an additional 260,000 customers.

By the spring and early summer of 1926, it was clear to most everyone in the Ford organization—except Henry Ford and one or two other executives also wearing blinders—that the Model T was failing. Despite an improved market, Model T sales in the April-June period dropped 154,000 from the comparable months in 1925. These figures were not lost on the press. Noting Chevrolet's 33 percent sales increase and its plan to expand production capacity to a million units annually by 1927, many observed that the Model T's dominance was being seriously threatened for the first time in almost two decades.

Speculation began immediately as to how Henry would turn things around. First reports were that he would replace the four-cylinder T with a six-cylinder car. When he denied this, it was next rumored that Ford would bring out a "Sheik Car" (a la Rudolph Valentino) to satisfy female demands for more style. Again Ford said no, remarking that he had already given the Model T colors and a nickel-plated hood. "Yes," a New York dealer was quoted, "you can paint up a barn, but it will still be a barn and not a parlor." Throughout the remainder of the year and into 1927 the rumors mounted: Ford would replace the T's planetary transmission with a selective gear shift; he would add a fourth speed; he would adopt a new carburetor capable of 30 mpg; he would produce an eight-cylinder model priced under $1000; he would enter the medium-price field with a car to be named Edison; he would build a super-flivver, a two-cylinder car with as much power as a four. Invariably Ford was asked to comment on these rumors, and invariably he denied them all. The Model T, he said, would endure.

1927

A nation remembers a faithful friend as Lizzie reaches the end of the road

courtesy Ford Archives, Ford Museum

Henry (left), son Edsel, the 1896 Quadricycle and the milestone 15-millionth Model T, in Dearborn, May 26, 1927

The Model T reached the end of its long road in 1927. Underneath all the cosmetic freshening up that had been done in the previous 10 years, the last Lizzie to roll out of the factory really wasn't that much different than the first one built in late 1908. That was one of her problems, of course, the thing that ultimately did her in, but it's also one of the many reasons why we remember the Model T with such affection some 60 years later. Cars built during this final year were equipped with the previously optional wire wheels as standard, replacing the old wood "artillery-spoke" types, and maroon and green were added to the color chart.

In mid-February, Henry Ford admitted for the first time that he needed to put a new car on the market. Acknowledging he had given some thought to its design, he refused to name an introduction date, claiming that "a statement at this time on the matter...might do serious injury to my competitors." A fresh crop of rumors at once sprang up. By early spring it was commonly assumed that the new model would be faster and would have a sliding-gear transmission. It would appear soon; some said as early as late June. But Ford was silent. Competitors complained this was responsible for a mild sales slowdown as prospects postponed buying until they saw what Ford had in mind. "The result is getting on everyone's nerves," said an Ohio newspaper, "as Ford himself probably realizes." Ford gave in: on the evening of May 25, 1927, Ford Motor Company confirmed that it would indeed build a new car.

As if to punctuate the announcement, the 15-millionth Model T rolled off the Highland Park assembly line the following afternoon, May 26th. The occasion was marked in an appropriately simple manner. There were no bands, no bunting, no speeches. With Edsel at the wheel and his father beside him, the car led a motorcade of company officials and 15 reporters and cameramen to the Dearborn Engineering Laboratory. On the plaza in front of the building, under gray skies, were Ford's earliest automobiles and the first Model T. For the benefit of motion-picture cameramen, Henry Ford drove both the older cars around the plaza. The ceremony was over.

Most newspapers and magazines commented on the Model T's demise. There were, as the Louisville *Times* predicted, "acres of humorous writing devoted...to 'hunky Elizabeth, chunky Elizabeth, spunky Elizabeth Ford.'" The Baltimore *Sun*, for example, remarked, "Since the Model T makes as much noise as any 10 other cars and the new Ford cannot possibly be noisier than the old, life will be pleasanter, we will all live longer." Most of the press, though, regarded this as a momentous event and treated it with a certain sentimentality. To the New York *Herald-Tribune*, the T's passing was "The End of an Epoch"; the Dayton *News* said a "world institution" was being "Retired with Honors." The Roanoke *News* spoke for many: "It will be long before America loses its affectionate, if somewhat apologetic, remembrance of the car that first put us on wheels. We probably wouldn't admit it to anyone, but deep in our hearts we love every rattle in its body."

There were many reluctant to see the Model T go. Hearst newspaper executive Arthur Brisbane, on adding a new Ford sedan and truck to the several he already owned, wired Henry that he should keep one plant running indefinitely to make half a million Model Ts a year; he thought they could easily be sold at higher prices by mail order. A Ford dealer in Newark, "believing in the great merit of the Model T and the continued demand for same," sought to arrange for its manufacture and/or assembly in New Jersey. Newark citizens, he assured the company, would finance the scheme. Soon after the May 25th announcement, many owners began to take better

Henry drives Quadricycle past photographers in May 1927.

care of their Tin Lizzies, eager to prolong their lives. One elderly lady of means in Montclair, New Jersey, purchased and stored away seven new Model Ts so that she would not be without one for the rest of her life. A man in Toledo bought six, and only wore out the last of them in 1967.

The perspective of time only served to increase affection and respect for "the first log cabin of the motor age." Archibald Henderson, writing in 1930, was typical in declaring that the Model T's impact was "greater by far than that of the telegraph, the telephone, rural free delivery, the phonograph, the radio, or electric light and power." E.B. White and Richard Lee Strout, in their classic 1936 epitaph "Farewell, My Lovely," said, "it was hard-working, commonplace, heroic...the miracle God

Edsel Ford wheels the 15-millionth T in May 1927 ceremony.

Lizzie went out with style, if not grace, as this 1927 runabout illustrates.

had wrought. And it was patently the sort of thing that could only happen once." To Philip Van Doren Stern, writing in 1955, the Model T "was, as no car before or since has been, truly the people's car...part of the fabric of American life, celebrated in song and legend and folklore." In 1959, *Fortune* magazine reported that 100 of the world's leading designers, architects, and design teachers ranked the T as the 82nd "best designed mass-produced product of modern times" (higher than all other Ford cars

except the 1940 Lincoln Continental, which ranked sixth, and the 1955 Thunderbird, rated 41st). In 1974, the T was voted "the world's greatest motorcar" by readers of *Motor Trend* magazine.

That the T helped to change America's psychology, manners, and mores as well as the national economy is beyond question. No other single device did so much to induce people of a provincial mind to begin thinking in regional and national terms. None did so much to knit together different parts of the county, state and, ultimately, the nation.

Ford produced 15,007,033 Model Ts in the United States through May 31, 1927, the figure and date often cited for total output and the end of production. But the company assembled 477,748 additional Ts during the summer of 1927. Ford of Canada had built another 747,259 Tin Lizzies, Ford of England an estimated 250,000. For several decades, automotive historians and journalists believed that the T's production mark would stand unchallenged. "No other model was ever produced in such numbers," asserted Allan Nevins and Frank Ernest Hill in their authoritative 1957 book *Ford: Expansion and Challenge 1915-1933,* "and it is safe to say that on this score alone its record will never be matched." But Germany's Volkswagen, amid much fanfare, produced its 15,007,034th Model 1200 Beetle on February 17, 1972, and smashed the T's worldwide production record the following year. For decades, the Lizzie shared honors with the Rolls-Royce Silver Ghost (1907-27) as the car with the longest life span. During the 1960s and '70s, however, several European models, including the Beetle, Volvo's PV444, the Citroen 2CV, and Fiat's 1100, exceeded the T's production life.

Contemporary cartoon captures a nation's sentiment.

Millions of Model Ts would prove as durable as flivver jokes and legend said they were. In March 1927, nearly 19 years after the first one was made, 11,325,521 Lizzies were registered in the United States. Despite its cheapness, the T lasted longer on the average (eight years) than other cars (6.3 years) because of its low-cost replacement parts, ease of repair, and the vast network of Ford dealers. The number of Ts in daily use declined rapidly with the end of production but, in late 1931, 5,432,000 Lizzies still plied the nation's highways; in 1941, an estimated 600,000-800,000. In 1948, when R.L. Polk and Company made the last actual count, 73,111 Model T cars and trucks were still registered. Many additional Ts were unlicensed, of course, stored in garages and farm buildings, while others could be found rusting where they had stopped running years before. In 1953, Ford estimated the number of surviving flivvers at 100,000. In 1971, automotive historian Leslie R. Henry, taking into account subsequent large-scale T restoration, put the number at 300,000. "If an antique buff finds a 'T' frame with a serial number on it," he noted "he's got enough to start building a car."

Many of the Lizzie's 4830 parts and some accessories are still readily available from old-car parts houses, some new old stock, others newly made reproductions from companies cashing in on the steady demand. The Sears, Roebuck catalog, which once devoted more space to T parts and gadgets than to men's clothing, still listed T en-

gine gaskets in 1975, though perhaps more for sentimental than business reasons. Today, every restored or restorable Model T sells for many times its original purchase price; even "basket cases" cost more than they did when new.

A few Ts remain in daily service, and they invariably make headlines when stolen or involved in accidents. The Windmiller family of Columbus, Ohio, still hauls produce for its farm in a truck it bought new in 1916. Samuel Treon, of Red Cross, Pennsylvania, continues to drive the flivver his foster father bought the same year. "There's no end of offers for it," observes Treon, "but I just say it's not for sale." Ernest Duhachek continually used a 1917 truck on his farm near Newman Grove, Nebraska until his retirement in 1974. He bought the chassis for $495, then added cab, seat, and cargo box.

Perhaps the most traveled T belongs to Mike Tonis, 85, of Sacramento, California. He claims his car, purchased in 1934, has more than 700,000 miles on it. Tonis put on most of that as manager of fruit-picking crews in the Sacramento Valley. People stop him every day, wanting to buy his car, he recently told the Associated Press. "Never," he responds, "I'll drive it forever." Mike isn't sure of his car's vintage. He spotted it wearing a "for sale" sign along a road near Sacramento. When he asked the price, the owner replied, "Whatever you've got." Mike forked over the $5 he had in his pocket.

Two international organizations serve Model T owners

An odd, but apt, expression of the Model T's enduring toughness and versatility. The flivver will live forever.

courtesy Ford Archives, Ford Museum

today: the Model T Ford Club International, founded in 1952 and one of the oldest old-car marque groups, and the Model T Ford Club of America, established in 1966. The Ford Club International, headquartered in Elgin, Illinois, has 53 chapters whose members own more than 10,000 Ts. The Ford Club of America has 66 chapters and 6000 members, many of whom also own more than one Lizzie. Both organizations publish bimonthly magazines that keep alive knowledge of and lore about the flivver. Virtually every old-car museum in the country has at least one Model T on display. Harrah's Automobile Collection in Reno, Nevada, has the world's largest collection—52 cars and trucks representing each model year. The Henry Ford Museum displays one of the first cars, the 15-millionth T, and several historically significant flivvers. Several individuals also have impressive T collections, among them Cecil Church of Harrisburg, Illinois, who houses his in a wooden replica of an early Ford dealership.

To this day the Model T continues to generate considerable attention. Since 1948, it has been given full chapters in at least 15 volumes, and has been the subject of six fiction and seven nonfiction books, not to mention a few movies and dozens of reprint owner and service manuals, parts catalogs, and sales brochures. In 1953, the Tin Lizzie was a focal point of Ford Motor Company's 50th anniversary celebration. It was heavily publicized again in 1958, the 50th anniversary of its introduction, and in 1963, when Ford marked the centennial of its founder's birth. The T was again trotted out during the company's 75th anniversary in 1978.

Ford and others still occasionally use the Model T to make points in advertising. On introducing its new Pinto in the early 1970s, ads signed by Henry Ford II declared the minicar "is the new Model T. The first Model T stood for sensible, simple motoring; it was 'lively and easy to handle and fun to drive,' and this new version of the Model T stands for the same things." It would even be available in "Model T Black." The campaign's early TV commercials showed a Model T being overtaken on the road by its successor, the Model A, and a Pinto. Rival auto companies like VW and a few non-automotive companies have also invoked the T, invariably complimenting

it and, in effect, saying "me too." One recent example: "What do the Apple personal computer and the Model T have in common? Ease of operation and affordability."

Over the years, "Model T" has been used as a way of saying "old-fashioned." The instances are too numerous to list. In 1963, *Life* magazine described the Navy's antiquated rescue vessel, Skylark, as a "small, prim, old-fashioned ship looking like a Model T." The New York *Journal-American* criticized the nation's "'Model T' highway program." Michigan Governor George Romney compared his state's then 55-year-old constitution to a "broken-down Tin Lizzie." Vassar College's British-born president said "the American mind chugs along like a Model T—persevering and rugged, but without much grace." More recently, in 1971, the chief justice of the Michigan Supreme Court described the state's judicial system as "a lurching Model T," after which the Detroit *News* declared the court was "a Model T, too." After Gerald R. Ford described himself as "a Ford, not a Lincoln" when sworn in as vice-president in December 1973, dozens of cartoonists pictured him at the wheel of a Model T—or *as* a Model T. Many journalists subsequently compared President Ford to a Model T, as well as to Edsel, Thunderbird, Maverick, and other Ford products.

"Model T" also comes up when durable, inexpensive, or widely accepted products are discussed. Persian lamb has been called "one of the great 'Model T's' of the fur industry, seemingly fashionable forever." Douglas Aircraft's DC-3 and Ford's trimotor airplane have been referred to as "the Model T of the air" or "the Model T of aircraft." And the Kodak camera is sometimes described as "the Model T of cameradom." The term has also become connected with simplicity, success, even quality. For example, a 1979 United Press International story said that the cooling plant for the Three Mile Island nuclear reactor "will use the same natural circulation process Henry Ford used to cool the Model T engine." The Detroit *Free Press* reported at about the same time that the owner of a local shirt printing company aspires to be "the Henry Ford of T-shirts" and is well on his way "to becoming Mr. Model T." An ad for a Japanese typewriter boasted the machine is "jampacked with quality like the Model T Ford and just as simple to repair." Such is the memory of the Tin Lizzie that it has become a part of America's thinking and vocabulary.

Nowadays, owning a Model T, especially one with brass fittings, is positively stylish, much more so than at any time in the past. Many old-car buffs would own no other antique. Others go to inordinate lengths to find an example like the one they knew as young adults or children. Perhaps more than any other object from our past, the Model T has a special niche in American hearts. Most older citizens had their first experience in automobiling when they rode in or drove a flivver. Today, the sight of one bobbing along warms them like a ray of sunshine. They smile, and some yell "get a horse!" If the car is pulled up at the curb, they may reminisce with the owner about the "good old days" and perhaps recall a Ford joke or two. If asked to take a spin, they'll immediately climb in. If invited to drive, many accept, eager to prove they

A face known round the world, remembered with affection

remember how to manipulate the T's pedals and levers. Younger people are similarly moved by the sight.

In the end, the Model T outlived its usefulness, but it hasn't been outlived by time. It has become almost immortal—as much a part of this country's heritage as the Fourth of July, a mixture of folk legend and nostalgic affection tinged with a bittersweet humor. Few cars, let alone one so humble, can claim as much.

1928

Starting over: problems and promises, popularity and pandemonium

As the curtain fell on America's most successful wheeled invention, the whole world wondered what "old Henry Ford" was going to do after his ailing Model T. About to turn 64 yet trim and youthful from a well-disciplined daily routine, the automaker was still in the prime of his extraordinary life. His handsome 34 year-old son Edsel, as president of the company, was showing great promise of following in his father's footsteps. There was nearly $250 million cash on hand, and total assets of the far-flung Ford empire stood at just under a billion dollars. But the ingenious Model T, the very foundation of this fantastic success, had run its course. As his company entered 1927 and sales continued to sink, it was becoming all too clear that Henry would have to work another miracle to bring forth a replacement.

Even as rumors of the Model T's demise swept the nation, the "wizard of motors" was already burning the midnight oil. He had steadfastly resisted the notion that the Model T was really finished. But if it was, he wanted something just as revolutionary to take its place.

For several years he had tinkered with different engines that might someday power such a car. One of these was

Ford's new Model A represented a dramatic break with the past, as this comparison with a mid-teens T demonstrates.

The 1928 Model A Standard roadster. "Henry made a lady out of Lizzie"—or rather Edsel did with his graceful styling.

the "X-8." It had four cylinders facing up, as in a V-type configuration, and four facing down where the oil pan would ordinarily be. It also had roller main bearings, a combination starter and generator, and a supercharger built into the flywheel. For Ford, this radical design would be a logical successor to his legendary four-cylinder Model T powerplant. It was also a chance to be one step ahead of the industry, rather than bring out another inline four or six. Unfortunately, extensive engineering and testing showed the X-8 far too complex for easy mass production, too heavy, and too prone to lower spark plug fouling by dust and mud kicked up from the roadbed. By the end of 1926, his hopes dashed that it would ever be practical, Henry reluctantly ordered development work stopped.

Now, as the company contemplated the inevitable end to the Model T, Ford and a handful of his most trusted aides began a top-secret rush to develop a new car along conventional lines. Edsel was closer to dealers and the sales department, and had presented the arguments to his father. What was urgently needed was an automobile that appealed to the same customer as in the halcyon days of the Model T, but one that could also compete head-on with the best the competition had to offer—namely, Chevrolet, Essex, and Plymouth. It would have to be faster, smoother, more durable, and must offer the kinds of features buyers were demanding.

One thing was certain: it would need a conventional select-shift transmission. Urban buyers, especially, preferred such a gearbox. Dealers had long complained of sales lost because the Model T had nothing better than the old pedal-operated planetary transmission. People were becoming more particular, roads were getting better, and there were more women drivers. The well-informed buyer was less inclined to lay out cash for a car that required a pedal held down hard just to select low gear or reverse. Though Henry staunchly defended this patented device and other features of his hallowed Model T, he nevertheless understood the language of sales. After great deliberation he finally gave the order to proceed with a design that would be entirely new from top to bottom, fender to fender.

Now, the most daring challenge for Henry was to prepare for closing his plants and scrapping the well-oiled Model T production lines to retool. For one thing, it meant losing incredible sums of money. For another, the grade-school-educated motor king had a well-known disdain of engineers and a preference for his own seat-of-the-pants approach. This plus the Model T's long-running success had left him remarkably shy of engineering and styling staff to handle the tremendous amount of work to be done in the transition. What he did have was a disciplined manufacturing operation led by one of the toughest, most brilliant production men in the business.

Charles Sorensen had been top man at Ford Motor Company, apart from Henry and Edsel, long before this. Starting in 1905 as a pattern maker, the tall Dane had always been a good idea man and when given a role in management had been one of the key figures in developing the moving assembly line for the Model T. A stern taskmas-

courtesy Ford Archives, Ford Museum

New to the Model A line was this Special Business Coupe, with leather-covered top, priced at $525.

ter with dynamo energy, he was the mainspring of the company's amazing expansion—creating new manufacturing and assembly techniques, building new plants at home and abroad, and carrying out Mr. Ford's orders with rapid-fire precision.

From the very beginning of the secret project, Sorensen and another top production man, Peter E. Martin, were part of the inner circle. By the time the idea had pretty well crystalized, three engineers had joined the group, selected quietly from the random projects that were always in progress around Dearborn. In charge of the new car's overall design was Eugene Farkas, former head of the X-8 project and a longtime Ford engineer who had played a major role in development of the Fordson tractor. Assisting him would be Frank Johnson, chief engineer at the Lincoln plant, and Lawrence Sheldrick, a young engineer who had caught Henry's eye on another assignment.

By inclination, Henry Ford was a chassis man. Intensely practical, he had little interest in the appearance of car, being more concerned about what made it run. Edsel, on the other hand, cared more about appearance, as well as things like passenger comfort and features. He had a natural eye for beauty, and had used that talent to make Lincoln one of the most prestigious nameplates in the industry. He had also learned the marketing lessons of updating models every year, something his father had stubbornly resisted with the Model T.

Partly because he was impressed with the job his son had done with Lincoln, but mainly because he was occupied with chassis ideas, the elder Ford gave the styling

job to Edsel—along with amiable veteran Joe Galamb. Galamb was a highly respected member of the Ford engineering staff who, for all intents and purposes, *was* the styling department. The Polish-born designer had laid out the first Model T and, when he wasn't called upon to make an occasional sheetmetal change on it, had charge of experimental engineering.

Edsel was known as the first-class gentleman, and he and Galamb hit it off right from the start. Young Ford would outline what he had in mind; Galamb would interpret it in sketches and clay models, which the pair would then discuss in great detail. The initial idea for the new car's basic body design was a scaled-down variation of the Lincoln. It would incorporate the same finely sculptured lines, rounded corners, just the right accent of nickel trim, nicely turned door handles, and a comfortable, well-appointed interior. 'He [was critical] of the interior quite a lot,'' Galamb would recall, ''and the instrument work. When we made the first body sample, Edsel was very particular about the trimming and the material. He knew what he wanted and insisted that we get it.'' But, while Edsel knew just what he wanted, nothing was approved without his father's critical—and often creative—contribution to it.

An example of the cut-and-try engineering that at times would affect the character of all Henry Ford's cars was the manner in which the height of the first prototype bodies was decided. All-round production man W.C. Klann was by now in on the project. ''The sample bodies were being built at the Highland Park plant,'' he recalled

The smart new Model A Tudor sedan for 1928 listed at $495, and was the best-selling single body style.

courtesy Ford Archives, Ford Museum

in a 1956 interview. "I built six bodies there...they were always under lock and key. We would bring the panels down [to Engineering] and assemble them and get the height of our seat cushions. Well, Henry Ford wanted to fit himself and Sorensen; Edsel Ford wanted to fit Mr. Martin and himself." Klann related how the elder Ford insisted he should be able to get in and out without knocking his hat off. The shorter Edsel supported Galamb's first drawings, which called for a lower profile. Naturally, Henry won out, and Klann made up a prototype 1½ inches taller. Said Klann, "When Henry Ford saw it it looked like an old hayrack. He said, 'Scrap that. It looks terrible!' So it remained the same as before."

First styling efforts involved the coupe and Tudor sedan. By March 1927, work was far enough along that a contract for a special set of body stampings was quietly given to the Murray Corporation of America. It may have been Henry's nature to leak a clue now and then—and secrets are hard to keep in Detroit. In any event, this was the first outside evidence that the Fords were working on a new model.

The next morning the press was speculating that, besides refined body lines, the new mystery Ford would probably be introduced with a select-shift transmission and modern distributor ignition.

Henry Ford instantly sparked a wave of national excitement when, in May 1927, he casually announced what he had been planning all along: to shut down the entire Ford system to retool. "We began work on this model sev-

eral years ago," he told the press with some truth. "In fact, the idea of a car to succeed the Model T has been in my mind much longer than that. But the sale of the Model T continued at such a pace that there never seemed to be an opportunity to get the new car started."

The shutdown would have enormous impact on a national economy in which Ford built nearly half the automobiles. Thousands of workers at 36 assembly plants across the country were immediately laid off, the once-booming Model T accessory industry was thrown into a tailspin, many suppliers and parts houses went broke, and only the strongest Ford dealers managed to survive. Also, thousands of potential car buyers decided to wait until they saw the new Ford offering. As their salesrooms gathered dust during what would be a long wait for the promised car, dealers could do little but wring their hands in frustration. Some of the more optimistic ones put up big colorful posters: "We are taking orders for the new car...speed, pick-up, flexibility, beauty, comfort, stamina, coming soon!" But as summer wore into autumn, then into winter, the new Ford had yet to appear. By now, dealer windows had grown cobwebs and the posters had faded.

Back in Dearborn, Henry Ford and his team were working night and day toward a single goal—launching a tough, spirited, smartly fashioned automobile the average man could afford. In design, it was already so new that it had been christened "Model A," significantly echoing the designation of the first Ford in 1903.

Engineer Harold Hicks, who was transferred from airplane work to help on the new car's engine and chassis details, was continually awed by Henry Ford's driving personality and the way he could get the best efforts from his staff. As an engineer, he was even more impressed with Ford's uncanny ability to shortcut extensive development time by being a bear for simplicity: "I remember that they had too many bolts holding the carburetor together. Henry Ford said to me, 'Cut those bolts down!' I had the Zenith company get out a design in which two bolts held the carburetor together. I felt quite proud that they had reduced it from about 14 little screws down to two bolts. I showed him the design. With his characteristic trait he said, 'Two is too many! Make it just one bolt!' So the carburetor came out with just a simple bolt down through it."

Henry Ford frequently offset his technical shortcomings and lack of education by overwhelming a problem with men and machines. Theodore Gehle recalls how this approach even rubbed off on Ford's chief lieutenant. Gehle worked in the Pressed Steel Department in Dearborn as the first Model A bodies were painfully taking shape in mid-1927. "Mr. Sorensen said, 'Now you go down...and you just live there until you get the first bodies out. When you see daylight for the first bodies, why, you let me know.' ...The quarter panel was what was holding up the bodies most, and fenders were second." An experienced Ford production man, Gehle worked virtually around the clock trying to straighten out the kinks. Finally, he reported back to Sorensen that he wasn't having much luck, but he had a suggestion: "Well, I suggest you issue an order for Pressed Steel to run off one hundred sets of stampings—the best they can make. Some of these are going to be horrible. Then issue an order to the Body Plant to build one hundred bodies with these sets of stampings. They will probably have to be scrapped, but it will give them knowledge. By relaying information back and forth (between departments), maybe out of the next one hundred bodies you may get a good one." Gehle was amazed the headstrong Sorensen went along with it. Said Gehle, "These first one hundred bodies were assembled and scrapped. On the next one hundred bodies we saved about ten. From there on we started the Model A production, the bodies having been the bottleneck."

Production bottlenecks proved almost countless. Starting at the end of May 1927, thousands of toolmakers, die and pattern makers, and millwrights had been hired or recalled to begin the massive overhaul that would have to be completed in record time, often without final plans and in many cases requiring duplicates for installation in the various assembly plants. In some departments, engineers and their assistants would work in relays, 24 hours around the clock, just correcting mistakes and designing and redesigning the special tools needed.

The Highland Park plant, once described as "the most productive piece of ground on earth," had to be gutted to the walls. Most manufacturing and all car assembly operations for that territory were transferred to Ford's new showcase factory complex rising on the banks of the River Rouge near Dearborn. Giant machines weighing as

The rugged Model A engine. Note winged distributor cap.

much as 240 tons had to be completely redesigned or rebuilt. Thousands of smaller tools and precision instruments had to be manufactured. Since the Model A would be composed of about 6800 different parts—compared to less than 5000 on the Model T—a multitude of new manufacturing sources had to be developed. Engines, some body stampings, rear axles, and brakes were among parts to be made at the Rouge plant. Shock absorber parts would come from Buffalo; bumpers from Chicago; wood body parts from the Ford lumber mills at Iron Mountain, Michigan; wood floorboards from a supplier in Vancouver, Washington; wheels from Memphis and from Hamilton, Ohio; glass from Dearborn and New Jersey; and radiators from the big Ford plant at Green Island, New York.

To supply the wide variety of smart new body types drawn up by Edsel Ford and Joe Galamb, the company would contract with outside suppliers for most of its stampings and built-up bodies. Briggs Manufacturing Company, a longtime supplier that also built custom coachwork for other auto companies, was given the contract to tool and produce the new Model A coupe. Major contracts were also signed with Murray and the Edward G. Budd Manufacturing Company. Briggs would come to specialize in stampings for sedan, coupe, victoria and panel delivery bodies, as well as furnishing completely built and trimmed cabriolet bodies. Murray provided much the same, plus assembly and finish for the wood-bodied station wagon introduced for 1929. Budd would become an invaluable supplier of special stampings and commercial bodies.

By mid-August, the Fords were satisfied with their

progress—enough that Edsel promised the press that the new car would be available "within the next few weeks." "Tests already made show that it is faster, smoother, more rugged and more beautiful than we had hoped for in the early stages of designing," he said. "Experiments have been made with a wide variety of color schemes and body designs, and all these have been decided upon." As it turned out, reporters had to wait a few months before they would get their first official peek at the car. Had they watched the gates at the Ford engineering laboratory more closely, they might have noticed that experimental cars, thinly disguised as Model Ts, had been leaving there for road testing since early spring. By the end of October, as many as 150 semi-disguised cars with new hand-built experimental chassis had been driven at night over Ford's only test track, the streets and countryside of Dearborn.

In the late afternoon of Thursday, October 20, 1927, after nearly a year's effort and millions of dollars, the first Model A engine approved for full production was built at Dearborn. Its number was ceremoniously hand stamped by Henry Ford as his son, Sorensen, Martin and two long-time employees, August Degener and Charles Hartner, looked on. The next day the engine was installed in a chassis rolling slowly down the pilot assembly line, and the tired auto magnate had his first real opportunity to stand back and assess his latest creation.

If the Model T chassis had been the paragon of mechanical simplicity, the Model A was certainly the ideal. True, Henry retained the familiar layout of his beloved flivver. Single, semi-elliptic transverse springs straddled the front and rear axles buggy-style; the "wishbone" radius rod acting as a front-end stabilizer was plain to see; and at first glance the overall spindly appearance seemed the same. But every suspension piece, from the spring perches and spright 21-inch welded wire wheels to the featherlight frame and forged axles, had been completely and ingeniously redesigned to make the car stronger and more nimble. And, for the first time on a Ford, rod-operated four-wheel brakes and shock absorbers were incorporated for a safer, smoother ride.

The cast-iron four-cylinder engine was still an L-head type, but was totally new in design. Rated at 40 brake horsepower, with a 3⅞-inch bore and 4¼-inch stroke for a 200.5 cubic-inch displacement, it was twice as powerful as the Model T powerplant, lighter, and considerably more efficient. And, sure enough, it was no longer bolted to a heavy, complex, planetary transmission but was coupled to a modern three-speed-with-reverse gearshift transmission controlled by a dry multiple-disc clutch. As predicted, engineers had also adopted a modern, less costly battery and ignition system, which did away with much of the clutter from the engine compartment. Instead of the old time-honored magneto ignition with its four vibrator coils and maze of wires running from dash to spark plugs there were just two wires between engine and dash, the high tension lead from the coil to the distributor, and the low tension lead to the ignition switch. A modern, specially designed distributor was now mounted atop the cylinder head, gear-driven by a vertical shaft off the center of the camshaft, with its tail end driving the oil

pump. The moulded plastic cap with a pair of winged extensions fore and aft would give the Model A distributor a character all its own. Encased in these wings were the leads connecting to the four spark plugs by means of simple brass straps secured with round finger nuts.

Assisting the smartly styled fin-and-tube radiator for cooling was a centrifugal water pump and two-blade fan unit. It was driven off the front crankshaft pulley by a V-belt, which also drove the "powerhouse" generator mounted on the engine's left side. And, to please the stylists, the respected engine crank handle that had always dangled below the Model T radiator could now be removed and stowed away.

As he watched the Tudor sedan body being tried on that first chassis, Henry Ford may have felt special pride in his ingenious fuel system. Unfortunately, though he had incorporated a similar design in his 1926-27 Model T, it would prove to be one of the most controversial features of the new car (insurance companies blindly labeled it explosion prone). The gas tank was simply part of the cowl, forming the roll over the front body from below the windshield to the hood beltline. The tank was filled by means of a knurled screw cap located on top. The fuel fed naturally to the Zenith double-venturi carburetor by gravity, flowing first through a handy sediment bulb installed in the line. The unit was designed in such a way that on the engine side it formed the firewall and mount for the hood and, on the driver's side, held the instrument panel.

Within a week of the day Henry Ford saw the first Model A completed, production had inched upwards as assembly problems were doggedly worked out. By November 1, 1927, the rate was about 20 a day. Two days later, selected Ford dealers and members of the press were at last invited to have their first look at the car. Describing that early Model A assembly line action, veteran auto journalist Fay Leone Faurote would write: "I stood and watched the men for a time. The job is new to them and they 'make haste slowly.' There are stops for fittings. Stops for minor parts and minor adjustments. In fact, the assembly line is just now crawling. But with each new machine a slightly faster pace is evidenced."

Arthur Hatch, manager of the Chicago Ford branch in 1927, reminisced in his retirement years about some of

The Model A Standard Business Coupe sold for $550 in 1928.

As nifty a truck as you're likely to see, the Roadster Pickup body style was continued in the new Model A line.

the trials and tribulations of getting the first Model As into production at his plant: "Finally, we got a car assembled and I took it out for a spin. I actually blocked the whole city of Chicago with the crowds that developed to see Henry Ford's 'well-kept secret'... We got into production and the next morning my wife calls me at my office. 'I've stalled,' she said. 'The car won't run! I've frozen my feet and hands trying to get it started!' She no more than hung up than I began to get calls from Ford dealers all over Chicago. They were complaining that the new cars wouldn't run. So, I went out in the plant and the superintendent said, 'There must be something wrong with the engineering...the cars are being put together right.' I called the Ford operator in Detroit and said, 'Get me Sorensen!' Sorensen came on and I said, 'I've just blown the whistle—shut the whole plant down. My wife is stuck in the park. I've got 300 calls this morning that people are stuck all over town!' Sorensen said, 'Don't leave the office! You stay right there! I'll fly six of our people over there that were supposed to have designed this automobile—are you sure you're right?' I said, 'I'm dead sure!'"

In Dearborn, Henry Ford took one of the newly assembled Model As home to have lunch with his wife Clara. When he got back in, it wouldn't start. The same thing happened to Sorensen. "Mr. Ford sent out an order at once to stop production," Arthur Hatch recalled. "It didn't take them long to find the problem. It was in the regulator which controlled the cutout between the battery and engine so it [the battery] wouldn't overcharge. He had all the assembly plants ship the faulty regulators—they cost about $4.50 each—back to Detroit,

where he made his engineers pile them in a big heap. I went down there and he had them piled up higher than the roof of the engineering laboratory. He'd lead you out and say, 'Look at those things. Look at all the dummies I've got around here!'"

Production problems continued to plague the Model A, but Henry wouldn't put it on sale until it was right. At the end of November, Edsel cautioned the press that it was "doubtful that the new Ford would be available to purchasers before the first of the year." He projected it would be months before the factories could turn out Model As on "anything like a peak production schedule," noting that the company had only shipped about 500 cars up to that time. Asked who was getting those first cars, Edsel let it slip that none were to be sold but that they were, at that very moment, speeding to different parts of the country for the forthcoming introductory shows.

So, the stage was set. On the morning of December 1, 1927, readers of 2000 daily newspapers across the nation opened to find a full page advertisement for the new Ford Model A.

"We believe the new Ford car is as great an improvement in motor car building as the Model T was in 1908." So wrote Henry Ford in a $2 million advertising blitz that hit the day before his long-awaited Model A went on sale. "In appearance, in performance, in comfort, in safety, in all that goes to make a good car, it will bear out everything I have said here..."

News spread like wildfire that the car would at last be shown in major cities the next day, Friday, December 2nd. That morning, hundreds of thousands of Americans lined up for a look. In New York City, people began gathering outside the big Ford showroom on Broadway at 3 a.m., and by midday the crowd had become so large that the manager had to move the display to Madison Square Garden. "Excitement could hardly have been greater," remarked the New York *World*, "had Pah-wah, the sacred white elephant of Burma, elected to sit for seven days on the flagpole of the Woolworth Building."

It was easily the greatest new-model introduction in history. And it even rivalled Lindbergh's transatlantic flight as one of the top news stories of the decade. In the U.S. alone an estimated 10 million people would flock to see the Model A in the first 36 hours after its unveiling. Some 100,000 descended on the show the first day in Detroit. In Cleveland, mounted police had to be called out to control the crowds, and in Kansas City an over-eager mob nearly burst the walls of Convention Hall.

Merrell "Mo" Jordan was a teenager in Illinois when the Model A was introduced and, later, would run a successful dealership in California: "You couldn't get near the car on introduction day. My dad owned the Ford agency but that didn't help me. I remember the long lines of people waiting to take a ride. We had a special route laid out that ended by crossing a plowed field. That first car would do 50 in second and I swear to this day that it was a faster model than the later ones." As a wide-eyed youngster, Jordan knew everything that went on at his dad's dealership—or thought he did. Noting that those first Model A demonstrators were taken into the shop and worked on all night, he will always believe that they were doctored to go faster. (The mechanics were probably just trying to keep the things running!)

The Model A was surprisingly quick. It could leap from 5 to 25 mph in a little more than eight seconds and had a top speed of 65 mph (against 43 mph for the T). Much of that acceleration, which compared favorably with that of even the best sixes and eights, could be attributed to modifications worked out by Harold Hicks—and to the use of aluminum pistons. The car was so quick that, the day after its introduction, the state of Massachusetts declared that for safety's sake it would "require all Model T drivers accustomed to the planetary transmission to take a test before they can operate the new models."

As for looks, the Model A was not sensational by standards of the day, but it had plenty of natural charm. From the shape and contour of the nickel radiator shell to the sweeping hoodline to the body details and the way the large, full-crowned fenders hugged the wire wheels, the family resemblance with Edsel's elegant Lincolns was obvious. By adopting some of the big car's finesse and incorporating a longer wheelbase and a higher beltline that reduced window height, the designers had fashioned a lower, much prettier car than the tall, boxy Model T.

Initially the A was offered in five body styles: Tudor sedan, coupe, sports coupe, roadster, and phaeton. The closed cars wore a smart cadet-type sunvisor, rounded roof corners, and fabric top covering. All bodies were nicely enhanced by the ample use of reveals to carry the contrasting paint and pinstriping. Naturally, Edsel's artistic eye had selected the four basic shades of Niagara blue, Arabian sand, dawn gray, and gunmetal blue.

Inside, the instrument panel was the epitome of form and function. Shaped roughly like a diamond and finished in satin-nickel, the main cluster was mounted to the back of the cowl fuel tank and contained a direct-acting float-

Like all Model As, this 1928 Tudor sedan boasted an impressive number of standard features for a low-priced car.

The Model A' stylistic relationship with Edsel Ford's big Lincoln design is evident in this 1928 photograph.

operated fuel gauge. The 80-mph speedometer was set off in a vertical oval at the bottom. The ignition switch was at the left, ammeter to the right. And in the center was the instrument lamp. As on the Model T, spark and throttle levers were mounted under the wheel on the steering column, but the former quadrants had been eliminated. In addition to the customary hand throttle there was also an accelerator foot pedal on the floor. A combination fuel regulator and choke rod extending directly from the carburetor was handily attached to the lower right side of the instrument panel. Surrounding the horn button at the lock nut of the hard rubber steering wheel was the headlight switch, controlled by a multi-position lever. Several grades of fine cloth upholstery were standard in the various closed models, with door panels, pleated door pockets, and side walls trimmed in the same material. Open cars came with imitation leather trim. Doors on roadsters and phaetons were opened by means of an internal lever (these models did not have external door handles in 1928). Windows in all models were crank-operated.

All this in the basic Tudor selling for $495, against a comparable Chevrolet at $585 and the Whippet at $535, was the attraction that had all those folks standing in line. A bonus was an impressive list of standard equipment. It now included Houdaille shocks all around, a combination tail and stop light, front and rear bumpers, windshield wiper, speedometer, swing-type one-piece ventilating windshield, and a Sparton horn.

It's an auto seller's dream when customers literally break down the doors, but Henry had laid down the law: none of the early demonstrators were to be sold. All through December, as the company worked to increase production, dealers were only allowed to take deposits on future deliveries while fending off every kind of offer on the one or two "bolt-down" models they had on the sales floor. Everyone it seemed, from grocery clerks to politicians, wanted to be the first to have one of the new cars—

but couldn't for love nor money.

The record is a bit hazy, but the honor of being the very first member of the public to receive a Model A Ford probably went to Thomas A. Edison. The famous inventor was invited to drive the first car off the Kearney, New Jersey assembly line on December 19th, and it was immediately turned over to him as a gift from his good friend Henry Ford. Senator James Couzens of Michigan—one of the original founders of Ford Motor Company—got the first car delivered in Washington D.C. It carried serial number 35, the same as his original 1903 Model A, and was also a gift from Henry Ford.

Officially publicized by the company as Model A "Purchaser Number One" was swashbuckling movie idol Douglas Fairbanks, who bought a sport coupe as a Christmas present for his equally famous wife, actress Mary Pickford. As arranged by Edsel, the car was delivered December 26th from the showroom of a Beverly Hills dealer where it had been a demonstrator. "America's Sweetheart" thanked Edsel by sending him an autographed pose with the car, signing it "Mary Pick-a-Ford."

Henry Ford had concluded he spent $100 million to bring out the Model A. His dealers had taken orders for 727,000 of them but deliveries still amounted to only a trickle at the beginning of 1928. It would be another full month before dealers would get even one of each model to put on display. "We probably gave back half our deposits eventually," said long-time dealer John Eagal. "People would wait five, six, or seven months and then buy something else. In fact, delivery took so long that we never did locate some of the buyers to give back their money!"

One of the main production hang-ups was controversy over the new single-system rod-operated brakes. Motor vehicle departments in several states had objected to the design in which both the foot and emergency brakes worked off the same pressure. The first cars had the emergency brake lever to the left of the driver, but the ruckus over the safety issue got so large that Henry ordered a re-design. By the end of January, some Ford plants had started building cars with the lever mounted in front of the gearshift and independent of the foot brakes. By the middle of the year, all Model A cars and Model AA trucks would have the modification.

As time passed slowly by, a confident Henry Ford urged his dealers to be patient. "The new car is coming along fine," he stated in a letter released in mid-February. "You can't get a great plant overhauled and converted from one type product to another in a day. It is easy to de-sign a car. It is a tremendous task to get into shape to produce it right in every detail and great quantity." Slowly, week by week, Model As finally began appearing on American roads, and it was becoming quite fashion-able to be seen in one. New York Governor Franklin D. Roosevelt bought a roadster for use around his Hyde Park estate. Actress Dolores Del Rio gadded about Holly-wood in her chic sport coupe. Will Rogers and movie producers Cecil B. DeMille and Louis B. Mayer bought Tudors to run around in. Billie Dove, Wallace Beery, Lon Chaney, and Lillian Gish were other celebrities who couldn't resist the Model A craze.

Unlike the Model T, the Fords had decided to make more features, colors, and accessories available on the in-creasingly popular Model A. They also decided to build more passenger and commercial body styles as well. By May a new Fordor sedan was in full production, and nearly every month for the balance of the year saw other new models, culminating with the introduction of the ele-gant Town Car on December 13th. Another of Edsel's cre-ations, it was intended for well-heeled customers who liked to ride in style but didn't want to appear overly wealthy. It featured a separate chauffeur's compartment, luxurious interior and more formal styling. Actress Joan Crawford preferred her Lincoln away from Hollywood, but bought one of the first of the spiffy Town Cars just to be one up on all the other Model As around.

1929

The Model A buying binge continues on the eve of The Great Crash

B y the beginning of 1929, all Ford assembly plants were working full steam—and still behind the steam-rolling demand for the Model A. A thousand boxcars a day moved in and out both the Highland Park plant and the Rouge facility to supply the mammoth assembly sys-tem as production soared beyond 100,000 units monthly. In January alone the company built 159,786 units world-wide, setting a pace that would make this its biggest pro-duction year before 1949. At the height of the Model A buying binge, in spring, rail shipments proved too slow, so Ford sent one of its freighters, the *Lake Benbow*, on an emergency rush with parts for the West Coast. Loaded at

Model A Town Car, priced at $1400, was cancelled after '29.

1929 Model A Standard Business Coupe. Note oval windows.

1929 Model A Fordor sedan, with body by Briggs

1929 Model A Standard roadster. Price: $450.

Standard roadster was available with trunk or rumble seat.

Closed-Cab pickup was offered in addition to Roadster model.

Station wagon was new to the Model A line for 1929.

This 1929 Model A Deluxe Phaeton sports the lovely, accessory radiator cap, which itself is highly prized today.

Chester, Pennsylvania, it sailed via the Panama Canal.

The 1929 models debuted with little fanfare, probably because they weren't outwardly much different from the '28s. What parts and sheetmetal had been modified during the previous year were designed to fit the newer models, so it was very common to see late-1928 cars with 1929-model parts and early 1929s with leftover 1928 items. The most noticeable change to open cars (and the commercial truck/pickup) was the appearance of external door handles. There were many other subtle differences, but one sure way to tell them apart is the sportier trim and colors on the '29s.

On January 16, 1929, the Model A cabriolet was introduced at the New York Auto Show, and on February 4th the 1-millionth Model A was built. The Town Sedan and wood-bodied station wagon were added to the line April 25th. Ford was on a roll now. On July 24th—less than 18 months after the first Model A was completed—the 2-millionth Model A, a cabriolet, came off the line.

The world-shattering stock market crash that broke suddenly in October would dampen Ford sales somewhat. But Henry Ford saw a positive side to the economic chaos that followed: falling wages and building materials costs created a good opportunity to expand operations. It was his philosophy that providing new construction jobs and lowering his car prices were ways he could help ease the general slump. As a result, brand-new Ford assembly plants were opened the following year at Long Beach, California; Seattle, Washington; Buffalo, New York; and Edgewater, New Jersey.

1930

The Model A is refurbished, but the competition is already catching up

Introduction of the 1930 Model A in the first week of the new year attracted nearly as much buyer attention as the 1928's had two years before—though it was a quieter, smaller crowd, estimated at just over nine million. Rumors had been flying for some time that major changes were in store, and Ford watchers were not disap-

pointed. A pleasing appearance improvement was the higher, smoother, hood-to-body lines on all models through elimination of the prominent cowl stanchion (first omitted on the 1929 cabriolet). A switch to smaller, 19-inch-diameter wheels and larger tires gave the car a more up-to-date stance. Another important advance was in the general use of stainless steel for the first time on a Ford. On the 1930 models this gleaming alloy would be used for much of the brightwork, including the radiator shell, a new cowl finish strip, and for the headlamp, cowl lamp and taillamp buckets and the doors. Rounding out the improvements were more generous fender shapes and roomier interiors. Colors and trim selections were, again, upgraded as had now become standard policy.

By this time the Model A's reputation for taking hard knocks had become almost legendary—like the tales told about rodeo star Alice Sisty's lovable roadster. The new (but already banged-up) 1930 ragtop faithfully carried the champion trick rider from show to show. And before awestruck crowds it served as the barrier over which she jumped her matched pair of horses in the daring "Auto Roman Standing Jump." The cars had also become exceedingly popular with the budding hot rod set at the dry lakes of California, where names like Riley, Winfield and Cragar were pioneering some great new Ford speed equipment—thus setting the stage for a whole new era of backyard mechanics and weekend racers.

More testimony to the Model A's fortitude was provided by an almost humorous accident near Spokane, Washington, in February. Two city officials were hurrying across frozen Fernan Lake in a 1929 coupe to greet Army aviators who had landed after completing a sub-arctic test flight. Suddenly, they hit a layer of thin ice. While the passengers bailed out in the nick of time, the Model A sank quickly through to the bottom. Twelve days later,

A literally flowery display of new Model As in a typical 1930 showroom.   Deluxe rumble-seat roadster is shown right.

Special-bodied Model As were not uncommon in the early '30s. This rakish dual-cockpit phaeton is an example.

the surrounding ice had hardened enough that a crew could bring a tow truck to the spot. A square was cut through the 14-inch-thick ice, and the coupe was located with a grappling hook and hauled to the surface. After draining the water from the body, crankcase and fuel tank, the car was towed to the Ford garage in nearby Coeur d'Alene, Idaho, and given fresh oil, gasoline, and a new battery. The only mechanical work deemed necessary was to clean the spark plugs, fuel bowl, and distributor.

The Ford dutifully fired up, and was driven back to Spokane, a little soggy but still good for many more miles.

Despite the economic downturn, 1930, like 1929, would be a banner year for Ford. However, in late summer some serious holes began showing up in the once-predictable sales patterns. On August 16th it was announced that because of strong demand, Model A production at the Chicago plant would be increased by 5000 cars per month. Four days later, assembly was cut drastically at Louis-

Another 1930 dealer scene. Note large accessories display.

1930 Model As used stainless steel for much of their trim.

The 2-door Deluxe Phaeton was a new body style for 1930.

Smart Victoria sedan debuted for 1930. Shown is the '31.

ville, Kentucky, because sales in that territory were off 33 percent. Though this was an early symptom of the faltering economy and contracting car market, Ford had other problems to contend with.

The main one was the competition, especially Chevrolet, which had not been idle during the Model A boom. Throughout 1928, Chevy engineers had been hard at work on a new six-cylinder engine, and by that Christmas it was available in a smart new line of cars priced just $100 over comparable Ford models. These Chevys fit nicely into a market segment that wanted something a little different, and were backed by a strong advertising campaign intended to win over four-cylinder buyers to the "smoother smoothness of the six-cylinder car." Sales of America's second most popular make rocketed to over a million units in just eight months. Throughout 1930, Chevy would continue to cut away at the Ford lead.

1931

Publicity efforts fail to prop up sagging sales as the Depression spreads

The 1931 Fords debuted in the midst of widening economic gloom and increased competition from rival makes. Except for a redesigned radiator shell with painted indentation, a restyled instrument panel, and one-piece runningboard splash aprons, there was little change. And as usual with Ford model changeovers, any old parts that fit the new cars were bolted on until stock was used up. So, it wasn't unusual for early-1931 As to have the old two-piece splash aprons and vice versa. In March, a distinctive new cabriolet and Fordor/Town Sedan were introduced with a noticeably different roofline. This was the racy "slant-windshield" design first seen on the bustleback Victoria sedan in late 1930. It was brought through in production by moving the front roof header back a bit and leaning the windshield stanchions to meet it.

Another major styling innovation appeared in June

with the arrival of the sensational new convertible sedan body style. This was a sporty, five-passenger two-door family car for all seasons, and also featured the slant windshield. The unique thing about it was fixed side window frames. This left the full door and quarter-window glass available for fending off the elements even when the canvas top was lowered. The top folded away neatly over the body behind the back seat, enclosed in a tailored boot. Seat trim in this Deluxe model was a fancy dark tan shade of genuine leather.

For the company and many of its dealers the promotional highlight of the year was the nationwide tour of the 20-millionth Ford. The milestone Fordor sedan came off the line at the Rouge on April 14th, and received an official send-off from Henry and Edsel Ford. Going first to New York, it was taken for a short spin by Governor Roosevelt's wife, Eleanor. The car and an accompanying caravan of other new Fords then headed west for whirlwind publicity stops at hundreds of welcoming dealers. Along the way, it paid a visit to Sidney Smith, creator of the Andy Gump comic strip, received the checkered flag at the Indianapolis Speedway, was inducted into the Sioux tribe, and was the first privately owned car to descend to the bottom of Hoover Dam. As it passed through various state capitols, specially minted "20,000,000" license plates were attached to it, and many governors signed the car's logbook. Other notables signing in were World War I hero Sergeant Alvin C. York, explorer Admiral Richard E. Byrd, and film stars

1931 Town Sedan with bodywork by both Briggs and Murray.

A day on the links. And what could be better for a spectator than this jazzy 1931 Model A Deluxe roadster?

Priced at $640, the new 1931 Deluxe convertible sedan combined top-down motoring with sedan-like weather protection.

For some reason, these two 1931 Model A buyers don't look all that happy. Shown are the Deluxe Tudor and Coupe.

Douglas Fairbanks and Mary Pickford. In Los Angeles, Fairbanks took the wheel as the car participated in that city's 150th anniversary parade. On its return to Dearborn the milestone Model A was put on display at Henry Ford's new museum, and was honored as the most widely traveled and photographed car in America.

But no amount of publicity would prop up Ford sales, which were now sagging terribly. From 1.5 million units sold in 1929, Model A production slipped to just a third of that in 1931. There had been rumors in the trade for most of the year that Henry was working on a small V-8 to counter the Chevrolet six. Some said it would be put in a new car to replace the faltering Model A and to be named the "Edison" in honor of his longtime friend.

Finally, on July 29th, the day before his 68th birthday, Henry Ford decided something had to be done. In the face of plunging sales he announced the layoff of 75,000 workers and the closing of 25 of his 36 U.S. assembly plants until the situation showed some kind of improvement. Privately, the wily auto baron had something up his sleeve. He knew it was all over for four-cylinder cars, and he was well along with the Model A's replacement.

1932

Henry confounds his critics with the country's first low-price V-8 car

In the summer of 1930, after returning from a trip to Germany, Henry Ford sent a trio of his most gifted experimental engineers to a small rustic building deep within his Greenfield Village showplace in Dearborn. He housed them in the replica of Thomas Edison's Ft. Myers, Florida laboratory, authentic right down to the old steam engine with its overhead shafts and belts that helped the prolific inventor in his work. One of the men, 28 year-old engineer Emil Zoerlein, had worked on a number of Ford's pet projects.

"There are two more fellows working back there," said Henry. "What you work on and what you see back there I want you to keep to yourself and not say a word to anybody about it. We are designing a V-8 engine. What do you know about electricity?" "I think I know quite a lot about it," replied Zoerlein. "Then, I'd like to have you work on the ignition system for this engine—and the generator and starter, and so forth," said Ford. "You work along with those two boys back there."

Reporting to the shop, Zoerlein found colleagues Carl Schultz and Ray Laird already at the drawing board laying out a small V-8 engine that could, in theory, be mass produced. They were working from rough sketches they had made of ideas suggested by Henry. "Schultz had already made a layout of the V-8 engine showing a box [distributor] in front with about the same position and shape as we finally developed," Zoerlein recalled in a 1972 interview. "I worked with him to get the basic configuration first of all. We designed a distributor with two pairs of breaking points and a four-lobe cam for an eight-cylinder engine . . . it was the same principle as the Model K Lincoln . . . except for a new housing." Looking to Lincoln was understandable. Ford already had considerable experience building large precision V-8s for his powerful luxury cars from the time he inherited the production facilities with the purchase of Lincoln Motor Company from the Leland family in 1922.

Though a pleasant thought, the idea of converting a Lincoln-type V-8 for use in the smaller Ford was scotched by high manufacturing costs. The Ford could be priced low because it was built in huge volume and had a simple four-cylinder engine cast and machined in one piece. One reason the big Lincoln had to be sold at 10 times the Ford's price was the labor-intensive methods required to build its complex V-8. Its block had to be cast and machined in pieces, and the whole engine was carefully bench assembled.

Of course, the V-8 configuration was nothing new in 1930. The French Antoinette had appeared way back in 1900, and Rolls Royce had one running in 1905. But just as in the days spent tinkering with the X-8 intended for the Model T's replacement, Henry Ford again wanted to bring out something truly revolutionary. The most radical aspect of this new project would be to do what the experts said couldn't be done: produce a *low cost* V-8 car.

Initially, Ford told no one about the project, not even son Edsel or Charles Sorensen, his closest aide. For nearly a year he would casually direct the three engineers. While Zoerlein experimented with the prototype engine's electrical system, Schultz and Laird wrestled with the real puzzle: how to design the complex V-8 block so that it could be cast in one piece. It was Henry Ford's peculiar habit to place obstacles in front of his engineers with the idea that it might bring forth new discoveries. This can be the only possible explanation for developing the new engine in such a primitive shop when his fully equipped Engineering laboratory sat just a few hundred yards away. Eventually, the team was allowed to recruit Herman Reinhold, head of the pattern shop. With his help they secretly built molds and then cast the first experimental block at the Rouge foundry. The first effort seemed satisfactory, and the team had it machined and fitted for running at the Ft. Myers workshop in early 1931.

"We didn't have any instruments in our Ft. Myers lab whatsoever," Zoerlein recalled. "We didn't even have an electric motor . . . I asked Mr. Ford if we could set one up. At that time we only had direct current, which was supplied by a generator driven by a steam engine at one end of the shop. The steam engine also drove an overhead line shaft, which provided power via belts to the various shop tools. Mr. Ford said he didn't want any electrical motors in this building even if direct current was available. He didn't give me any reason for that and I didn't ask for it."

Because of the antiquated equipment they had to work with the team faced another problem: how to test the engine. Henry Ford wouldn't allow any bolts or nails to be driven into the planking of his cherished Edison building, so the trio had to devise a wooden test stand for the engine. They braced this on the floor by running wood beams to the ceiling in such a way that it was forced to stay in position without nailing directly into either surface. "We put a pulley on the back end of the engine and ran it up to the steam engine-powered transmission shaft of the shop to get it started by belt drive," Zoerlein remembered. "We were so busy getting the engine set up that it wasn't until the last moment . . . that we noticed that we lacked a carburetor. We sent one of the engineers running and he came back with one that we stuck on . . . The engine started and the whole building shook. As it ran it would drive the line shaft and the steam engine, to give it load, until the belt slipped off. We were very happy

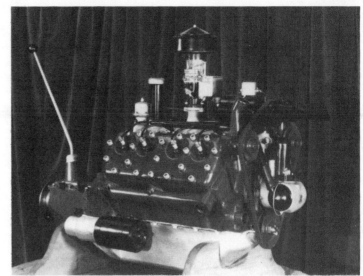

An historic engine: Ford's monoblock flathead V-8

Henry strikes the serial number of the first '32 V-8 car.

because before starting the thing we didn't know whether it would run forwards or backwards!"

While that first experimental V-8 did, at times, not only run backwards but very rough as well, Henry Ford was pleased enough with it that he invited Edsel and production bosses Sorensen and Martin out for a look in June 1931. Also let in on the project was Lawrence Sheldrick, who had exhibited such talent in the Model A's development that he now headed the Ford Engineering Department. Edsel was easily convinced of the engine's potential but the others flatly declared that a 90-degree cylinder block with right-angle crank throws simply could not be cast in one piece at mass-production speeds—and that any attempt to do so was a good way to go broke. Henry listened impatiently to their arguments, then groused, "Anything that can be drawn up can be cast!" With that, he ordered them to get the V-8 into production.

By early August, Henry was personally working full bore on the project, just as he had to perfect the Model T and the Model A. On through fall, more people were

New flathead V-8 was a costly gamble for Henry Ford.

brought to the task of engineering, casting, and testing blocks. For every success there were a hundred failures from core shifts and pinholes. Still, Ford was convinced he was on the right track. By the first week of December, he was so sure that he decided to stop all Model A car production to concentrate on development of a V-8-powered replacement. Thus began a $300-million race to solve the casting problems in time so the new car could be brought to market without undue delay. "It was an awful gamble," said one automobile man in retrospect. "There is not a man in the business today who would—let alone could—make that bet."

"We were scared because of the rush," said one foundry worker. "I worked night and day. We even forgot to go home, right through Christmas season. One day in the foundry we had exactly 100 percent scrap. Everything was wrong. Not one engine came out right. Just think of this: there were 54 separate cores in that mold—54 sand cores that had to stay put just exactly right for the valve sections and cylinders and everything in that engine block."

As the Rouge shops worked against the clock to perfect the production engine, Edsel Ford and Joe Galamb teamed again to style a full line of open and closed bodies for the new car. Once more they took their cue from the highly successful Model K Lincolns that so embodied Edsel's artistic taste. The objective was a smaller-scale adaptation that would incorporate the same sculptured lines and fine detailing. Body design was coordinated with a new chassis being developed under Henry Ford's close supervision by engineers Eugene Farkas and Emery Nador. Also heavily involved were body suppliers Briggs, Murray, and Budd, who fine-tuned the approved stamping designs in anticipation of production orders.

Farkas contributed the major chassis innovations, and his frame design proved both novel and functional. It originated in an idea, first sketched by body designer Galamb, where the side rails functioned in place of the traditional runningboard splash aprons. Farkas cleverly developed this so that the actual production rails were stamped out extra deep and with a long contour on their outer faces. When the body was installed, the frame members would provide a natural enamel finish between the underbody and the runningboards. The methodical Hungarian also had the task of designing a conventional fuel tank, which was to be relocated from above the driver's knees, as it was in the Model A, to the rear of the new frame. Ford gas tanks had been up front since 1926, but this had drawn a lot of criticism mostly because of largely unproved allegations that it constituted a fire hazard. As with the frame, Farkas and Galamb designed the tank so that it very nicely formed the enameled sheetmetal to finish out the detail at the lower rear bodyline.

While all this was going on, Ford's great plants lay mostly idle. At the end of 1931 their only serious activity was manufacturing replacement parts and assembling Model AA commercial vehicles, which continued to find a market. As this near sequel to the events of mid-1927 was being played out, the entire Ford organization was edging toward the brink of financial disaster. The company's cash flow had all but dried up, its trained labor force had been largely laid off, and already hard-pressed dealers across the country were either struggling to stay alive selling parts and used cars or going broke.

It wasn't just dollars lost from having no cars to sell; it was also the enormous expense of tooling for the new model. "The cost was incredible," recalled one production man involved with the V-8 project. "If it wasn't for Henry Ford's great personal wealth, the company could have gone broke in casting that engine."

It didn't take Charles Sorensen long to understand the gravity of the situation. Setting aside his earlier prejudices against the complexities of casting the new engine, he rolled up his sleeves and pitched in at the foundry. Armed with a knowledge of pattern making (as noted, his first job at Ford 27 years earlier), Sorensen barked orders, made changes, and drove his men relentlessly. The last stubborn obstacles were overcome, largely through his personal touch. From that time on he would carry the nickname "Cast Iron Charlie."

Henry Ford was now confident he could actually mass-produce and sell his low-price V-8. After months of rumor and speculation, he began promoting it. In a press statement on February 11th, he said: "I have just got back my old determination to get the price of an automobile down to the mark where the public can buy it." Besides introducing the new V-8 within weeks, he said his company would continue building four-cylinder cars to be designated Model "B." Henry knew that was important, too. It would satisfy those who had written in urging that a "four" be continued. It was also a hedge—just in case the V-8 should fail.

Details of Henry's latest creation came together on March 9, 1932, when the first car authorized for production drove off the assembly line at Dearborn. By the 29th,

Millions turned out to see Ford's new V-8 cars. This showroom scene featuring the Deluxe V-8 coupe was typical.

every dealer in the land had at least one car to show. On April 2nd, the public got its first look at this new mechanical marvel.

Though many Americans were out of work, nearly six million people turned out nationwide for a close-up look at the long-awaited Ford V-8. It was a subdued crowd, but one enchanted with the idea that a Ford could be had with twice the cylinders under the hood. From a distance, the new car didn't seem all that different from the Model A, but closer inspection revealed it to be an all-new species from radiator cap to taillight. Edsel Ford, and those who helped him, could certainly take pride in it, for this was far and away the best-looking Ford yet. That opinion would soon be confirmed by the nation's youth, who would covet the 1932 Ford for hotrodding above all others.

For the first time, low price and performance had been combined with beauty to give the Ford a youthful, sporting appeal. An impressed newsman at the San Francisco preview would write, "In the new Ford car the eye is caught by the bright beauty of the rustless steel headlamps and travels along the bead on the side of the hood toward the rear of the car—giving the impression of an arrow in flight. The bodies are fresh and modern, from the gracefully rounded V-type radiator to the rear bumper. The convex lamps, full-crowned fenders and long, low running boards harmonize with the balance of design."

Inside, the V-8 was nearly as revolutionary in design—for Ford—as it was on the outside. While the light switch remained at the horn button, as on the Model A, the key

and ignition switch were sensibly combined in a single anti-theft unit at the steering column bracket. With the ignition toggle in the "off" position and the key removed, the steering gear locked the front wheels for parking. It was a wonderful idea (still in use today), but it took some getting used to. Drivers new to the car were forever removing the key before coming to a complete stop—and

One of the all-time great Fords: the 1932 Deluxe V-8 roadster

The 1932 Deluxe V-8 roadster with rumble seat. Price: $500.

The 1932 Deluxe coupe could be yours for $575.

Arriving in style with the 1932 Deluxe V-8 roadster

The V-8 line also included this handsome Phaeton at $545.

ending up in all sorts of locked-up trouble. On the dash, the 80-mph speedometer and other instruments were grouped in a handsome, engine-turned oval trimmed with a stainless bead strip and mounted in a mahogany-colored panel. Sunvisors were hinged to move out of the way, and the windshield opened out on a pair of adjustable swing arms. Following what had become tradition, a selection of fine wool, mohair, and leather upholstery was offered. There were no fewer than 14 separate models, arrayed in Standard and Deluxe series, with prices ranging from $460 to $650. Following Model A practice, fenders on all models were dipped in black enamel, while bodies came in a fair choice of colors, with contrasting reveals and pinstriping.

Under the hood was the ingenious flathead V-8. Its twin four-cylinder banks were cast together with the crankcase and flywheel housing, which allowed a short, powerful crankshaft. As a result, the 65-bhp, 221-cid engine could be installed in about the same space needed for the four in the Model A. Up front, a single belt drove a pair of water pumps and a combination generator/fan off the crank pulley. The belt was adjusted by turning a nut (1932 only) on the generator post mount. The aluminum intake manifold was topped by the Detroit Lubricator carburetor, and a fuel pump that worked by way of a pushrod operating off the camshaft. Engine pans were initially made of cast aluminum, later stamped steel.

The compact V-8 was mounted on rubber in a double-drop frame of all-new design. Suspension was by the traditional Ford transverse system with a single leaf spring straddling each axle. However, the rear one was now placed behind the differential, which helped lower frame

height by nearly two inches overall. That—and the new 18-inch wire wheels—gave the V-8 chassis better handling, the car a smarter road-hugging appearance. The front axle was stabilized with a radius-rod wishbone per Ford practice since the Model T. A system of rods and levers operated the four-wheel mechanical brakes. Shock absorbers were by Houdaille. At the rear of the chassis, the gas tank neatly formed the underbody finish. Above it was the spare tire mount, which also served as a frame member. The transmission was a three-speed with synchronized second and high.

For the diehard "four-banger" believer, this most modern Ford yet was also available with an improved version of the Model A engine. There were some very sound business reasons for this. One was the persistent (and as-yet unpublicized) problem of casting perfect V-8 blocks every time. Another was the buyer who would take a lot of convincing that an eight could be as cheap to operate as a four. The four-cylinder cars were assembled on the same line as the V-8s since they shared bodies and basic running gear. The only noticeable difference was the lack of V-8 emblems on headlamp bar and hubcaps, the latter bearing "Ford" script instead. For parts identification purposes the 1932 V-8 cars were designated "Model 18," while the fours were labeled "Model B." Somehow, Model B prevailed in the common description of all the new cars, and to this day many people erroneously apply it to the '32 V-8s.

These were hard economic times. And, nicely tooled and beautiful though it was, the fast new V-8 proved terribly tough to sell. Not only was it introduced at the very depths of the Depression, when consumer dollars were scarce and competition from other makes doubly fierce, there was also a natural wariness about the unproven engine among potential buyers. "Twice the cylinders take twice the gas!" was one often-heard remark. "Cylinders layin' on a slant like that will wear out on the down side!" was another. Rural folk were some of the most skeptical in brushing off the V-8 as a passing fad, preferring to carry on with the old four instead. Some of those doubters weren't far off the mark. Within days of taking to the road, the V-8 cars began earning a reputation for guzzling oil. Also, it was discovered that oil in the pan would surge away from the crankshaft bearings in hard turns, causing engine seizure. Worse yet, pinholes were discovered in many blocks that had been poorly cast, and many of the early cars had to be recalled by dealers for engine replacements.

This situation worried Henry Ford. While his engineers hurried to correct the problem, he directed his outlying branches to begin sponsoring some reliability events in an effort to counter the bad publicity. The most widely reported of these was run in California's Mojave Desert during that summer. Over a 32-mile course, veteran race driver Eddie Pullen, driving a stock Ford V-8 Victoria, logged 33,301 miles in 33 days—and averaged 20 mpg—without engine failure. "After the first run of orders, we had some very difficult selling of the V-8," recalled long-time Stockton, California Ford dealer John Eagal. "With the excessive oil consumption on the early deliveries it was a hard thing to explain to customers . . . and hurt the V-8 cars more than anything else. It was during this period, also, that Ford lost the lead to Chevrolet. With the engineering problems, production lagged behind . . . the

dealers couldn't get cars and the salesmen became discouraged. Chevrolet simply out-produced Ford."

What might have been a great new-car launch became a mediocre one instead. Even lending a fleet of V-8s as official cars for the Indianapolis 500 failed to generate much public response. With sales sluggish and dealers going broke in droves as business conditions worsened, word finally came down from Dearborn to get the V-8 out in the hands of the public.

The best idea put forth to accomplish that was the "Ford Open Air Salon." During the summer, dealers attempted to generate customer interest with carnival-type shows in vacant lots where demonstration rides, movies about making Fords, lectures on the V-8's finer points, and other activities were staged. For the event in Marysville, California, the dealer rented a local peewee golf course to benefit from its night lighting. Besides his entire selection of new models for prospects to try, the highlight of his show was the appearance of Eddie Pullen's durability Victoria, fresh from its Mojave run. The 1932 Michigan State Fair was chosen as the site for the company's own "Open Air" exhibit. Alongside a modest cluster of tents shading a display of new cars and trucks, a half-mile-long oval track was graded and fenced so visitors could have a free demonstration ride in the "smooth" V-8. By fair's end, 63,000 visitors had taken test rides in the new Fords.

But the nation's economy was still on a downslide, and no amount of stimulation would help the general automobile sales slump. The V-8 regained some of its lost momentum, and was now outselling the four-cylinder Ford nearly nine to one. Nevertheless, by the first of August

The new 1932 Model B shared styling with the V-8 cars but used an improved Model A four. Shown is the station wagon.

most of the company's assembly plants were down to a four-day week, operating at just a fraction of their total capacity.

Then, on November 7, 1932, the company issued a terse statement with some somber news. "As the situation has stood," read the news release, "we have been operating plants two or three days a week, getting out from 50 to 100 cars a day at each plant. This is neither good from a manufacturing point of view, nor does it provide workers with a livable wage. We are, therefore, for the time being concentrating our production at points where shipping factors are more advantageous."

In other words, Ford was gearing down. Over the next two months all but 6 of the 30 plants operating that summer were closed. Ford production had fallen to its lowest point since 1914, presenting Henry with another in what would become a series of yearly challenges to stimulate the market.

1933

Sorting out V-8 problems plus elegant new styling for a tough market

To Henry Ford, the practice of changing models every year was "the curse of the industry." Here it was, late summer 1932—barely beyond the ordeal of his multi-million-dollar V-8 launch—and already it was time to start work revamping his new design for the 1933 season. Badgered from all sides by bad news, his cars falling farther behind Chevrolet in the sales race, Henry had at last realized that if he couldn't sell his V-8 line on performance alone, he would have to sell it with a combination of speed and sporty good looks.

Always the motor and chassis man, Henry spent time improving the V-8's running gear while his quietly artistic son Edsel and stylist Joe Galamb were completing the rush job of creating a totally new look. This time, they would get invaluable assistance from body suppliers

Briggs, Murray, and Budd, which by now were accomplished enough to provide clients such as Ford with ideas and mock-ups expressing the latest, most fashionable styling trends. While cars were becoming more streamlined on the drawing boards, the industry still lacked the technology to produce such shapes. So, the design Edsel approved for 1933 wasn't the teardrop it might have been, but it was nevertheless more graceful, with the sort of low-slung, racy lines characteristic of the early and mid-1930s, the remarkable era that produced some of America's all-time classic automobiles.

Though hampered by a strike at Briggs plus other production problems associated with building their second all-new design in two years, the Fords debuted their latest creation on February 9, 1933—about three months later than the customary introduction date. The new passenger line was designated "Model 40." Describing the beautifully executed 1933s, one journalist would write: "The new Ford V-8, with much roomier bodies, entirely new and decidedly attractive appearance, is out. Its beauty is enhanced by the rakish angle of the radiator grille which coincides with those of the windshield, hood, and door lines. Fenders are of modern design, with wide skirts, and the construction eliminates the need for the old splash aprons below the radiator and above the running boards. Wire spoke wheels have been reduced to 17-inch in size and full-length bumpers, front and rear, are styled with a painted horizontal stripe and a slight dip in the center." The writer neglected to mention the new longer 112-inch wheelbase, longest in Ford history.

By the beginning of the year most of the V-8 engine block problems had been ironed out, and there were several internal improvements that boosted output to 75 bhp. These were aluminum cylinder heads, a higher compression ratio, and better cooling and ignition. An all-new stiffer X-type frame, which retained the traditional transverse springing, and axles stabilized with radius rods gave the Model 40 great flexibility over rough roads and an exceptionally soft ride. And, once again, buyers had the less expensive alternative of ordering a four-cylinder engine instead of the V-8. The designation for this car was Model C. Like its 1932 counterpart it was easily identified by the lack of V-8 emblems on hubcaps.

All in all, the 1933 Ford line was brilliant. Unfortunately, it was introduced quite late in the model year and,

1933 Deluxe V-8 cabriolet displays this year's new styling.

The 1933 Deluxe V-8 cabriolet. Rumble seat was no charge.

The 1933 Deluxe V-8 Fordor sedan listed at $610.

All doors on the '33 Deluxe V-8 wagon were rear-hinged.

Deluxe V-8 Victoria looked more like the Tudor for 1933.

The 1933 Deluxe V-8 coupe featured standard rear-mount spare.

Price on the 1933 Deluxe V-8 Tudor sedan was $550.

A quintet of '33s in a Tacoma, Wahsington, showroom

with little price advantage and the absence of a good publicity buildup, the cars never earned the kind of success they deserved. The late start and Ford's long-standing policy of prohibiting his 9000 dealers from using high-pressure sales tactics like the rest of the industry, enabled high-rolling Chevy to take another commanding market lead—and Plymouth to move up another notch. Even so, sales for the calendar year would run some 100,000 units ahead of 1932.

As the Model 40s took to the road, there were growing signs that the V-8 was catching on at last—especially among the leadfoots of the nation. Dirt track and speed boat racers were among the first to discover that with only a few simple modifications, a Ford V-8 would outperform most everything else its size and weight. In fact, its success on amateur and professional racing circuits from the Detroit River to Pike's Peak would set off a flathead

speed craze that continues to this day. Stock car drivers, especially, had found that by stripping the runningboards, fenders and top from a regular V-8 roadster and making a few chassis adjustments they could just about beat anything on the dirt tracks. At the nationally famous Elgin (Illinois) Road Race held in August, stunned onlookers watched as seven stripped Fords took the first seven places against a highly touted pack of Chevrolets, Plymouths, and Dodges. The winner, in a '33 roadster, was Fred Frame, 1932 Indy 500 champion, who led the field over the tricky 8.5 mile course for 203 miles at an average speed of 88.22 mph. The Elgin event proved a tremendous tonic for Ford sales. In October, when Henry invited his suppliers to Detroit for a special Exposition of Progress, Frame's winning roadster was the featured attraction.

Encouraged by this happier turn of events, Henry Ford

Ford's flathead V-8 was the favorite of early hotrodders. Here, two stripped roadsters line up for a 1933 speed run.

began directing Model 40 refinements for the coming year. At the same time, he swiftly began planning for a major company presence at the 1934 World's Fair in Chicago, and began stepping up his advertising and promotional programs.

1934

More refinements—and an unsolicited testimonial from Bonnie and Clyde

On December 6, 1933, the Fords hosted newsmen at the best publicized event of its type since the onset of the Depression: a Dearborn preview of the nicely updated Model 40 for 1934. Held a month earlier than other automakers' press shows, it was praised almost as much for the cars as for the fact that this was the first time

Henry Ford had ever served an alcoholic beverage at a company function. While beer and cigarettes were passed around, reporters were openly enthusiastic about the glamorous new models and gave them a very flattering review.

"Changes in the appearance of the attractive car include new hood, radiator and grille lines, a new instrument panel, and luxurious new upholstery treatment," wrote the reporter for *Automotive Industries*. "The curve in the grille has been eliminated and there is a new ornament surrounding the radiator cap. Hubcaps and the spare tire-lock cover are also new, as is the V-8 insignia on the grille. The fashionable bodies have the new 'clear vision' ventilating system similar to that in the new Lincoln cars." The last was a reference to a redesigned window winding mechanism. As it wound down the front door glass first moved rearwards to a "vent" position, then dropped vertically. This required a design change to the door window frame, so the closed 1934 bodies differ from 1933's in that respect. The most noticeable interior change was deletion of the engine-turned instrument panel insert in favor of a plain painted dash of similar lay-

The elegant 1934 Deluxe V-8 Fordor sedan, priced at $625

Out for a carefree spin in the '34 Deluxe V-8 Phaeton

A tiny trunk was featured on the '34 Deluxe V-8 Victoria.

out. New accessories for 1933 had included either a glove compartment-type or ashtray-mounted radio, plus dual wipers and heater. To these, Ford added a beautifully cast radiator cap in the image of a running greyhound for '34. And for the first time in Ford history body-color fenders were no-charge.

The Detroit Lubricator carburetor was replaced by a better-engineered Stromberg dual-downdraft type. This yielded 10 extra horses, the V-8 now rated at 85 bhp. Most other engineering changes this year were minor fit and wear improvements of existing hardware.

With all the good press and the company's renewed interest in promotion, sales of the dandy '34s began taking off once people had a chance to get behind the wheel. Among the new model's earliest champions were police officials who used its explosive speed to chase crooks—and crooks who stole new Fords to outrun the law. Infamous bank robber Clyde Barrow was one unabashed admirer who took time from his criminal pursuits to praise V-8 virtues in a letter sent to a surprised Henry Ford. Postmarked Tulsa, Oklahoma, and dated April 10, 1934, it read:

Dear Sir:
While I still have got breath in my lungs I will tell you what a dandy car you make. I have drove [sic] Fords exclusively when I could get away with one. For sustained speed and freedom from trouble the Ford has got ever [sic] other car skinned and even if my business hasn't [sic] been strictly legal it don't hurt enything [sic] to tell you what a fine car you got in the Ford V8.

Yours Truly,
Clyde Champion Barrow

As fate would have it, Clyde and his wife Bonnie would meet their maker in a 1934 Ford sedan, gunned down in a sheriff's ambush.

On May 26th the Ford exhibit opened at the Century of Progress in Chicago. It was by far the most ambitious undertaking of its kind ever attempted by the company. The show buildings were laid out on an 11-acre landscaped site fronting Lake Michigan. Dominating the area was the magnificent gear-shaped Rotunda building. Along the lakeshore ran a .4-mile "Roads of the World," where visitors could ride over short reproduction stretches of his-

1934 Deluxe V-8 3-window coupe

1934 Deluxe V-8 5-window coupe

toric world thoroughfares in the new Ford of their choice. Inside the Rotunda and an adjoining industrial show wing was a dazzling display of the latest Ford automaking technology, plus supplier exhibits, live demonstrations of parts manufacturing, and displays of antique models and the newest Ford cars and trucks. As a centerpiece, three fully equipped V-8 Victorias were hung as on a chandelier from a single 17-inch-diameter wheel—to show the strength of its welded steel spokes. It was Ford's greatest show ever, and few would forget the sights and sounds, the free souvenirs, and the beauty of the cars. The 1934 models seemed to have just the right balance of details, which made them a sensation in their day and would assure their place in the hearts of car fans everywhere as some of the classiest Fords of all time.

1935

An improved chassis, new bodies, and the return of the convertible sedan

By the mid-'30s, competition in the auto industry was fierce as a dwindling number of companies fought for an ever-smaller number of sales. In this climate, Ford had found it necessary to update its cars annually. Besides, this was clearly recognized by now as a major factor in establishing Chevrolet's sales leadership. With the Model 40 of 1933, the company inaugurated a two-year design cycle that it would adhere to for the rest of the decade. Accordingly, the 1935 Fords received a revised frame, a newly styled bodyshell, and a new Model 48 designation.

The theme for 1935 was "Greater Beauty, Greater Comfort, and Greater Safety." Styling took on a more rounded look. Bodies were longer and wider, there were more curves, windshields were more steeply raked, and radiators were narrower. Wheel diameter was reduced an inch, to 16 inches. The result was a sleeker, more streamlined appearance, though nothing nearly as radical as Chrysler's Airflow design, which had been a disaster in its debut year of 1934.

Engineering refinements included a beefed-up frame and rear axle, better mechanical brakes, nicer steering, and a new "easy-action" clutch. Horsepower on the flathead V-8 remained at 85 bhp, as it would for the remainder of the decade, but there was a new camshaft and crankcase ventilation was improved. The suspension still consisted of a single transverse spring at each end, an archaic arrangement that would persist in Ford chassis design for the next 13 years. This and the use of mechanical brakes were two areas in which Ford was distinctly behind the times, but old Henry refused to believe any of his ideas were outdated.

A significant body change this year that was unrelated to styling was first-time availability of a built-in trunk on the Tudor and Fordor sedans. A step in this direction had appeared on the 1934 Victoria 2-door. Unfortunately, this trunk didn't provide much space, and it was awkward to get at because its bottom-hinged lid didn't tilt open very far. This year's sedan trunk was more useful, and added a mere $20 to the cost of the standard "fastback" sedans. The "trunkback" style, as it was called, would prove increasingly popular as the years passed.

Model offerings were broadly the same as in recent years, though the Victoria now disappeared. The most expensive of the regular line was the new 4-door convertible sedan at $750. Unlike the Model A version of this body style, the 1935 had no permanent side window frames, and its center pillars were removable. Still around were the glamorous Deluxe Phaeton at $580, the rumble-seat Convertible Cabriolet at $625, and the youthful Deluxe Roadster at $550. All open models this year sported front-hinged doors, a definite safety plus. Rear doors on sedans remained the "suicide" rear-hinged type.

A possible sign of renewed prosperity was the reopening of Ford's Long Beach, California, plant in February 1935.

The Deluxe V-8 Fordor sedan with new-for-'35 built-in trunk

1935 Deluxe V-8 3-window coupe

The romantic Phaeton returned for '35, priced at $580.

1935 Deluxe V-8 5-window coupe

Convertible sedan was revived this year with four doors.

1935 Deluxe V-8 Convertible Cabriolet, priced at $625

According to Paul R. Woudenberg, author of *Ford in the Thirties*, styling for the 1935 line can be credited to Phil Wright of the Briggs body company. "There were two styling sections at the firm," he notes, "one headed by John Tjaarda being charged with experimental car design exercises, while the [second] group did speculative designs for Briggs' regular customers, notably Ford and Plymouth. Phil Wright reportedly did the renderings for the 1935 Ford at his home, then showed them to his boss, Ralph Roberts, who in turn showed them to Ford management including Edsel Ford. Ford officials were so pleased that the order went out to go right to a full-scale mockup of wood, rather than through the customary 1/24th clay scale models. Famed stylist Bob Koto, a compatriot of Wright...was later assigned to facelift the '35s into the following year's 1936 Model 68."

Woudenberg also observes that by the end of the 1935 selling season "Ford had decisively regained industry leadership in sales with 826,519, compared to Chevrolet's 656,698 and Plymouth's 382,925." While the new styling surely played a part in this success, so too did a redesigned 1935 chassis. Engineer Lawrence Sheldrick, responding to GM's new "Knee Action" independent front suspension, cleverly managed to relocate the Ford's front transverse leaf spring from behind to in front of the axle. This permitted the engine to be shoved up some 8.5 inches and, more significantly, allowed the spring to be longer and spring rates both front and rear to be softer. The result was what Ford called the "front seat ride" for all passengers. Compared to the Model 40 frame, the 1935 design "was much stronger, using more box sections and heavier bracing throughout," according to author Woudenberg. The car felt more solid, and the chassis racking, still noticeable on Model 40 when negotiating sharp road angles, was gone."

The 1935 lineup made its first public appearance at the prestigious New York Auto Show in late December, 1934. It had been 25 years since Ford last exhibited at the annual event, and the company went all out to capture attention. Besides a sparkling bevy of cars there were cutaway "motion" exhibits, installed on all three levels of the show hall. These drew crowds of admirers, and ranged from a motorized "exploded" V-8 engine and chassis to a demonstration of rapid engine assembly, run against the clock by two workers from the big Rouge plant.

The 1935 models saw the last of several longstanding Ford features. They were the last Fords with standard wire-spoke wheels, external horns, and outside radiator cap. One item moved inside, though: the parking lamps, now housed within the headlamps. And there was a first this year as Ford began manufacturing its own sub-assemblies for station wagon bodies. Previously, the Mingel Company of Kentucky had supplied the wood panelling; Briggs or Murray in Detroit handled assembly. Hereafter, wagon panels would be fabricated in a plant at Iron Mountain, Michigan, an ideal location because Ford owned hardwood forest acreage nearby, which minimized transportation costs. Final assembly took place at the company's own branch assembly plants.

Besides its New York appearance, the '35 Ford also starred at Indianapolis, where a sporty Convertible Sedan was selected as pace car for the annual 500-mile racing classic. The promotional highlight of the year was the California-Pacific International Exposition in San Diego, where the company put on a huge show in a specially erected building.

1936

A new "face" and hidden features keep Ford moving right along

Keeping to its two-year design cycle, Ford issued a mildly restyled lineup for 1936 in mid-October 1935. Detailed to enhance the V-8 engine's growing reputation for performance, the new Model 68s sported a number of minor styling changes that, taken together, produced a smart, new, graceful look. Industry design practices of the day dictated hiding some components that had previously been exposed, so the horns were now placed behind "catwalk" grilles in the front fender aprons. The hood became longer and more pointed, and the radiator grille was given a more pronounced V-shape to match. Wheels were changed from wire-spoke to a new drop-center all-steel type with full disc hubcaps.

A new body style was added in March, the five-passenger Convertible Club Cabriolet. This featured a longer top to enclose a rear seat. The regular single-seat two-passenger Deluxe cabriolet and the Deluxe roadster were still around for those who preferred rumble seats—and by this time, fewer people did. Prices were $675, $625, and $560, respectively, for these Deluxe-trim open cars. The most expensive of the line was the new Convertible Touring Sedan, featuring integral trunk and priced at

The Deluxe V-8 Phaeton sold for $590 in 1936.

Top of the '36 line was the $780 Convertible Touring Sedan.

Whitewalls add spiff to this 1936 Deluxe V-8 3-window coupe.

New '36 Convertible Club Cabriolet retailed for $675.

$780. All '36 Fords except the roadster and coupe could be ordered with a built-in trunk. Counting utility models the model count totalled 21.

Engineering alterations for the Model 68 weren't earth-shaking, but they were important in the neck-and-neck sales battle with Chevrolet where every little talking

1936 Deluxe V-8 Convertible Touring Sedan

Trunkback '36s like this Fordor were called Touring models.

The Deluxe V-8 Tudor "flatback" sedan cost $565 for 1936.

1936 Deluxe V-8 convertible sedan (center posts removed)

Center posts were removable on '36 convertible sedans.

A special 1936 V-8 Town Car with coachwork by Cunningham

The '36 Ford lineup poses in V-formation with salesmen.

1936 Deluxe V-8 5-window coupe

point counted. Among these were an increase of 3.5 inches in rear elbow room, new pivoting rear quarter windows in Fordor sedans, reduced steering effort, and an increase in cooling system capacity and radiator area to alleviate the overheating problems that were still dogging the V-8.

The pace of razzle-dazzle promotion quickened in 1936 as Ford put on big shows at the Texas Centennial in Dallas, at the Atlantic City boardwalk, and at the Great Lakes Exposition in Cleveland. Those attending these events saw a parade in which a float bearing a 1936 roadster passed by, proclaiming the Ford ride as "The Car in

A classy Ford from a classic era: the 1936 Deluxe Phaeton

New Convertible Club Cabriolet offered seating for four.

That's actor Clark Gable at the wheel of this custom-built Ford roadster with bodywork by Jensen of England.

the Clouds." Another crowd-pleaser was the "Human Ford," a '36 roadster that appeared on stage to ask and answer audience questions in a "mystical" voice (no doubt that of a local ventriloquist).

Ford logged two production milestones in close succession in 1935-36. The 2-millionth V-8 car had rolled off the lines in June 1935. Less than a year later, in May 1936,

the 3-millionth was built. Though the country was now only inching its way out of the Depression—and slowly at that—Ford was rolling right along, surely a tribute to the inherent "rightness" of its cars. Nevertheless, the model year saw Chevy retake the number-one sales position, with 930,000 units to Ford's still substantial total of some 764,000.

1937

A smaller companion V-8 and streamlined styling for a splashy debut

All-new styling and a number of new features made 1937 a vintage year for Ford. Billed by company publicists as the most stunning Ford yet, the '37 inaugurated another two-year design cycle, and was clearly a radical departure from past styling practice.

The new look was more evidence of Ford's work in streamlining, first seen in the futuristic Lincoln-Zephyr of 1936, styled by Tom Tjaarda. Headlamps were now incorporated into the front fender aprons. The prominently

vee'd grille was stretched and sloped back. Fenders were curvaceous. Slim louvers matching the fine horizontal grille bars adorned the sides of the pointed hood, which was now hinged at the rear to open "alligator" style, as on the Zephyr.

The '37 Ford was one of the handsomest cars of the decade—even President Roosevelt bought a convertible sedan to use at his Warm Springs, Georgia retreat. In a year of questionable styling for the industry as a whole,

Accessory fender skirts grace this '37 Deluxe Fordor sedan.

The handsome 1937 Deluxe Club Cabriolet sold for $760.

The Deluxe V-8 roadster made its last appearance in '37.

Ford was a standout—proof that streamlining didn't have to mean an end to distinctive, timelessly styled automobiles. The new car might have been even more attractive had it not been for Henry Ford, who personally directed a reduction in overall length of 3-4 inches—most of it in the front—from the original prototype. The "flatback" trunkless sedans probably suffered most from the resulting extra stubbiness.

In the late '30s, styling was one of Ford's few strong points. By this time, Henry Ford, who had brought the automobile to the masses in his youth, was a hardened man in his mid-70s. Though his son Edsel remained company president, Henry continued to rule with an iron hand. Aside from stifling new product developments, he adamantly refused to let his factories unionize. His right-hand man, Harry Bennett, employed a sort of private army to ensure that Henry got his way. In 1937, men distributing union handbills took a brutal beating from Ben-

nett's troops, resulting in the worst public image Henry Ford ever had.

By contrast, the 1937 line was introduced in one of the splashiest extravaganzas ever seen. On the morning of November 6, 1936, some 7000 Ford dealers from all over the country packed the Detroit Coliseum. The mood was one of excitement and anticipation: at long last, the nation seemed to be breaking out of its economic gloom. The auditorium was darkened, and a slim shaft of light picked out a large V-8 emblem on the center of the elevated stage. There, golden-haired "elves" unwound themselves up from the floor and, rising one at a time, began tossing various car parts into a big cauldron. Steam began to emerge as engine components, wheels, radiators, and other bits and pieces were thrown into the brew. Then, in a fantasy of light and color, the fumes cleared, the elves disappeared, and a new 1937 Club Coupe rose up on a ramp, traversed the stage, then drove down onto the

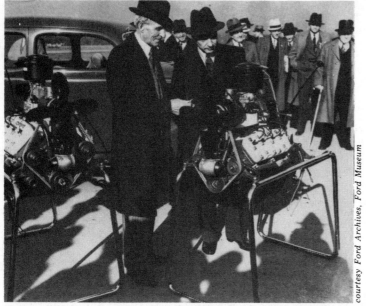

Henry, Edsel, and reporters at the 1937 Ford press preview

main floor. It was a new way to introduce cars, one that would be widely imitated as the industry became increasingly enamored of such razzmatazz for hawking its wares. Certainly Ford dealers must have come away feeling 1937 was going to be a banner year.

And in most respects it was. For the first time, closed body styles lacked the traditional fabric roof insert as Ford followed GM's lead the previous year with all-steel "turret-top" construction. Also for the first time, there was a smaller version of the flathead V-8. Sized at 136 cid and rated at 60 bhp, the new engine had originally been conceived for use in Britain and France, where it had powered locally built Fords for more than a year. The reason for it was European tax laws, which were based on engine displacement, not vehicle size (in Britain, on bore but not stroke), but in the U.S. the "V-8/60" was marketed as an economy engine. Available on all but Deluxe models, it featured a much reduced bore compared to the V-8/85 (2.6 versus 3.1 inches). It was hoped this option would attract a large number of buyers looking for a standard-size car that was cheaper to operate. It was a sound idea, but it didn't work. The 60-bhp V-8 was underpowered for most Americans, and failed to garner many sales. It lasted only through 1940.

There were several other noteworthy engineering refinements this year. For the V-8/85, the capacity of the water pump was increased and the unit relocated, both of which improved cooling efficiency. Larger insert bearings and new cast-alloy steel pistons were also used. While Ford clung persistently to mechanical brakes, the old system of rods used to actuate them was discarded in favor of a more modern cable linkage, housed in a protective conduit. Finally, the steering ratio was again lowered to

The Deluxe V-8 5-window Club Coupe, a new 1937 body style

Sans trunk, the '37 Deluxe V-8 Tudor sedan sold for $675.

Plush seats dominated 1937 Ford Tudor's front cabin.

reduce effort at the wheel, though it did mean an unseemly number of turns lock-to-lock.

Ford offered 18 different models for 1937. Body styles with the difficult-to-use side curtains of old continued to decline in popularity as the decade wore on, so this would be the last year for the true roadster. After '37, it would be effectively supplanted by the more popular Convertible Cabriolet with roll-up glass. The 4-door phaeton was still listed (at $750), but would continue only through 1938. New to the roster and quite popular was the four-passenger five-window Club Coupe, priced at $720. It had a roof length halfway between that of the conventional Tudor sedan and the normal coupe, which this year acquired rear quarter glass to become a five-window style. The woody wagon again came with roll-down glass in the front doors only; side curtains were provided instead of rear door and quarter glass. As an option, you could order an "all-glass" wagon for $20 additional, bringing the price up to $775. Once again, the top-line offering was the glamorous Deluxe convertible sedan, priced at $860.

In all, the more modern '37s lived up to customer expectations—aside from persistent comments that the cars would have been safer with a hydraulic brake system like that on most competitors. The sales race saw Ford beaten by Chevrolet by a mere 2000 cars. However, Ford trucks sold better, putting the division ahead of Chevy in gross totals. Unfortunately, Ford would not do as well for the next dozen years.

1938

Ford divides its model line to conquer more sales in a difficult year

A new marketing ploy was adopted with the 1938 Ford line: different styling for base and Deluxe models. The former, now called Standard, were essentially warmed-over versions of the previous year's Model 78 bodyshell. Its main distinction was that the upper horizontal grille bars were swept back almost to the cowl, thus eliminating separate hood louvers. The new Deluxe models, like the Standards designated Model 81A, got a more heavily reworked front end. A longer hood curved over and down into the grille, which was now rounded off at its upper corners, and separate hood louvers were retained. The reason for all this was to give Ford broader market coverage, as a sizable demand still existed for less expensive, more austere standard-size cars. It was a practice Ford would continue through the 1940 season.

Engineering changes were almost nonexistent. The Standard coupe and Tudor and Fordor sedans were available with either V-8. The Deluxe line, which included

The 1937 Deluxe V-8 Fordor Touring Sedan

Standard 1938 models like this Tudor used 1937 tooling.

A '37 convertible sedan displays its new "alligator" hood.

Here's the Deluxe 1938 Tudor, with all-new styling.

1938 Deluxe V-8 convertible coupe

1938 Deluxe V-8 Fordor sedan

courtesy Ford Archives, Ford Museum

The glamorous Deluxe V-8 convertible sedan remained the top-of-the-line offering for 1938, priced at $900 even.

these styles plus four convertibles, the club coupe, and the station wagon, was offered only with the larger 85-bhp engine. All models featured a built-in trunk as standard equipment this year. Accessory fender skirts were a new dressup item, and they suited the open cars particularly well, especially the romantic phaeton, now in its final year. All-round glass windows became standard equipment for the station wagon.

The relative lack of change for '38 signalled that some-

thing was going on in Dearborn besides old Henry's railing against progress. And indeed, it was: the company was busy preparing an all-new Ford for 1939—and a new companion make. The "split" 1938 model line was, in a way, a preparatory move designed to provide an orderly price progression between Ford and the forthcoming new Mercury. As we know now, the new make would be a slightly larger, more powerful, higher-priced derivative of the '39 Ford, intended to give Dearborn a more direct

A 1938 Deluxe V-8 Club Coupe shares a Tacoma, Washington, dealer's showroom floor with a bare Ford chassis.

competitor in the medium-price field against Pontiac and Oldsmobile from GM, and Dodge and DeSoto from Chrysler.

A recession this year blunted the pace of the national economic recovery, and car sales slipped throughout the industry. In Ford's case, total volume was only about half what it had been in 1937, some 410,000 units. Chevrolet sales also sank, but not quite as much. In some respects, this disappointing result also reflected the fact that Ford was still behind the competition: old-fashioned transverse-spring suspension and mechanical brakes remained the most glaring anachronisms. By now, Henry Ford's intransigence, his refusal to bow to what he considered engineering "fads," was hurting the company. And that would continue to be the rule well into the following decade.

1939

Hydraulic brakes at last—but the new Mercury steals the limelight.

Overshadowed by introduction of the new medium-price Mercury in early October 1938 were several significant developments for the 1939 Ford. Aside from pretty new lines on Deluxe models, the big news was hydraulic brakes. Old Henry had finally given in—three years after Chevrolet and 11 years after Plymouth. The hydraulic system answered one long-standing Ford criticism, but the antiquated chassis was untouched again this year.

Work on the new brakes had begun in 1938 at Henry's direct order. However, the aging motor magnate suffered a stroke soon afterwards, and from this point on would be less and less involved in running the company and developing its products. Henry continued to rely heavily on the advice of Harry Bennett, even over that of his own son Edsel, who was still—at least in name—company president.

Mercury was really Edsel's idea. Though a new design from the wheels up, it could more accurately be described as a "super deluxe" Ford, with scaled-up price, proportions, and power. Its wheelbase was longer than the Ford's by four inches, and it consequently offered a roomier interior and a nicer ride. It should be noted, however, that some of the development work on the Mercury project spilled over to this year's Fords, especially the Deluxe models. For example, the Mercury used an enlarged 239-cid version of the flathead V-8, with larger-diameter bearings, heavier rods and crankshaft, and other strengthened internal components. Most of these changes were also adopted for the 221-cid engine in the Ford. Also, there was an obvious styling kinship between Mercury and this year's Ford Deluxe, especially at the front. Both wore low vee'd grilles, the Mercury with horizontal bars, the Ford Deluxe vertical bars. Headlamps on both were completely absorbed into the front fenders, but retained the oval shape of previous years (circular sealed-beam units were on the way). Hoods were deeper and bereft of side louvers. Stylist Bob Gregorie had created two of the prettiest Ford products ever. The 1940 editions would be even prettier.

Meantime, the Ford Standard soldiered on again as a mild rehash of the previous year's Model 81A. Its grille and hood detailing was busier and less organized now in the contemporary fashion. The lower-price line gained a station wagon, joining the two sedans and five-window coupe from '38. The broader Deluxe range was abbreviated as the phaeton, club coupe, and convertible club coupe all disappeared. The lovely convertible sedan was in its final season, but was no longer alone at the top of the line: the Deluxe wagon carried an identical $920 price. Curiously, the convertible 4-door would resurface the next year—and that year only—as a Mercury.

Apart from the new brakes, engineering improvements were few. The V-8/85 retained its customary power rating despite the stronger internals, though some tests suggested it was slightly greater than before.

General interest in the '39 Fords was heightened throughout the year by the company's exhibit at the New York World's Fair. Here as at Chicago, Dallas, and San Diego in past years, a special building was put up to showcase the Ford story. Visitors found their greatest

The Deluxe 5-window coupe was priced at $700 for 1939.

Snappy Deluxe convertible coupe for '39 could seat six.

1939 Ford Deluxe front end was similar to the new Mercury's.

On the dais at the '39 press preview, the Deluxe Fordor.

Pointed prow marked all Deluxe '39s, like this Fordor sedan.

thrills on the "Road of Tomorrow," an elevated highway encircling the entire main building where everyone had a chance to ride in Fords, Mercurys, and the elegant Lincolns.

In what was expected to be a better sales year than it turned out to be, Ford sold over 481,000 cars, trailing Chevrolet by nearly 100,000. Worse, third-place Plymouth was closer than ever on the strength of its smart new 1939 design. Ford also faced strong competition in the new six-cylinder Studebaker Champion. Ford was doing well enough, but so were most rivals.

The decade coming to a close had been a difficult one for Ford. The technical advances made with the Model A and the flathead V-8 were counterbalanced by Henry Ford's growing eccentricity and the loss of supremacy in the low-price field to Chevrolet. Yet after several years of hasty, often confused new-model programs, Ford seemed to be sorting out its various problems, while looking forward to real national prosperity that presumably was just around the corner. As 1939 moviegoers were being captivated by *The Wizard of Oz* and *Gone With the Wind*, the ominous rumblings of war could be heard.

1940

Benchmark styling makes this year's Fords among the most coveted of all

Unveiled in October 1939, the Model 01A 1940 Ford is remembered today primarily for its styling. It had little in the way of engineering refinement to speak of, except for addition of a front anti-roll bar or spring stabilizer on the 85-bhp Deluxe models. Workmanship, never a Ford selling point, was better, perhaps because of the fact that the company was now producing all its passenger-car bodies owing to labor problems at its body suppliers' plants. Still, Ford trailed its competitors somewhat in fit and finish. But, oh, that styling!

The 1940 design was good indeed—so good that these Fords have become some of the most desired cars ever built in the eyes of enthusiasts. Designed principally by Bob Gregorie with guidance, as always, from Edsel Ford, the new Deluxe was dominated by a crisply pointed hood

meeting a handsome chrome-plated vee'd grille composed of delicate horizontal bars and flanked by painted side grilles. Headlamps—circular sealed-beam units for the first time—were nestled into neat chrome nacelles faired into the fenders. The fenders themselves were artfully curved to complement the body contours, and could be skirted at the rear for a more streamlined look. The rear end was distinguished by distinctive chevron taillights. This deft facelift of the 1939 bodyshell worked amazingly well, and even the cheaper Standard models looked fresh, much less frumpy than in the past. They used body-color headlamp housings and vertical grille bars with a simple chrome cap on the grille peak.

This would be the last year for the split Standard/Deluxe model line. The sole remaining open body style

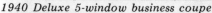
1940 Deluxe 5-window business coupe

1940 Deluxe Fordor sedan

Deluxe convertible coupe was the only open model left in the 1940 line. Price was reasonable at $850.

this year was the rakish convertible coupe, offered only in Deluxe trim, priced at a reasonable $850. Demise of the convertible sedan left the wood-bodied wagon the costliest '40 at $950. A new entry was the business coupe, a replacement for the club coupe. Featuring fold-up rear jump seats and a large trunk, it was commonly referred to as the "opera coupe" by most buyers. It was available in both Standard and Deluxe trim, priced at $680 and $745, respectively. In future years, these coupes would prove to be popular as hot rod material. The 3-passenger five-window coupes without jump seats were still offered at $660 for the Standard and $721 for the Deluxe.

In April, the 28-millionth Ford car, a Deluxe Fordor sedan, came off the line at the Edgewater, New Jersey assembly plant. Over the next few months, this car would tour the country, stopping in major cities and state capitols to collect specially numbered license plates and celebrity signatures in its logbook. Another milestone was observed a few months later, in June, as Ford built its 7-millionth V-8 engine.

Sales of the 1940 Ford were encouraging. The total comfortably exceeded a half-million units, a gain of about 10 percent on 1939. Plymouth and Chevrolet had both been busy, though, and each scored healthy sales gains. Ford was, once again, not quite as up-to-date as the opposition. All that would change in 1941.

1941

The biggest Fords ever debut as war looms on the horizon

Many Americans were happy-go-lucky at the end of 1940. True, there was a worrisome war raging abroad, but President Roosevelt and his New Deal had put many workers back on the job, and the country was hopeful that it could avoid the conflict while enjoying renewed prosperity. A body painter at Ford Motor Company was making good wages for the time—$1.10 an

1941 Super Deluxe sedan coupe listed at $850.

New top-line Super Deluxe series included the convertible.

The 1941 Super Deluxe Fordor, one of the "big" new Fords

hour—and fender stamping repair workers had the best pay on the line at about $1.15.

Into this optimistic climate, Ford rolled out its 1941 cars at a big Dearborn press reception in September 1940. Henry Ford was 78 now, and this would be his last appearance at such an event. Reporters must have somehow sensed this, for nearly 500 turned out to see and hear the auto industry's elder statesman. True to form, he had little to say. Instead, he escorted the party to a nearby site where his workers were busily erecting a huge new factory that would turn out fighter airplane engines. Like many other companies, Ford was now deeply involved in a growing number of defense projects as government geared up not to fight, but to supply its European allies with war materiel.

The '41s were the biggest Fords yet—longer, lower, wider, flashier, and heavier. Wheelbase stretched by two inches, bodysides ballooned outward, interior space increased, and a stouter frame slid in underneath. Curb weights rose by some 300 pounds on the average compared to the lithe 1940s. Styling was evolutionary, marked by a rather busy front end with a vertical center grille flanked by low-riding "scoop" grilles, all with vertical chrome bars. Said *Ford News:* "Probably the most outstanding advancement in this year's car is improved riding, made possible by a number of factors including a wheelbase increased to 114 inches. That the 1941 Ford is a big car is indicated by the fact that the front seat in the Fordor Sedan is a full seven inches wider than in any pre-

vious Ford car. The front seat width is why so little runningboard shows outside. The unusually wide bodies, with doors that round out at the bottom to cover all but a narrow strip of the runningboards, are trim and sleek. Headlamps are mounted far apart on the massive front fenders to increase nighttime visibility, and the separate parking lamps are set high on the fenders."

Ford was right in step with its "big" '41. In fact, rivals Chevrolet and Plymouth had enlarged their cars substantially the previous year, a move that met with considerable buyer approval. If Dearborn had been behind the times, it was certainly catching up fast now. The clean, ready-for-action look of the '41 Ford was quickly accepted as the latest in high-fashion motoring.

The big engineering news this year was the arrival of a new six-cylinder engine, the first at Ford since the Model K of 1906. An L-head design, it displaced 226 cid—5 more cubes than the flathead V-8—and produced 90 bhp at 3300 rpm—5 bhp more than the V-8/85. This new six came about from dealer reaction to the Mercury back in 1939, namely that a "Ford Six" would have been a better seller than a puffed-up V-8 car. Edsel Ford, always respectful of and often sympathetic to what dealers had to say, promised them one. He even managed to get his father's approval in one of those strange turnabouts for which Henry was noted.

Replacing the unpopular V-8/60, the new six was offered as an alternative to the V-8/85 throughout a revised '41 model line. Replacing the Standard was the new Special, offered as a coupe and Tudor and Fordor sedans. The middle-priced Deluxe series offered five body types—coupe, business coupe, the two sedans, and the wagon. At the top was a new Super Deluxe group comprising all the Deluxe types plus convertible and a new 2-door six-passenger model dubbed the Sedan Coupe. The new six with its more modern design and greater power must have been a slight embarrassment to Ford, for the V-8 cost only about $15 extra model for model. Prices ranged from $684 for the basic six-cylinder Special coupe up to $1013 for the V-8 Super Deluxe wagon. The latter marked the first time the price of a regular-line Ford had exceeded the magic thousand-dollar mark.

Ford was making up for lost time in another way for '41. If it had been late with hydraulic brakes, it could at least have the industry's largest—12 inches drum diameter. Other engineering alterations included widening the front and rear transverse leaf springs, which allowed softer spring rates for a more cushioned ride. Numerically higher gear ratios from the previous V-8/60 transmission were adopted on both six and V-8, mainly to make up for the performance losses expected with the greater heft of the '41 models. The result was comparable low-end getaway at some expense in low-speed flexibility in second and third gears.

Once again, Ford faced formidable competition in the low-price field—particularly from the new '41 Chevrolet, which would rank as one of the best Chevys of all time. Plymouth, fielding a restyled version of its new 1940 design, managed to pull within 100,000 units of Ford by some accounts, and Chevy finished the year far ahead of Ford. Overall model year totals were about 692,000 for Ford, slightly over a million for Chevy, and some 546,000 for Plymouth.

Another milestone was recorded on April 29th this year as the 29-millionth vehicle to bear the "Ford" script since the company's founding in 1903 was built. It would be the last such production feat for several years: World War II was looming ominously closer.

The 1942 Super Deluxe sedan coupe, a six-passenger model

Price of the Super Deluxe Fordor rose to $920 for 1942.

Wood-body Super Deluxe wagon broke the $1000 price barrier.

1942

Ford gears up for defense production in an abbreviated model year

H istorically, a newly designed Detroit automobile is usually given only a mild reworking for its second year of production. The 1941 Ford was no exception, and the '42 edition was little changed in most important respects. But 1942 would hardly be the usual sort of model year at Ford or anywhere else in the industry. Less than three months after Ford introduced its '42s on September 12, 1941, the nation was at war.

Henry Ford was a renowned pacifist, and had felt the winds of war blowing in Europe. Accordingly, his company was already engaged in an increasing amount of war

work long before the events of December 7th. Three days before the Japanese attack on Pearl Harbor, Ford and other automakers were ordered by the government to freeze all future civilian projects and to cut back on excessive options and use of brightwork. These orders were made all the more sober by the sudden declaration of war and the assumed consequent total conversion of American industry to military production. The assumption became reality on February 10, 1942, when the government ordered a halt to all civilian car production for the duration. Since January 1st, only 43,307 Fords had been built. The total 1942 production run was just 160,432, making these the rarest Fords since 1910. They would have to last, for there would be no more new cars for four very long years.

Mounting defense work in 1940-41 had left Ford stylists and engineers little time for anything except only minor alterations on the '42 models. Styling was marked by runningboards now fully concealed by the lower door sheetmetal, and by a more cohesive front end treatment.

Customers inspect the '42 Fords in a local showroom.

Later '42 press photos had a definite military flavor.

courtesy Ford Archives, Ford Museum

The grille was now set in a chrome frame, and was lower, more horizontal, and close to full-width, in line with contemporary industry trends. The only vestige of the prominent central grille on the '41 was a slim chrome strip running down from the hood, almost like an animal tusk. Above this ensemble were square parking lamps, mounted in what remained of the front fender "catwalks."

The model lineup was unchanged for '42 except that the low-price Specials were restricted to the six-cylinder engine only, while Deluxe and Super Deluxe offerings could also be had with the V-8. Ford dealers must have tired of trying to explain to customers why the six had more horsepower than the V-8, so the flathead engine was now rated at the same 90 bhp even though it was mechanically unchanged from 1941. Prices *were* changed—up about $100 across the board—making the convertible (at $1080) the first Ford aside from wagons to sell for more than $1000 since the Model A town cars of 10 years earlier.

Per Washington's decree, the final '42 Fords were assembled with many parts painted instead of chrome-plated, mainly because military applications now had priority over civilian ones for this metal. This makes the "blackout" '42s the rarest of a rare breed, something that can also be said for all Detroit cars built in the final days of this abbreviated model year.

1943-45

The war years: Fords that never were and an historic change in leadership.

It hardly needs saying that Ford Motor Company was one of the nation's most important defense contractors during World War II. Though it had ceased to be the nation's largest automaker in the '30s—at least in sales—it was still a vast corporation with huge resources in the early '40s. And, Henry Ford saw to it that those resources were mobilized as quickly as possible for the war effort. He had built a huge new factory at Willow Run, which would turn out scores of the famous B-24 "Liberator" bomber aircraft. Ford Motor Company also stepped in to produce the military's new light utility car, the Jeep, designed by the failing American Bantam Car Company of Butler, Pennsylvania, which proved unable to cope with the tremendous number of vehicles demanded by the government.

Ford's other wartime production involved a wide array of different military vehicles, ranging from amphibious and armored personnel carriers and light tanks to various conventional and all-terrain trucks. The firm also built a limited number of 1942-style cars, mostly standard Tudor and Fordor sedans, with government approval. Most of these saw service as military staff cars, but some remained stateside for "essential" civilian uses.

Unfortunately, the war years witnessed some major personnel changes in Dearborn, changes that would have a profound effect on company operations and products in the immediate postwar period. Perhaps the most significant of these was the untimely death of Edsel Ford on May 26th, 1943 at the age of only 50. Never a robust figure, Edsel was a victim of fever, stomach ulcers, and cancer. Though he remained in the shadow of his legendary father right to the end, Edsel had emerged as his own man, an auto executive of rare taste and ability. He had almost singlehandedly established styling as a distinct and important function within the Ford organization, and his absence would be keenly felt. His death was, perhaps, hastened by his father's continuing reliance on Harry Bennett, whose strong-arm tactics had led to major labor unrest in the late '30s and created dissention among top company executives.

It was shortly after this, in June, that the elder Henry Ford was reelected to another term as company president, the end of which he would not complete. Two months later, in August 1943, Henry Ford II, then only 26, was given early discharge from Navy service with the express understanding that he was urgently needed to take over from his grandfather as head of one of the nation's most important businesses. Meanwhile, Clara Ford threatened to leave her husband if he continued to stand in the way of union organization at Ford Motor Company. The old man ultimately relented, but not before he had

continued on page 129

Above: The Model T touring car, a once-familiar sight on American roads. Below: This snazzy special-bodied 1914 Model T speedster sports Frontenac ohv engine.

Opposite page, above: Another special speedster-bodied Tin Lizzy, this 1913 car sports the distinctive "monacle" windshield in vogue at the time. Below: Early Model Ts (to 1912) were not assembly-line built. Shown is the 1911 touring, one of many types available. This page, above: Optional wire wheels, standard balloon tires helped jazz up the looks of this 1926 Model T coupe. Left: The Model T Fordor for 1926, Lizzie's last full production year.

Opposite page, above: The new Model A caused a rush to Ford showrooms in late 1927. Shown is the dashing 1929 cabriolet. Below: The 1930 Fordor sedan offered no-frills transporation at its rugged best. This page, above left and right: Under Edsel Ford's direction, styling became sleeker in the mid-'30s, as seen in this 1935 DeLuxe 5-window coupe. Left and below: Swept-back grille, ovoid headlamps mark this 1937 DeLuxe convertible sedan. That year's closed body styles adopted all-steel construction.

This page: Two of the most coveted flathead V-8 models in the engine's 21-year lifespan, the 1939 DeLuxe coupe (above) and 1940 DeLuxe convertible (right). Both command premium prices today. Opposite page: Low-volume Sportsman convertible (1947 top, prototype 1946 middle right) helped keep buyer interest alive in Ford's carryover postwar line. Wood trim was similar to that used on the DeLuxe wagon (1946 shown middle left). Except for engines, the '49 Ford (Custom V-8 coupe shown bottom) was all-new.

This page: The 1949 Ford line proved a great success—enough to pull the company back from the financial brink. Shown are the station wagon (above) and convertible (right), both from the Custom V-8 series. Opposite page: Advertised as "50 Ways Better," the 1950 Fords were quieter and more stable than the '49s. Joining the convertible (bottom) in the top-of-the-line Custom V-8 series was the spiffy Crestliner Tudor (above), an interim offering pending the arrival of a true pillarless hardtop.

Opposite page: Twin-bullet grille marked the 1951 Fords, represented here by the Custom V-8 convertible (above). The new Victoria hardtop proved more popular, though, by almost 3 to 1. Ford's first overhead valve V-8 arrived for 1954, along with the novel Skyliner hardtop (below) with green-tinted "see-through" roof. This page: The first of the classic two-seat Thunderbirds debuted for 1955 and proved instantly popular. With standard 292-cid V-8, steel body, and more civilized cockpit, Ford's new personal car quickly outsold its main rival, Chevy's slower, more spartan Corvette. Detachable hardtop (below) was an extra.

More power, a fractionally longer wheelbase, wrapped windshield and more colorful styling were among many changes for the 1955-56 standard Fords. Fairlane was the new top-line series, and included everything from Fordor sedans (near right) to the chromey Crown Victoria 2-door (1955 shown center spread and opposite page top), available with or without see-through top. A 4-door Town Victoria hardtop (opposite page center) joined the familiar 2-door (opposite bottom) for '56.

This page: The standard Ford was all-new again for 1957. The broadest-ever lineup consisted of five series on two different wheelbase lengths. A sample (clockwise from top left): Fairlane 500 Town Victoria hardtop sedan, 2-door Ranch Wagon, Custom 300 Fordor sedan, and the fascinating Skyliner retractable hardtop-convertible. Opposite page: 1957 also saw a completely restyled Thunderbird, the last but most numerous of the two-seaters. A few of these packed a supercharged 312 V-8 engine.

Above: The innovative Skyliner retractable hardtop-convertible in its 1958 form. About 14,700 were built. Right and below: Like other models, Skyliner was heavily facelifted for 1959, its last year. Continued slow sales was the reason. The mid-season debut of the new Galaxie series led to a change in rear fender script as these two illustrations reveal.

A more integrated grille proposal for the stillborn '43s

This Volvo-like wagon was part of Ford's small-car project.

Clay was slapped on this production car in early-'42 trial.

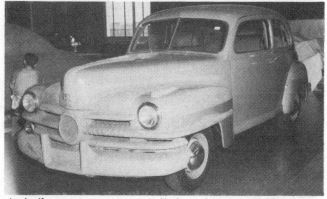

A similar treatment was applied to this prewar Mercury.

1943 sketch may have inspired 1946-48 Sportsman.

continued from page 112

suffered further losses to his own prestige and in the loyalty of his employees.

On top of this turmoil within the Ford family came a breakup of the company's top managerial staff. Actually, the problems had begun as early as 1939, but they ultimately led to a wholesale walkout by several top Ford designers on March 4, 1944. Among them were engineer Lawrence Sheldrick and chief stylist E.T. "Bob" Gregorie. "Cast Iron Charlie" Sorensen was also a victim of the political power struggle. Shortly after Henry II was named executive vice-president, in late January 1944, Sorensen left the company to assume the president's chair at troubled Willys-Overland.

All this intrigue and drama—surely worthy of any modern-day soap opera—made it difficult to plan for the return of civilian car production after the war. But not impossible. In fact, proposals for an entire, completely revamped line of 1943 Ford Motor Company cars were already well advanced before the outbreak of hostilities. And even during the war years designers still managed to find time to work on refinements of these as well as to develop new ideas. Some of this work would emerge in the all-new 1949 Lincoln and Mercury. Other efforts wouldn't appear in products for the American market.

If it hadn't been for the war, Ford's 1943-45 models would have appeared in completely new clothes. Since the Lincoln line had been radically facelifted for '42, the 1943 models would have been changed only in detail. Bob Gregorie recalled Ford's wartime activities in an interview with Michael Lamm published in *Special-Interest Autos* magazine in 1970. The tremendous surge of work toward what would have become the 1943-45 models came to a screeching halt with the outbreak of war: "Suddenly, overnight, everything and everybody stopped. All at once the whole company changed gears and got down to war work . . . Yet, in the backs of our minds, we knew that after the war we were going to have to start building cars again. At the beginning, nobody knew whether the U.S. would win or not, but there seemed little point in planning on any assumption except that we would. So slowly, in between wartime assignments, this little skeleton group we held together would go back to the sort of nebulous business of designing after-the-war cars.

"The Ford lines were the ones we worked on most, because they were past due for a change. Edsel Ford was very busy with war production matters in 1942, but did spend what time he could with us on future planning. This lasted until his illness and death in the spring of 1943. The elder Mr. Ford took virtually no interest in design or styling activities, leaving this phase of operations to Mr. Edsel Ford and myself. There were no committees, etc., as is the usual practice. Decisions were quick and simple, which possibly accounts for some of the cleaner, simpler, straightforward styling we were able to accomplish. Mr. Edsel Ford and I were usually pretty much in agreement.

"What was intended as the larger Ford became the first all-new postwar Mercury . . . At the time, we considered this design for the Ford of that era. Then, an entirely new Ford was developed, with lighter construction, new suspension, etc., and this became the 1949 Ford.

"One idea we had back then, and it came to fruition in 1949, was to associate the Mercury more closely with the Lincoln via certain body interchanges, as well as tie them together in advertising, sales, etc. Before, the Merc was based on the Ford. We figured the Mercury might gain some prestige by becoming a baby Lincoln, rather than a blown-up Ford.

"So during the war, our Lincoln designs did have some importance toward that end. We laid down the basic lines for what would become the 1949 Mercury in a painting that Ross Cousins did in 1943. That painting showed a five-passenger coupe driving past the Rouge plant. We called it a Lincoln, but the profile is very much what the 1949 Mercury became. Then too, all those early Lincoln clays show a lot more of what we had in mind for the Mercury—as well as the Lincoln Cosmopolitan.

"As for the Continental, we weren't too sure about that one. We didn't know whether it would be continued after Mr. Edsel Ford's death in 1943. We made some renderings and full-size models of the Cosmo with a spare tire mounted on the trunk, but it was too ponderous and clumsy to project the true Continental image. I think the only reason Ford Motor Company kept the Continental after the war was because they already had the body tooling. If the 1946-48 Continental hadn't used 1942 tooling, it probably wouldn't have been built those years. With the strong demand for postwar cars, the Continental did sell, and it really carried Lincoln prestige into the postwar period and to later Continentals. After Mr. Edsel Ford's death, though, no one had the heart to come up with a completely new Continental design."

The upgraded 1949 Mercury that Gregorie mentioned was not supposed to resemble the Lincoln—an important historical point. The original plan called for two separate models between Ford and the big Lincoln: the Mercury on a 116-inch wheelbase, and the Lincoln-Zephyr on a 118-inch chassis. The Zephyr would have had the "baby Lincoln" styling Gregorie recalls, while the '49 Mercury would have continued as a more luxurious Ford. The Ford line would have included a standard full-size model and a small car.

Thoughts of a small postwar Ford started a flurry of design and model-making activity in Dearborn as early as 1942. The first ideas centered on a low-priced four-cylinder model using the dimensions, power output, weight, and price of the prewar Willys-Overland as targets. Later, it appears some executives saw the new car as a rival for the Studebaker Champion in size and price. The Champion, of course, had a six-cylinder engine, and its dimensions had grown from 1939 to 1942. It turned out that Studebaker based its entire postwar line on the Champion, with dramatic restyling planned for 1947.

In late spring 1944, a group of executives led by sales manager John R. Davis and production boss Mead L. Bricker came to young Henry Ford II with the idea for forming a separate committee to prepare new products for the postwar market. This became the Engineering Planning Committee, representing key departments from manufacturing to market research. Hudson McCarroll took the lead in defining future products and their techni-

An early attempt at integral front fenders from April 1942. This clay would evolve into the 1949 Mercury.

First full-size clay for the eventual '49 Mercury

This scale model, probably a Lincoln study, is strikingly similar to the "pregnant" '48 Packard.

Grille theme on this wartime Lincoln scale clay did turn up in modified form on the 1946-48 facelift.

Opposite side of above model differs in fender details.

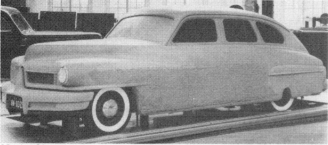

Note the prominent vertical grille theme on this Lincoln study: it predates Edsel by many years.

Postwar Mercury became the "baby Lincoln" envisioned here. "Bathtub" look was clearly preferred in mid-'42.

Front-end treatment of this Lincoln mockup from 1943 shows heavy Buick and Olds styling influence.

This wartime clay is somewhat more advanced than the other designs shown here, seems to forecast the '50s.

Senior 1949 Lincoln styling was based directly on this wartime study. Hidden headlamps didn't make production.

cal makeup. This included what he saw as a new kind of economy car, designed to sell at two-thirds the price of the standard-size Ford.

The committee looked at the company's last small-car project from before the war. This was known by code number 92-A, and was completed in 1938 by a team led by Eugene Farkas, who had played a big part in designing the Model A, Model B, and Ford V-8. Project 92-A was quite small, about 600 pounds lighter than the standard-size Ford, with a shorter wheelbase and a narrower track. Cleverly, Farkas had proposed using the anemic V-8/60 rather than developing and tooling up for a new four- or six-cylinder engine. But Project 92-A was scrapped because of high production costs. As calculated in 1938, they would have been too close to those of the big cars to give the smaller model a significant price advantage. Ford planners knew the cost/profit problem would be even more troublesome in the postwar world.

Ford had produced various smaller cars in Europe before the war, starting in 1932 with the four-cylinder British Model Y Junior, a Sheldrick design. All these were considered too small for American buyers, however, and they offered nothing technically that could be profitably applied to a smaller U.S. model.

Clearly, the new small American Ford had to be designed from scratch in Dearborn. Frantic and furious work brought forth many ideas—some intelligent, some much less so. One featured front-wheel drive and a four-cylinder engine installed transversely ahead of the front wheel axis. The radiator was placed slightly higher than the engine and behind it, backed by a cowl structure that carried the fuel tank. This made for a short hood and a low flat floor for unusually generous interior space. Another had a conventional chassis with an inline five-cylinder engine. This was the elder Henry's doing. Although he was ostensibly no longer connected with the company's product engineering, he still maintained a private laboratory where he had been toying with five-cylinder engines since about 1936.

Soon, the experimental department was humming with new and original powerplant designs. Air-cooled four- and six-cylinder engines were built and tested. Cast-aluminum cylinder blocks were tried for several water-cooled units, including the five-cylinder job, but were ruled out as too costly. Rear-mounted engines were not even considered. Front-wheel drive was quickly discarded because of its many unknowns in addition to its high costs.

As time went on, the small V-8 was increasingly preferred, along with other basic design elements of Farkas' 1938 proposal. A new prototype incorporating its main features was completed in mid-1944. In September, Henry Ford II announced his company intended to produce a smaller, lower-priced model.

Gregorie had been doing sketches and clay models of small cars for two years when the Engineering Planning Committee ordered full-scale versions that winter. A 98-inch wheelbase was selected, and a fastback two-door sedan was the first body style developed. The overall proportions that emerged were quite similar to the standard-size '42 Ford's, but the lines were more modern, with a slab-sided body and a lower, wider grille. A continuing flow of fresh market information led to completion of several prototypes that differed in many ways from each other. These were further modified and a 100-inch wheelbase was tried. Although the five-cylinder engine was still in the running at this point, development concentrated on the V-8/60.

In January 1945, the small car was defined more precisely than before, and planners settled on the 100-inch wheelbase. Within six months, the five-cylinder engine had been scrapped, and development work went ahead on the V-8 alone. The frame was designed as a smaller version of the Ford and Mercury chassis being prepared for 1949. The new coil-spring independent front suspension and parallel rear leaf springs were adapted for the small car as well. Clyde R. Paton, former chief engineer of Packard, was hired to direct the project from prototype to production-ready stage. His understanding was that the car should start coming off the lines within six months after the end of the war in Europe. But the small car soon ran into the same snag that killed Farkas' project: cost.

Hudson McCarroll, who was officially promoted to engineering director in 1945, didn't know how to handle this hot potato—and ended up listening to everybody. Sales manager Davis had a buyer for every car Ford could build. Why put a lot of money into a brand-new model that the public might not accept? He saw no need for a smaller car—even as a loss leader—until 1948 or '49 at the earliest. In that event, Clyde Paton thought it would be necessary to redesign the car completely—preferably with a unit body. As a result, the 100-inch-wheelbase prototype was shelved.

Paton and his staff went to work on two larger versions of the Light Car, one with a 106-inch wheelbase to be sold as a Ford, the other with a 112-inch wheelbase for the Mercury nameplate. To handle development and production, Ford created a new Light Car Division in April 1946. By then, the program was seen as so important that no one questioned a corporate reorganization of this scale. But in the immediate postwar years, steel, copper, lead, zinc, and other metals were hard to come by. Henry Ford II knew it was not good business to add a whole new model line to vie for scarce resources with cars that were already selling well. Although management did not officially stop small-car development, the Product Committee told the Light Car Division to defer production plans in 1946. The result was the same: the Light Car was dead in Ford's U.S. future. But by then, the 106-inch-wheelbase version was fully engineered and could be considered a production prototype.

The Light Car's production problems in the U.S. made it easier for Maurice Dollfus, a prominent Paris banker and president of Ford France. He had long argued that the new small car should be built in Europe. At last, he got his wish. In June 1946, Dearborn's engineering department released all data and blueprints to him.

The 106-inch-wheelbase prototype was redesigned at Poissy for production on metric tools, and specifications were adjusted to accommodate locally produced components. Under the name Vedette, it started coming from the French factory in the fall of 1948. However, it was

Ford's Light Car project envisioned four body styles.

Prototype Light Car had bare interior to keep costs down.

Light Car became the 1948 Vedette built by Ford France.

hampered by relatively high fuel consumption and stiff competition from class rivals, and proved a sales disappointment.

There was a funny thing about all these wartime machinations, and Gregorie sums it up perfectly: "It never dawned on any of us that right after the war, anything on wheels would sell, whether it was restyled or not. We just never sat down and thought about it enough to figure that out. So we went right ahead as though the first thing we'd have to do after the war was restyle the Ford and Mercury, not realizing until the last minute that a suitable facelift would do as well. In fact, we had until about 1948-49 before we'd have to come up with anything really different."

1946-48

The new order takes charge with a beautiful—and rare—stopgap model

With conclusion of war in the Pacific, American industry rapidly turned from military to civilian production. For Ford Motor Company, this transition would be fraught with significance. The war years had seen the untimely death of Henry's son Edsel and the departure of the brilliant designers who had gravitated to him. Their loss, wrote historians Allan Nevins and Frank E. Hill in *Ford: Decline and Rebirth*, were "body blows to the Ford Motor Company." Into the breech stepped two determined and ruthless men: Charles Sorensen and Henry's crony, bodyguard, and all-around "iron man," Harry Bennett. Henry soon decided that Sorensen had to go. "Cast

Iron Charlie" was told about it through intermediaries. He had become too ambitious; he wanted to succeed Henry as president; Henry would not have it. Sorensen departed in March 1944. The way now seemed clear for Bennett. But the optimistic Bennett hadn't counted on the well-knit family that still controlled the Ford Motor Company (and would for many years to follow). Clara Ford was the only person willing to tell Henry he was wrong. He must now resign, she told him, in favor of his grandson, Henry II. The old man, wrote Nevins and Hill, "was peevishly reluctant." The scales were tipped by Mrs. Edsel Ford, who took Clara's side: "If this is not done," she announced, "I shall sell my stock." Henry capitulated.

In August 1945, Henry Ford II, still in uniform, was summoned to Fair Lane, his grandfather's Dearborn estate. There, the elder Henry said he was ready to step aside. HF II knew what he was up against. "I told him I'd take it only if I had a completely free hand to make any changes I wanted to make," he said. "We argued about that—but he didn't withdraw his offer."

Henry Ford submitted his resignation as president on September 20th. The Board of Directors accepted it the next day, and named Henry Ford II to replace him. Harry Bennett left the company that day, with the window-dressing of a one-month directorship. Angrily he had told the new president, "You're taking over a billion-dollar organization here that you haven't contributed a thing to!"

Henry II was about to start contributing. By bringing new, young, talented people into the organization, he would turn its fortunes around in less than a decade and make Ford a near rival to mighty General Motors.

As World War II drew to a close, most U.S. automakers faced a dilemma. Should they get back into volume production quickly with warmed-over prewar models, or should they put the rush on all-new postwar designs? Studebaker, after a brief run of 1942 lookalikes labeled

Actress Ella Raines waves from her spiffy 1946 Super Deluxe Sportsman convertible. Wood trim was structural.

Sportsman convertible was pricey, didn't sell in high volume.

An early 1947 Super Deluxe Fordor sedan

Later '47s and all '48 Fords have round parking lights. An outdoors theme was used on this 1948 press photo.

1946s, did the latter. Most everyone else did the former. Henry Ford II had no choice. His company, though financed to the tune of nearly $700 million, was heavily in debt, and faced the massive cost of winding down its war machine. Above all, Ford needed to get back into civilian production: the road back was going to be a long one.

The Ford Sportsman and its second cousin, the Mercury Sportsman, were the first product decisions made by the new man in charge. He reasoned that if the first postwar Fords couldn't be all-new, at least some of them could be strikingly different on the surface—enough to lure buyers into newly reopened showrooms. Paneling convertibles in maple or yellow birch with mahogany-veneer inserts seemed like a pretty good way to do that.

Before his departure, styling director Bob Gregorie had designed a convertible of this sort, and HF II liked it. Furthermore, the company already had a massive timber forest and a processing plant up at Iron Mountain, Michigan. This operation had supplied raw materials for build-

ing station wagon bodies since 1936, so there was no lack of wood. And because the panels could be grafted easily right onto the existing Ford convertible body, building such a car would be no more difficult than turning out woodie wagons. This is not to imply that the Sportsman's panels were mere appliqués. They were, in fact, structural body elements made from solid wood blocks and mitred together with handcrafted precision.

Wood is nature's product, not man's, so no two Sportsmans were exactly alike. Three different types of trim were used during the production run. Style "A," according to Sportsman enthusiast Dr. Thomas B. Garrett, "had horizontal pieces running full length across the doors and quarters. In the 'B' and 'C' styles, the full-length members ran vertically from top to bottom. All 1946 Sportsmans used the 'A' panels wheras '47s were divided between all three." (Ford lists only 28 Sportsmans for the 1948 model year, all actually reserialed 1947s.)

Incidentally, the woodie conversion had a problem—the

1946 Super Deluxe Fordor sedan

1948 Super Deluxe convertible, available with V-8 only

The price tag read $1975 for this '48 Super Deluxe wagon. Like all early postwar Fords, it was a warmed-over '42.

production 1946 rear fenders. They wrapped around too much at the rear, which would have cut into the wooden trunklid. The solution was to use fenders (complete with taillights) from the 1941 sedan delivery. Sportsman body panels from the cowl forward were shared with other Ford models. The car was offered only with the L-head V-8 engine, not the Ford six, and hydraulic window lifts and vanity mirrors on both sunvisors were included as standard equipment.

Ella Raines, the Hollywood actress, took delivery of the first Sportsman on Christmas Day 1945, a scant three months after Henry Ford II had assumed the presidency. Despite only incidental publicity, the model was a fair success considering that it cost $800 more than the V-8 Fordor sedan and $500 more than the standard all-steel convertible. A total of 3487 were built for the three model years plus 205 of the longer-wheelbase Mercury Sportsman, offered only for 1946.

The significance of the handsome Sportsman is not so

much its qualities as a car as its mission of luring prospective buyers back to Ford dealerships. Most who did buy, of course, drove out in one of the plain sedans. The Sportsman's objective was to add a touch of class to an otherwise very ordinary group of 1946-48 models based on prewar tooling.

Performance was not one of the Sportsman's assets. It weighed about 100 pounds more than the standard convertible and 200 pounds more than the Fordor sedan. It had the flathead V-8 and moved along well, but wasn't sensationally quick. The typical Sportsman would do about 85 mph maximum and run the 0-60 mph dash in a bit less than 20 seconds. Definitely an understeerer, the Sportsman had adequate handling for a car riding antediluvean transverse leaf springs front and rear. It still copes well with today's roads and traffic conditions including 55-mph freeways. Most examples are unusually solid for convertibles, testifying to their very careful construction. Altogether, the Sportsman is an entertaining piece of

Two views of the 1948 Super Deluxe Fordor. In the postwar seller's market there was no need for all-new designs.

transportation—and certainly the most noteworthy production Ford of the early postwar years.

If the rest of the Ford line in the immediate postwar period looked familiar, it was. The 1946 models were essentially warmed-over 1942s, with a simplified front end as the main styling distinction. The only mechanical change was a bore increase for the flathead V-8, which boosted displacement to 239 cid and output to an even 100 bhp. The L-head six remained at its customary 90 bhp rating. The prewar Special series of low-priced sixes was eliminated, leaving the Deluxe and Super Deluxe six- and eight-cylinder models. Body styles comprised Tudor and Fordor sedans, coupes, wagons, convertibles, and an "open express" pickup, a one-ton utility model with standard 4-speed transmission. The convertible was offered only with V-8 in the Super Deluxe line.

Little outward change was made for 1947-48. Alterations involved a shuffle of nameplates and lower-mounted round parking lights for '47, and no styling changes occurred for '48. The six was now rated at 95 bhp. Responding to postwar inflation, Ford raised prices in 1947 by an average of $100. A similar increase was made in '48.

While all this sounds boring, no styling or engineering changes were really needed in the booming postwar

On April 7, 1947, Ford Motor Company observed a milestone of a different sort: the passing of Henry Ford at age 83. Despite the bitterness and disappointments of his later years, Ford's achievements remained untarnished. And to the end, he himself remained irascible, unpredictable, enigmatic—and endlessly fascinating. Wrote Michael Lamm in the Ford 75th Anniversary Issue of *Automotive News* in 1978: "Almost anything anyone says about...Henry Ford contains a contradiction. Newton's third law of motion applies about equally to physics and to the elder Mr. Ford. It seems that every action...had an equal and opposite reaction...[He] was an immensely complicated man, consistently inconsistent, and his personality changed not only from day to day, but a good deal over the course of his long life. Men close to Ford could read his mood by the lines around his mouth and the color of his complexion. When his face looked gray and furrowed, people tended to stay out of his way.

"It's hard to believe that a man enlightened enough to revolutionize labor via the $5 Day of 1914, revolutionize industry through the moving assembly line, who believed in lowering profits, who tried to stop World War I with the Peace Ship of 1915, who supported Wilson and the League of Nations and paid all bills for the Neutral Conference on Continuous Mediation; who founded schools, a hospital, an orphanage, and a museum, who ultimately gave away at least a third of his life's net income—it's hard to believe that [this man] would later harass his workers with a private police force; resist the National Recovery Act; come to despise Roosevelt; admire the Nazi government and accept a citation from Hitler in 1938; lash out at Jews, banks, and Wall Street and fire most of his closest colleagues."

If ever there were a folk hero to come from the ranks of the automobile industry, Henry Ford was surely that figure. Along with the Wright Brothers and his friends Thomas A. Edison and Harvey Firestone, he was an inspiration for millions—a symbol of the dreams, drive, and inventiveness that sparked America's unparalleled growth and prosperity in the first half of the 20th Century. He had established his company purely on venture capital and an idea, and would see it blossom into a multimillion-dollar worldwide organization. He had taken just five years to produce a mechanical device that enabled a nation to conquer its vast size. No geographically large country had ever before built a world-class economy; for her's, America was in his debt. No less important were his manufacturing and product innovations, such as the simple, reliable Model A, and engineering benchmarks like the monobloc flathead V-8, which pioneered a whole new approach to affordable transportation.

For a man who once remarked "History is more or less bunk," Henry Ford certainly did more than enough to earn a permanent place in it.

seller's market. Ford output exceeded 429,000 in 1947, but was only 236,000 in '48. That decline was not a sign of trouble, only an early end to 1948 production. Ford management had realized a new car was needed, and had begun work on an all-new design in early 1946. Set to debut for the 1949 model year, it would be a car of major importance to the still-struggling company. It would also be the first to bear Henry II's imprimatur.

1949

The most dramatic new Ford in a generation debuts in a fateful year

---

It's difficult to overstate the importance of the 1949 Ford. It was, primarily, a design revolution for Dearborn, all-new from road to roof and the most dramatically different Ford since the Model A had replaced the Model T a generation earlier. Wrote veteran auto tester Floyd Clymer, "It is no more like the prewar Ford than day and night. It does not operate like any previous Ford car and in its roadability, ease of operation and control there is just no comparison between the new and old models." The '49 design was also the one that literally saved Ford Motor Company. Had it not succeeded as it did, it's doubtful whether Ford would have survived to see its 50th birthday in 1953.

During Henry Ford II's first two years as president the firm's losses ran as high as $10 million a month. Young Henry was amazed—and appalled—at the business methods he found in use. One department figured out how much business it had done at the end of a day by weighing the paperwork! The 27-year-old auto chief began looking for help. Late in 1945 he found it in an unexpected place: Litton Industries. Litton chairman Tex Thornton had written Ford to offer the services of himself and a group of talented young officers just being dis-

charged from the Air Force. To Thornton's surprise, Henry accepted. Thornton's people became the nucleus of the "Whiz Kids," the bright managerial team that would turn Ford's fortunes around. Then, in early 1946, HF II coaxed Ernest R. Breech to Dearborn from the Bendix Division of General Motors. Breech served as his right hand until he was unexpectedly fired in 1959.

Along with GM and Chrysler, Ford would completely overhaul all its car lines for 1949—its first all-new postwar models. Designs for the new Lincoln and Mercury had been laid down by Bob Gregorie before he'd departed during the war. The '49 Ford assignment was handed to two key men: engineering vice-president Harold Youngren, a recent arrival from Oldsmobile and a Breech recruit, and design consultant George W. Walker. Youngren initially envisioned two Ford lines: the standard 114-inch-wheelbase car that ultimately emerged and a 100-inch-wheelbase compact (which was eventually built by Ford of France as the Vedette).

Although both Ford engines would stay the same, the rest of the 1949 specification was completely different from '48. Wheelbase was not changed, but every other dimension was. The '49 was three inches lower and fraction-

The dramatic new 1949 was especially appealing as a convertible, offered only with Custom trim and V-8 power.

The station wagon reverted to two doors for '49, but kept its wood trim. It was part of the Custom V-8 series.

External spare tire mount was standard on the '49 wagon.

1949 Custom Tudor sedan

A new 1949 Custom Fordor stands side-by-side with its Model T forerunner. A standard Fordor was also available.

Henry II, Benson, William Clay Ford, and a milestone '49.

ally shorter and narrower than the '48, though its new, flush-fender styling gave it a much sleeker appearance. Despite the more compact body, Youngren's people managed to increase seat width by half a foot, find more legroom, maintain headroom, and create a much larger luggage compartment. Although the new car seemed more spacious as a result, careful attention to detail brought it in at the targeted curb weight of under 3000 pounds; only the convertible and woodie wagon were slightly heavier. By contrast, no 1948 Ford tipped the scales under 3000 pounds, and some were over 3500. Less weight made the '49 livelier despite the carryover engines.

The new car was also dramatically different underneath in a way that probably would have upset the elder Henry Ford. His traditional beam front axle and transverse-leaf-spring suspension were gone. In their place were an independent front suspension acting through coil springs and wishbones, and longitudinal leaf springs used to locate the rear axle. Final drive was now of the hypoid, instead of spiral-bevel type, and torque-tube drive was replaced by Hotchkiss. The transmission was completely re-engineered, and the old two-speed rear axle gave way to a modern optional overdrive. (Ford-O-Matic, the new automatic then under development, did not arrive until 1951. Ford had tried without success to purchase Studebaker's automatic for the '49 models.) The redesigned brakes were given greater swept area. All these new components were hung onto an up-to-date ladder-type frame that replaced the heavy X-member frame on all models except the convertible.

The '49 was so desperately needed that Henry Ford II personally told development engineer Bill Burnett to forget last-minute efforts to reduce noise, and to concentrate instead on the remaining problem of front-end geometry caused by the engine's extreme forward location. According to *Special-Interest Autos* magazine, however, the engineers "kept right on improving the car after introduction, insulating it, changing the fan pitch, the camshaft, body mounts, and exhaust system for less noise." By the time the similar-looking '50 model debuted, they had made it a very quiet automobile.

There are several conflicting claims as to who deserves the credit for the 1949 design, which was presented to management in final form by styling consultant George Walker. Walker had instituted a crash program among all his assistants, who produced at least a dozen different proposals. The one accepted was that of Richard Caleal, a freelance stylist working for Walker and previously associated with the Loewy team at Studebaker. Caleal worked so hard to sell his car to Walker that friends nicknamed him "the Persian rug salesman."

Caleal's shape was clean if slab-sided. Only recently has it been learned that he was strongly influenced by Loewy concepts. Facing a tight deadline, Caleal asked his former associates, Bob Bourke and Holden Koto, to help him perfect the clay model for Walker. Remembers Bourke: "The final clay model was baked in Dick Caleal's kitchen oven in Mishawaka, Indiana, greatly affecting the quality of cuisine in the Caleal household for months. Our influence was the bullet-nose grille, which was similar to the component on Studebaker front ends for 1950-51." Caleal's model was approved with hardly a change. Walker did turn its vertical taillights horizontally and gave them accenting "pods" that ran forward along the rear fenders to add visual interest to the slab sides.

The '49 Ford was an expensive program for a company only just recovering from some pretty lean years. It took 10 million man hours and $72 million just to get it into production. Its debut date was moved up to June 1948, because Ford literally could not afford to wait for the usual fall introduction. But the effort paid off handsomely, and Ford recorded a gratifying $177 million profit for calendar year 1949. And it bested Chevy in actual model year production by over 100,000 units.

To give the '49 the big sendoff it needed, Henry II staged an extravagant press party at New York City's Waldorf Astoria Hotel. It began on June 8, 1948, just 10 days before the official public announcement, and lasted six days. An estimated 300 reporters attended, brought in by car or train at company expense, along with almost every high-ranking Ford official. The result was a nationwide barrage of favorable publicity for the new model. By the time the car was unveiled in dealer showrooms, the public was primed and eager. An estimated 28.2 million visitors choked Ford dealerships during the first three days, and more than 100,000 of them placed orders the first day alone. For sheer impact, it was an introduction to rival that of the Model A 30 years before.

Ford must still have had a soft spot in its heart for limited-edition specials, because we might have had a Sportsman version of the all-new '49. At least one proto-

1949

type, a Tudor sedan, was mocked up, with bold front fender script and a long wooden "frame" running from rocker panels to about mid-bodyside, split laterally by a thick chrome molding. The car also wore rear fender skirts and a low-hanging windshield visor. Unlike the 1946-48 Sportsman, the wood side trim here was used only as a highlight or "outline," and the inserts were painted body color. No doubt this was a prelude to the Custom Crestliner, which appeared the following year, but it would have made an interesting addition to the line.

"Sportsman" prototype based on 1949 coupe

Studebaker styling concepts were evident in the '49 Ford's distinctive bullet-nose front as on this Custom convertible.

"Sportsman" prototype didn't make the 1949 lineup, but may have inspired the limited-edition Crestliner the next year.

Detail refinements for a winner and a jazzy new limited-edition model

Advertised as "50 Ways News . . .50 Ways Finer," the 1950 Fords bore little outward sign of change. A simple crest replaced block letters over the bullet grille, and the same basic model lineup returned—six-cylinder Deluxe coupe and sedans and Custom V-8 coupe, sedans, convertible, and the 2-door wood-trimmed wagon, now called Country Squire. The tremendous cost of tooling the all-new 1949 design had prevented Ford from responding to a new body style introduced at GM that year, the pillarless "hardtop convertible." This rakish new design had

found immediate buyer favor among GM's senior nameplates. More important for Ford was the fact that Chevy would have one for 1950, the stylish Bel Air. What to do? Why not a spiffy Tudor sedan with the look, if not the function, of a hardtop? George Walker's design staff went to work, and the Crestliner bowed late in the season as the newest offering in the Custom V-8 series.

The Crestliner's colorful styling was influenced by Gordon M. Buehrig, famed designer of the mid-'30s Auburns, Cords, and Duesenbergs. Buehrig, at this time a member of the Ford design staff, likened the new model's two-tone paint treatment to the classic "LeBaron sweep" of the custom-body era. This was a reference to the Crestliner's elliptical chrome moldings delineating the area for the contrasting color insert. The car also wore a vinyl roof covering, emphasizing the convertible aspect, and rear fender skirts. Final touches included anodized-gold fender nameplates and luxurious color-keyed interior.

The Crestliner was the most expensive model in the

Crestliner featured black top and bodyside color sweep contrasting with yellow, maroon, or green primary paint.

Crestliner was Ford's stand-in for a true hardtop.

Rear fender skirts, vinyl top were standard on Crestliner.

The Custom convertible for 1950 was priced at $1948. As on all Fords this year, there were many detail refinements.

Ford crest replaced block letters on 1950 front ends.　　*Base series for '50 was renamed Deluxe. Shown is the Fordor.*

The 1950 Custom Fordor, photographed in front of the Henry Ford Museum at Greenfield Village in Dearborn

1950 line, priced at $1711, $200 above the Custom Tudor. Despite that and its late start, this "factory custom" scored respectable sales of 17,601 units. Today, it is a highly prized collectible.

A number of detail revisions were made to all Fords this year, partly because the '49 had been such a rush job and the company knew certain things about it had to be cleaned up. Among the improvements listed were new pistons, a three-blade cooling fan, a new design for the emergency brake lever, larger defroster vents with greater air flow, water-resistant brake drums, increased use of sound-deadening material, wider sunvisors, higher-capacity heater, and a new gas filler tube and cover.

1951 Custom Fordor sedan. Price: $1553.

Custom convertible displays 1951's new twin-bullet grille.

1951

Two firsts for Ford: a new automatic transmission and a genuine hardtop

For 1951, the third and final year for the significant 1949 design, the Crestliner was joined by a true pillarless hardtop, christened Victoria. With its dashing appearance, developed by Gordon Buehrig, not to mention plush interior and V-8 performance, the Victoria was a sales smash. Altogether, 110,286 were sold, a figure that beat both the Chevrolet Bel Air (103,356) and Plymouth's new Cranbrook Belvedere (about 30,000) in this first year of the battle of the low-priced hardtops. The Victoria's success rendered the Crestliner redundant and, with sales of only 8703 units this year, the model was dropped after 1951.

All '51 Fords had a new face courtesy of a thick horizontal grille bar with two smaller bullets at its outboard ends instead of one large central bullet. Inside was a handsomely redesigned, asymmetrical dash. Except for the addition of 2-speed Ford-O-Matic Drive, the company's new automatic transmission, there were no mechanical changes. Custom models retained their classic flathead monobloc V-8, still at 100 bhp; the cheaper Deluxe models continued with the 95-bhp 226-cid flathead six.

Victoria was billed as the "Belle of the Boulevard... smart as a convertible... snug as a sedan." And, as the brochure pointed out, it was the only car in its price range with a standard V-8. Popular when new, the Victoria is treasured by collectors today, even though its road manners and performance pale by modern standards. The seats offer little lateral support, the large steering wheel

Rear fender pods were lengthened slightly on '51 Fords. Shown is the Deluxe coupe with optional V-8 and wide whites.

A '51 Tudor body meets its chassis on the Dearborn assembly line. Note flathead V-8's distinctive appearance.

Priced at $1925, Ford's first true pillarless hardtop, the Victoria, proved a great success in its debut year of '51.

The good-looking 1951 Custom Tudor sold for $1505.

Wagon was dubbed Country Squire for '50. Here's the '51.

than on the 1949-51 cars yet somehow managed to look boxier. There were now 11 models in three series instead of two. Mainline and Customline took over for the old Deluxe and Custom designations. Both were offered with standard six-cylinder engine, a new overhead-valve unit rated at 101 bhp. The new top-line offerings were called Crestline, and comprised Victoria hardtop, newly named Sunliner convertible, and a new four-door Country Squire wagon. Standard power for Crestline models was the time-honored flathead V-8, mechanically unchanged but now packing 10 more horsepower, probably a paper increase. The V-8 was also standard for the new four-door Country Sedan wagon in the Customline series. Together with the Squire and the Mainline 2-door Ranch Wagon, these were the first all-steel Ford wagons. The Squire's side trim no longer used any wood at all, being composed of a steel frame with insert decals resembling wood.

Underneath the new body was an equally new chassis. Called the "K-bar" frame, it had five crossmembers welded to box-section side rails, and was claimed to be more rigid than the previous ladder-type chassis. At the rear were longer and stronger "Para-Flex" multi-leaf springs, and rear shocks were relocated to reduce side sway in turns. Brake seals were redesigned for better protection against dust and water. At the front were what Ford called "Hydra-coil" springs that gave easier steering and more precise control. Altogether, the new chassis/suspension package gave what was described as "automatic ride control." With its longer wheelbase, lower center of gravity and wider tracks, the '52 Ford did indeed exhibit a notable improvement in both ride and handling compared to the 1949-51 cars. Extra weight may also have played a part as the '52s were heavier model for model. The Victoria hardtop, for example, was about 100 pounds more portly, and the Sunliner convertible weighed in about 70 pounds more than its '51 counterpart.

Inside, the driver peered through Ford's first modern one-piece windshield, and operated brake and clutch pedals with suspended instead of floor-mounted pivots. The new instrument panel featured speedometer and gauges mounted in a simple arc cluster directly ahead of the steering wheel. The new '52 was about as roomy as previous models, and offered similarly upright seating

with its inverted-V spokes can be slippery, and the car corners with considerable body roll and great howling from the optional 6.70 × 15 4-ply whitewall tires. Yet performance is sprightly if not dramatic, the ride comfortable, and engine noise low. In one respect, the Victoria is literally head and shoulders above most newer cars; its interior is positively cavernous, with a flat floor and lots of stretch-out space for tall adults. As a roomy, handsomely styled touring car, the Victoria was hard to beat. No wonder it sold well right off the bat.

1952

An all-new body and chassis design mark the first Fords of the '50s

Ford Motor Company instituted a top-to-bottom corporate restyle for 1952, and for the second time in three years Ford appeared all-new. Proclaimed as the "big" '52, the new design employed a longer 115-inch wheelbase and styling that was actually lower and wider

Crestline was top '52 series. Sunliner soft-top is shown.

1952

Crestline Sunliner convertible displays new 1952 styling, with boxier contours and new one-piece windshield.

1952 Country Sedan, one of Ford's first all-steel wagons.

All '52 Fords sported round taillamps, a new design hallmark.

Although boxy, the '52 styling was at least clean and trim. More important, it was new in a year when both Chevy and Plymouth were essentially carryovers in appearance. The front end reverted to the familiar center-bullet theme, but the horizontal grille bar was now slotted instead of solid. Discreet bulges around the rear wheel openings helped relieve the slab sides, and the squared-off rear deck was flanked by small round taillights, a Ford hallmark that would carry on for many years. A neat touch was the fuel filler, relocated from the left rear fender to the lower rear valance panel, where it was hidden by a pull-down license plate holder.

The advent of hostilities in Korea resulted in an industry-wide production decline. Ford's model year total thus fell from slightly over 1 million units for 1951 to about 672,000. Chevy's total dropped by about the same amount.

1953

The fabled flathead V-8 makes its final bow for Ford's 50th birthday

Though 1953 marked Ford Motor Company's 50th anniversary there were no special changes in this year's Fords to celebrate the occasion—except for an increase in prices. Ford Division built 1.2 million cars this year, and was closing in on Chevy, having enjoyed four years of solid sales success. That had restored the company's financial vigor and firmly cemented the reputation of

The 1953 Crestline Victoria hardtop wore the then-current Ford look quite well. Styling changes were minimal.

Benson Ford at the wheel of the 1953 Indy 500 pace car

Crestline Sunliner convertible listed for $2043 in 1953.

Midrange Customline Fordor was the most popular '53 model.

Wood trim on '53 Country Squire wagon was strictly decorative.

Henry Ford II as a manager to be reckoned with. However, to achieve such high production, Ford had had to strain its dealers. In an all-out effort to wrest the number-one sales spot from Chevy, a massive campaign later known as the "Ford Blitz" was instituted starting this year. The effort reached its peak in 1954, when new Fords were being advertised at "less than cost." Chevrolet was not seriously damaged by this onslaught, but the independent automakers were. Unable to discount as much, Studebaker, American Motors, and Kaiser-Willys dealers were hit hard, and the warfare contributed heavily to the demise of Kaiser-Willys in this country. The Ford Blitz is generally considered one of the most important factors in the decline of the independents in the mid-'50s.

This Sunliner convertible served as pace car for the 1953 Indy 500, a fitting honor in Ford's 50th Anniversary year.

Styling changes this year were minor, mostly confined to a reworked bullet grille with a slimmer crossbar. Mechanical changes were next to nil, but 1953 did mark a milestone: it was the last year for Ford's durable flathead V-8, the workhorse spearheaded by the senior Henry Ford back in the early '30s.

1954

Ford steals a march on its rivals with a new V-8 and a see-through hardtop

The big event for 1954 was a new engine, the first modern, high-compression V-8 ever to power a Ford. Actually, it was the last of three overhead-valve engines to appear in the early '50s at Ford Motor Company. All stemmed from a project initiated in early 1948 under engineering director Harold T. Youngren. The idea was to develop a common block that could serve as the basis for three engines: a new Ford six, a small V-8 for Ford and Mercury, and a larger V-8 for Lincoln. All were needed in the shortest possible time, and the program was completed with remarkable speed. Test engines went on the dynamometer late that year. Before the test phase was over, some 400 prototype engines had run the equivalent of nearly a million miles in the laboratory and on the road. Final specifications were approved for production by mid-1950, and two of the three new engines—the Ford six and the Lincoln V-8—debuted for 1952. For a variety of reasons, the Ford/Mercury version had to be delayed another two years.

But it was worth the wait. Though the new V-8 had the same 239-cid displacement, it was much more efficient than the old flathead. It was also capable of being enlarged, while the flathead had reached the limit of its expansion by the early '50s. The most distinctive thing about the new engine family was its deep crankcase. This gave the V-8s a Y-shape cross section, hence its name Y-block (the six was called I-block). Bore and stroke for the Ford/Mercury version were 3.39 × 3.30 inches, and it delivered 145 bhp on a 7.2:1 compression ratio. This would turn out to be short of expectations, so a displacement increase to 254 cid was ordered for 1955. When Ford learned Chevy would have a new V-8 with 265 cid, it enlarged its engine even more, taking bore out to 3.625 inches for 272 cid and a handsome 182 bhp. There was also a 292 rendition, with bore stretched again (to 3.75 inches) as the standard powerplant for the 1955 Thunderbird. Principal engineering on this engine family was the work of Victor G. Raviolo. In determining cylinder spacing he had aimed for a V-8 displacement range of 230 to 320 cubic inches. As it turned out, that wouldn't be enough for the horsepower race of the '50s, and it led to other new Ford engines beginning in 1958.

Despite its ultimate size limitations, Ford engineers were quite proud of the Y-block. It exhibited no valve bounce at all below 5500 rpm. Hard tappets, full-pressure-lubricated rocker arms, umbrella-type valve guides, and dampening coils on valve-spring ends contributed to quiet running and low oil consumption. The combustion chambers followed the Ricardo principle in being shaped like a kidney, with the larger end away from the spark plug. Combustion began in the larger area progressing to the smaller, where gases were cooled by con-

Big innovation for 1954 was Ford's first modern ohv V-8. It's shown here both in cross-section and as installed.

tact with the head and piston. It was quite a contrast to the Chrysler hemi-head V-8 and its symmetrical combustion chambers.

It's worth noting that Chevrolet and Plymouth would trail Ford by a full year in offering a powerful, lightweight V-8 engine. And as styling and engineering were essentially carryover for all the low-price three in 1954, the new engine was undoubtedly the single most important factor in putting Ford on top in the industry production totals. The margin over Chevy was slim to be sure—less than 23,000 units for the model year—but it was an important moral victory and an indication of just how far Ford Motor Company had come in a very short time. In fact, Dearborn was now solidly entrenched as the world's second largest automaker, having passed Chrysler Corporation in 1951—and this despite having only

three makes to GM and Chrysler's five. Much of this is attributable directly to the success of the Ford line.

Ford had another exclusive for 1954, though it wasn't nearly as significant as the ohv V-8. This was the novel Skyliner hardtop, a special version of the Crestline Victoria with something previously seen only on show cars: a see-through top. Designers had begun thinking about "bubbletops" in the '30s, when plastic began to be accepted as a structural as well as decorative material. The first such application was by John Tjaarda for Briggs, a one-piece plastic top for a 1939 Plymouth convertible sedan. Even before the end of World War II, half a dozen manufacturers titillated the public with promises that see-through cars would be the wave of the future in the postwar years. But nobody ever built a bubbletop production model—until Ford.

Grilles, hubcaps, minor trim were altered slightly for '54. The Crestline Sunliner convertible was now priced at $2164.

1954

Impetus for the Skyliner was probably helped by the arrival of Gordon Buehrig. Buehrig had come to Ford to design the Crestliner and Victoria, and would later play a role in developing the beautiful 1956 Continental Mark II. He had previously worked with Raymond Loewy, a leading proponent of the see-through top. As a freelance designer, Buehrig had created the stillborn TASCO car, which had hinged transparent plastic roof sections, an idea he patented. He was later moved to take issue with General Motors when it showed something similar on an experimental Corvette. "But I settled," he said. "They were too big to sue."

A forecast of the Skyliner was seen in the XL-500 experimental car, a 1953 exercise featuring a clear plastic top bisected by a forward-leaning center pillar that wrapped up and over the roof. In 1955, the same idea ap-

The Crestliner Victoria hardtop for '54: $2055

An inviting view of the 1954 Crestline Sunliner

"Bubbletop" Skyliner cost $2164, same as the convertible.

1954 Skyliner hardtop was part of the top Crestline series.

The eight-passenger Country Squire wagon remained the most expensive model in the 1954 lineup, priced at $2339.

peared on the Mystere show car where the pillar served as the only structural roof member.

Ford's production bubbletopper was considerably less radical, of course. The Skyliner was essentially a 1954 Crestline Victoria hardtop with a see-through Plexiglas roof insert forward of the "B-pillars." With standard six-cylinder engine, the Skyliner was priced at $2164, $109 more than the normal steel-topped Victoria. Aside from the top and minor identifying trim, the two models were virtually identical.

1954 Skyliner displays new "toothy" grille used this year.

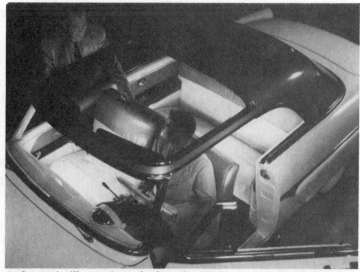

A dramatic illustration of what the Skyliner was all about.

Instrument panel was simple, almost plain, but convenient.

Snap-in sunshade helped keep Skyliner occupants from baking.

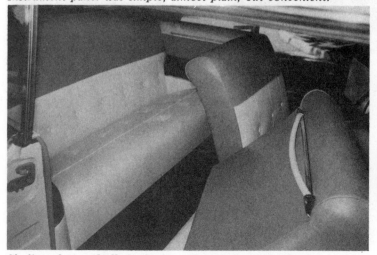

Skyliner featured all-vinyl trim. Note pulls on seatbacks.

Valve covers on 1954 Ford V-8 bear large "Y-block" insignia.

Selling mainly on novelty value, the Skyliner scored a respectable 13,344 sales in the 1954 model year.

Forward-leaning side trim on the 1954 Country Squire was quite in keeping with "jet age" design trends of the '50s.

Concept for the '54 Skyliner originated in these two Ford show cars, the Mystere (left) and XL-500 (right).

Ford described the Skyliner in rather flowery prose, claiming for it "a freshness of view, a new gaiety and glamor, vast new areas of visibility, a whole new concept of light and luxury...you're comfortably 'out of doors' all year long...with that wonderful feeling of being fashionably first." This happy puffery wasn't entirely accurate. To reduce heat and glare, Ford tinted the Plexiglas section green, which made for a kind of bilious interior ambience that was more than a little weird. *Motor Trend* magazine's Walt Woron quipped: "It may cause many a young lady to check her makeup. She might as well switch to green lipstick."

There was another problem: perspiring passengers.

Though desert tests indicated only a five-degree difference in interior temperature between the Skyliner and the standard Victoria, there's little doubt it got quite warm inside the bubbletopper on a sunny day. And remember that air conditioning was not a common item in the mid-'50s. Accordingly, Ford provided an accessory sunshade that could be snapped on over the headliner inside. This made the Skyliner at least reasonably comfortable.

Novel though it was, the Skyliner proved something of a flop: only 13,344 were made. The idea would be continued for two more years with even less success, but at least Ford was trying to give the public something it couldn't get anywhere else.

1955

The Thunderbird takes wing, while the standard cars get new glitter and go

Ford dealers gained their first-ever companion model for the 1955 selling season. This, of course, was the sleek, two-passenger Thunderbird, a "personal" car with sports car overtones. However, the standard line was hardly overlooked: restyled from stem to stern and offered with Ford's most powerful engines yet. In what would be the industry's all-time record sales year up to that point, the traditional battle between Ford and Chevy was especially fierce. Ford was again relegated to second spot on the sales chart, but enjoyed unprecedented volume of over 1.4 million cars for the model year. Robert S. McNamara, one of the "Whiz Kids" hired by Henry Ford II shortly after the war, was elevated to the post of division general manager in 1955, and his influence on Ford design and marketing would be felt into the next decade.

By the mid-'50s, Ford Motor Company's fortunes had improved dramatically. This encouraged management to begin taking on General Motors product-for-product. Wherever a market gap existed, Ford moved to fill it. For example, in the late '40s and early '50s, sports cars like Jaguar and MG had started selling consistently, though hardly in large numbers. Several American automakers decided that a home-grown sports car would do much better owing to customer loyalties and the easier parts and service availability domestic makes enjoy. Accordingly, there appeared the Nash-Healey, the Kaiser Darrin, and—most important in Ford's eyes—the Chevrolet Corvette. Dearborn replied with the 1955 Thunderbird.

The Thunderbird project came together from two directions. Ford styling director Franklin Q. Hershey, ably assisted by young Bill Boyer, had been doing sports car renderings since 1950, hoping to interest management in

Displayed at the Detroit Auto Show in early 1954, this wood mockup differs in detail from the production '55 Thunderbird.

putting such a car into production. Nothing much happened until Ford Division general manager Lewis D. Crusoe went to Paris for the 1951 automobile show. Strongly supported by his companion, George Walker—who was still an outside consultant working separately from Hershey—Crusoe felt a yen for a Ford answer to what he saw in Paris: the Spanish Pegaso, the revived Bugatti, the Jaguar XK-120, and the General Motors LeSabre show car. Crusoe reportedly asked Walker, "Why don't we have something like that?" Oh, but we do," replied Walker—who then grabbed a phone to tell his people back home to get a sports car going. Both Walker's and Hershey's staffs started drawing up ideas for the sports-car-to-be. After GM introduced the Chevy Corvette in

Hooded headlamps marked the production '55 T-Bird.

The "Fairlane Bird" prototype, Lewis Crusoe's personal car

'55 T-Bird's main instrument pod was flanked by tach, clock.

T-Bird 292 V-8 delivered 193 bhp or, with automatic, 198.

Profile of the wood mockup shown on the previous page emphasizes the low-slung sleekness of Ford's new personal car.

1953 the project got going in earnest, which underlined Henry Ford II's determination to meet GM in every market sector.

The production Thunderbird was the work of Hershey and Boyer. The design was rapidly pushed through the usual stages of renderings, clay models, and steel prototypes, during which basic styling was gradually refined. Among ideas that went by the boards were canted fins and taillights; a wide, eggcrate grille with a high-set bumper; numerous sheetmetal sculptures of the scoop-and-scallop school; fins and fangs of unmemorable proportions; and a bolt-on hardtop similar in appearance to the roof of the already-locked-up Continental Mark II. A sweepspear fender molding, similar (but not identical) to that of the 1955 Ford Fairlane, was shown in two early ads for the car, but was scrubbed before production began. The result was a timeless look that could hardly be improved upon. Meanwhile, there was the problem of what to call the thing. The eventual choice was one of about 300 candidates that included such monikers as Sportsman, Sportliner, Roadrunner, Runabout, Arcturus, Barracuda, Savile, El Tigre, and Coronado.

The first production Thunderbird came off the line on September 9th, 1954. The new model received generally favorable reviews. The only feature it shared with the Corvette was having two seats. A boulevard tourer rather than an all-out sports roadster, the Bird shunned snap-in side curtains for more convenient roll-up windows, fiberglass bodywork for traditional steel, and a six-cylinder engine for a potent V-8, a 292-cid Mercury engine derived from Ford's 1954 Y-block. With 193 horsepower, the T-Bird had plenty of zip to go with its good looks, and a respectable 16,155 of the 1955 models were sold.

In retrospect, the two-seat Thunderbird was a fluke. Though it was a good idea, it didn't, in the end, sell in sufficient volume to satisfy company accounts—or Robert S. McNamara. Because of that, it was made into something entirely different: the post-1957 "Squarebird" with four seats. Interestingly, the change was underway even as the first two-seaters were being sold. Given the industry's normal three-year new-model lead time, it's clear that forward planning for a four-seater had to have begun no later than 1955. Though the two-seat Birds always outsold Corvette, their volume was never enough to impress management, and was never as high as that of the later four-seat cars. As almost everyone knows now, the "classic" two-seat 1955-57 Thunderbirds are highly prized—and high priced—collector cars.

The bread-and-butter line for 1955 was thoroughly overhauled and boasted a number of new features. Designer Frank Hershey gave a rakish new look of motion to what was essentially the 1952-54 bodyshell. Highlights

Chrome-trimmed headlamp bezels didn't make '55 production.

1955 Thunderbird's twin exhausts exited through bumper guards.

Crown Victoria 2-door was top of the new 1955 Fairlane series, could be had with or without see-through roof.

1955

were a trendy wraparound windshield, full-width concave grille, deeply hooded headlamps, artfully angled "speedlines" in the sheetmetal around wheel openings, and modestly finned rear fenders. The lineup was now divided into four series, with wagons as a separate group. Replacing Crestline at the top of the heap was the new Fairlane (named after the Ford estate in Dearborn), identified by bold chrome side moldings running from the tops of the headlamps to the rear fenders and saucily dipped at the A-post.

Besides two sedans, the Sunliner convertible, and Victoria hardtop, the Fairlane line included the new Crown Victoria, a hardtop-styled 2-door sedan available with or without the see-through top of the '54 Skyliner. In essence, the Crown Vicky was a revival of the Skyliner. Its styling was created by L. David Ash, a young designer working under Hershey, who had created the X-100 and Mystere show cars. These undoubtedly inspired the new model's roof treatment, which featured a wide chrome band raked forward from bottom to top to conceal the B-

1955 Fairlanes were often two-toned like this Crown Victoria. Wrapped windshield was common to all models.

Crown Victoria's chrome wrapover roof band was purely decorative, concealing the solid 2-door sedan B-post.

pillar, and wrapped up onto the roof and down the other side. Though the band looked like a rollbar it didn't act like one, and engineer Harold Youngren thought enough of the car's body flex to specify the stiffer X-braced frame from the Ford convertible. Consequently, the Crown Victoria was very tight and solid-feeling. The Plexiglas roof was available as an option in place of steel forward of the band. As before, it was ¼-inch thick. As the star in the new Fairlane series, the Crown Victoria was usually fully equipped and painted in bright two-tone color schemes. It added zest to an already very impressive Ford line.

Although the plain Crown Victoria had appeal, the plastic-top version didn't: only 1999 were built against 33,165 steel-topped models. By 1956, the idea seemed to be dead. Of only 9812 Crown Victorias built just 603 had the plastic roof. Price was not the deciding factor, for the difference was only $70. What caught up with the bubble-top was its impracticality. Air conditioning was uncommon and very expensive; in a Ford it seemed almost an excess. So, it was the heat buildup inside a non-air-conditioned car that was without doubt the biggest factor against the Skyliner and Crown Victoria's success.

On the mechanical side for 1955, Ford was ready for Chevy's new V-8 with a pair of larger engines. First came a bored and stroked version of the 239-cid unit from 1954. At 272 cid it was rated at 162 bhp with single two-throat Holley carburetor. For more horses, a four-barrel carb and dual exhausts were offered, good for 182 bhp. Next, Ford went to the parts bin for the 292 V-8 previously reserved for Mercury. Since it was just a bigger-bore 272, it fit the smaller Fords easily, and available horsepower went up to 198 bhp. Later in the year, a special 205-bhp "Interceptor" 292, ostensibly for police use only, appeared on the equipment list, an outgrowth of the factory's efforts in NASCAR stock-car racing. Ford was attempting here to match its chief rival Chevrolet in the horsepower race, and to prevent defection by speed merchants and hot rodders who had quickly acclaimed the Chevy V-8 for its freer, higher-revving valvetrain and superior hop-up potential. At the other end of the spectrum, the basic Ford six was now rated at 120 bhp, up five from the previous year.

To provide best performance, Ford stressed what it called "Torque-Tailored" rear axle ratios this year. This

Ragtop Sunliner was a Fairlane for '55. Price was $2224.

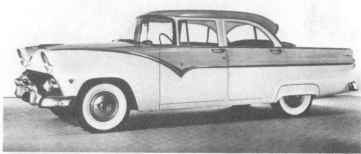
1955 Fairlane 4-door was called Town Sedan, not Fordor.

Small rear fender vents on this solid-color 1955 Fairlane Town Sedan are ducts for the rare air conditioning option.

157

1955 Ford radio dials were circular in "Astra-Dial" panel.

A handsome wagon, the '55 Fairlane Country Squire: $2392

1955 Victoria wore its name in script above sweepspears.

meant that final gearing was matched to the body style, engine and transmission, resulting in what was claimed the "right over-all ratio for brilliant response at all driving speeds." Transmission choices were 3-speed manual, manual with overdrive, and "speed-trigger" Ford-O-Matic. On this last, the brochure explained "for a real 'speed-trigger' start, just press the accelerator to the toe-board and you'll flash away in low gear." Chassis alterations for '55 included a slight rear tilt to the ball-joint front suspension so that road shocks were absorbed from

the front as well as vertically. Brakes were enlarged by about 10 percent, and had harder linings that lasted 40-50 percent longer.

A typical bit of '50s kitsch was the "Astra-Dial" instrument panel. Three circles in the lower center of the dash were provided (left to right) for heater controls, radio, and clock. Directly ahead of the driver was a semicircular speedometer mounted on top in a housing with a little window cut into it "for daylight illumination."

In all, 1955 was a good year for Ford cars and the company. Though not as highly appreciated today as comparable Chevys, these Fords stand as worthy collector cars in their own right. The fast-looking Fairlane models especially had a lot going for them, and they seem destined to appreciate in value as the years pass.

1956

Safety or performance? Ford tries both in an effort to beat Chevrolet.

Ford moved in two different directions for 1956, safety and performance. All models wore a conservative rehash of 1955 styling. The standard cars received larger parking lamps and taillamps plus a grated insert for the grille cavity. Following GM's lead the previous year, Ford introduced its first hardtop sedans—called Town Victoria—in the Customline and Fairlane series. They were priced about $75 above the 2-door hardtops at $1985 and $2249, respectively, and enjoyed strong sales of over 65,000 units.

Horsepower continued to climb. Joining the 272 and 292 V-8s was a new 312-cid enlargement of the Y-block (bore and stroke 3.80 × 3.44). It produced 215 bhp in standard form or 225 bhp with four-barrel carb, the latter supposedly available only with Ford-O-Matic. At midyear, a twin four-barrel setup with 245 bhp was announced as an option for Thunderbird. The standard Ford wasn't included, though it's possible a few cars got it.

This year the company tried to make safety a selling point. Standard for all models were a dished steering wheel, breakaway rearview mirror, and crashproof door locks; padded dash and sunvisors cost $16 extra, and factory-installed seatbelts cost $9. The public took to "Lifeguard Design" in a modest way early in the model year. But the rush to install seatbelts overtaxed Ford's supplier, and only 20 percent of the cars were so equipped. Ford continued to stress safety for a few years, but after it failed to catch Chevrolet in 1956, a lot of dealers said performance was more important.

Curiously, Ford had offered factory-fitted seatbelts in 1955, but made no effort to sell them. This may reflect a controversy within the company over safety features in general. While division manager McNamara and engineer Alex Hayes lobbied for the Lifeguard Design program, only Henry Ford II among other senior company officials really favored the idea. Of course, having the president's blessing was enough. While most of those opposed to the safety campaign probably felt vindicated when it didn't help to increase sales measurably, having the items in the catalog must have been a relief when the Automobile

Manufacturers Association came down hard against factory-sponsored racing and performance advertising in 1957.

The most marked difference in the '56 Thunderbird was its new "continental" style exterior spare tire mount. This last-minute change was likely made more as a way to

1956 Fairlane Town Victoria 4-door hardtop (prototype)

Trunklid crest is all that's missing on this '56 Sunliner.

A mild facelift was ordained for the standard 1956 Fords. Sunliner ragtop here displays revised sweepspear moldings.

Another view of the prototype '56 Sunliner seen above. All Fairlanes wore their series name on the hood below crest.

Middle Customline series included this 4-door sedan at $1985.

New-for-'56 Fairlane Town Victoria sold for $2249.

New '56 body style was the 4-door hardtop. Fairlane is shown.

Second most popular '56 Ford was the Victoria 2-door.

The Fairlane Sunliner was priced at $2359 for 1956.

Special side moldings marked '56 Customline models.

increase trunk space than for styling, though it did come off well visually. The front fenders now sported flip-open cowl ventilators to answer complaints of excessive engine heat in the '55 cockpit. Another appearance fillip that came off well was the now-famous porthole windows, a new option for the accessory hardtop. Though the round shape didn't relate to anything else on the car, it somehow looked right. More important, it improved over-the-shoulder visibility. Whether it was because of that or their slightly nautical air, the portholes were preferred by buyers four-to-one over the blind-quarters hardtop. Standard T-Bird power remained the 292 V-8, now rated at 202 bhp with manual transmission, and the new 312 engine was added as an option.

Writer Karl Ludvigsen regarded the 1956 Thunderbird as a better balanced car than the '55, mainly due to a more equal front/rear weight distribution created by slinging the spare out back. Nevertheless, the roadability of early Birds was not genuinely sporting. The '55s used fairly stiff rear springs and quick steering. These were softened and slowed, respectively, for '56 because most buyers wanted it that way. As a result, the '56 (and 1957) Bird plowed a bit more on corners than the '55, and response to steering input in the 50-mph range was rather vague. The all-drum brakes were adequate for normal driving if not track work. The steering, though imprecise, was not completely robbed of road feel by excessive power assist. Today, however, the two-seaters still seem entirely up to date, and give away little in comfort or driving pleasure to cars several decades younger in the same weight and size class.

Despite its expected disadvantages as a competition car, the Thunderbird was raced—and did surprisingly well. In fact, it was far more capable than most people appreciated. At the 1955 Daytona Beach Speed Weeks, A T-Bird sponsored by Tom McCahill of *Mechanix Illus-*

Sporting a mild facelift, the 1956 Thunderbird offered a new 312-cid V-8 at extra cost, but only with automatic.

Though external spare tire mount was the most obvious change, front-fender ventilator doors also identified '56 T-Bird.

T-Bird's accessory hardtop was available with "blind" quarters as in '55, but new porthole windows proved more popular.

trated magazine swept all honors among American production sports cars. Driven by Joe Ferguson, this car averaged 124.633 mph on a two-way run—better than any Austin-Healey, Porsche, and all but one Jaguar XK-120M.

The T-Bird did even better in 1956, when Ford hired ex-racing driver Pete DePaolo to prepare its cars. Chuck Daigh drove a carefully set-up '56 to 88.779 mph in the standing mile, winning the production title in that class and very nearly besting a modified-class Corvette driven by Zora Arkus-Duntov (89.735 mph). But the Birds weren't entered in Daytona's long-distance race, and a Chrysler 300 won the Grand National that year. And the car wasn't competitive in road racing because of its soft suspension and indifferent brakes.

Ford pulled a lot closer to Chevrolet in the model year production race, building a bit more than 1.4 million cars for '56 compared to Chevy's 1.56 million. Thunderbird output tailed off slightly to 15,631, perhaps a result of slightly higher prices. In March, Ford Motor Company announced a $437 million profit for calendar 1955, a new record. Now all that remained was to pull ahead of its perennial rival and stay there. Ford wouldn't do that, but it would beat Chevy once again the following year.

The 1956 Thunderbird with optional "porthole" hardtop

Here's how the '56 Bird looked with its soft top in place.

1957

Pulling out all the stops to top the sales charts in a vintage year

Ford pulled out all the stops for model year 1957, considered by many enthusiasts today as *the* vintage year of the decade. Ford certainly contributed its share of the harvest: a line of totally restyled standard cars; the last of the two-seat Thunderbirds, now handsomely facelifted; and a vast array of V-8s, ranging from a mild 190-bhp "300" powerplant on up to a supercharged 312 engine with 300 bhp. Such a massive product overhaul coming only two years after the totally new 1955s would be unheard of—and prohibitively expensive—today. But anything was possible in the extravagant '50s, and the huge investment necessary to bring out its 1957 cars paid off for Ford. The race with Chevrolet, which fielded only heavily facelifted models this year, was close and hard-fought as always. In calendar year output, some statisticians showed Ford ahead of Chevy for the first time since 1935, but the final tabulation indicated Chevy ahead by a scant 130 cars. However, Ford's margin in model year production was substantial: better than 170,000 units. The grand total: over 1.67 million cars. It was a new high for Ford Division, an achievement it would not surpass until well into the '60s.

Certainly a big factor in Ford's popularity this year was one of the industry's broadest lines of powerplants. Starting at the bottom was the ohv six, the base engine in the standard Fords (save one) and rated at 144 bhp. V-8 offerings began with the 190-bhp 272, then jumped to a 212-bhp 292 engine, the latter the standard Thunderbird powerplant. Then came a raft of 312 V-8s, commencing with a four-barrel 245 bhp version, and extending through twin four-barrel 270- and 285-bhp units. Finally, there were two supercharged 312s, rated at 300 and 340 bhp on 8.5:1 compression. It's doubtful any of the latter were actually built, but some 208 of the 300-bhp engines did find their way into Thunderbirds this year.

The 1957 standard Fords gained an all-new bodyshell designed around two different wheelbase lengths. The model lineup was accordingly rearranged, and there were now five separate series. Built on the shorter 116-inch platform were the bottom-end Custom and slightly flashier Custom 300 sedans (replacing Mainline and Customline, respectively), plus 2-door plain and Del Rio Ranch Wagons, two 4-door Country Sedan wagons, and the woody-look Country Squire 4-door. The longer 118-inch wheelbase was reserved for two Fairlane series, a four-model standard line of 2- and 4-door hardtops and sedans and the Fairlane 500 group, which offered these body styles plus Sunliner convertible and the unique Skyliner retractable-hardtop convertible. The new styling was particularly simple for the period: clean, full-width rectangular grille, rakish side moldings, tiny tailfins, and large round taillamps. The new bodyshell was distinguished by a more severely wrapped windshield, with the "dogleg" A-posts angled farther back than on the 1955-

The 116-inch-wheelbase '57 Fords consisted of Custom and Custom 300 series. This Custom 300 4-door sold for $2157.

Fairlane was the second-echelon series for '57. Bullet-like side trim was featured as on this Victoria 2-door.

Fairlane 500 was the most expensive series in the '57 line. This Town Victoria hardtop sedan retailed for $2404.

Ford built exactly 183,202 of these Fairlane 500 Victoria 2-door hardtops for '57. Model sold new for $2339.

1957 Ford wagons like this $2864 Country Squire were built on the shorter 116-inch wheelbase.

The '57 Fairlane Town Sedan offered hardtop styling for $2286.   *The same applied to the $2281 Fairlane 500 2-door club sedan.*

Ford pioneered a new concept in the '57 Ranchero, a car/pickup based on the station wagon chassis.

A good-looking car even nearly 30 years later, the '57 Fairlane 500 Sunliner is emerging as a collectible today.

The 1957 Country Sedan wagon sported gold-colored anodized aluminum side trim borrowed from the Custom 300 series.

Stylist George Walker with the '57 Sunliner and guest

The spiffier '57 2-door wagon was called Del Rio Ranch Wagon.

Liftgate glass wrapped a bit on '57 wagons like Country Squire.

1957 Custom 300 2-door sedan. Price new was $2105.

The Fairlane 500 Town Victoria hardtop sedan for 1957

56 design. In line with the longer-lower-wider look then in vogue in Detroit, Ford switched from 15- to 14-inch wheels and tires, and all models sat about three inches lower than before. Overall length and width were both noticeably greater, approaching dimensions that had distinguished Mercurys of only a few years earlier.

By far the most interesting—even curious—model in the lineup was the new Skyliner, the first and *only* retractable hardtop. Introduced slightly behind the rest of the line, it was the ultimate expression of '50s gadgetry, almost like something from Mars. And Ford advertising helped stimulate interest in this new hybrid body style by making a legitimate point: "How can it be a 'hardtop *convertible*' if the top doesn't go down?"

There's nothing new under the sun, and the retractable hardtop idea can be dated at least as far back as 1941. That's when Briggs Body Company stylist Alex Tremulis designed the Chrysler Thunderbolt show car, of which six were made. The Thunderbolt's top was relatively small, just large enough to cover the cockpit with its single bench seat, so the top could be easily withdrawn into the car's trunk. But unlike the Thunderbolt, the Skyliner (a name revived from "bubbletop" days) was a full-size, six-passenger car. At first glance, it did not look different from any other Ford. However, its rear fenders were longer by three inches and its top shorter by nearly four inches. From the rear, the Skyliner had a "bustle" look that clearly set it apart from its linemates.

The Ford stylist who suggested the retractable concept was Gilbert Spear, whose designs convinced William Clay Ford to earmark $2.2 million for development. Bill, the younger brother of Henry II, was at that time the head of the Special Projects Division, which was working hard on a new Continental, the Mark II. The retrac was originally intended for that car until Special Projects decided to go with only a conventional fixed top in 1955. Ford Division then got the retrac project, but only after another $18 million had been invested for testing. The all-new 1957 Ford was only two years from introduction when the transfer was made, so a crash program had to be instituted for the Skyliner to be ready in time.

Most of the work, of course, went into the rear structure. There had to be room enough for that big roof and all the hardware needed to raise and lower it. The long rear decklid was hinged in the only possible way, at the rear. The greenhouse was shortened, and the roof was given a hinge 10 inches from its leading edge, creating a flap that would fold under the top as it slid back. The new model was mounted on the convertible chassis with frame rails set closer together to create the outboard room necessary to accommodate the top's control linkage. Remarkably, rear seat legroom was not affected. The gas tank took up valuable storage space in its standard location under the trunk floor, so it was put behind the rear seat, an "accidental" benefit to safety in a rear-end collision. The spare tire was placed in a small floor well. Because of its greater weight, the newcomer carried the base 272 V-8 option as standard equipment.

The Skyliner's "nervous system" was composed of 600 feet of wiring running to no less than 10 power relays, eight circuit breakers, 10 limit switches, three drive mo-

Shorter roof, higher rear deck are evident in this view of the unique 1957 Skyliner retractable hardtop/convertible.

Complex electrics often failed, leaving Skyliners at "half mast" like this. Fortunately, top could be stowed manually.

With its top stowed, this Skyliner looked at a glance much like the normal 1957 Sunliner soft-top convertible.

tors, and a safety interlock that prevented anything from happening unless the transmission was in Neutral. If all that sounds complicated, it was—but when everything was working properly, the whole operation was simple.

Here's how it worked. First, the driver would depress a switch (located on the steering column) with the ignition on (and preferably the engine running to minimize battery drain). This activated two (1957-58) or three (1959) switches to start the deck motor, which lifted the long lid via twin shafts mounted at each edge. As the deck locked into full-open position, it tripped the switch for another motor, mounted behind the rear seat, that raised the

1957 Skyliner's longer rear deck is evident in this view of a near-final styling prototype.

package shelf behind the seat to deck level. This in turn started another motor that unlocked the top. After this, two more motors (one on the 1959 model) started running to raise the top and send it rearward into the open trunk cavity. A separate servo folded the hinged front roof section as the roof eased its way back and down. A dashboard warning light, which glowed during the whole sequence, was then extinguished, telling the driver to release the switch. This process could be reversed at any point. It was remarkably trouble-free considering the number of stages involved. In case of failure, the point at which the sequence stopped told a mechanic immediately where to look. A hand-cranked emergency manual override feature was provided so an unlucky owner wouldn't have to drive with the top stuck at half-mast.

The 1957 Skyliner sold for $2942 or $437 more than the soft-top Sunliner convertible. For a car this specialized selling mainly on novelty value, it did respectably well. Ford built 20,766 units for the model year. It was just the thing to usher in the space age. This sales figure, as *Special-Interest Autos* magazine has pointed out, almost matched the two-seat Thunderbird's record year—and was more than twice the number of Corvette sales through 1960. Yet the retrac was *less* unique, and therefore involved less development expense, than either of those cars because it shared so much with the standard Ford line.

Though it would be continued through 1959, the Skyliner was inevitably doomed by its inconvenience and high cost. The price premium over the regular Sunliner, which had the same open-air appeal, grew each year; other models went up, too, but not as much. Also, the Skyliner had hardly any trunk space—none with the top stowed. To segregate baggage from the top and its retracting mechanism, Ford provided a small fitted luggage box measuring only 6.5 cubic feet. And you couldn't get to that with the top down or up except by manhandling it out from the side. Perhaps the most telling factor in its demise was Robert S. McNamara, who deplored such "gimmick engineering" and turned Ford steadily toward no-nonsense high-volume products as the '60s approached.

The Skyliner remains a fascinating artifact of a unique

time in automotive history. Of the total 48,394 built in 1957-59, a fair number have survived, and today there's a large national club dedicated to them. Skyliners of all years have also been named Milestones—outstanding cars built between 1945 and 1967—by the Milestone Car Society.

Rumors of a new, larger Thunderbird started circulating in 1957. Some people suspected the two-seater was on the way out, while others hoped it would continue as a companion to the "family" Bird. As we all know now, the former view proved correct, but at least Ford saved the best of the two-seaters for last.

A serious facelift was mandated for '57. The front wore a bold combination bumper/grille, an idea Bill Boyer had proposed for 1955 that was then considered too radical. The back end sprouted modest tailfins—a nod to Chrysler, but much less vulgar—flanking a longer rear deck. "We extended the trunk largely to get rid of the spare tire," Boyer remembered. The 1957 Thunderbird was nevertheless four inches shorter than the '56 thanks to the spare's reabsorption into the trunk. (An optional exterior spare tire was listed for '57, and some models were so equipped.) Inside was a handsomely redesigned dash with a telescopically adjustable steering column (a feature revived from the '55). Door panel trim was modified, and featured a repeating Thunderbird logo.

The 1957 model was the most "styled" of the three-year two-seat generation. Still, Ford sales and product planning personnel resisted stylists' attempts to gook up the car with extra chrome, two-tone paint, and sheetmetal creases. They deserve a lot of credit, because what emerged looked good—and still looks good today. Production lasted longer than usual due to delayed release of the '58 Thunderbird, so the '57 set the two-seat sales record at 21,380 units.

Mechanical changes were small but significant. A new rear axle with straddle-mounted pinion gear was fitted, and fuel tank capacity was increased from 17 to 20 gallons. The strong frame and coil-spring front suspension were retained. Engineer Bill Burnett specified five-leaf rear springs (as in 1955) instead of six-leaf (as on the '56), and wheel diameter shrank from 15 to 14 inches. Engineers considered—and rejected—Edsel-style pushbutton

At $2942, the Skyliner was the priciest of the '57 Fords. A total of 20,766 were built for the model year.

T-Bird sported a handsome facelift for 1957.

Modest blade fins topped longer rear deck on '57 T-Bird.

'57 T-Bird's bold bumper/grille was first proposed for '55.

Most '57 T-Birds were sold with the porthole hardtop.

Due to an extra-long model year, the '57 T-Bird set the production record for the two-seaters at 21,380 units.

The 1957 Thunderbird's longer rear deck was necessitated by relocating the spare back inside the trunk.

Four versions of the 312 V-8 were listed for the '57 Bird.

Engine-turned appliques made '57 T-Bird cockpit glittery.

Spare tire ate up much space in the '57 T-Bird trunk.

The '57 would be the last of the "classic" two-seat T-Birds.

automatic transmission controls. While transmission choices for '57 were the same as before, the engine range was greatly expanded—and now included the two supercharged mills mentioned earlier.

The Paxton-McCulloch supercharger was supplied by McCulloch at the behest of driver Pete DePaolo, who had learned that Chevrolet might offer a blower on the 1957 Corvette. A $500 option, this centrifugal unit delivered up to 6 psi of compressed air to a sealed carburetor. It did wonders for performance. Where the 245-bhp model would do 0-60 mph in 10 seconds and top out at 115 mph, the blown car would almost certainly see 125 mph maximum and run 0-60 in well under 7 seconds. A Ford-O-Matic "F-Bird" driven by the editors was timed at 5.5 seconds in the 0-60 sprint (a time not corrected for speedometer error, which couldn't have been far off).

Only 208 supercharged Thunderbirds were built, and only another 1500 were fitted with the 270- and 285 bhp engines with twin four-barrel carb. But Ford was not doing all this for fun; Daytona was again on management's

Joe Weatherly's '57 Sunliner leads Billy Myers Mercury in a NASCAR convertible race on the beach course at Daytona.

Chuck Daigh before his record-setting runs at Speed Weeks '57

More NASCAR action: a '57 in the pits at Darlington

mind. Accordingly, 15 blown cars with the 300-bhp setup were run off in order to homologate the package as "stock" in time for the 1957 Speed Weeks. There, Chuck Daigh scored 93.312 mph in the standing mile, and a privately entered Bird was clocked at 146.282 mph one-way, 138.775 mph both ways, in the flying mile. Unfortunately, the Automobile Manufacturers Association decided shortly after this to deemphasize competition, and the T-Bird's racing career was nipped in the bud before DePaolo could develop the car further.

By this time, however, the Thunderbird had proven its merit. A sports car it wasn't—certainly not on a road course. A high-performance car it definitely was—at least the '57 could be with the right options. Had competition development continued, it showed every sign of becoming a serious super-stock contender in NASCAR. It is remarkable that this sort of performance was offered in a car so luxurious and lovely. It is an accomplishment in which, regardless of what happened in later years, Ford Division can take a great deal of pride.

1958

Big-block V-8s and the birth of the definitive personal-luxury car

The first four-seat Thunderbird and the first of the so-called "big-block" V-8s carried Ford Division through the recession-riddled 1958 model year. The standard Fords were heavily facelifted, and bore an obvious kinship with the new T-Bird. Overall industry sales were down this year, and the big Fords suffered along with most every other make. Thunderbird, however, bucked the trend on the strength of its new design, selling 50 percent better than the last of the two-seaters and nearly 100 percent above its first-year 1955 pace.

New to the Ford engine chart this season were two V-8s, 332 and 352 cid. These were part of the new FE-series family devised principally by Robert Stevenson, who had been named chief engineer at Ford Engine & Foundry in 1957. Though derived from the Y-block design, the FE-series incorporated all the lessons learned in the field. Cylinder centers were chosen so that enlargement up to 425 cubic inches would be feasible—an arbitrary figure so far above forseeable needs that a long production run seemed assured. The FE's main internal improvements were bigger valves and bigger bearings,

1958 Fairlane 500 Town Victoria hardtop sedan. Price: $2499.

the latter allowing the use of a low-cost, precision-cast crankshaft. Combustion chambers were fully machined and located in the head (as opposed to the block). The valve arrangement was such that no two exhaust valves were adjacent to each other, thus minimizing the possibility of overheating and valve warpage. Cylinder heads were smaller but intake manifolds larger than usual, which allowed engineers to make the manifold passages

All standard Fords wore a massive bumper/grille for '58, inspired by the new T-Bird. Shown is the Skyliner "retrac."

Like the rest of the industry, Ford adopted quad headlamps for its '58s. Shown here is the Custom 300 2-door sedan.

of about equal length to insure more even fuel distribution. A bonus was added engine rigidity and elimination of separate tappet chamber covers. Besides the two Ford versions, FE-series engines appeared in this year's new Edsel (361 cid), and Mercury (390 cid). As installed in the Thunderbird, the 352 was rated at an even 300 bhp with four-barrel carburetor and 10.2:1 compression. The FE-series would prove to be an extremely long-lived design,

continuing in production into the 1970s.

The other important mechanical development for '58 was Cruise-O-Matic, a new 3-speed torque-converter automatic derived from the existing Ford-O-Matic transmission. It offered so-called "dual-range" drive, with first-gear starts in position D1 and second-gear takeoffs in D2. Cruise-O-Matic also incorporated a hill-holder feature so that the brakes did not need to be applied to keep

The 1958 Ranchero continued its stylistic relationship to Custom 300s, but lacks the cars' T-shaped grille bar.

Price went up on the '58 Skyliner—to $3163. Production fell by some 6000 compared to '57.

The '58 Skyliner flips its lid. Note small hinged roof flap. As before, sequence could be reversed at any point.

the car from rolling backwards when stopped on an incline. Like the FE-series V-8s, this would prove a very long-lived component, and is with us today.

The standard—what would soon be called full-size—cars were given a heavy facelift this year in the spirit of the times. The front end was marked by a combination bumper/grille stylistically linked to that of the new Thun-

derbird, plus quad headlights and taillights and, on some models, flashy anodized-aluminum side trim. The previous model lineup returned, but prices were higher across the board. The fascinating Skyliner "retrac" remained the priciest of the bunch at $3163 basic, $513 more than the Sunliner soft-top and a whopping $728 more than the fixed-roof Fairlane 500 Victoria 2-door

The '58 Skyliner nears the end of its disappearing act. Considering its complexity, the top mechanism worked well.

Like other members of the '58 Fairlane 500 series, the Skyliner sported flashier gold anodized-aluminum side trim.

hardtop. Only 14,713 examples were built, some 6000 fewer than in 1957. Overall, the entire line suffered a heavy sales reversal despite offering exactly what the market seemed to want: more glitz, glitter, and go.

The new four-seat Thunderbird introduced this year pioneered a totally new concept: the personal-luxury car. And though it would take a few years, it would be widely imitated. Seen in this light—and in view of its remarkable success in an otherwise bad sales year—the Thunderbird's transformation from two-seater to four-seater seems perfectly logical. Of course, at the time nobody—and that probably included division general manager Robert S. McNamara—was certain that the four-seat concept would "play in Peoria."

Skyliner's bustle tail is evident in this rear view.

'58 standard Ford dash was unusually simple for the period.

No, it's not a Skyliner. It's the '58 Sunliner soft-top.

Thunderbird product planner Thomas Case had recommended retaining a two-seater for 1958 as "a marketing device to add some spiff to the program. It was not set up to be a profit program per se, although it turned out to be profitable." But McNamara, who had succeeded Lewis Crusoe as division general manager in 1955 when the decision was being made, wanted the '58 Bird to be a solid profit-maker, not just a glamor item. When he heard Case was angling to keep a two-seater in production he gave the young product planner what Case described as a chewing out: "Tom, it's dead. I don't ever want to hear of it again. I don't want anybody to do any more about it." McNamara should not be viewed as a villain, because without him the Thunderbird might have died after 1957.

Said stylist Bill Boyer, "McNamara really fought for it. He thought it was a good concept; he went in and fought for it [with the board of directors] and won." Part of McNamara's pitch was, of course, that a four-seater would make *real* money—which it did.

The most innovative aspect of the '58 Thunderbird was its unit body—a fresh idea for Ford, but a concept that had been around in Europe since the '20s and in Detroit since the '30s. Inspired by aircraft design practice, unit construction does away with a separate steel body attached to a frame with flexible mounts. Instead, it is a combined structure designed to be strong yet light, and able to absorb stresses evenly. Also known as the monocoque principle, it tends to result in a tight, rattle-free automobile that weighs less.

Unit construction was also ordained for the 1958 Lincoln and Continental Mark III, so Ford erected a new assembly plant at Wixom, Michigan to build these cars and the new Thunderbird. This made sense, because all were low-volume luxury models but accounted for enough volume between them to keep a plant busy. This also made unit construction economically feasible, since their lower volume would have made the cost of separate frames far higher than in the case of a high-volume car like the standard Ford.

Despite the fairly revolutionary nature of the '58 Thunderbird, Ford Division was allotted only $50 million for the whole project—$5 million for styling and body/chassis/engine engineering and $45 million for tooling. To economize on R&D, management decided to farm out body engineering to the Budd Company and the convertible prototype program to Wettlaufer Engineering. A few problems cropped up, but were solved in rapid-fire succession. "For instance," says body engineer Bob Hennessy, "we started in figuring the movement of the rear suspension [and found that] the car wasn't wide enough. We would be rubbing the sides of the wheel housing. . . . Since we were about two-thirds into engineering with die models in progress, we literally split the drawing down the centerline of the car and spread it apart.

"Inside the car there was really incredible room when you consider we had reduced the overall height from the standard sedan by about 10 inches. This height had very much to do with the package drawing we engineers furnished Bill Boyer to style a vehicle around. . . . With a five-inch ground-to-floorpan height, 2½ to three inches for a seat track and electric seat motor, plus four inches of actual seat height, the driver's fanny was only 12 inches off the ground. This left us with a high tunnel on the inside, and, of course, the main integral frame sill section above the floor on the outside of the seat. The front seats were literally in a deep well." But Bill Boyer and his designers developed an ingenious dashboard extension that took advantage of this—one of the first uses of the central tunnel console in a modern production car.

Styling work began during 1955, with Boyer increasing the proposed wheelbase from 108 to 113 inches. A "formal" roofline with wide rear quarter pillars was adopted for its distinctive appearance and to keep decklid height down for the ultra-low stance the sales department was demanding.

All-new 1958 four-seat Thunderbird was an immediate success, easily outselling the two-seaters by almost 50 percent.

Honeycomb mesh filled the '58 T-Bird's gaping grille cavity.

The same pattern appeared out back around the taillamps.

A convertible body type was in doubt until quite late in the game. It wasn't actually approved until May 1957, and didn't appear in dealer showrooms until June 1958. As a result, only 2134 convertibles were built for the 1958 model year. Once production hit its stride, however, soft-tops were turned out in decent numbers: 10,261 for 1959 and 11,860 for 1960. But this was only a small fraction of hardtop volume, which reached 57,195 units for 1959 and 76,447 for 1960. Also for '60, a third model with a gold-colored padded-vinyl top and special trim was offered at about $4000 base, and scored another 2536 sales.

The convertible's top mechanism was a complicated af-

fair, similar in design to that of the Skyliner. The driver first unlocked the rear-hinged decklid by means of a remote-control button, then unhooked two windshield header clamps, manually raised the decklid, and lastly pushed another button to activate the folding mechanism. Late in the '59 model run the device became fully automatic via a single dashboard pushbutton.

The 1958 Thunderbird was such a success that Ford had to put Wixom on heavy overtime to keep up with demand, a refreshing change in a generally poor sales year. (The only other American make to gain that season was Rambler.) "We were making money so fast we didn't

The 1958 Thunderbird's stylish, wide-quarter squared roof and center console proved two of its most popular features.

know what to do with it," said engineer John Hollowell. "It came, as I recollect, to somewhere around $1000 per car."

Despite the general sales downturn, Ford still moved over 950,000 cars for the 1958 model year, compared to Chevrolet's 1,057,000. The bottom line, however, was that Ford came out ahead since it had less invested in development costs than Chevy with its new Corvette and what would turn out to be a one-year-only bodyshell for its standard cars. The seesaw battle for sales supremacy was as fierce as ever.

1959

Conservative styling pays off: the T-Bird and its look prove big hits

Buyers had a clear styling choice among the low-priced three for 1959: Chevy's radical "bat-fin" design, Virgil Exner's "shark fin" Plymouth, or Ford's conservative squared-up look. Though Chevy emerged the winner in model year production by slightly less than 12,000 units, it's clear the public preferred Ford, which outsold its perennial rival for the calendar year by about the same margin.

Mechanically, the '59 standard cars were similar to the '58s, but Ford settled on the longer 118-inch wheelbase for all models. This and major appearance alterations to the 1957-58 bodyshell made for a bulkier, more important look. The facelift involved cylindrically shaped upper rear fenders (about as close as Ford ever got to fins), simple if broad side moldings, a more integrated hood and front fender treatment, and an uncomplicated rectangular

grille filled with floating star-like ornaments. Windshield headers were raised so that the glass almost wrapped up into the roof. All this was clearly influenced by the '58 "Squarebird." The four-seater would lend one more styling element—its fashionable wide-quarter squared roof—to a new line of hardtops and sedans announced at mid-year as the Galaxie series. Actually, this name was a late substitution for Fairlane 500 on the rear fenders of all the top-line standard Fords, including the Sunliner and Skyliner, and forecasted a shakeup in the big-car line the following year. In any case, grafting a T-Bird-style roof onto the big Ford proved to be a popular move. The technique would be used again to enhance appeal of some smaller Fords in the '60s.

Engine availability was reduced from five to four this year as the 265-bhp 332 V-8 was discontinued. This left the base 145-bhp six and the usual assortment of V-8s. Once again, the 200-bhp 292 was standard for the Skyliner retractable, appearing for the last time, a victim of declining sales and Robert McNamara's dislike.

Thunderbird was refined with minor trim changes, a new engine option, and a redesigned rear suspension. The new engine was the big-block 430-cid Lincoln V-8, rated at 350 bhp. It was the largest member of the "MEL" family, introduced the previous year to power various Mercury, Edsel, and Lincoln models. T-Bird's standard engine continued to be the 300-bhp 352.

The reason for the rear suspension change was a change in company plans. Ford had originally planned to offer Ford-Aire suspension on the '58 T-Bird, and had accordingly engineered complex coil-spring and trailing-arm rear geometry specifically for use with air bags. Ford-Aire was also offered in the standard '58 line, but the system proved so trouble-prone that it was withdrawn before the new T-Bird went on sale. With Ford-Aire dead, the '59 T-Bird reverted to conventional rear leaf springs. More minor mechanical modifications were a new auxiliary coolant tank and radiator fan and a relocated windshield washer system.

T-Bird's boxy roof suited the standard '59 Ford's foursquare lines. This is a prototype for the Galaxie hardtop.

Compared with the '59 Chevy and Plymouth, this year's Ford was quite tasteful. Shown is the $2958 Country Squire wagon.

Less ornate Country Sedan sold for $2745 in six-seater form.

The early-season 1959 Fairlane 500 Victoria 2-door, $2537

179

In profile, the '59 Thunderbird didn't look much different than the '58. Note reshuffled trim, newly styled hubcaps.

'59 T-Bird grille changed from honeycomb to horizontal bars.

Again, the taillight applique mimicked the grille pattern.

Externally, the '59 T-Bird could be distinguished by its thin horizontal-bar theme on grille and taillight appliqués (the '58s had a honeycomb pattern), plus front fender ornaments, pointed chrome moldings on the door bullets instead of the previous hash marks, relocated name script, and revised wheel covers. Inside, white replaced black on the instrument dials, and interior (as well as exterior) colors and combinations were shifted. Prices were up by about $50, to $3695 and $3979 for the hardtop and convertible, respectively. Thunderbird production moved up smartly. In fact, total model year output of close to 67,500 was nearly double that of 1958.

The 1959 Thunderbird convertible. Production was 10,261.

The hardtop was much more popular at 57,195 units.

1960

The big cars get bigger, and a new smaller Ford gets back to basics

Ford Division opened the "Soaring '60s" with a brand-new compact, a totally restyled big-car line, and a refined version of the four-seat Thunderbird. Taking over as division general manager this year was one Lee A. Iacocca, who would go on to become the driving force behind Ford's most single successful new product of the decade, the Mustang. A born car salesman with a keen sense of what turned on the public, Iacocca would also spearhead Ford's Total Performance campaign, injecting excitement into almost every Ford of the '60s.

The new small car was named Falcon. It arrived this year as one of the Big Three compacts along with the Chevrolet Corvair and the Valiant from Chrysler Corporation. This trio was Detroit's response to the growing popularity of small imports like the Volkswagen Beetle and to the economy-car craze spawned by the 1958 recession. That had given new life to the Rambler, and had enabled Studebaker to make a comeback with its Lark. Work on Falcon had been started as early as 1957, originally under the code name "XK Thunderbird." It was one of several small-car projects in progress throughout the worldwide Ford organization at the time (another was a front-drive model that would eventually lead to the stillborn Ford Cardinal in 1962), and it was completed in a remarkably short 19 months.

To many, the Falcon was the ultimate throw-away car, built to sell at a low price and designed to be driven and then discarded within a few years. Compared with the Corvair, its main rival, it was deadly conventional: ordi-

Rear view of the 1960 Sunliner convertible highlights Ford's attempt at matching Chevy's "bat-fin" styling.

Pert and practical, Ford's new 1960 Falcon quickly became the top-selling compact. This 2-door sold for a low $1912.

1960 Falcon styling was clean and simple. Compare standard hubcaps on this $1974 4-door with full wheel discs above.

1960 Falcon offered plain metal dash, large windshield.

Trunk space in the 1960 Falcon sedans was quite good.

nary front-mounted six-cylinder water-cooled engine, rear drive, live-axle rear suspension. Chevy's approach, on the other hand, was to mimic the layout and construction of the Beetle: air-cooled rear engine, all-independent suspension ("the engine's in the back where it belongs," ran the ads). But while the Corvair's unusual specifications intrigued mainly car buffs, the Falcon's anvil simplicity had much wider appeal, and the new little Ford quickly established itself as the top seller in its class.

Riding a 109.5-inch wheelbase, the Falcon was initially offered in 2- and 4-door sedan body styles. Later in the year, 2- and 4-door wagons were added. Styling was simple in the extreme, almost severe, with a large concave grille flanked by dual headlamps, attractive bodyside creases, rounded corners and fenders, and a simple rear end punctuated by large round taillamps. At 181.2 inches overall it measured more than a foot shorter than the full-size Fords, yet it offered a surprising amount of room inside. Power was supplied by a 144-cid cast-iron pushrod six developing 90 bhp, hooked to either a 3-speed manual transmission with column shift or optional 3-speed automatic. The interior was plain (some said stark), but it was all part of the plan.

In a very real sense, Falcon was a return to the Model A concept: a simple, reliable, no-nonsense car, easy to buy and cheap to own. Fuel economy, as reported in the press, reached upwards of 27 mpg. Prices were low. The 2-door sedan listed at just $1912, and the most expensive version, the 4-door wagon, sold for a reasonable $2287. There weren't many options available, though there would be in short order, but that, too, was part of the plan. Ford was on to another winner.

The successful Thunderbird package was left pretty much alone this year. One new option was a snug-fitting, sliding metal sunroof, the first among postwar American cars. Styling changes were confined to hash marks on

Falcon wagons were added at mid-1960. The 2-door cost $2225.

Falcon was the first Ford wagon without a separate liftgate.

rear fenders, cleaner side trim, a square mesh behind a large horizontal grille bar with three vertical dividers, three-element taillight clusters, standard outside rearview mirror, polarized day/night inside rearview mirror, revised interiors with built-in armrests, and a raft of new color combinations. Prices went to $3755 for the hardtop, $3967 for the sunroof hardtop, and $4222 for the convertible.

After three years on the big-car platform, the Ranchero car/pickup became a derivative of the new compact Falcon for '60.

The first four-seat Thunderbird design was in its final year for 1960. Sales hit a new high, nearly 91,000 units.

Large cross-hatch grille bar marked 1960 T-Bird's grille.

T-Bird tail acquired extra taillamps, close-checked applique.

The four-seat Thunderbird was regarded as more luxury than performance car, but don't think it wasn't quick. With the 430-cid Lincoln V-8 it would typically sprint from 0 to 60 mph in nine seconds flat, but used fuel at the drunkardly rate of 12 miles per gallon. Its main faults were a lack of nimbleness and, perhaps, practicality. In a test of the 1960 model, *Motor Trend* magazine noted: "Steering is slow and not precise. The driver's position limits visibility and makes control clumsy and restricted...[it has] some of the dimensional attributes of a compact and yet lacks some of those same characteristics of maneuverability associated with the type...[It is] nearly as costly as any standard luxury car, yet it has quality comparable only to a standard low-priced Ford...Its styling is distinctive but certainly not notable." These were curious comments considering the magazine had named Thunderbird "Car of the Year" for 1958.

But *MT* concluded on a sweeter note: "There were many cars that would outperform the four seater," it said. "But somehow the T-Bird has never been measured by these standards...It is a car apart, and like royalty, rarely required to count for ordinary deficiencies...These other qualities are, after all, quite common-place. The Thunderbird is different, and that is all it has ever had to be."

Thunderbird popularity reached a new high, nearly 91,000 of the 1960 models finding homes. It was a record that would not be broken until 1964. A unique variation this year was a special high-trim model with gold-colored vinyl top, of which about 2500 were produced. Most T-

The 1960 Thunderbird with newly optional sliding sunroof

Slick Starliner hardtop was a new body style in 1960's top Galaxie series in the full-size line. Price was $2610.

The 1960 standard Fords like this Fairlane 500 4-door were the biggest in history. Note compound-curve front, rear glass.

Birds this year carried the standard 352-cid Ford V-8; only about 3900 were equipped with the big-block Lincoln mill.

Now that compacts had arrived, auto writers coined a new term for the largest U.S. cars like the Ford Galaxie: full-size. And for 1960, the big Fords grew even larger, gaining a much longer, lower, wider bodyshell. Wheelbase grew an inch (to 119 inches, where it would remain for the rest of the decade), but overall length was up by 5.7 inches and width swelled by 5 inches to a massive 81.5. The new styling was a hastily contrived attempt to match the radical bat-fin 1959 Chevrolet, but was far more tasteful. Ford quickly learned it didn't need such extremes, however.

Ford built 11,860 of the 1960 Thunderbird convertibles.

1960 Fairlane 500 4-door sedan, priced at $2388.

One of Ford's 1960 "fastbacks," the basic $2586 Ranch Wagon.

1961

A beguiling new Bird and a burly new V-8 headline a successful season

Headlining the 1961 Ford lineup was the all-new third-generation Thunderbird and a trimmer, restyled big Ford. The division offered more horsepower up and down the line, from a larger Falcon six to a brawny new 390 V-8. These and a raft of mechanical and cosmetic refinements helped Ford slip past Chevrolet in model year production by over 20,000 cars.

The new 390 V-8 was essentially an enlarged version of the 352, created by stretching bore 0.05 inch (to 4.05) and lengthening stroke 0.28 inch (to 3.78). Dubbed the Thunderbird Special 390 V-8, it produced the same 300 bhp as the previous top-tune 352, but packed more torque (427 lbs/ft versus 381 lbs/ft, both developed at a lazy 2800 rpm). In this form, the 390 was the new standard—and only—powerplant for the new Thunderbird, and was the largest engine option for this year's big Fords. All Ford V-8s now bore the Thunderbird name, whether they were available in the T-Bird or not. This applied to the 352, which was still around as a regular-fuel 220 bhp offering, and the 292, now at 175 bhp.

There were also two other versions of the 390 available: a police-only 330-bhp Interceptor engine and a Thunderbird 390 Super edition rated at a conservative 375 bhp. At mid-year, the single four-barrel engine initially offered was supplemented by one with triple two-barrel carbs and higher compression, good for 401 bhp. Author Phil Hall in *Fearsome Fords* notes that all 390s differed internally from the smaller FE-series Y-block engines. Specific changes included stronger castings, thicker main bearing webs, enlarged oil passages, and larger intake manifolds. The cast-iron exhaust headers from the previous 352-cid Interceptor 360 were retained, as were its larger dual exhaust outlets. The 375-bhp unit could be ordered in any full-size '61 Ford except wagons, but it was strictly for performance: power steering, power brakes, and automatic transmission weren't available. With all this, Ford was now firmly in the big-inch league with Pontiac's 389 V-8 and the new Chevy 409.

None of this mattered much to Thunderbird fanciers, who this year had an all-new version of their car to drool over. What they got was a larger, sleeker interpretation of the personal-luxury theme so successfully established by the 1958-60 design. Ford coined a new slogan for the '61 that perfectly described it: "Unique in All the World."

Throughout its history the Thunderbird has generally kept to a three-year styling cycle. Thus it was that the 1961 model was to be all-new. Two clay mockups were in contention for '61 styling, one by long-standing Bird designer Bill Boyer, the other by Elwood Engel, both working under the then vice-president for styling, George Walker. Engel's angular, crisply lined proposal was eliminated when then division general manager Robert McNa-

Nevertheless, the '60s were quite pretty in their way. Headlamps moved down into the grille, which announced a lower, broader hoodline. The old windshield dogleg disappeared in favor of simple slanted A-posts. Bodysides were marked by discreet contouring below a full-length extension of the beltline sheetmetal, which swept back into modest horizontal fins and a flat rear deck. Altogether, the big Ford was arguably the best-looking of the Big Three standards this year.

Once again the model lineup was shuffled. From the bottom the order read: Custom 300, Fairlane, Fairlane 500, and Galaxie; the separate Station Wagon series paralleled these as before in trim and equipment. An attractive new body style in the Galaxie series was the Starliner hardtop, with an airy, gently curved roofline that almost qualified as a fastback. Of course, there was more to this than looks: the roof was aerodynamically superior on the NASCAR supertracks to the T-Bird-like Galaxie roof, and there's reason to think that winning races was the Starliner's main mission in life.

Engine choices for the 1960 big cars still involved the familiar 292 and 352 V-8s. After a few dormant years following the AMA's 1957 anti-racing edict, the Big Three were beginning to engage in performance skirmishes again, and Ford's maximum 300 bhp just wasn't enough. Accordingly, the division released its first performance engine in three years for 1960. Dubbed "Interceptor 360," it was a tuned 352 packing a single four-barrel carburetor and 10.6:1 compression, good for 360 bhp. Initially, it was available only with 3-speed manual transmission. In the summer of '59, *Motor Life* magazine got hold of a prototype Starliner with the new engine, and was startled to find the car would zip from 0 to 60 mph in 7.1 seconds. And despite its 4141-pound bulk, it would do an honest 150 mph. The magazine described it as a "new bomb." By contrast, *Motor Trend* magazine tested a Starliner with the 300-bhp 352 and automatic, and recorded an 11.7-second 0-60 mph time. The best news for performance seekers was the Interceptor's price: just $150. The Total Performance era had begun.

Ford retailed more than 68,000 of the 1960 Starliners, making it one of the division's most popular models. The Starliner's life was brief—it lasted only two years—but sweet. It was, as one enthusiast observed, "the kind of car you never forget, never."

mara decided it should be the basis for the "compact" 1961 Lincoln Continental, so Bill Boyer's work was once again the starting point for a new-generation Thunderbird.

Boyer remembered that his model "was very rocket-like in concept—very much aircraft-oriented, with big round 'flowerpot' taillights. It had what I called a 'fleet submarine bow.' We wanted to keep the thing very youthful, and of course that meant aircraft and missile-like shapes—a model as aerodynamically aesthetic as possible. In contrast, Elwood's was a very formal job, [thus] was perfectly suited to Lincoln." The two new cars, Boyer

This 1961 Thunderbird convertible served as pace car for the 50th anniversary year of the Indianapolis Speedway.

A total of 10,516 of the sleek '61 T-Bird ragtops was built.

'61 T-Bird convertible top aped the hardtop's appearance.

As with the "Squarebirds," the convertible top on the '61 Thunderbird was completely hidden when stowed.

Base sticker price on the '61 T-Bird convertible was $4639.   *The companion hardtop listed for $4172.*

'61 T-Bird front featured headlamps sunken in odd-shaped wells, a touch also used on this year's new Lincoln.

continued, had much in common: "Both featured very highly integrated bumper/grille combinations, for example. There was much similarity in the windshield and side glass, a lot of interchangeability."

From its sharply pointed front end, Boyer's design was tapered cleanly along the fuselage, with only the merest suggestion of a tailfin on the rear fenders. The 1958-60 "Squarebird" roofline was retained, but in a more rounded rendition. The original 1961 front end was a bit on the chromey side, and remained so through grille insert revisions for 1962 and '63.

Meanwhile, careful attention was being paid to interior design, guided by the talented hand of Art Querfeld, a 40-year Ford veteran. "I wanted to emphasize and delineate the positions of the driver and front seat passenger," Querfeld said. "I conceived of two individual compartments separated by a prominent console, which swept forward to the dash, curved left and right, meeting the doors and continuing around on the door panels." The console/divider was finished in brushed aluminum with horizontal lines. Stuart Fry of the packaging team created the '61 Bird's unique "Swing-Away" steering wheel. This moved 10 inches laterally to the right (with the transmission in Park) to assist entry/exit. Pop-up roof panels were also considered, but rejected due to cost and complexity.

The third-generation Bird was not greatly changed in dimensions from the 1958-60 series. It retained a 113-inch wheelbase and 52.5-inch height, but was half an inch shorter and about an inch narrower overall. Body construction now followed the "dual unitized" principle, with separate front and rear sections welded together at the cowl. The cowl structure was shared with the '61 Continental, which helped keep tooling and production costs down and provided greater rigidity than in previous models.

Most engineering work for the '61 went into its completely redesigned chassis. There now appeared what engineers called "controlled wheel recession," which meant extensive use of rubber bushings to allow fore/aft as well as up/down wheel movement. This idea, then familiar Mercedes-Benz practice, marked another T-Bird "first" that would later be copied for many other U.S. cars.

The front suspension employed coil springs located above the upper wishbones. The lower control arm was a single bar instead of a wishbone, with a strut running from its outer end to a rubber bushing mounted on the unit body. At the rear, the forward spring mounts were also carried in rubber bushings. Arms extended from the leaf shackles to each bushing to allow fore/aft movement. Stability was improved by increasing track width one inch at the front and three inches at the rear. Steering had a quicker ratio, which reduced turns lock-to-lock to 3.5 and allowed use of a smallish 16-inch-diameter steering wheel. The power-assisted, self-adjusting brakes had 14 percent more lining area than in 1960.

The thoroughly overhauled chassis made the '61 T-Bird a much better handler than its predecessor. It took high-speed turns with little body lean, and would plow heavily only in tight corners. The quicker steering was more responsive, the enlarged brakes had better stopping power, and the "controlled wheel recession" made the '61 the smoothest-riding Thunderbird yet. Certainly it was the most comfortable American car on a wheelbase of less than 115 inches. And it was the best-engineered Thunderbird in history. Ford sold 73,051 units for 1961, of which 10,516 were convertibles.

The full-size Fords were treated to a heavy facelift for '61, and became slightly shorter and lighter than the pre-

vious year's boats. Changes included a concave grille with a texture similar to that of the '59, a shorter rear deck, and round taillamps topped by subtle blade fins. The model line stayed basically the same. All closed Galaxie models save the Starliner wore squared-off wide-quarter rooflines a la Thunderbird, which buyers definitely preferred. Starliner sales declined to under 30,000 units for the model year; only the Galaxie 2-door sedan was less popular among the non-wagon offerings.

Less maintenance was heavily emphasized on the big cars this year. Lubrication intervals were extended to a full 30,000 miles, made possible by using a special molybdenum-disulphide lubricant for key points, which were protected by polyurethane caps or liners. Normal grease fittings were eliminated, replaced with threaded

The Galaxie Sunliner convertible for '61, priced at $2849

The Galaxie 2-door sedan retailed at $2538 for 1961.

Big Ford styling became cleaner, less contrived for 1961. Shown is a styling mockup for the Galaxie 4-door sedan.

Starliner hardtop's semi-fastback roofline mated well with the new 1961 lower body styling. Model sold for $2599.

Fewer than 30,000 Starliner hardtops were built for '61.

1961 Falcon 4-door wagon. Price: $2270.

New convex grille marked all '61 Falcons, like this 4-door.

Base price on the plain Falcon 2-door rose just $2 for 1961.

'61 Falcon 4-door carried a patriotic price tag: $1976.

plugs that could be removed if lubrication ever became necessary. Oil change intervals were also extended this year, to 6000 miles. Other mechanical alterations comprised thinner main leaves for the semi-elliptic rear springs, recalibrated shock absorbers, and standard self-adjusting brakes. Steering effort with optional power assist was reduced by about 50 percent, a less welcome change.

Falcon returned for its second year with a bit more chrome and a new convex grille. Responding quickly to the success of the bucket-seat Corvair Monza, introduced midway through the 1960 season, Ford bowed the Falcon Futura for "1961½". A more uptown version of the standard 2-door sedan, Futura offered standard bucket seats separated by a Thunderbird-like glovebox, plush carpeting, higher-grade vinyl trim, and special emblems. A floorshift manual transmission was optional. The Futura pointed the way to success in the compact class, notching close to 45,000 sales despite an abbreviated model year. Newly available for all '61 Falcons was a stroked version of the sturdy pushrod six, delivering 101 horsepower from its 170 cid. This powerplant would remain in service at Ford through the early '70s, when it powered the Falcon's spiritual successor, the Maverick.

1962

Opening up the market with a new-size Ford and a significant new engine

The Ford lineup became even more specialized for 1962 with the arrival of the new-size Fairlane and the full-size XL sub-series, the first of the big performance Fords. The year also saw the birth of an important new engine, the small-block V-8, and a near-revival of the two-seat Thunderbird. In model year production, Chevrolet opened up a wide gap over Ford, partly on the strength of its new conventional compact, the Chevy II. Still, Ford's overall total was better than 150,000 units higher than the 1961 tally.

A new market class emerged this year, the intermediate-size car. Ford led the way with an all-new Fairlane sized between the Falcon and the standard Ford. In a way, this Fairlane was a kind of grown-up compact. Its wheelbase for example, was 6 inches longer (115.5 inches) than Falcon's, and it was 16.5 inches longer overall and 500 pounds heavier. However, it utilized unit construction like Falcon, the same kind of conventional engineering and conservative styling, even the Falcon's optional 170-cid six as its standard engine. Model choices were restricted to 2 and 4-door sedans in standard and glitzier 500 trim.

Coincidentally, Fairlane appeared in the same year Plymouth and Dodge fielded smaller full-size models of similar dimensions. Whether it was because of their smaller size or oddball styling, these cars didn't sell well,

Division chief Iacocca and the 1962 Fairlane 2-door sedan

and Chrysler hurriedly revived the big Dodge at mid-model year. Fairlane had no such difficulty, however, and more than 297,000 copies were sold. A plus for Ford was that most of this represented new business and did not come at the expense of other models.

Fairlane development was well along in 1960 when Ford product planners determined that an engine larger than the Falcon six would be needed for the new model as an extra-cost option. Unfortunately, there were none in the company stable. The 223-cid six from the big Fords was getting old and besides, it wouldn't fit. Even the smallest FE-series V-8 available, the 292, was too bulky—and thirsty. But a new V-8—smaller, lighter, and more efficient than any then-current Ford engine—would be just right. Accordingly, engineering director Harold C. McDonald convinced management to approve a $250 million program to develop a new so-called small-block V-8, with displacement pegged at 220 to 230 cubic inches. The project was handed over to a team headed by George F. Stirrat, who had joined Ford in 1949 and had worked his way through the ranks at the company's Engine & Foundry operation.

Stirrat's major objectives for the new engine were lightness and compact size. His targets were 20 inches maximum width and an installed weight of 450 pounds. He went to new extremes in order to make the block compact, selecting a 3.50-inch bore and a short stroke of 2.87 inches, plus short connecting rods and low piston height. He extended the block only as far as the crankshaft centerline instead of farther down into a deep, rigid crankcase. This layout did not even leave room inside the

crankcase for full counterweighting—30 percent of the engine's total unbalanced forces had to be handled by adding external masses. Bore centers were spaced at 4.38 inches, which allowed considerable freedom for later enlargement beyond the engine's initial 221 cid. On a compression ratio of 8.5:1, the new Fairlane V-8 delivered 145 bhp at 4400 rpm.

Stirrat's valvegear design was new to Ford, but was familiar Pontiac/Chevrolet practice. Rocker arms were mounted on ball-studs, thus eliminating rocker shafts. Valves were conventionally sized relative to bore, with head diameters of 1.59 inches for the intakes and 1.39 inches for the exhausts. Timing was fairly conservative, even for a volume-production V-8, at 21-51/57-15, giving an intake duration of 252 degrees and 36 degrees of valve overlap.

Despite weight-paring measures, Stirrat couldn't have met his 450-pound limit had it not been for newly developed foundry techniques. The man behind Ford's advances in thin-wall, high-precision casting was Harold C. Grant, a leader in the development of nodular-iron castings and the shell-molding process using resin-filled cores. His work enabled Ford to keep out a lot of needless metal.

And more or less incidentally, the cast-iron Fairlane V-8 was a knockout blow for the aluminum-block engines then built in America: Buick's 215-cid V-8, and sixes from Chrysler and American Motors. The Buick and AMC engines were lighter, but Chrysler's 225-cid six was heavier. All were far more expensive to produce. The Ford engine sent these rivals scurrying back to the iron foundries to copy its construction.

Auto writers were quick to note that the Fairlane marked the revival of a size of car not seen from a U.S. manufacturer since 1955. The success of Ford's new intermediate—and its lively V-8—wasn't lost on GM. Just two years later, Chevy fielded a 1955-size car of its own, the Chevelle, available with a descendant of that make's original V-8.

One step down the size ladder, the compact Falcon carried on with a new "electric shaver" grille theme and Deluxe-trim versions of all body styles. New was a Squire version of the wagon, with the same sort of imitation wood side paneling found on the big Country Squire. The Falcon name also appeared for the first time on two passenger models of the Econoline forward-control van, but these don't concern us here.

Bucket-seat Falcon Futura returned from mid-1961. All '62 Falcons had a busy new grille, minor trim changes elsewhere.

Full-size Fords took on a more rounded, bulkier look for '62. Shown is the Galaxie Sunliner convertible at $2924.

1962 Galaxie 2-door sedan. Price new was $2453.

Falcon Futura acquired T-Bird style roof from 1962½.

Vinyl roof covering was optional for the mid-year Futura.

Big-car brawn at its best: the 1962 Galaxie 500XL Sunliner

The bucket-seat XLs differed little externally from other 1962 Galaxie 500s. Emblems here are actually airbrushed.

The big Fords were thoroughly restyled for the third year in a row. Sheetmetal was more rounded everywhere and the overall look bulkier. The model lineup contracted to make room for the new Fairlane. Galaxie was now the base series, while a new Galaxie 500 line was added above, offering a full range of body styles. The complementary wagon lineup returned minus the 2-door, and the pretty Starliner 2-door hardtop vanished. Engine availability at the start of the model year was unchanged from '61.

A marketing technique favored by division chief Lee Iacocca was the "half" model year, when special trim and/or mechanical options would be introduced for existing models. The purpose: to give familiar models added zest for the spring selling season, traditionally the year's busiest. Iacocca inaugurated the practice at Ford this year, and three "1962½" models appeared in April under the "Lively Ones" theme. All were intended to capitalize on growing buyer interest in bucket seats, console, floorshift, and other youth-oriented features popularized by Chevy's Corvair Monza. Predictably, then, the bucket-seat Falcon Futura 2-door was restyled with a squared-off T-Bird-type roof. The new Fairlane 500 2-door was spiffed up with buckets and special trim to become the Sports Coupe. The same treatment was applied to the big Galaxie 500 2-door hardtop and Sunliner convertible, and the XL designation was tacked on. While some thought the letters stood for "Experimental Limited," the true meaning was nothing more than "extra lively."

Also at mid-year, Ford upped its ante in the performance game by bringing out its largest V-8 yet—a 406-cid unit created by boring out the 390 by 0.08-inch. Available only for the big Fords, it was offered in two versions: a 385-bhp unit with single four-barrel carb as the Thunderbird High-Performance V-8 and with three two-barrel carbs as the Thunderbird Super High-Performance V-8, rated at 405 bhp, nearly 1 bhp per cubic inch. The latter was clearly not for the faint-hearted, and it added a sizable $380 to the XL's base price. Nevertheless, the 406 gave the big bucket-seat Fords the go-power to match their sporty pretentions. Contemporary road tests showed 0-60 mph acceleration times ranging from the mid-6s to a bit over 7 seconds—fantastic for a quiet, smooth-riding freeway flyer weighing nearly two tons.

The 406 would have made the big Ford a fine stock-car racer but, aside from its heft, the big Galaxie had a problem. As writer Phil Hall explained: "When the Starliner was dropped, so were Ford's superspeedway chances. The squared-off sedan roof just didn't cut through the air as quickly as the sleek Starliners." Ford's answer was the Starlift, a removable roof that fitted the big convertible and made it look a lot like the Starliner. Though ostensibly available to the public as well as race teams, the Starlift was banned by NASCAR officials after but a single race. Ford would improve the aerodynamics of its full-size cars with racing in mind, but not for another year.

Thunderbird remained much the same for '62, but there were several interesting developments. One was a new op-

Proposed "Starlift" roof was Ford's unsuccessful attempt to sneak around NASCAR rules for '62 racing season.

"Starlift" made convertible look like the previous Starliner, but NASCAR banned the option after only one race.

Clever tonneau cover made the four-place Bird convertible into the dramatic-looking 1962 Sports Roadster.

The regular '62 T-Bird convertible saw 7030 copies.

By contrast, Sports Roadster was rare: only 1427 were built.

A prototype '62 T-Bird convertible minus its fender skirts

New '62 T-Bird Landau was a hardtop with dummy landau bars.

tional version of the 390 V-8, the M-series engine, with triple two-barrel carbs and 10.5:1 compression. So equipped, the Bird packed 340 bhp, sufficient for 8.5 seconds in the 0-60 mph dash and a top speed of 125 mph.

The two-seat T-Bird returned this year—in spirit if not in fact—in the unusual Sports Roadster. Ever since the days of the 1955-57 models, Ford had received a steady stream of inquiries from dealers and customers who, although happy with the four-seater, wanted a little Bird, too. Lee Iacocca was sympathetic, but he didn't want to spend money reviving the two-seater as a separate model. A solution came from stylist Bud Kaufman. It was a fiberglass tonneau cover, with a pair of faired-in headrests

for the front seats, designed to cover the rear seat area of the standard T-Bird convertible. Through careful detail engineering, the tonneau didn't interfere with raising or lowering the top, and the front seats were still free to hinge forward so luggage could be stuffed in underneath it in back. But the tonneau was too big to carry in the trunk, so you had to leave it at home if you wanted to travel four-up. This, plus a tall price—about $5500—limited the Sports Roadster's appeal, and only 1427 of the '62s were built.

Still, the Roadster was a dramatic package. It was set off by standard Kelsey-Hayes wire wheels and skirtless rear wheel openings. The spinner hubs made the wire wheels too bulky to fit under the normal T-Bird skirts (and they were too pretty to hide, anyway). Because of its rarity, the Sports Roadster has become the most desirable Thunderbird of the 1960s. The most exotic versions were equipped with the M-series engine, installed on only 120 of the '62s.

Another new "package" model for 1962 was the Landau, a high-line hardtop distinguished externally by dummy landau bars on the roof quarters—another Bill Boyer flashback to Classic-era styling. The Landau accounted for about a fourth of all Thunderbird hardtops. Its popularity stemmed not only from its looks but also a competitive price: at $4398 it cost only $77 more than the standard hardtop.

1963

More models, more power, more go: Ford calls it "Total Performance"

More models, more engines, more horsepower: Total Performance was in full swing at Ford for 1963. Major highlights were new body styles for Falcon, Fairlane, and the big Galaxie series, plus larger versions of both the small-block and big-block V-8s. Much of this activity was reserved for mid-year introduction. Ford built over 1.5 million cars for the model year—its highest since 1957 and a new record—but trailed Chevrolet by a significant 600,000 units.

As was becoming standard Ford practice, the 1963 models bowed with the most powerful engines offered at the end of the preceeding model year. An exception was a bored extension of the 221-cid Challenger V-8 (from 3.5 to 3.80 inches), with 260 cid and 164 bhp on a tighter 8.7:1 compression ratio. The Galaxie's engine chart was revised by cancelling the 292-cid Y-block. A single 352 and a brace of 390 and 406 V-8s comprised the initial power options.

All four Ford lines were facelifted. Falcon sedans adopted the squared-up roofline used on the mid-'62 Futura 2-door, and all models displayed more pointed front fenders and a more pleasing convex grille. The Futura was expanded into a separate series, replacing the former Deluxe, with 2- and 4-door sedans and a new convertible. Spear-like side trim marked these more expensive Falcons. Galaxie was fractionally longer and wider this year, marked by a handsome new concave grille, more prominent round taillamps, and twin bodyside moldings on Galaxie 500s. Added to the XL sub-series was a square-roof 4-door hardtop complete with bucket seats. This year's Thunderbird was identified by square-top wheel openings and modest horizontal creaselines in doors and front fenders, plus new wheel covers and the usual nameplate shuffling. The intermediate Fairlane was facelifted to more closely resemble the Galaxie, acquiring a similar concave grille. Two new body styles were offered, a 2-door hardtop in the Fairlane 500 series and a 4-door wagon, available in three versions including a fancy Squire with imitation-wood side trim.

Ford saved its most interesting 1963 developments for mid-season. Starting at the bottom of the line, Falcon gained a pretty 2-door hardtop body style marked by a graceful semi-fastback roof. It was offered both as a Fu-

The pretty Falcon Futura Sprint hardtop for mid-1963. Six was standard on Sprint, but 260 V-8 gave it lots of snap.

tura and, along with the convertible, as the new Sprint. Equipped with standard bucket seats, 4-speed manual transmission with floorshift, dash-mount tachometer, and simulated wire wheel covers, the Sprint could be made into a neat little GT by ordering the Challenger 260 V-8, available in the Falcon for the first time.

The 164-bhp, 260-cid small-block made the humdrum Falcon into an honest performance machine. *Car Life* magazine, which called the Sprint "Le Petite Sport," noted that it reduced the normal Falcon's power-to-weight ratio from 31.4 lbs/bhp to 21.0. The 260, *CL* said, was "a willing engine. If it seems unaware of the choking restrictions of its single 2-barrel carburetor, it is because of somewhat generous valve sizes and relatively clean intake and exhaust designs. Its ability to readily surpass

the 5000-rpm redline would have one believe it is fitted with mechanical lifters, but, of course, it isn't. The engine is completely devoid of fussiness, and exhibits a surprising amount of torque from rather ridiculous rpm levels. Despite the ease of over-revving, there is a decided leveling off of output at the power peak, so that raising the shift points makes no improvement in acceleration. This engine is much happier in the Falcon surroundings than it ever seemed to be in the Fairlane, particularly when it had been teamed (in the latter car) with the 2-speed automatic transmission." *Car Life* recorded 0-60 mph in 12 seconds, the quarter-mile in 18 seconds at 75 mph, and a top speed of 105 mph for its four-speed model.

The Ford small-block was used to give Fairlane an added dose of excitement. Another bore increase (to 4.00

1963½ Fairlane 500 Sports Coupe hardtop. Price was $2504.

Fairlane 500 4-door was the most popular mid-size '63.

This Fairlane show car appeared on the 1963 auto show circuit. Note rounded rear wheel arches, "sedanca" roof.

Mid-season Fairlane 500 Sports Coupe was available with up to 271 bhp from the newly enlarged 289-cid small-block.

inches) yielded 289 cid and 271 bhp with four-barrel carb and 11:1 compression. (There was also a 195-bhp version, which replaced the 260 as base power for the big Galaxie at mid-year.) Heralding the 289 was another bucket-seat special, the Sports Coupe hardtop, which offered center console and deluxe wheel covers with simulated knock-off spinners.

In June 1962, Ford had declared it would no longer honor the AMA racing ban from 1957. The first evidence of that appeared in the Galaxie line for 1963½ in the form of a new slantback Sports Hardtop. Sitting about an inch lower than the formal-roof models, it had sloping rear roof pillars and a smallish backlight. While not as smooth as the old Starliner, it was a step in the right direction for stock-car racing—as events would prove. In fact, Ford enjoyed one of its best NASCAR seasons this year. Commencing with Dan Gurney's win in the Riverside 500 in January, Fords were in the winner's circle at every 500-mile event, and took 23 Grand Nationals in all. The big XL was also a winner. Model year production was 12,596 of the 4-door square-roof hardtops, 29,713 of the 2-doors, and 18,551 convertibles. The new fastback was the most popular of all, scoring 33,870 deliveries of the XL version and another 100,000 in normal Galaxie 500 trim.

Matching competitors' moves in the big-inch engine wars, Ford once again bored its FE-series block, this time by .10-inch, bringing displacement up to 427 cid. With single four-barrel carb, output was 410 bhp, and a new twin four-barrel setup (plus aluminum intake manifold) pushed that up to 425. Both versions used a tight 11.6:1

The price tag on this 1963 Galaxie 2-door read $2453.

Designed for NASCAR: 1963½ Galaxie 500/XL Sports Hardtop

1963 Galaxie 500/XL Sunliner, one of the "Super-Torque" Fords

Bucket-seat 4-door hardtop was new 500/XL model for '63.

Like the new "fastback," the square-roof 2-door hardtop was available in XL or (pictured) normal Galaxie 500 form.

The Thunderbird Sports Roadster returned for '63, but only 455 were built. Of these, just 37 had the M-series V-8.

Sports Roadster's 1963 price was a hefty $5439.

Bodyside creaselines distinguished all 1963 Thunderbirds.

Grille insert was subtly changed for the '63 T-Bird.

Most popular '63 Thunderbird was the $4445 standard hardtop.

A mere 5913 of the regular '63 T-Bird ragtops were built.

compression ratio. Price was discouraging—the lower power unit cost $405 additional—but if it was power you wanted, at least Ford made it relatively easy to get. A 4-speed manual transmission, which had first appeared as a late 1961 option, was mandatory with the 427. You also got a beefed-up chassis and suspension, more powerful brakes, and larger tires with this option, which helps to explain why it was so expensive.

There was also a limited-production 427 for the dragstrip. Despite its higher 12:1 compression, it was rated at 425 bhp—same as the more powerful street version—though that was mainly to satisfy the rulebook. By now, lighter mid-size cars were beginning to rule the quarter-mile circuits, but Ford tried to keep its big cars competitive by offering an S/S kit. This consisted of fiberglass body panels and other changes that lightened the front end by some 160 pounds. Ford even built a few cars with this kit and stripped interiors at the factory. However, the lighter Plymouths and Dodges were faster in Super/Stock action, and the typical XL rolled out the door by means of a Thunderbird 390 V-8 and automatic.

The same applies to the interesting Thunderbird Sports Roadster, now in its second—and final—year. A mere 455

were built. Personal-luxury buyers were now clearly moving away from open cars. Consider that Ford built 10,516 of the '61 T-Bird ragtops, 7030 of the conventional '62 convertibles, and just 5913 of the '63s. T-Bird convertible sales would rise again with the advent of the fourth-generation for 1964, then decline the next two years. When the fifth-generation design appeared for 1967, the convertible would be gone.

Nowadays, of course, ragtops are making a comeback, and there must be many Bird lovers hoping Ford will revive one.

1964

Escalating excitement and extra luxury make an award-winning Ford line

Ford's biggest success of the decade arrived during the 1964 model year. As most enthusiasts know, Mustang was officially designated a 1965 model, reflecting another Lee Iacocca merchandising technique, the "early" or advance model year introduction. Therefore, we cover Mustang's background (and the distinctions between the first "1964½" models and the "true" '65s) in the next section.

Of course, Mustang wasn't the only noteworthy development for '64. The division had a brand-new Thunderbird and a heavily reskinned Galaxie to show, plus facelifted Falcons and Fairlanes. This was a good year for Ford, with production up by well over 60,000 units. But Chevy did considerably better, topping the 2-million mark for the third year in a row and notching better than 160,000 more sales compared to 1963. The gap with Ford

Falcon Sprint convertible listed for $2671. 4278 were made.

The 1964 Falcon 2-door sedan: economy plus for $1996

All Falcons were reskinned below the belt for '64, achieving a busier, bulkier look. Shown is the Sprint convertible.

Priced at $2436, the 1964 Falcon Futura Sprint hardtop saw total production of 13,830 units for the model year.

was better than 700,000, but Dearborn would close that up substantially—thanks largely to Mustang—in the 1965 tally.

Though you wouldn't think it from just looking at them, the full-size 1961-63 Fords had been based on the bodyshell and inner structure introduced with the 1960 line. Ford reskinned this platform for one last time this year, achieving a distinctive if rather busy look compared with earlier models. The most noticeable highlights were "pontoon" bodyside sculpturing, a longer rear deck, rounded nose, and a horizontal-bar grille with three distinct vertical peaks. The previous Galaxie and 300 names were abolished at the bottom end, replaced by the Custom and Custom 500 designations. Galaxie 500 and the bucket-seat XL sub-series continued at the top. Except for one special mid-year power option that we'll get to shortly, there were no major alterations to drivetrain specs or availability.

The '64 Sprint cockpit. Note pod-mounted tachometer on dash.

Historically, the '64 Ford may not seem significant—basically just a five-year-old design set to be phased out for the all-new 1965s, the most changed Ford passenger cars since 1949. But for collectors, it is perfect. Wrote Tim Howley in *Special-Interest Autos* magazine: "The '64 Ford stands quite alone as the ultimate Total Performance Ford." Howley called it evolutionary, but noted that it reached near perfection in the process. Though mechanical specs were basically the same as in 1963, "styling had been carefully dictated by the aerodynamics of racing. Even the body panels were designed to be lighter than the '63s." There were three 500XL models: the convertible and two- and four-door hardtops both with the fastback roof from 1963½. Production totaled 58,306 two-doors, 15,169 convertibles, and 14,661 four-doors. Evidently the public agreed with *Motor Trend* magazine, which gave its "Car of the Year" honors to the entire 1964 Ford line, including the full-size models. Because of a strong quality-control effort begun in 1961, XLs and other big Fords wore like iron. "With that kind of quality," according to Howley, "all too many of them were driven for 10 years or 200,000 miles, and they just don't show their age. Rare is the low-mileage '64XL, as this was not the kind of car you bought to put away in your garage."

The performance of the '64 500XL seems awesome today. In a contemporary magazine comparison test of 390- and 427-cid models, the milder car did 0-60 mph in 9.3 seconds, which is fair going, but the 427 clocked it in 7.4 seconds—remarkable for a two-ton, full-size car that could only be described as luxurious.

No engine changes were made on the '64s, nor was advertised output boosted on any powerteam. Ford's drag racing colors were now carried by the lighter and more competitive Fairlane. But the big cars still ran in the Grand Nationals, and did well. Chrysler Corporation brought back its fabled hemi-head V-8 for the '64 campaign, planning to beat the stuffing out of any GM or

The ultimate evolution of Ford's early '60s big-car design, the '64 Galaxie 500/XL enjoys a growing fan following today.

Besides the convertible above, '64 XL models included 2- and 4-door hardtops, both with "fastback" roof styling.

The big '64 XL cockpit. Dash design was similar to 1963's.

Most '64 XLs had the 390 V-8. Virile 427 was optional.

Ford challenger. Ford told NASCAR this was unfair. If Chrylser could race the hemi, Ford ought to be allowed to use its overhead-cam 427. Not quite, NASCAR replied, but the non-ohc 427 could have a high-rise manifold and a higher rev limit, both of which Ford quickly attended to.

The hemis grabbed the limelight: Plymouth won the Daytona 500 and the World 600 at Charlotte, NC. Mopars also finished 1-2-3 at the Darlington 500. But when the smoke cleared, Ford was still the star of the show: 30 NASCAR victories.

The 1964 Galaxie 500/XL 2-door hardtop. Price was $3233.

The companion drop-top XL retailed for $3495 this year.

1964 Galaxie 500 4-door hardtop carried a $2750 base price.

1964 XL front cabin featured these thin-shell bucket seats.

1964 Galaxie 500/XL mockup in the Ford Styling viewing yard.

The 1964 Galaxie 500 4-door hardtop

That mid-year performance option we mentioned showed up dramatically in a very small number of Fairlanes built strictly for dragstrip duty. Called Thunderbolt, they resembled the stock Fairlane 500 2-door sedan, but were different in almost every other way. The purpose of the Thunderbolt was to beat the similarly sized big-inch Plymouths and Dodges in NHRA competition, something Ford was deadly serious about. According to Phil Hall, author of *Fearsome Fords*, some 54 Thunderbolts were built by Dearborn Steel Tubing, which undertook special projects of this kind for Ford in those days. The heart of the car was the new High Riser, a fortified version of the already awesome 427, boasting two four-barrel Holley carbs on an aluminum high-rise intake manifold, plus high-rise heads, machined combustion chambers, domed pistons, high-lift cam, and a modified Galaxie driveshaft mated to a Detroit Locker differential. Compression ratio was a stratospheric

12.7:1. Because of its physical size, the big-block V-8 wouldn't fit the stock engine compartment, so the Fairlane's front suspension and much of the 427 exhaust system had to be modified and/or custom-fabricated to accommodate. Naturally, weight was removed wherever possible: fiberglass hood, front fenders, and doors; gutted interior; Plexiglas rear and side windows. Two transmissions were available, a very heavy-duty 4-speed with Hurst linkage or 3-speed automatic. The latter proved troublesome in actual use.

The amazing thing about the Thunderbolt was, as Hall points out, that "you could order [it] through your dealer, race ready, for about $3900. Considering what you got, it was stealing." Few people realized the car was a "catalog" item—except those drag racers who wanted to put Ford on the NHRA throne. Their efforts were generally successful, though the automatic proved a handicap against the MoPar 4-speeds. Highlighting the year was

Fairlanes were modestly facelifted for '64 and now shorn of their tiny rear fins. This is the 500 Sports Coupe.

The 500 4-door was again the best-selling Fairlane for '64.

1964 Fairlane 500 Sports Coupe hardtop retailed at $2502.

the S/S win by Butch Leal at the NHRA Nationals at Indianapolis Raceway Park on Labor Day. He hurled his Thunderbolt through the quarter-mile in just 11.76 seconds at 122.78 mph—in what some said at the time was the closest competition in memory. Partly because of the Thunderbolt's success, Ford won the NHRA Manufacturer's Cup for 1964.

As the "Total Performance" competition victories were making headlines, Ford released a very different sort of car this year: the fourth-generation Thunderbird. This third series of four-seat models made absolutely no gesture toward sportiness. There was no more Sports Roadster—though some dealers fitted leftover tonneaus and wire wheels to some 45-50 standard convertibles—and no more M-series engine. The plain 390 V-8 was again the only powerplant listed, still carrying the same 300-bhp rating it had three years earlier.

Planning for the fourth generation evidently took note

of the competitive challenge from the new Buick Riviera, which Ford knew about some time before GM launched its answer to the T-Bird for 1963. The Bird was given completely new sheetmetal featuring busy bodyside sculpturing, a bulging hood, and a dropped-center rear deck. Still keeping to a 113-inch wheelbase, designers put strong emphasis on quiet and refined luxury. The roofline retained the formal air of past models, but had a new feature in its "Silent-Flo" ventilation. By flicking a lever on the console, the driver could activate a servo that opened a full-width air vent under the rear window. The result was an extraction effect that pulled air entering at the cowl through the car and out the vent into the slipstream behind.

Exterior styling was overshadowed by a very jazzy interior, built around a dash that would have done justice to an airplane. No sporting driver liked the ornate speedometer with its red-banded drum pointer, or the chrome-

Thunderbird was all new for '64, and sales hit a new high. The Landau hardtop pictured saw nearly 23,000 copies.

Convertibles were on the decline, though: 9198 of the '64s.

1964 Thunderbird Landau, with anachronistic wide whites.

trimmed minor gauges, or the plethora of highly styled buttons, knobs, and levers that sprouted from every corner. But Ford would have Mustang for the enthusiast crowd; Thunderbird owners simply loved their cars. Despite rivalry from the elegantly muscular Riviera, the T-Bird ran up satisfying sales totals. The '64 broke 1960's record with 92,465 units; the '65 sold 74,972 copies; and the '66 scored 69,176. No three-year generation did better. The 1964 figure was not exceeded until Ford adopted the mass-production LTD II bodyshell for 1977.

Advertising said these Birds were "Begadgeted and Bedazzling," which was a fair description. But they were not simply "luxurious bombs." A '65 Landau tested by *Car Life* magazine, for example, was said to be ideally suited for high-speed motoring: "So quiet and effortless was the running that the...speedometer too often crept well past the 80-mph mark...This is precisely the type of service for which the Thunderbird was designed—covering vast distances between two points in the shortest legal time with the least extraneous intrusions upon the passenger's serenity." *Car Life* ran 0-60 in 10.3

seconds, recorded a top speed of 115 mph, and scored 13 to 16 miles per gallon.

Road & Track magazine, which almost by definition favored the design attributes of small imported sedans and sports cars, was less sanguine about the Thunderbird than its then-sister publication. *R&T* said the '65 had "more symbolism than stature. Only the blessedly ignorant view it as anything more than what it is: a luxury-class car for those who want to present a dashing sort of image, who worry about spreading girth and stiffening arteries, and who couldn't care less about taste."

But it misrepresents *R&T* to quote that remark out of context. "Even when viewed in that light," the editors continued, "the Thunderbird must be admired. It is extremely well done for its purpose. Its roofline, its bucket seats, and console have inspired dozens of lesser imitations which, by their very imitation, proved the Bird a better beast. And certainly when viewed from outside, the body lines of the present version have an overall cohesiveness and sense of dynamism that few mass produced automobiles seem able to match."

1965

Mustang gallops in as new full-size cars set the pace in NASCAR

During the 1965 model year a new name was added to the long roster of memorable Fords in the tradition of the Model T and V-8. That name, of course, was Mustang. The car bearing it pioneered a brand-new concept: a sporty compact with long-hood/short-deck proportions. Though Mustang was by far this year's most successful development for Ford, the division also presented an all-new big-car line that included what would become another favorite, LTD. Together, these products pushed Ford's model year production total well over the 2-million mark, a postwar record. More significantly, Ford pulled to within 203,000 units of industry-leading Chevrolet, whose sales improved by a much smaller percentage.

Ford wishes it had a winner like the 1965 Mustang today. When it was introduced on April 17, 1964 as a 1965 model, the Mustang made more news than Barry Goldwater sewing up the Republican Presidential nomination. America went wild over this sporty, long-hooded Ford—the first in a long line of automobiles that would become known, in its honor, as ponycars. Ford had projected first-year sales of 100,000 units. The final model year total (through December 1965) was an astounding 680,989. A legend had been created overnight. And the legend's base price was only $2368 f.o.b. Detroit.

The Mustang was born during 1961 meetings of the Fairlane Group, an informal eight-man executive committee headed by Lee Iacocca that met regularly at the Fairlane Inn in Dearborn. The group's assignment came from the division chief: to come up with a new, youth-oriented car to capitalize on growing buyer interest in

One of many Mustang styling studies completed under the "Allegro" project code in '62 was this racy fastback.

Wearing "Torino" badges and a "Cougar" grille emblem, this 1963 clay was directly related to the Oros Mustang design.

Mustang's ultimate proportions were evident in early mockups.

A show car called Allegro was publicly displayed in 1963.

This Allegro clay featured rather odd front fenderlines.

A convertible was part of the Mustang program early on.

Front view of above proposal shows pointy bumper/grille.

Above design was also mocked up as this Falcon-like coupe.

Mid-engine Mustang I idea car had V-4 power, only two seats. It was interesting, but potential market was too limited.

bucket-seat compacts with four-on-the-floor. Working under the project code T-5, the group considered and decided against both a revival of the 1955-57 Thunderbird (the "XT-Bird") and a production model patterned after the experimental Mustang I, a lightweight, mid-engine design with all-independent suspension and Triumph/MG proportions. The reason in both cases: only two seats. Iacocca's team shrewdly realized that such a car would have limited appeal—and none for young couples with children, or indeed anybody who occasionally needed back seat carrying capacity. The decision was made to go with the "median sports car," a four-seat proposal that established size and packaging requirements for the new model. Now, all Styling had to do was to develop an appropriate character for it.

During late 1961 and throughout 1962, Ford stylists produced scores of proposals. The one that ultimately impressed Iacocca most was a white-painted clay model dubbed Cougar. This low, sleek hardtop came from the Ford Division studio under Joe Oros, Gail Halderman, and David Ash, one of several teams competing in what

amounted to a not-so-friendly intramural design contest. A running prototype styled around this car called Mustang II was constructed, and very closely resembled the production car-to-be. It was shown to the crowd at the United States Grand Prix in the autumn of 1963. By then, of course, the production model had been nearly locked up in all aspects. All indications were that it would meet Iacocca's goals: 2500 pounds curb weight, a base price not more than a dollar a pound, and looks that said "young."

The Mustang was mainly a body engineering project. This was because, again at Iacocca's direction, the chassis, engine, suspension, and drivetrains would all be off-the-shelf Falcon and Fairlane bits, an essential part of the plan to keep the new car affordable. At 181.6 inches, the Mustang had the same overall length as the 1964 Falcon, though wheelbase was slightly shorter. Both hardtop and convertible body styles were planned, and Ford engineers projected the use of both the Falcon six-cylinder engine as well as the efficient 260-cid Fairlane V-8. The 170-cid six would be standard, along with three-speed

Variations on the Allegro theme were near limitless.

One of a parallel series of studies called "Stiletto"

Mustang II running prototype was shown at Watkins Glen in late 1963, provided sneak preview of production model.

Comparison of two production-approved Mustang prototypes shows "Cougar" name was in contention until quite late.

The handsome Mustang convertible in its "1964½" form

The convertible cockpit, with console and Rally-Pac gauges

Mustang's high-set grille looked awkward to some critics.

Spinner wheel covers, vinyl top adorn this Mustang hardtop.

This prototype '65 hardtop wears GT-style front foglamps.

Over 101,000 convertibles were built during Mustang's long debut model year. Price for the ragtop was $2614 basic.

manual gearbox with floorshift, full wheel covers, padded dash, bucket seats, full carpeting, and a color-keyed interior.

A key part of the Mustang concept was a veritable smorgasbord of optional equipment so each customer would be able to personalize his or her particular car. The menu included self-shift Cruise-O-Matic, four-speed manual, and three-speed-with-overdrive transmissions; a choice of three different V-8s; limited-slip differential; "Rally-Pac" (tachometer-and-clock combo wrapped in a small pod around the steering column); handling package; power and front disc (late 1965) brakes; power steering; air conditioning (except with the Hi-Performance 271-bhp V-8); center console; deluxe steering wheel; vinyl roof covering; pushbutton radio; knock-off style wheel covers; 14-inch styled steel wheels; and whitewall tires. There were also option packages: a Visibility Group (mirrors and windshield washers); an Accent Group (striping and rocker panel moldings); an Instrument Group (needle gauges and round speedometer); and a GT group (disc brakes, driving lights, and special trim). The most expensive extra was air conditioning at $283. Many desirable accessories were bargain priced: handling package ($31), disc brakes ($58), Instrument Group and Rally-Pac ($180).

Engine options played a big part in any Mustang's personality. During the long 20-month 1965 model run, powerplant offerings were shuffled slightly. The smaller V-8 offered for the 1964½ models was the 260-cid small-block with 164 bhp. Derived from it was the 289-cid version that produced 195 bhp with two-barrel carburetor or 210 bhp with optional four-barrel. A "Hi-Performance" version of the 289 four-barrel had 271 bhp. After September 1964, the 260 was discontinued, and a two-barrel 289 with 200 bhp became the base V-8. Output of the four-barrel unit was then boosted to 225 bhp, while the 271-horse HP was left unchanged. The four-barrel 289 cost $162 extra, the 271-bhp unit was $442.

The Hi-Performance 271-bhp engine was the ultimate factory powerplant. It developed .95 hp per cubic inch, and offered 312 foot-pounds of torque at 3400 rpm. It featured a high-compression cylinder head, high-lift camshaft, free-breathing air intake system, free-flow exhaust, solid valve lifters, low-restriction air cleaner, and chrome-plated valve stems. Although the HP's power seemed to be the answer to every dragster's dream, there were ways to improve performance even more. The $73 Cobra "cam kit" consisted of solid valve lifters and a 306-degree-duration cam with .289-inch lift. The $222 "cylinder head kit" comprised two stock HP heads with extra-large intake and exhaust valves and heavy-duty valve springs and retainers. Matched pistons combined with the cam and head kits made up the $343 "engine performance kit." Then there were carburetors and manifolds. A single four-barrel carb and a big-port aluminum manifold cost $120. With dual four-barrels it was $243, and with triple two-barrels the price was $210. As a final touch, a dual-point centrifugal distributor was available for $50. For stopping power to match the go power, front disc brakes were offered late in the 1965 model year as a $58 extra, and were well worth the money. Built by Kelsey-Hayes,

From bottom: Mustang I and II, the '65 hardtop and GT-350

they were cast-iron units of one-piece construction. Disc diameter was 9.5 inches.

Though Mustang was certainly attractive, it was not exotic or earth-shaking in appearance. But it looked light, agile, and clean, and suffered only by a few lapses. The most criticized were the non-functional bodyside "scoops" ahead of the rear wheel openings and the shallow, high-set grille that looked a bit awkward. Space utilization, given a fairly ample wheelbase, was poor, leaving the rear seat only marginally habitable by adults. Sports car magazines took issue with the driving position, the sloppy standard suspension, and the "borrowed" (from the Falcon) dash.

Properly optioned, however, the Mustang was a horse of an altogether different color. A 271-bhp model tested by *Road & Track* magazine returned blazing acceleration (0-60 mph in 8.5 seconds, the standing-start quarter-mile in 15.6 seconds at 85 mph, and a top speed of 120 mph). Its optional handling package (larger front anti-roll bar, 5.90 × 15 Firestone Super Sports tires, quick steering ratio) "eliminated the wallow we experienced with previous Mustangs [and tied] the car to the road much more firmly, so on a fast run the point of one's departure into the boondocks is delayed very considerably...There is a certain harshness to the ride at low speeds over poor surfaces, but this is a small price to pay for the great improvement in handling and roadholding." The editors called the Mustang 271 "a big step in the right direction."

Road & Track was the harshest of the reviewers. Most other publications liked the car about as much as the buy-

Mustang was purposely designed for Ford's small-block V-8s.

vide flow-through ventilation. Priced about $200 above the hardtop and mere pocket change below the convertible, it was a sales winner. Over 77,000 were sold for the model year, against 102,000 convertibles and—the really stupendous figure—over half a million hardtops.

A limited-production, high-performance offshoot of Ford's new ponycar arrived in mid-1965, about a year after the Mustang itself. This was the Shelby GT-350, a heavily modified Mustang fastback created at Ford's behest by former race driver Carroll Shelby. It was one of the few truly dual-purpose American production cars: brilliant on the street, superbly capable on the track. The impetus for it was Ford's desire to give the Mustang a solid performance image. And what better way to do that than by taking the Sports Car Club of America's B-Production championship from Chevy's Corvette?

The GT-350 accomplished precisely what it was built for: Jerry Titus won the B-Production national crown in 1965. Walt Hane won it again—with the same car—in 1966, and another GT-350 owned the class in 1967. The GT-350 was also successful on the dragstrips. It was, in a word, a thoroughbred. Today, it stands as one of the most coveted Fords of all time—surely one of the hairiest.

Carroll Shelby's involvement with Ford began in the early '60s, shortly after heart trouble forced him to retire from racing. Settling in Southern California, he operated a tire distributorship and, later, opened the first high-performance driving school in the U.S. At the same time, he nurtured the dream of building the world's fastest production sports car. But without sufficient capital and no firm design ideas or resources, his dream remained only that. Then Shelby had an idea. A.C. Cars Ltd. of Surrey, England, had a lovely, lightweight sports car called the Ace, but was about to go under for lack of engines. Ford

ing public. *Motor Trend* magazine's 271 did 0-60 mph in 7.6 seconds, and ran the quarter-mile slightly faster than *R&T's* car. It was obvious that with the right equipment, a Mustang could be a very interesting and satisfying automobile.

To mark the start of the official 1965 model year, Ford added a fastback body style (called "2+2" in the brochures) to the notchback hardtop and convertible in the autumn of 1964. Rear legroom was scanty—even less than in the other models—but it was sleek-looking. In place of quarter windows in the rear roof pillars it had little air vents, which functioned as air extractors to pro-

A near-final mockup for the Mustang 2+2, introduced in autumn, 1964. Hood ornament was fortunately scrapped.

1965 Mustang 2+2 fastback listed for $2589, and slightly over 77,000 were sold for the model year.

Here's the 2+2 with the optional GT Equipment Group. It included front foglamps, rocker stripes, dual exhausts.

Look carefully: this fiberglass mockup is for a two-seat Mustang, photographed two months after the ponycar's launch.

Mustang 2+2 mockup shows how stylists continued to play with details even after final design was locked up.

had just developed a powerful, small-displacement V-8 for its 1962 Fairlane that just might fit the traditional British roadster. After some adroit negotiations, Shelby modified the Ace to accept Ford's 260-cid V-8, and the Cobra was born. It was quite fast initially. With larger engines, the later versions were downright awe-inspiring.

As a hybrid sports car built in tiny numbers, the Cobra was never commercially important to Ford. But it was important in two other respects. First, it garnered a great deal of favorable publicity for Ford—and Shelby—by winning races left and right. And that *was* important for polishing up the image of anything powered by Ford. Second, despite its small numbers, the Cobra established Shelby as a manufacturer. Indeed, he had opened a small-scale assembly operation in Venice, California by 1962. Thus, when Lee Iacocca decided Mustang needed an extra dose of excitement, Shelby was the most logical choice. He had racing experience, he was a fine engineer, and he had made a name for himself—especially in Dearborn—with the Cobra.

Shelby's assignment was deceptively simple: modify the Mustang into a race car capable of winning the national championship in SCCA's hotly contested B-Production class. There were two requirements. First, the racer had to be readily identifiable as a Mustang if Ford were to get any sales benefit from the effort. SCCA rules also tended in this direction. Second, the rulebook stipulated that any model raced in a production class had to be built in quantities of at least 100 units annually. For this reason, two versions of the modified Mustang were planned from the start: a street model and a full-house ready-to-race car. Both would be available through the network of performance-oriented Ford dealers that Shelby had established earlier to sell his Cobra.

For no particular reason, Shelby's more muscular Mustang was called GT-350. Each started out as a white Mustang fastback built at Ford's San Jose, California plant and fitted with the 271-bhp high-performance 289 V-8 and Borg-Warner T-10 four-speed transmission. After delivery to Shelby, a High-Riser manifold, big four-barrel carb, hot cam, and free-flow exhaust headers were added, bringing engine output up to 306 bhp at 6000 rpm. The factory supplied the car with a Ford Galaxie rear axle instead of the stock Falcon unit. This gave a heavier center section and 10 × 3-inch drum brakes, which were fitted with metallic linings. The GT-350's rear axle location was by trailing arms. Koni shocks were used all around. The front suspension was heavily modified with relocated front mounting points and Ford's optional Kelsey-Hayes disc brakes. Shelby also fitted a large front anti-sway bar to provide extra roll stiffness and a heavy steel-tube brace that connected the tops of the front shock absorber towers to eliminate body flex under hard cornering loads. The GT-350 rolled on cast-aluminum, 15-inch-diameter wheels (with 6-inch-wide rims) made by the Shelby factory and shod with Goodyear high-performance tires. The stock Mustang steering box was replaced by one with a quicker ratio. The result of all this was near neutral handling, in contrast to the standard Mustang's strong understeer. The GT-350 driver could thus exploit the car's extra power for cornering to the limit.

The exterior was just as carefully thought out. The standard Mustang's prancing pony was plucked from the grille, leaving a simple rectangular opening. The steel hood was replaced by a fiberglass replica with a functional, built-in scoop. The dummy scoops ahead of the rear wheels were eliminated to clean up the car's side appearance. Finally, blue racing stripes were applied along the rocker panels. Another pair of much wider stripes split the hood, roof, and rear deck down the center to set off the white paint job. Some later cars were painted blue and had white striping.

The street GT-350 interior was only mildly altered from that of the production Mustang. The most obvious changes were three-inch-wide competition seatbelts, a mahogany-rim steering wheel, full instrumentation—and no back seat. The last was because of SCCA rules that took note of a car's passenger capacity. Shelby made the GT-350 a two-seat sports car by the simple measure of removing the stock back seat and relocating the spare tire to the empty space. For owners who occasionally needed to carry rear riders, a kit was available with a small bench seat that put the spare back in the trunk. All the street models used black interior trim and stock Mustang buckets.

The R-model full-race version was basically the same as the street car, but more highly tuned and specifically set up for the track. The competition engine was the same as the street mill except for special heads, and was rated at 340-460 bhp. In fact, it was the same unit used in the racing Cobras. The T-10 four-speed was unchanged except for an aluminum case to save weight. The interior was stripped except for a racing bucket seat, rollbar, safety harness, and necessary instruments. A heavy-duty suspension was used along with racing tires. The final touch was a new fiberglass nose that eliminated the front bumper, leaving a rudimentary air dam with a large central slot that acted as an air intake for an oil cooler. Some cars also had four-wheel disc brakes. The GT-350R weighed only 2500 pounds compared to 2800 for the street machine.

The GT-350 was homologated for SCCA Class B-Production, which meant it would compete against small-block Corvettes, Sunbeam Tigers, Jaguar E-types, and the occasional Ferrari or Aston Martin. A total of 562 Shelby-Mustangs were built as 1965 models, but no more than 30 of these were built to racing specifications. However, since all the special parts were available to private customers over the counter (per Shelby philosophy), anyone could turn a street car into the racing machine simply by removing and/or substituting parts. Many owners did just that.

In 1965, the GT-350 sold for $4547, about $1000 more than a standard V-8 Mustang and an equal amount less than a Corvette. This pricing put it right in the middle of the performance market. With 0-60 mph times averaging 6.5 seconds, a top speed of 130-135 mph, and race-car handling and braking, the car drew rave reviews.

The first-year Shelby-Mustangs would be the purest of the breed, and as such are the most highly prized today. Beginning with the 1966 models, the car was refined and softened until, ultimately, it was simply a plusher, more stylized version of the production Mustang, something completely different from Shelby's original concept.

While Mustang was setting sales records, the big Fords were giving the division its best-ever year in NASCAR, winning 48 of the 55 scheduled events. Although a rules dispute kept the factory Plymouth and Dodge teams out for most of the season, these and other makes were still represented by intermediates—which makes the big Ford's track record all the more impressive. Veteran Ford pilot Fred Lorenzen won that year's prestigious Daytona

A month after its launch, Mustang paced the 1964 Indy 500.

Fred Lorenzen's NASCAR Galaxie at Daytona

Lorenzen won the '65 Daytona 500.

First of the Shelby-Mustangs was the 1965 GT-350.

Ford's best NASCAR year was '65; 48 wins in 55 events.

Though little different from the production Mustang outside, GT-350 got numerous engine and chassis modifications.

The Galaxie 500 LTD hardtops debuted mid-way through the '65 model year.   The 4-door shown here notched 68,038 sales.

This limousine stretch conversion on the '65 LTD 4-door was produced in small numbers on a contract basis.

Popularity of the Galaxie 500XL slid for '65 despite new design.   Only 9849 of these convertibles came off the line.

Galaxie 500XL convertible retailed at $3498 for 1965.

1965 Galaxie hardtops retained the 1963-64 slantback roof.

1965 LTD 4-door hardtop carried a $3313 price tag.

Chrome was sparingly used on full-size Fords like this XL.

XL 2-door hardtop scored a bit over 28,000 sales for '65.

500, averaging 141.539 mph in a rain-shortened race. Bobby Johns placed third, also in a Galaxie. Of course, the stockers bore little resemblance to the all-new showroom models, now billed as being "quieter than a Rolls-Royce." Pride of the line was the limousine-like LTD, and all big Fords acquired more square-cut body lines. Yet the

500XL hardtop retained its semi-fastback roofline from 1963-64, and this undoubtedly contributed to Ford's victory streak on the supertracks.

Underneath its new styling and luxury demeanor, the full-size Ford was radically different. Author Phil Hall summarized this year's chassis engineering in his book, *Fearsome Fords:* "The frame and concept were new. There were now coil springs front and back. The front units were redesigned for strength utilizing the experience from stock car racing. Conventional coils were still between the upper and lower control arms. The design was so strong that it became the standard for NASCAR stock cars, regardless of make...right into the 1980s...The rear coil springs were mounted just ahead of the rear axle with two control arms anchoring the axle and springs to the body. A third member was attached to the right-hand side of the differential. There was also a panhard rod from the right side of the axle to the left frame member...Frames contained torque boxes for added strength. In addition, the bodies were strengthened similar to unitized bodies [and] the number of frame attachment points was reduced...While this had little to do with performance it did make for a quiet ride, something Ford would make a lot of noise about."

As before, the big-car lineup consisted of Custom and Custom 500 sedans, the full-range Galaxie 500 series, and parallel Station Wagon offerings. The '65 bodyshell brought with it cleaner, more stately lines, announced by a horizontal-bar grille flanked by stacked quad headlamps. The fussy pontoon bodysides of the '64 gave way to more flowing sheetmetal sculpturing. At the rear, Ford abandoned round taillamps for the first time since 1960 in favor of large, roughly hexagonal lamps. There were few changes in the engine department, but there was a new base powerplant, the 240-cid "Big Six" to replace the old 223-cid unit that had been around since 1952. There were six V-8s available, with horsepower ranging from 200 to 425 bhp, including two 427 big-block mills.

The mid-season debut of the posh LTD was a forecast of future big Fords, and it hastened the demise of the overtly sporty, bucket-seat XL. In fact, XL production this year totalled only 37,990, compared to its 1963 high of nearly 95,000. The LTD, offered in both 2- and 4-door hardtop models, scored over 100,000 sales this year alone. Overall sales for the full-size line were up for the third year running, but it was clear that buyer interest in bucket-seat big cars was on the wane. From here on, Ford's emphasis would be on luxury. Total production of the full-size 1965s was 978,519.

Fairlane was in the last year of its original 1962 design and, as is often the case in Detroit, was treated to a bevy of alterations to keep customers interested. A reskin below the beltline resulted in a more important, square-shouldered look, with some attempt at aping the new big-car appearance. Wheelbase grew half an inch (to 116 inches), and there were minor gains in rear track, overall length and width—and weight. The engine chart was redrawn by making a redesigned version of the 200-cid six, now with seven main bearings, the new standard offering. Optional choices comprised three 289 V-8s, with the high-performance 271-bhp version still top dog. New to the list

Ford bulked up its mid-size Fairlane for '65, last year for the original 1962 design. Pictured is the Sports Coupe.

The Falcon Futura convertible for '65, priced at $2481.

1965 Falcon Futura hardtop. Price now stood at $2226.

Last Falcon convertibles were the '65s, like this Futura.

Futura 4-door was second most popular 1965 Falcon at $2192.

All Falcons wore simplified grilles for '65, but retained '64 sheetmetal. Pictured is the Futura hardtop.

was a 225-bhp version with 10:1 compression and four-barrel carb. Despite the unusual number of revisions, Fairlane suffered in popularity. Production dropped to a new low of 223,954.

Falcon had been reskinned for 1964 and, except for mild trim shifting, retained this basic look for '65. Here again, Ford stylists had attempted a more important look, but somehow the extra sheetmetal and its plethora of creases and folds just looked silly on the 1960 body dimensions. Model choices remained the same. The most interesting variants were still the Sprint hardtop and convertible, but they were not popular in their final season. Only 2806 and a mere 300, respectively, came off the assembly lines. However, these hot little Falcons were still two of the year's best buys, priced at $2337 and $2671, respectively. Falcon finally got the 289 V-8—substituting for the little 260, which disappeared from Ford Division this year—but it was only the easy-going 200-bhp version, nothing to get excited about. Incidentally, Falcon was also in the

final year for its original platform. For 1966, Ford's compact would become a larger, heftier car.

Thunderbird was only mildly facelifted in this, the second year of the fourth-generation. A Bird emblem replaced block letters on the nose, chrome "C-spears" adorned front fenders, and taillamps were segmented into thirds for sequential turn indicators, a new gimmick. More significant was standardization of front disc brakes for '65, something this weighty personal car had long needed. In late March a fourth model—actually a trim package—was added. Called the Limited Edition Special Landau, it boasted "Ember-Glo" metallic paint and matching wheel covers, a parchment-color vinyl top, pseudo-wood interior trim, color-keyed carpeting and vinyl upholstery, and a console plaque bearing the owner's name. Priced less than $50 above the regular Landau, it saw only 4500 copies. Total Thunderbird production for the model year was down, sliding to about 75,000 units, a drop of some 18,000.

1965 Thunderbird Limited Edition Special Landau

Thunderbird convertible production fell to 6846 for '65.

Fourth-generation T-Bird received only minor trim changes in its second year. Pictured is the standard hardtop.

1965 Thunderbird convertible displays new segmented taillamps, which lit up in sequence to signal a turn.

1966

Getting serious about the muscle-car wars with a handsome new intermediate

Prototype Fairlane looks much like production model.

In an ad claim that bore some justification, Ford Division modestly touted 1966 as "the greatest year yet for Total Performance." Stars of the show were the totally redesigned intermediate Fairlane and its compact Falcon derivative. The year also saw the largest extension yet of the venerable FE-series V-8, still going strong after eight years. Ford had a very successful season, as production figures show. Its year-end tally was some 2.2 million, a shade over 6000 units ahead of Chevrolet's. Much of this success is attributable to continuing strong demand for Mustang, the mainstream big cars, and the new intermediates.

Pontiac had created a new kind of automobile in 1964: the muscle car. The formula was simple: a big-inch V-8 in a comparatively light, intermediate bodyshell. GTO was the first of the new breed, basically the larger '64 Tempest LeMans stuffed full of 389 V-8. It was an instant hit and, predictably, rivals were not long in following. Oldsmobile, in fact, fielded its 400-cid 4-4-2, a heated up F-85 Cutlass, the same year, and Chevrolet dropped its 396 V-8 into the Chevelle during 1965 to produce the SS-396. Ford, meantime, had to sit on the sidelines. The reason: its Fairlane hadn't been designed with sufficient underhood room for anything larger than one of the division's small-block V-8s. While these engines provided fine performance and made more sense from a weight/handling standpoint, the Fairlane was simply put in the shade by GM's muscular new middleweights.

Ford caught up quickly this year with an all-new Fairlane. Though dimensionally similar to the 1962-65 models, the '66 had more pleasing styling—and had been purposely designed to accommodate any big-block mill the engineers wanted to shove in. The GT hardtop and convertible were the muscle models. They packed a standard 335-bhp 390 engine with higher-lift cam, larger four-pot Holley carb, and a lower-restriction air cleaner compared to the next engine down the ladder, a 315-bhp 390. Standard gearbox was a 3-speed manual, but many buyers opted for the 4-speed unit with floorshift or the new "Sport Shift" Cruise-O-Matic. With the latter, you got special "GT/A" badges on trunklid and front fenders. "Sport Shift" referred to a new-design range selector (with console mounting) that permitted the driver to hold first or second gear to maximum rpm as with a manual. By contrast, other Fairlanes seemed pretty tame. They carried a modest 120-bhp six as standard, with options of 200-bhp 289 V-8, a 390 with 265 or 275 bhp depending on transmission, and the 315-bhp unit.

Besides the new GTs, Fairlane model choices comprised the usual body styles plus a new convertible arrayed in base and 500 series. The convertible was also available as a 500 or, along with the 2-door hardtop, as the new 500/XL. Both GT and XL came with all-vinyl front bucket seats and center console.

Styling for the '66 Fairlane was clean, crisp, and

All-new bodyshell made 1966 Fairlane sleeker—and provided room for big-block engines. Shown is the 500 hardtop.

contemporary—a complete break from the dowdy look of the past. A new front-end appearance was achieved by stacking the quad headlamps either side of a wide horizontal-bar grille, much as on the big '65 Ford. The fall-away front fender contour swept back past the broad, flat hood to mildly kicked-up "coke bottle" rear fenders terminating in a truncated rear deck with neat vertical taillamps. Hardtops were graced by a nicely integrated semi-fastback roofline.

While these hotter, smoother Fairlanes seemed to be just the weapon Ford needed for the muscle-car battle, competitors had not been idle. Pontiac, for example, offered up to 360 bhp in the GTO this year, and Chrysler made a street version of its fabled 426-cid hemi V-8—producing 425 *very* strong horses—available as the top power option for its mid-size 1966 Plymouth Belvedere and Dodge Coronet. Ford's response was to run off a very limited number of Fairlane 2-door sedans (about 70) equipped with the mighty 427, still rated at 410 bhp with single four-barrel carb or—that magic figure—425 bhp with twin quads. These cars also carried special fiberglass hoods with functional air scoop, and were destined solely for dragstrip service. Interestingly, no GTs were built this way.

Despite being down on ultimate power compared to its rivals, Fairlane enjoyed a near sensational sales year. Production totalled over 317,000, second only to the 1963 figure and an impressive 42 percent higher than the lackluster '65 total. The new GTs proved quite popular, outselling the tamer, less expensive XLs by some 8000 units. The GT ragtop was a rare bird: only 4327.

Falcon became more mid-size car than compact this year, and the reason had to do with developments at Lincoln-Mercury Division. Back in 1960, Mercury had fielded the compact Comet, a longer, slightly plusher version of the Ford Falcon based on the same unit body/chassis structure. When Ford introduced the Fairlane for '62, Mercury got its own version as usual, the Meteor. But Meteor failed to sell as well as Fairlane, and was dropped after only two years. For 1964, Comet was spruced up and elongated to fill in as Mercury's "intermediate," though it continued to share the Falcon platform.

4-door sedan was most popular Falcon Futura.

Club coupe was the cheapest '66 Falcon at $2020.

Company planning for 1966 decreed a new mid-size design, so Comet was moved up the size scale to share tooling with the new Fairlane. As it would have been too costly to tool up a wholly separate Falcon, the compact was cleverly turned into a short-wheelbase version of the mid-size cars. At the same time, Falcon would lose its hardtop and convertible body styles, the latter transferring to the Fairlane line.

Out of all this emerged the 1966 Falcon, from the cowl back nearly identical to the Fairlane. Front and rear styling was different, of course, as were wheelbases. The Falcon and Fairlane wagons shared an identical 113-inch wheelbase and, consequently, bodies. However, on Falcon

Fairlane 500XL 2-door hardtop was an addition to the revamped 1966 lineup. Price: $2533.

1966 Falcon Futura Sports Coupe.   Window sticker said $2328.

Mustang convertible's price rose slightly to $2653 for '66.

Hardtop was again the most popular Mustang in 1966.

The 1966 Mustang 2+2, here with GT Equipment Group option

4-door and 2-door "club coupe" sedans, wheelbase was 110.5 inches, an inch longer than before but 5.5 inches less than the new Fairlane's. There were no changes to the 1965 powertrain lineup, which returned with the mildly tuned 200-bhp 289 as the top power option. The most interesting model was the bucket-seat 2-door Futura Sport Coupe; the interesting Sprints were discontinued. In all, this new Falcon offered mid-size interior room and comfort combined with more manageable exterior size. Still, it wasn't that much cheaper than a Fairlane, and was eclipsed by the intermediates in both marketing emphasis and sales.

Mustang had been such an overwhelming success in its inaugural year that Ford understandably wanted to leave well enough alone. However, there were some minor alterations for the follow-up 1966 edition. Up front, the single horizontal grille bar was replaced by several thin bars as backdrop for the galloping horse emblem. The fuel filler cap was modified, but nothing else changed at the rear. Along the bodysides, the simulated scoops were decorated with wind-splits, nameplates were mildly revised, and wheel covers were restyled. Inside, the bargain-basement standard gauge cluster with strip speedometer was replaced by the more comprehensive five-dial instrumentation previously listed as an option, and Rally-Pac remained an extra-cost item. Engines were reduced to

Mustang demand continued strong for '66, but convertible output fell sharply to a little more than 72,000 units.

Trunk space was a Mustang shortcoming, as this 2+2 shows.

four. The base unit was now a 200-cid ohv six (the 170 was dropped). Optional were three 289 V-8s offering 200, 225, and 271 bhp. The option list was extended to include a stereo tape system and deluxe seatbelts with reminder light.

Overall sales of the '66s were not as high, because the '65 model year was longer than normal owing to the Mustang's early introduction. But for comparable 12-month periods, the '66 actually did better—by 50,000 units. Of course, Mustang still had no direct competitors. Chevy was a year away from launching its new Camaro, and sales of its Corvair were dwindling. Plymouth's hastily created Barracuda was recognizably just a fancy Valiant with a glassy fastback roof, and its sales were way behind

Mustang's. So, Ford happily counted the proceeds from selling a model year total of 35,000 fastbacks, 70,000 convertibles, and nearly a half million hardtops.

Dealer and customer feedback were behind most of the changes to this year's version of the high-performance Shelby GT-350. The most obvious ones were external: fixed Plexiglas rear side windows in place of the stock Mustang fastback's air-exhaust vents, side scoops for rear brake cooling in place of the stock windsplits, and the thin-bar grille adopted for the production Mustang this year, still minus the big galloping pony. Aside from these, there's no clear distinction between the 1965 and '66 models. The main reason is that Shelby did not always incorporate specific changes with the first car of a new model year, preferring instead to use up parts on hand before stocking new ones—just like in the days of the Model A. Thus, the first approximately 250 of the '66s were actually leftover '65s with all the new cosmetic touches but the previous suspension, interior, and blue-on-white paint scheme.

When actual 1966 production began, color choices were expanded to red, blue, green, and black, all with white racing stripes. A fold-down rear seat, standard on the Mustang fastback, now became a Shelby option. Batteries were left in their stock underhood location. Heavy-duty Ford-installed shock absorbers were now used, but the special Pitman and idler arms that gave the 1965 its sharp steering were retained. The 1965 and early-'66 Shelbys used rear traction bars that ran from inside the car to the top of the rear axle; later models used Traction Master underride bars. Early cars also had lowered front A-arms that altered the steering geometry for improved cornering. This refinement was determined not to be "cost-effective," and was discontinued on later '66 cars.

Engines and drivelines remained the same. The Detroit

Rear side scoops, rear quarter windows marked '66 GT-350.

The 1966 Shelby GT-350 was a bit more civilized than the '65.

One of the special black and gold GT-350H cars for Hertz

Color choices were expanded on the 1966 Shelby GT-350.

Shelby-Mustang production totalled 2380 cars for the 1966 model year. Every one is a blue-chip collectible today.

Special stretched LTD 4-door was continued for 1966. It's probably the world's only pillarless hardtop limousine.

Individual front seats identify this big '66 Ford as the XL version of the convertible. Base price was $3480.

"Locker" rear end was made optional, as was an automatic transmission. Large disc brakes in front and large drums with sintered metallic linings in the rear were also retained. Extra pedal pressure was required with these brakes, but they just didn't fade. The early 15-inch mag wheels (actually aluminum centers with steel rims) were replaced by 14-inch rims. These were either chrome styled steel or cast-aluminum alloy, at the buyer's option.

While the 1966 GT-350 wasn't quite as loud or fierce as the previous version, Shelby nevertheless kept it interesting. As an option, he offered a Paxton centrifugal supercharger. (A special GT-350S was envisioned, but never actually released.) The blown engine was advertised with a horsepower increase of "up to 46 percent."

Increased production was planned for 1966 so that every Shelby dealer who wanted cars could get them. Shelby also sold the Hertz rental-car company on the idea of buying about 1000 special GT-350H cars, all of which were finished in black with gold stripes. Hertz made them available at major airports throughout 1966. A lot of them returned from a weekend's use with definite signs of competition. Not surprisingly, Hertz soon found the GT-350H venture a mite unprofitable.

Shelby-Mustang production for '66 totaled 2380 units, including 936 Hertz models and six specially built convertibles that Shelby gave away as gifts at the end of the model year. No R-model racers were constructed, though a few leftover '65s were registered as 1966s. Shelbys continued to race and win this year, although they were essentially the same cars that had run the year before.

Further up the scale, the full-size Fords were treated to detail appearance changes. Taillights became more square, the grille and hood were pushed forward a bit, and rear wheel arches were enlarged slightly, but the balance of the '65 styling remained intact. Pride of the line was the new Galaxie 500 7-Litre convertible and hardtop coupe. The model designation referred to its 428-cid V-8 (7.0 liters in metric measure). A new engine at Ford for '66, the 428 was created by combining the 4.13-inch bore from the old 406 with the 3.98-inch stroke of the 410-cid Mercury V-8. Displacement actually worked out closer to 427 cubes, but Ford called this new FE-series engine a 428 to avoid confusion with the high-performance big-block. Though it used 10.5:1 compression, a big four-barrel carb and hydraulic lifters, the 428 was not a performance engine. Rather, it was intended as a torquey, low-revving mill with the kind of low-end pulling power needed in the big cars, which were growing ever heavier and acquiring more and more power accessories. Output was rated at 345 bhp in standard tune, and there was a 360-bhp police version that was at least theoretically available to civilians.

Only 6360 of the '66 Galaxie 500 XL ragtops were built.

Big Ford power options for '66 went to 427 and 428 V-8s.

'66 LTD hardtop sedan was quite popular: 69,400 deliveries.

The 1966 Galaxie 500XL convertible, also shown above

Most of LTD limousine's stretch was in the rear doors.

The popular full-size Country Squire wagon for 1966

1966

Despite its heft (curb weight was over two tons), the 7-Litre was quite fast. *Car Life* magazine tested one with automatic, and ran the 0-60 mph dash in a very creditable 8.0 seconds flat. But the 7-Litre was really a luxury car with just a hint of sport—much like the XL, in fact. (It even shared the XL interior with all-vinyl bucket seats and center console.) As such, it would find a limited audience. Only 8705 hardtops and a mere 2368 drop-tops were sold. The XL, too, was waning in popularity, though it fared considerably better: sales totalled 25,715 hardtops and only 6360 convertibles. By now, buyers looking for *real* performance looked to the mid-size muscle brigade, not big-inch, buckets-and-console full-size cars. However,

it should be noted that Ford's powerhouse 427 (at its customary 410 and 425 bhp ratings) was still available in this year's full-size line.

Though the 7-Litre wouldn't prove to be a success, its engine would. It was an option for other '66 full-size Fords as well as this year's Thunderbird, and would continue as such for several years. Other powerteam choices remained as before. As a group, the big Fords did quite well. Production topped the 1-million mark for the first time in six years. As usual, the mid-line Galaxie 500 4-door sedan and 2-door hardtop were far and away the best-sellers.

A mild restyle and a couple of new options marked the

1966 T-Bird hardtop shows off new wall-to-wall taillamps.

Town Landau was the most popular '66 Thunderbird model.

Hood and grille were restyled for the '66 T-Birds.

Ford's 428 V-8 was new optional equipment for '66 T-Bird.

New 1966 Thunderbird Town hardtops had ultra-wide rear roof pillars.   Landau retained its previous S-bar trim.

last of the fourth-generation Thunderbirds. Joining the lineup were the new Town Hardtop and Town Landau, the latter with dummy, S-shaped landau bars. They differed from the normal hardtop by the absence of the small, triangular rear quarter windows, replaced by C-pillars extended right around to the doors. Unique to both Town models was a standard overhead "console" (optional on the base hardtop) housing a bank of warning lights above the windshield header. The new roof gave the T-Bird a bulky, formal look—even more so when the accessory rear fender skirts were added—but it proved very popular with style-conscious Bird buyers. Combined Town hardtop sales were well over 50,000 units, while the "plain" version found only a little over 13,000 sales.

The T-Bird's standard engine remained the trusty 390 V-8, now rated at 315 bhp, and the new 345-bhp 428 was available at a modest $64.30 extra. A new feature was a cruise control system with buttons mounted in the steering wheel spokes for convenience. Ford initially called it "Highway Pilot Controls;" later, it would be known as "Fingertip Speed Control." Leather upholstery with reclining front passenger seat was another new extra at $147, as was 8-track stereo tape player combined with AM radio at $81.55. All models featured a new checked grille pattern adorned with a wide-winged Bird emblem, and taillamp lenses spread completely across the back panel for the first time, still with sequential turn signals.

Significantly, 1966 would be the last year for the factory-built T-Bird convertible. Buyers in this market had long shown a preference for the greater comfort of closed models with air conditioning, reflected in sales of the final rag top, only 5049. Overall Thunderbird sales slipped this year, dipping to near 69,000 units, a loss of some 5000 cars.

Bird no longer needed any pretense of sportiness, especially since Mustang and the attractive new Fairlanes would cater admirably to the younger, performance-oriented crowd.

The fifth-generation Thunderbird announced for 1967 was, perhaps, the purest expression of the personal-luxury concept yet, and it firmly fixed the Bird's shape, size, and character for the next decade. This new Bird was larger, heavier, and plusher than any that had gone before. In place of the convertible was a new 4-door Landau sedan, built on a 117.2-inch wheelbase—nearly as long as that of the full-size Fords. Base and Landau 2-door hardtops—with wide C-pillars and tiny quarter windows that slid back into them—returned on a 114.7-inch chassis, up 1.5 inches from the 1964-66 models. Powerteams remained the same: standard 315-bhp 390 V-8 or optional 345-bhp 428. Both were available only with Cruise-O-Matic, now with the manual-hold feature (renamed SelectShift) introduced with the '66 Fairlane GT.

For the first time in 10 years, Thunderbird returned to body-on-frame construction. Richard M. Langworth in *Personal-Luxury: The Thunderbird Story*, points out this was "a move dictated by cost and a desire to reduce the price of body work. The frame consisted of two straight side rails joined front and rear by torque boxes. Rigidity lost through the departure of the unit body was largely replaced by stiffening ribs, sheetmetal crossmembers, and a full-length tunnel stamped into the floorpan. All 14 body mounts were located ahead of or behind the passenger compartment, to reduce noise and vibration within."

In appearance, the '67 Bird was quite fresh—almost striking—though vestiges of previous themes remained, especially around the sail panels and at the rear. The drop-center decklid was retained in muted form and tail-

1967

A new definition of personal-luxury, new competition in the ponycar field

For this final year before federal safety and emissions regulations took effect, Ford presented a totally new Thunderbird, plus full-size cars and a Mustang both re-skinned from the beltline down. The compact Falcon and mid-size Fairlane, new the previous season, were given only minor touch-ups, though the intermediates now offered their most powerful engines ever. Demand for Mustang remained strong and the new T-Bird turned in a better sales performance than its 1966 predecessor, but declines in mid-size and big-car sales brought the division's total way down. Model year production plummeted by half a million units—down to a little more than 1.7 million—while Chevy maintained its previous volume.

Earlier in the '60s, Ford officials had steadily debated the pros and cons of a Thunderbird sedan. By 1965, division chief Lee Iacocca and others were satisfied that the

Thunderbird 4-door was big news for '67--and a big car.

Landau name was shared by new sedan and this hardtop.

1967 Thunderbird models were the new Landau sedan (foreground) and base and Landau hardtops (above left and right)

All '67 T-Birds featured hidden headlamps for the first time. Front-end design was the work of L. David Ash.

lights still stretched all the way across the back, but the rear fenders now had fashionable "hippy" contours, bodysides were more massive, and hidden headlamps appeared for the first time, set in a massive, "wide-oval" grille.

In an interview with Langworth, longtime T-Bird designer Bill Boyer revealed that the '67 styling was actually the work of two separate studios, joined together: "It was a compromise in a way . . . [L. David] Ash had at that time what I think was called the Corporate Projects Studio, which was in competition with the Thunderbird Studio. My studio essentially did the roof, backlight, and rear half of this car. Dave was responsible for the front end. He had a design that he considered a giant Ferrari. Management liked [this] front end and our rear end with its hopped-up rear quarter. What we ended up with was an amalgamation, I would say just about down the middle . . . The 4-door version just sort of happened . . . We did a rendering in black cherry with a black vinyl roof, a 4-door with center-opening doors and a 'sail' on the rear door where it hinged to the body. Iacocca saw this and just about flipped. 'Let's get that 4-door nailed down,' he said."

The '67 T-Bird sold well, mainly on the strength of its new styling and greater size. Interesting gimmicks also helped, like the new Tilt-Away steering wheel, which not only moved out of the way laterally like the Swing-Away wheel of 1961-66 but also tilted up to the right. The most popular model was the 2-door Landau, but the new sedan scored respectable sales of nearly 25,000 for the model year. However, this would be the highest it would ever achieve, and the 4-door's popularity fell with each passing year until this body style was phased out after 1971.

The full-size 1965 bodyshell received a heavy "mid-life" facelift to carry it through two more years. While still massive, the new look was more flowing and less straight-edged than before. Main distinctions included hopped-up rear fenderlines, elliptical wheel openings, and a new two-element horizontal grille, still flanked by vertical quad headlamps. Rooflines on 2-door hardtops took on a faster slope. The LTD version had very wide C-pillars angled vertically at their leading edges, while Galaxie 500 and XL hardtops had larger, triangular rear side windows and correspondingly slimmer pillars.

Powerteam availability for the 18-model big-car line was unchanged, but the 7-Litre hardtop and convertible

The 1967 Galaxie 500XL convertible was a handsome and powerful brute, but only 5161 examples were built.

Full-size hardtops featured a faster roofline for 1967. Pictured is the XL version, now priced at $3243.

from '66 were transmogrified into an option group exclusive to the bucket-seat XL. Priced at $515.86, it included the 428 V-8, uprated suspension, and power brakes with front discs. The 427 V-8 was still available, but on a more restricted basis. Features new to the big Fords this year were Fingertip Speed Control, 8-track tape player, and SelectShift Cruise-O-Matic. The XL's standard engine remained the 200-bhp "Challenger" 289 small-block, and its standard equipment included "leather-smooth" all-vinyl trim, Thunderbird bucket seats, and "command" console with T-bar shift lever.

Big Ford production declined 15 percent for the model year, and XL sales hit a new low, barely 23,300—including a paltry 5161 convertibles. The luxury LTD subseries, bolstered this year by addition of a 4-door sedan, scored over 110,000 sales. Once again, the most popular single big-car offering was the Galaxie 500 hardtop coupe, at over 197,000 units.

The hot-selling Mustang ponycar finally got some competition for '67. Chevrolet fielded its new Camaro, rival Lincoln-Mercury Division introduced a plusher pony called Cougar, and Pontiac debuted its Firebird, a reworked Camaro, at mid-year. The Plymouth Barracuda,

which had appeared as a "glassback" version of the compact Valiant at about the time Mustang was launched, received a handsome new look all its own for '67, plus coupe and convertible body styles. Of course, Dearborn knew something of its competitors' plans in advance, and had readied some new features for the '67 Mustang. Chief among these was a bold engine option, the broadshouldered Thunderbird 390 V-8 with four-barrel carburetion and 320 bhp. With the carryover 200-cid six and the trio of 289 V-8s, the total number of available powerteams now stood at 13.

Though Mustang retained its customary 108-inch wheelbase for '67, sheetmetal was revised from the beltline down for a beefier look. Overall length went up by two inches, width by 2.7 inches and, most significantly, front track was wider by 2.6 inches, the latter to make room for the new big-block engine. The 2 + 2 became a true fastback this year, with a sweeping roofline to replace the semi-notch effect used for 1965-66. Other appearance changes were a concave tail panel and a few extra inches in the nose to go along with a more aggressive grille. Engineers pitched in with new rubber bushings at suspension attachment points for reduced noise

227

and vibration. The wider track also improved handling response. A general front suspension rework decreased the car's understeering tendency without the stiff springing that previous models had needed for good handling.

The 390 made the Mustang very brawny, but unfortunately it also brought a heavy front-end weight bias. Agile handling was not its forte despite standard F70-14 Firestone Wide Oval tires. The optional competition handling package (stiff springs, thick front anti-sway bar, Koni shocks, limited-slip differential, quick steering, and 15-inch wheels) was almost mandatory with the big-inch mill. It was also available with the 271-bhp 289, making a Mustang so equipped a grand tourer in the international idiom. But if you wanted to run seven-second 0-60 mph wind sprints and 15-second quarters, the 390 was the only way to go. Drag racers loved it.

Inside, Mustang shed another vestige of its Falcon origins with a completely restyled dash for '67. This featured two large circular dials in front of the driver surmounted by three smaller gauges. Ordering the optional tachometer eliminated the ammeter and oil pressure gauges in the large righthand dial, a retrograde step. The new Competition Handling Package was available only with the GT Equipment Group, and was not commonly specified, making it quite rare today. The GT package could still be ordered and, as before, was limited to V-8 cars. It included foglamps for the grille, rocker panel stripes, dual exhausts, power brakes with front discs, and fat wide-oval tires. You could also get an Exterior Decor Group with thin bars over the taillight panel and turn signal repeater lights mounted in a twin-scoop hood. And, as on the Fairlane, combining the GT group with automatic got you "GT/A" badges on the lower front fenders. The T-Bird's Tilt-Away steering wheel option was listed for all models.

It was almost a foregone conclusion that Mustang sales

Price for the restyled '67 Mustang hardtop was $2461.

Mustang 2+2 got a true fastback roofline for 1967.

A new option for the '67 Mustang convertible was a glass instead of plastic backlight, hinged to fold in the middle.

Mustang 2+2 shows off 1967's more aggressive lower-body sheetmetal. Car pictured has the desirable GT equipment.

would decline in the face of competition, and indeed they did—by about 25 percent. Most of the loss was sustained by the hardtop, but convertibles also suffered, trailing fastbacks for the first time. Yet the 1967 model year total of 474,121 units led the ponycar field by a wide margin. Interestingly, that was still better than *double* the most optimistic estimates of Ford's marketing mavens for the Mustang's *first* year.

The Shelby GT-350 was markedly altered along the lines of the restyled '67 Mustang. And, in typical Shelby style, Carroll went Ford one better by offering an even larger big-block engine than the Mustang's new 390. This was the Ford 428-cid V-8, warmed up to an advertised 355 bhp but closer to 400 horses by most estimates. As installed in the new GT-500, this unit featured an aluminum intake manifold breathing through a matched set of 600-cfm Holley four-barrel carbs. The GT-500 was highly popular, and outsold the smaller-engine GT-350 by a two-to-one margin. The latter still carried the Hi-Performance 289 V-8 with Shelby tweaks except the former steel-tube exhaust headers. Power output was still listed at 306 bhp, which is odd because without the headers and straight-through mufflers it was certainly lower than this.

To keep the car's weight down and its appearance distinctive, Shelby stylists created a fiberglass front end to complement the production Mustang's longer hood. They also put two high-beam headlamps in the center of the grille opening. (Some later cars have these lamps moved to the outer ends of the grille to comply with state motor vehicle requirements specifying a minimum distance between headlamps.) The 1967 Shelbys had a larger hood scoop and sculptured brake cooling scoops on the sides. Another set of scoops on the rear-quarter roof panels acted as interior air extractors. The rear end received a spoiler and a large bank of taillights. As a total design,

'67 Mustangs got this new, more imposing instrument panel.

The 1967 Shelby GT-350 at an apt place: the dragstrip

The Shelby-Mustang was restyled at each end and gained a new big-block companion model for 1967, the GT-500.

Mustang took the SCCA's Trans Am championship in 1966-67. Pictured is one of the Jerry Titus '67 racers.

Fairlane appearance was little altered for 1967. "GT/A" badges on this convertible signify automatic transmission.

After several years as a Falcon, the Ranchero car/pickup returned after a one-year hiatus as a Fairlane for 1967.

the 1967 Shelby was stunning. It looked more like a racing car than many racers. There was still nothing else quite like it.

Because the '67 Shelby was heavier than its predecessors, and because customer feedback indicated a preference for a more manageable car, power steering and power brakes were mandatory options. The new interior received some special appointments not shared with the production Mustang: a distinctive racing steering wheel, additional gauges, and a genuine rollbar with inertia-reel shoulder harnesses.

Shelby-Mustang production forged ahead to 3225 units for the '67 model year, much of it due to the new GT-500. Unlike the past two seasons, there was no attempt at racing the '67s—and for a very good reason: the new Shelbys were about equal parts luxury and performance, while the 1965-66 cars were primarily designed for performance, more like thinly disguised race cars that could be used on the street.

It should be noted here that Mustang won the SCCA's new Trans-American Sedan Championship in its first two years. Created especially for ponycars as well as U.S. and import compacts, the series was staged on road courses, and quickly earned a wide fan following. The initial 1966 Trans-Am schedule comprised six races, four of which went to Shelby-prepared Mustangs. The sophomore 1967

season saw serious competition from the Roger Penske Camaros and Bud Moore's Mercury Cougars, but Ford again won the manufacturer's crown as Jerry Titus took the Mustangs to four wins.

The intermediate Fairlane received only detail refinements this year. Exterior trim shuffling was confined to badges, taillights, use of wider bodyside moldings, and a new grille with a chrome horizontal divider bisected by three vertical bars. Engineering changes were minimal, but 390 V-8 offerings were cut to two, a 270-bhp two-barrel unit and a four-barrel rated at 320. The high-performance 427 engine was ostensibly available to give Ford an edge in advertised horsepower over the likes of the Pontiac GTO, Buick GS, Olds 4-4-2, and Chrysler's hemi-engine intermediates, but few saw the light of day.

Fairlane production fell by nearly a quarter for the model year, landing not far above the 1965 nadir. The total was 238,668. The 500XL and GT convertibles were quite scarce: only 1943 and 2217, respectively, were built. The hardtops were more numerous—14,871 and 18,670, respectively.

Falcon flew along basically unchanged. A new "crosshair" grille bar marked the front, and back panels on Futura models gained a brushed-metal horizontal applique between the taillights. The one new engine option for the year was a four-barrel 289 packing 225 bhp.

Mario Andretti won the '67 Daytona 500 with this Fairlane.

Fairlane 500XL hardtop sold for $2724 in 1967.

Ford built only 2117 Fairlane 500XL/GT convertibles for '67.

A NASCAR Fairlane makes a pit stop in Daytona time trials.

Falcon Futura Sports Coupe changed little for '67.

1968

Running to win with a new mid-size line and a raft of "better ideas"

A reasonable $3001 bought the 1968 Torino GT convertible.

A soon-to-be-famous, soon-to-be-quoted ad slogan arrived with the 1968 model year: "Ford has a better idea." Actually, what the division had mainly was a collection of new little ideas, plus one big one: a completely restyled intermediate line. The government had had a few ideas, too, and these were quite visible on all 1968 cars. Like the rest of the industry, Ford was required to fit certain safety items at no cost, like shock-absorbing collapsible steering column, front and rear side marker lights,

anti-glare interior brightwork, and non-protruding, more difficult to open inside door handles. The list would lengthen in future years. Also, exhaust emissions standards applied to all 50 states, not just California.

Overall, the division had a good year, reflecting a generally improved sales picture industry-wide. Model year

Rear quarter angle emphasizes the sleekness of the 1968 Torino GT fastback. Roofline was inspired by Mustang 2+2.

Distinctive bodyside C-stripes could be ordered to set off the '68 Torino GT fastback's slick lines. Model cost $2447.

The formal-roof Torino GT hardtop listed at $2772.

Mid-size ragtop was offered in Fairlane 500 trim at $2822.

production rose some 534,000 units despite a lengthy strike and a considerable drop in Mustang sales, but Ford still trailed league-leading Chevrolet in the perennial race by a healthy margin.

Mid-size cars took the limelight for '68 as each of the Big Three issued newly styled and/or engineered editions

of these increasingly popular models. Like its Mercury sister, Ford introduced a new name for the high-trim versions of its 1968 intermediates. The name was Torino, the famous Italian city. It graced a six-model group comprising five body styles: standard formal-roof 2-door hardtop, 4-door sedan and Squire wagon, plus hardtop, convert-

New Torino was honored by being selected as the pace car for the 1968 Indianapolis 500 Memorial Day race classic.

Slick Machete show car, based on the new Fairlane/Torino fastback, toured in 1968, hinted at future Ford designs.

This 1968 Mustang fastback carries the optional GT Equipment Group, distinctive bodyside C-stripes, styled wheels.

ible, and a new fastback hardtop in sporty GT guise. The Fairlane name returned on the lower-priced companion line, which offered the same body styles arrayed in base and 500 series. Chassis design and its 116-inch wheelbase (113 on wagons) was the same as in 1966-67, but overall length grew by about 4 inches, width by a half inch, and weight increased by around 120 pounds on the average.

With dimensions that now approached the full-size class, the new Fairlane/Torino was styled to bear an obvious relationship with the big Fords. Rear fenderlines had the now-obligatory hop-up so popular in the late '60s, and bodysides were more radically tucked under, as on the Mustang. Front and rear ends were pleasingly simple. Quad headlamps reverted to side-by-side positioning within a recessed grille cavity and front fenders jutted ahead slightly to house combined parking/side marker lamps. The new fastback 2-door hardtop was the real head-turner, with a roofline taken directly from the '67

Mustang 2 + 2. However, unlike previous sloped-roof intermediates like the AMC Marlin, this one managed to avoid looking fat and heavy mainly through an upward angled rear side window line and a deep backlight.

Fairlane/Torino engine selections were the usual array, but there was a new number among V-8s: 302. This small-block unit was simply the 289 with the same 4.00-inch bore but a longer 3.0-inch stroke. Rated at 210 bhp, it had been engineered with the new emissions standards in mind. It was standard for Torino GTs at the beginning of the year, but was made an option at mid-season, when it was replaced by a two-barrel 289. That engine lost 5 bhp to 1968 emissions tuning (now rated at 195), as did the optional two-pot 390 (now 265). The four-barrel 390 gained five ponies, though (moving to 325). Standard for non-GT models was the sturdy 200-cid six. It, too, fell victim to emissions controls at 115 bhp, five fewer than before.

The performance mills for '68 changed during the year.

New Sports Trim Group option package is illustrated on this '68 Mustang convertible. It included two-tone hood paint.

At the start, Ford listed one version of the big 427, a single four-barrel unit rated at a lower 390 bhp through a switch to a milder cam profile and first-time use of hydraulic lifters. However, it was available only with automatic—not what the drag set had in mind. Accordingly, it was phased out by spring in favor of the new 428 Cobra Jet, a huskier version of the engine used in the Thunderbird and full-size Fords. For drag racing and insurance purposes it was advertised at 335 bhp on 10.7:1 compression, but was undoubtedly much stronger than that.

After a lackluster NASCAR season in 1967, Ford roared back with a vengeance in '68. It captured 20 victories—more than any other make and twice as many as it had in each of the previous two years. David Pearson won the championship. The new mid-size fastback was a big help, of course, with much superior aerodynamics that had been designed with an eye to long-haul superspeedway events. In USAC racing it was the same story, with A.J. Foyt's Fairlane on top. And in ARCA (Auto Racing Club of America), Benny Parsons was king in a Torino. Despite all these wins, Ford still had one problem: the rival Mercury Cyclone fastback. It was faster still in the long-distance sprints because of its smoother front end, a fact Cale Yarborough and company rubbed in every chance they got.

Of course, the one race that mattered to Ford accounts was the sales race, and here the new Fairlane/Torino was a real champ. Production climbed better than 50 percent over the '67 total, setting a record at over 372,000 cars. Significantly, the most popular single offering was the slick GT fastback at 74,135 sales, and more than 32,000 of the Fairlane 500s were sold. Convertibles, by contrast, were falling out of favor: just 5310 of the GTs and a mere 3761 of the Fairlane 500s.

Mustang seemed to be falling out of favor, too. Model year sales topped 300,000—good but not great compared to the early years of Ford's ponycar. On paper the losses were difficult to explain given the improved overall market and the fact that Mustang offered the widest selection of engines and other options in its history. The probable explanation is continuing strong competition—and there was even more this year with the arrival of AMC's handsome new Javelin. Another factor may have been Mustang's familiarity. Since a major facelift had been carried out only the year before, the car wasn't altered much for '68. Besides, Mustang had been on the market longer than any of its competitors, and was a familiar "face" by this time. And as so often happens, fa-

Mach 1 name was first used on this '68 Mustang show car.

'68 Mustang Mach 1 show car featured early hatchback design.

A convertible body style expanded Shelby-Mustang offerings to four. It was offered as a GT-350 or GT-500 as shown.

miliarity leads some car buyers to shop elsewhere.

Styling changes for '68 were minimal. The grille was more deeply inset and the crossbars omitted, leaving the running horse to "float" in its chrome frame. The grid-pattern dummy rear fender scoops on the '67 were erased. A new option was a distinctive C-stripe tape treatment, so called because it started at the leading front fender edges and swept back to the rear fender indentations, where it looped around and ran forward again.

The Mustang engine chart was redrawn. Compression drops robbed the base six and optional two-barrel 289 V-8 of 5 horses each, but output on the optional 390 rose by 5 to 335. Transmission choices remained as before, except that sixes could no longer be teamed with 4-speed manual. The 390, however, was still available with a heavy-duty 3-speed. The 289 was phased out at mid-year, replaced by the new 220-bhp two-barrel 302. As in the Fairlane, it was a reasonable performance/economy compromise between the base six and the high-power V-8s, and it was reasonably priced at about $200 additional. A 250-cid six with 155 bhp, lifted from the Ford truck line, was also added at the same time.

To counter Chevy's growing escalation of the horse-power war, Ford offered its mighty 427 V-8 as a new Mustang option. Priced at a formidable $755, this semi-hemi powerhouse ran on 10.9:1 compression and packed a 390-bhp wallop. Its steep price and its heaviness (which tended to overwhelm the front suspension) kept it from being very popular. It was sold only with Cruise-O-Matic, though it would have been something else with four-speed and a stump-pulling axle ratio. The 427's typical 0-60 mph times were in the blistering neighborhood of six seconds, the fastest yet for a showroom-stock Mustang in

An early '68 Shelby GT-500 fastback. Production was 1253.

The Shelbyesque California Special, a '68 limited edition

a straight line. However, in anything other than a straight line it tended to oversteer or understeer heavily, depending on how hard your right foot was working, which may be why all but very serious drivers shunned it.

As had been the case with Fairlane/Torino, the 427 was hastily retired from the Mustang program at mid-year, and the 335-bhp Cobra Jet 428 was substituted. A quarter-mile zip of 13.56 seconds at a trap speed of 106.64 seconds caused *Hot Rod* magazine to sing the praises of the new big-inch Mustang. Also announced was a high-tech version of the 302, with special high-compression heads, larger valves, wilder cam timing, and a pair of four-barrel carbs. Rated at a humorous 240 bhp, it was clearly developed around the Trans-Am formula. After it got an OK from SCCA, Ford had trouble getting it into production, and few were actually made. But it didn't make much difference. Mark Donohue won 10 events with his Camaro, and Chevy collected the manufacturers' trophy. Mustangs only won three events.

Predictably, other Mustang options proliferated for '68. New to the list was the Sports Trim Group, consisting of woodgrain dash trim, two-tone hood paint (also available separately), Comfort-Weave vinyl seat inserts, and wheel lip moldings on sixes, plus styled-steel wheels and larger tires with V-8. A spring/summer Sprint package offered GT C-stripes, pop-open gas cap, and full wheel covers plus, with V-8, styled wheels and wide-oval tires. The GT Equipment Group itself remained essentially the same:

The 428 Cobra Jet V-8 as installed in the Shelby GT-500KR

Shelby GT-500KR replaced GT-500 at mid-1968. Chief difference was substitution of Cobra Jet 428 for normal 428.

grille-mounted foglamps, side striping, dual exhausts with chrome "quad" outlets, pop-open gas cap, heavy-duty suspension (high-rate springs and shocks, front anti-roll bar), styled steel wheels, and fat rubber. Despite all the go-go goodies, equipment installation rates this year indicated buyers were shifting from strict sport to a combination of sport and luxury. Other new '68 options were

rear window defogger and Fingertip Speed Control.

A somewhat rare, limited-production Mustang was offered this year only. This was the California Special, a customized version of the standard Mustang hardtop, available primarily to Golden State buyers. Styled along the lines of the Shelby-Mustangs, it was marked by a rear ducktail spoiler above a deep back panel housing wide

Just 933 of the GT-500KR fastbacks and another 318 convertibles were built for '68. Ford now handled assembly.

This Galaxie 500 was one of two convertibles in the 1968 full-size line. Price was $3108 list. Production: 11,832.

taillight clusters, plus mid-bodyside tape stripes and a plain grille cavity with foglamps but no Mustang emblem.

This year's edition of the Shelby-Mustangs got a facelift. Hood and grille were restyled and more conventional, taillamps were segmented to incorporate sequential turn indicators, and there was a new convertible body style, complete with built-in rollbar, available in both GT-350 and GT-500 form. The new 302 enlargement of the Ford small-block became standard power for the GT-350,

mainly for emissions reasons. Luxury options like air conditioning, tilt steering wheel, tinted glass, and AM/FM stereo now almost outnumbered the performance features. At mid-year, the GT-500's 428 V-8 was superseded by the new Cobra Jet unit and the model retitled GT-500KR (for "King of the Road"). Again, the big-block Shelbys proved more popular, outselling the GT-350s by two to one. Total model year production was up for the third year in a row, reaching 4450 units. Convertibles, as you'd expect, were more rare than fastbacks. The totals

The big Country Squire wagon returned for '68 at $3539.

LTD 4-door hardtop listed at $3206 for '68.

Hidden headlamps marked '68 LTDs like this 2-door and XLs.

A bit more than 50,000 of these '68 XL fastbacks were built.

The Thunderbird Landau sedan for '68, priced at $4924. Like all Birds, it was outwardly little different from the '67s.

are 404 of the GT-350s, 402 of the early GT-500s, and a mere 318 of the KRs.

Carroll Shelby had begun to tire of the car business by this time. It had lost much of its original attraction because Ford was now calling most of the shots and the "feds" were enacting rules that threatened to make his brand of car antisocial if not illegal. Perhaps the most significant change for the '68 Shelbys, therefore, was the transfer of production in late 1967 from Shelby's Los Angeles facility to Michigan. There, the A.O. Smith Com-

pany was contracted to carry out Shelby conversions of stock Mustangs. From here on, Ford would handle all promotion, advertising, and, future model development.

The fifth-generation Thunderbird entered its second year with only minor trim shuffling and one new engine. Sales dipped some 13,000 units to 64,931, the lowest since 1963. At the start of the season the familiar 315-bhp 390 V-8 was listed as standard and a new 429 engine was the lone option, but by the end of December 1967, only the larger V-8 was fitted.

Landau 2-door hardtop proved far and away the most popular 1968 Thunderbird. Production totalled 33,029.

The $4716 standard '68 T-Bird hardtop. Production: 9977.

1968 Thunderbird Landau 2-door retailed at $4845.

Chop-top Fiera show car dramatized the inherent sleekness of the full-size fastback hardtop styling.

Engineering V-P Harold C. McDonald with 1968 Techna show car

Lateral-opening doors were among many unique Techna ideas.

The 429 was one of the new "385" series engines (so-called because 3.85 inches was the stroke of the first design) offered for the first time this year. It was a cousin to Lincoln's big 460-cid unit also new for '68, and both would soon spread to lesser Ford and Mercury models, including intermediates. With bore and stroke dimensions of 4.36 x 3.59 inches, the 429 was rated at 360 bhp in the T-Bird. Its major advantage over the old FE-series was its greater adaptability to emissions control. The 429 would continue as the Thunderbird's powerhouse well into the '70s.

The full-size Fords were mechanically unchanged for '68 apart from emissions-tuned engines. Another round of lower-body sheetmetal surgery plus fresh nose and tail grafts yielded a more massive, yet still flowing, appearance. Sail panels on the "formal" notchback hardtops became less imposing (and obstructive to driver vision). On LTD, XL, and the Country Squire wagon, headlamps were hidden behind retractable "doors" matched to a special grille with a cross-hatch pattern unique to these models. The hoary old 427 V-8, considerably tamer than in previous years, remained the top power option

The 1968 Custom 500 2-door sedan, a big-car bargain at $2699

The Falcon Futura wagon retailed at $2728 for 1968.

Falcon was little changed for the third straight year, apart from federally required equipment.

throughout the model run (unlike Fairlane and Mustang, the big cars did not get the 428 Cobra Jet in 1968). The XL fastback and convertible lost their standard bucket seats at mid-year, but putting in a front bench and deleting a few other equipment items allowed Ford to cut advertised list prices. The 7-Litre package was replaced by a new GT Equipment Group, a $205 option available for the XL but only with the 390 or 427 V-8s. It included heavy-duty suspension, the requisite GT stripes and emblems, power front disc brakes, and wide-oval tires.

Sales of the full-size Fords dropped fractionally from 1967. After several consecutive years of decline, XL demand shot up to its highest level since 1964. Most of the more than 56,000 sold were fastbacks; the convertible accounted for only 6066 orders.

Falcon was largely ignored for '68. The only cosmetic changes of note were a new twin-element mesh grille, which would be continued through the compact's demise in 1970. As elsewhere at Ford, the 302 V-8 was offered as an alternative to the base six and optional two-barrel 289. With automatic transmission, buyers automatically got the SelectShift manual override feature.

Ford was still playing with two-seaters even in the late '60s. This one was called both Cobra II and Cougar II.

1969

A dramatic management shift brings more of everything to Ford Division

For 1969, Ford was "The Going Thing!"—or so said the ad writers. There certainly was a lot going on at Ford Division this year: a new-generation Mustang, a larger small-block V-8, the last of the compact Falcons, and larger, redesigned big cars. Also, two *very* hot new intermediates arrived to carry Ford's performance colors on and off the race track, while the Shelby-Mustang was about to depart. Two significant executive shifts were in place by '69-model announcement day. In a move that sent shockwaves through the industry, company chairman Henry Ford II appointed Semon E. "Bunkie" Knudsen, recently resigned as a General Motors executive vice-president, to be the firm's new president in early 1968. Also, John B. Naughton was promoted to the general manager's post at Ford Division.

In production, Ford's model year total improved by about 75,000 units (not counting 3150 Shelby-Mustangs), rising to a little more than 1.8 million. Chevrolet lost about 25,000, but still tallied slightly above 2.1 million cars. Interestingly, the full-size Fords accounted for the bulk of 1969 sales, slightly more than a million units.

Knudsen's defection from General Motors left Detroit gasping in astonishment. There probably hadn't been such a startling shift between rival automakers since Bunkie's father, William S. Knudsen, had left Ford after an argument with the elder Henry and went to Chevrolet. In the 1920s, "Big Bill" had built Chevrolet into a Ford beater, and now his son was trying to make Ford more competitive with Chevrolet for the '70s. Rumors about a drastic shakeup in Ford management began flying almost as soon as Bunkie went to Dearborn.

Knudsen's presidency meant a renaissance for performance Fords. He wanted lower, sleeker cars, with particular emphasis on fastbacks. In fact, Knudsen said that while "the long-hood/short-deck concept will continue...there will be a trend toward designing cars for specific segments of the market." While he denied Ford had any intention of building a sports car, he did hint that an experimental mid-engine car was being developed. (This turned out to be the Mach 2, a design exercise begun in 1966 making liberal use of off-the-shelf Mustang components wrapped up in a curvy two-seat coupe package.) He also assured the press that Ford's efforts in stock car racing would continue.

The compact Falcon, once one of Ford's biggest money-spinners, celebrated its 10th birthday for 1969—and was virtually unchanged from its 1968 form. The four-barrel 289 V-8 was deleted, leaving the 220-bhp 302 as the most powerful engine you could buy. The model lineup still

Mid-engine Mach 2 was strictly experimental, mainly an image-boosting show piece. Mustang mechanicals were used.

Falcon was in its last full model year for '69, and was little changed. Shown is the bucket-seat Futura Sports Coupe.

1969 Falcon Futura 4-door sedan listed for $2498.

The 1969 Falcon wagon, priced this year at $2660

comprised base and Futura series, each offering 2- and 4-door sedans and 5-door wagon, with the vinyl-topped Futura Sport Coupe 2-door continuing as a specialty item. Production was down almost all across the board as buyers deserted compacts in favor of the slightly more costly intermediates or lower-priced smaller imports. Ford had sensed the shift, and had readied a new compact to replace Falcon. Called Maverick, it was introduced on April 17, 1969, a date perhaps chosen for luck: that was the day on which Mustang had been launched five years before. (Because it was officially a 1970 model, Maverick is covered in detail in the next section.) Falcon would hang around, unloved and unpromoted, through the end of calendar 1969, when it was unceremoniously dropped.

Thunderbird returned for '69, again with few changes. Aside from the usual different grille texture and rearranged exterior brightwork, the one appearance alteration was elimination of the vestigial quarter side windows on the 2-door Landau hardtop. This created what author Richard Langworth describes as "one of the all-time great blind spots." Ford engineers did a bit of chassis tuning to give the 2-door Birds flatter cornering response and less roll, but except for a slightly lower ride height the basic all-coil suspension adopted for '67 was left intact.

There was one major new option for '69, one that would be widely seen in future years. This was an electrically operated sunroof, a rectangular panel cut into the roof that slid back to give the feel of open-air motoring without the drawbacks of a convertible. Sunroofs had been popular for years in Europe; T-Bird helped popularize them in America. Bucket seats had moved to the options column for 1968, and Landau sedan and hardtop buyers showed a marked preference this year for the now-standard front bench.

Overall T-Bird production declined by about 15,700 units for the model year to slightly more than 49,000. That was the lowest point since the abbreviated 1958 model run, and the picture wouldn't change much for the next few years.

Ford filled a rather obvious displacement gap in its engine lineup by introducing a new 351 V-8 engine for 1969. This was basically the existing 302 small-block redesigned by Phillip A. Martel, who had come to Ford from GM back in 1950. (Martel was also responsible for the new "385" series engine family that debuted for 1968 in 429- and 460-cid form.) A direct descendant of the 221/260/289 Fairlane family first seen in 1962, the new V-8 was stroked .5-inch (to 3.50 inches), but used the 4.00-inch bore of the 302. Author Phil Hall points out in his book *Fearsome Fords* that actual displacement worked out to precisely 351.86 cid, but the division decided to use "351"

The Landau 2-door hardtop was far and away the most popular '69 Thunderbird model. Base price now stood at $4964.

to avoid confusion with the earlier 352 Y-block engine. The 351 was optional for Fairlane/Torino, the full-size Fords, and all Mustangs except the new Mach 1, where it was standard.

It should be noted that the 351 we're talking about here is the "Windsor" unit, not the more famous "Cleveland" engine. It went into production at the Canadian plant from which it got its nickname in the fall of 1968, a full

year before the Cleveland arrived. While both V-8s had the same bore/stroke dimensions, the Windsor featured increased bulkhead strength in the block, a deck height raised 1.27 inches, and a new crankshaft with larger main and crankpin journals. Its intake manifold was of drop-center design, and its valvetrain included "positive-stop" rocker arm studs. The bore spacing of 4.38 inches, as in the original Fairlane 221 V-8, was also retained for the

Thunderbird 4-door Landau declined in popularity for '69. Only 15,700 were built, each costing $5043.

Ultra-wide rear roof pillars reappeared on '69 T-Bird hardtops after a two year absence. Shown is the Landau.

Cleveland engine. When that unit came into production, the Windsor was relegated to a secondary role, used mainly with low compression and two-barrel carburetion. The Cleveland engine became the basis for nearly all the high-performance Fords from 1970 through the end of 1974.

Ford spent some $100 million in tooling for the Cleveland engine. Its block casting was different than the Windsor's, with an integral timing chain chamber and water crossover passage at the front end. Its deck height was increased exactly 1.00 inch above that of the 302 block. Cylinder heads were dramatically different from the Windsor's. Valves were canted 9.5 degrees from the cylinder axis to give a modified wedge-type combustion chamber. In addition, the intake valves were tilted 4 degrees, 15 minutes forward and the exhaust valves 3 degrees backward to give shorter port areas with more direct gas flow. The valves were placed as far apart as possible so they could be as large as possible. Intakes had a 2.19-inch head diameter, and the forged-steel exhaust valves were 1.71 inches across their aluminized heads.

The Cleveland V-8's valvegear was also new in several important details. Independently mounted rocker arms had wide cylindrical fulcrums in place of the usual ball-stud mounts. These fulcrums were seated in guide slots milled into the mounting pedestals of the cylinder heads to give more positive control over rocker arm movements. Valvetrain durability was enhanced by shorter, stronger pushrods, a new camshaft, and stiffer valve springs (with inner dampers on four-barrel engines).

Fresh from the tires up described the 1969 full-size Fords. Though basic chassis and suspension design were altered only in detail, wheelbase was increased two inches to 121 (where it would remain through 1978), the first such stretch since 1960. Overall length went up, and there were fractional gains in track and overall width. The 21-model lineup began with Custom and Custom 500 sedans and wagons, progressing through seven Galaxie 500s, two XLs, and finally, the pinnacle, the LTD sedan, 2- and 4-door hardtops, and Country Squire wagons.

Styling was a nice mixture of Lincoln-Mercury pretense

The '69 XL "cockpit" dash. Note U-shaped shift selector.

The 1969 LTD 2-door hardtop. All full-size Fords were completely restyled on a longer 121-inch wheelbase.

At $3251, the '69 LTD 2-door hardtop saw 111,565 units.

Big XL fastback listed at $3069 for '69. 54,557 were built.

1969 Galaxie 500 "SportsRoof" 2-door hardtop. Price: $2930.

"Flying buttress" roof marked '69 Galaxie 500 fastback.

and the svelte brawn of earlier big Fords. Hoods were longer, rear decks shorter, and bodysides more shapely. Once again, headlamps were concealed behind flip-up doors on LTD, Country Squire, and XL models, which also shared an imposing, full-width eggcrate grille with protruding center section. Lesser models had a flatter, plainer face. The fastback 2-door hardtop, offered as a Galaxie 500 or XL, was renamed "SportsRoof" (as were all Ford fastbacks this year), and acquired "tunnel roof" or "flying buttress" styling with a near vertical backlight and sloping "outrigger" sail panels. Inside was what Ford called its "front room," a curved cockpit-style in-

strument cluster, with the rest of the dash swept away to give passengers, as the brochure boasted "room to relax, more room than Ford has ever offered before."

The big-car engine lineup was rearranged. Replacing the old 427 as the top option was the new "Thunder Jet" 429 V-8. There were two versions, a two-barrel 320-bhp unit and a four-barrel 360-bhp engine both running 10.5:1 compression and requiring premium gas. The 240-cid "Big Six" with 150 bhp was base power for all models except the LTD and Country Squire, which had a 200-bhp 302 as standard. Also available were a lone 390 rated at 265 bhp with two-barrel carb and, at mid-season, the new

351 Windsor in 250-bhp two-barrel form. For shifty types, a 4-speed manual gearbox was still optional, but only with the four-barrel 429.

This swankier package seemed to be a hit in the marketplace. As noted, big-Ford sales broke the 1-million barrier this year, the last time they would do so. Ford tried half-heartedly to promote the XL, listing the convertible and SportsRoof as a separate series and even bringing back the GT Equipment Group as an option with the big-block engines. However, bucket seats still cost extra, and other enthusiast-oriented features had long since been the province of intermediates and the ponycars. Still, XL sales blipped upward for '69. However, the drop-top remained a low-demand item. Of the nearly 62,000 XLs sold, only 7400 were convertibles, making this one of the rarest production-line '69 Fords.

Major changes had been planned for the Mustang long before Bunkie Knudsen took over as Ford Motor Company president. The ponycar had suffered three straight years of sales declines, but Knudsen appeared untroubled about its future prospects. "We are comparing today's Mustang penetration," he told reporters, "with the penetration of the Mustang when there was no one else in that particular segment of the market. Today [that field is] much more competitive." Knudsen, of course, had put Pontiac on the map years before with an extensive emphasis on performance and sporty features despite GM policy. He had then done much the same thing for Chevrolet. While Bunkie wouldn't have much influence on Mustang design or any other Ford until the 1971 models, he was able to make some last-minute alterations to the '69 lineup.

One of Knudsen's more productive personnel raids on his former employer was hiring stylist Larry Shinoda to head Ford's Special Design Center. Shinoda had worked under GM design vice-president William L. Mitchell since the early '60s, and had been involved with such stunning show cars as the 1960 Sting Ray racer, the Corvette Mako Shark, the Monza GT, and the Corvair Super Spyder. He favored wind-cheating shapes and eye-catching aerodynamic addenda: spoilers, front air dams, low-cut noses, voluptuous lines. Many characteristics of the "GM look" would show up later on Mustangs and other Fords.

Styling for the '69 Mustang was mostly completed by the time Shinoda arrived, with dimensions that marked a departure from the original ponycar concept. The new Mustang retained its customary 108-inch wheelbase, but was four inches longer (most of it in front overhang), about a half-inch wider, and some 140 pounds heavier than before. The bodyshell was completely new, but unit construction was retained and successful appearance themes continued. There was a more prominent "mouth" grille with eggcrate insert that carried two extra headlamps at its outer ends in place of the optional (and mostly ineffective) foglamps of previous years. The old side sculpturing was erased, but rear fenders now bulged noticeably above the wheel arches. Taillights were still vertical clusters, but no longer recessed in the tail panel, which was now flat instead of concave. The same three body styles were fielded, and the fastback—now named SportsRoof—acquired flip-out rear side windows. Driving

The 1969 LTD 4-door hardtop, luxury at $3278

Over 113,000 LTD 4-door hardtops were built for '69.

Handsome hauler: 1969 LTD Country Squire wagon, $3661

Country Sedan 6-passenger wagon sold for $3661 in '69.

Fleet favorite: 1969 Custom 500 4-door sedan, $2790

Mustang "Aspen" wagon was briefly considered for '69 line.

A pre-production prototype for the '69 Mustang Mach 1

range was increased by enlarging the fuel tank from 17 to 20 gallons.

Dimensional increases were evident inside, too. The new Mustang offered 2.5 inches more front shoulder room and 1.5 inches more hiproom than previous models due to a reduction in door thickness. A modified frame cross-member under the front seat allowed rear legroom to be increased by a significant 2.5 inches. Trunk capacity was enlarged "13 to 29 percent," according to bubbly Ford

press releases, but actually this wasn't much of a gain because there wasn't much space to begin with. A Mustang trunk could still only just manage a two-suiter and not much else.

Mustang model choices expanded for '69 with four new permutations. Two appeared at the beginning of the year, the other two at mid-season. Taking careful aim at the personal-luxury ponycar represented by Cougar and Firebird, Ford released the six- and eight-cylinder Mustang

Racy new Mustang Mach 1 sold strongly in its debut year. Car pictured has optional 428 Cobra Jet V-8.

Ultra-strong Boss 429 sold for $4798. Only 852 were built.

Boss 429 V-8 was a shoehorn fit, put out 360-375 bhp.

Factory publicity photo shows a Mustang Boss 302 in Trans Am trim. Ford bowed to Chevy in the '69 race series, though.

Grande hardtop. Priced at about $230 over the standard hardtop, it offered a vinyl-covered roof with identifying script, twin color-keyed outside rearview mirrors, wire wheel covers, a two-tone paint stripe just below the beltline, and bright wheel well, rocker panel, and rear deck moldings. Its dash and door panels were decorated with imitation teakwood trim, a very good copy of the real thing, and its body was hushed by some 55 extra pounds of sound insulation.

A much more exciting newcomer was the Mach 1 fastback, with a $3139 base price. As an intruder into Shelby territory, it featured simulated rear-quarter air scoops, decklid spoiler, and a functional hood scoop, nicknamed "The Shaker" by Ford engineers. Attached to the engine air cleaner, it stuck up through a hole in the hood, and earned its name by vibrating madly, especially at high revs. Though its dimensional differences were slight compared to other Mustangs, the Mach 1 was definitely the raciest of the new breed. Its broad, flat hood and sweeping roofline combined with NASCAR-style hood tie-downs and that aggressive scoop to create the aura of genuine performance.

Engine availability also expanded for '69. The base powerplant for all Mustangs except Mach 1 was the hardy 200-cid six. For $39 extra, you could have the 250-cid six with 155 bhp. Ford improved six-cylinder smoothness with "center percussion" [forward located] engine mounts. Competition manager Jacque Passino was optimistic about it: "We've been putting out Mustang sixes kind of artificially since '64 to fill up production schedules when we couldn't get V-8s. I think there is a real market for an inexpensive hop-up kit for the 250-cubic-inch engine." But he was whistling in the wind. A kit never materialized, nor did a fuel-injected six he also predicted, though both probably should have. V-8 offerings began with the 220-bhp 302-cid unit and ran to the top-line Cobra Jet 428, available with or without Ram Air induction and rated at 335 bhp. The standard Mach 1 powerplant was the new 351, a 250-bhp two-barrel regular-fuel V-8 available at extra cost on other Mustangs. There was also a high-compression four-barrel unit with 290 bhp, optional across the board. Rounding things out was a four-barrel 320-bhp 390 running on 10.5:1 compression.

For all-out performance the Cobra Jet was king. Developed by Ford's Light Vehicle Powertrain Department un-der Tom Feaheney, it made the Mach 1 one of the world's fastest cars. For this application it was thoughtfully combined with a tuned suspension designed by engineer Matt Donner. Donner used the 1967 heavy-duty setup, but mounted one shock ahead of the rear axle line and the other behind it to reduce axle tramp in hard acceleration. Result: a street machine that handled like a TransAm racer. The big-engine Mustang still exhibited final over-steer, but the rear end was easily controllable with the accelerator.

Plush Grande hardtop was a second new Mustang for '69.

Grande sales totalled 22,182 units. List price was $2866.

249

Priced at $3588, the mid-1969 Boss 302 was offered on a limited basis, but it was mainly for Trans Am racing.

"The first Cobra Jets we built were strictly for drag racing," Feaheney said. "The '69s had a type of the competition suspension we offered in '67. Wheel hop was damped out by staggering the rear shocks. It was not a new idea but it worked. Another thing was the [Goodyear] Polyglas tire. I really can't say enough about this...In '69 every wide-oval tire we offered featured Polyglas construction." All this talk of handling may obscure the matter of straightline performance. The Cobra Jet Mach 1 would run the quarter mile in about 13.5

Rear wing and "sports slats" louvers were standard on Boss 302.

seconds, as quick as the fastest four-seater in production at the time.

At mid-model year, Ford released two very exotic Mustang fastbacks, the Boss 302 and Boss 429. Both were created primarily to qualify for racing. The Boss 429 was built partly to satisfy NASCAR officials but mainly for drag racing. Priced at $4798, it was powered by a modified version of the 429 V-8 with thinwall block and semi-hemispherical—or, as Ford termed it, "crescent-shaped"—combustion chambers. Other features included aluminum cylinder heads, beefed-up main bearings, and cross-drilled steel-billet crankshaft. There were actually two Boss 429 engines. The "S" version had hydraulic lifters, and was fitted to the first 279 cars. The later "T" version had different rods and pistons, and used mechanical or hydraulic lifters. Both were nominally rated at 360 bhp in street form or 375 bhp in race trim.

To accommodate the big-block mill, the Mustang's stock front suspension had to be heavily modified for the Boss 429. The battery was relocated to the trunk, and an oil cooler was added to prolong engine life. On the outside, the Boss 429 sported a discreet "chin" spoiler, a large functional hood air duct, Magnum 500 chrome wheels shod with massive F60 × 15 tires, and no gaudy stripes or decals save for small i.d. lettering on the front fenders.

Conceived as a low-production "homologation special," the Boss 429 required too many modifications for Ford to be able to produce it economically, so construction was farmed out to Kar Kraft in Brighton, Michigan, a contractor that undertook such small-scale projects for Ford at the time. Even so, Ford undoubtedly lost money on every one sold. After a slow start, some 852 of these monster Mustangs were completed for the '69 model year.

Shelby Mustangs (GT-500 fastback shown) were restyled for '69, ended up busier-looking than the production model.

The Boss 302 was created to compete with the Camaro Z/28 in SCCA's Trans-Am series. To qualify it as a production racer, Ford had to build at least 1000 copies, but actually 1934 of the '69s were constructed. Despite its limited numbers, the Boss brought people into Ford showrooms like the original Mustang had back in 1964. Among its design touches were front and rear spoilers, effective at any speed over 40 mph. The four-inch-deep front spoiler was angled forward. The rear one was an adjustable, inverted airfoil. Matte-black rear window slats,

like those of the Lamborghini Miura, did nothing to enhance airflow but looked terrific. The aerodynamic aids resulted in a gain of perhaps 2.5 seconds per lap at Riverside Raceway in California with no increase in engine power.

Of course, there was an increase in power—a big one. The Boss 302 V-8 was advertised at 290 bhp at 4600 rpm, but estimates of its actual output ranged as high as 400 bhp. It had "Cleveland" heads with oversize intake valves and huge 1.75-inch exhaust valves, which were in-

A mere 335 of these '69 Shelby GT-500 ragtops were built. Price was $5027 compared to $4709 for the fastback.

Shelby GT-500 fastback for '69

1969 Shelby GT-500 convertible

clined in the big ports to improve fuel flow. Other engineering features were an aluminum high-rise manifold, Holley four-barrel carburetor, dual-point ignition, solid lifters, bolted central main bearings, forged crankshaft, and special pistons. To help prolong engine life, Ford fitted an ignition cutout that interrupted current flow from the coil to the spark plugs between 5800 and 6000 rpm, thus preventing accidental over-revving.

Boss 302 hardware also included ultra-stiff springs, staggered shocks, four-speed gearbox, 11.3-inch power front disc brakes, heavy-duty rear drum brakes, and F60 × 15 Goodyear Polyglas tires. Ford hadn't missed a trick: even the wheel wells were radiused to accept extra-wide racing rubber. On the street, the Boss was unmistakable, with matte-black center hood section and grille extensions plus special striping with "Boss 302" lettering. On the track, however, the Boss 302 bowed to Penske, Donohue, and Chevrolet in the '69 Trans-Am series, accounting for but a third of the dozen events on the card.

Car Life magazine tested both Boss Mustangs, and found the little guy quicker to 60 mph—6.9 seconds compared to 7.2. But the 302 lost in the quarter-mile at 14.85 seconds and 96.14 mph compared with 14.09 seconds and 102.85 mph for the 429. Top speed for both was shown as 118 mph. Axle ratios on both ranged from 3.50 to 4.30:1. The magazine also discovered that the Boss 429 was actually slower than the 428CJ Mach 1.

Mustang's expansion into both the luxury and performance ends of the ponycar field showed interesting results. Out of 184,000 cars delivered in the first half of 1969, only about 15,000 were Grandes but close to 46,000 were Mach 1s. On cue, division general manager John Naughton predicted "heavy emphasis on performance" for what he (or his press writers) saw as the "Sizzlin' '70s." Said Naughton: "We're going to be where the action is, and we're going to have the hardware to meet the action requirements of buyers everywhere."

Because Mustang changed for '69, so did its Shelby GT cousins. The heavier, longer, busier production styling was made to look considerably more rakish, but the effort was Ford's in Dearborn, not Shelby's in California. Highlighting appearance was a longer hood with a prominent bulge and NACA-type scoops, a loop bumper/grille with

single headlamps instead of the production car's quads, the customary bodyside scoops for rear brake cooling, a fiberglass spoiler, taillamps *a la* Mercury Cougar, and center-mounted twin exhaust outlets. The GT-350 was upgraded from the 302 V-8 to the new Windsor 351, while the 428CJ continued for the GT-500, which lost its KR designation. Convertibles were still available and, as usual, were outsold by the fastbacks. Also as usual, the GT-500 maintained its sales lead over the GT-350.

At the end of the model year, Carroll Shelby called it quits as an ostensible manufacturer. There were many

1969 Torino GT fastback. Base engine was now 220-bhp 302.

Torino GT fastback sold for $2840 in 1969.

Hot new Cobra packed standard 335-bhp 428 Cobra Jet V-8. Fastback version shown here was attractively priced: $3189.

reasons. Ever the individualist, he had begun by building the sort of car he himself had wanted to drive, but by this time he had to accept decisions made by committees, where lawyers and accountants usually overruled engineers and test drivers. The niche he had created in the Ford lineup was being usurped by production Mustangs like the Mach 1 and Boss 302, and competition from other makes was much keener. His cars weren't being raced much any more, and the newer models bearing his name were softer, slower, and far less virile. Shelby announced his retirement as race car developer and team manager on October 4, 1969. Shortly after that, Ford executive vice-president Lee Iacocca agreed to terminate the Shelby-Mustang program quietly. Cars still in the production pipeline at the end of 1969 were given Boss 302 front spoilers, black hood panels, and 1970 model year serial

Hood tie-downs, cartoon snake insignia, minimal chrome trim identified the '69 Cobra, Ford's budget muscle car.

All '69 Ford intermediates wore a modest restyle of the all-new '68 design. This is the Torino 4-door sedan: $2733.

Low production—just 2552 units—makes the 1969 Torino GT convertible a likely collector's car of the future.

numbers. A little over 600 were made, thus ending one of the most remarkable chapters in high-performance history.

The intermediate Fairlane and Torino returned for '69 appreciably unaltered, except for minor trim changes and optional availability of the 351 V-8. However, there were two hot newcomers to the ranks. One was the Cobra, a no-frills muscle car in the image of Plymouth's highly popular Road Runner, introduced the previous year. The Cobra wasn't fancy, just fast. It was offered as a 2-door hardtop with either the formal notchback roof or fastback SportsRoof. Although exact production figures aren't available (because Cobra body designations were shared with corresponding Fairlane 500s), we'll bet most of those built were the slinky sloped-roof kind. Regardless, standard equipment included the big 335-bhp 428 hooked to a 4-speed manual transmission, plus heavy-duty suspension, six-inch-wide wheels, and F70 × 14 wide-oval belted tires. The outside was devoid of extraneous doodads save for cartoon snakes (decals on early cars, emblems on later ones) on the tail and front fenders. Interiors were as plain as any taxicab's. Options included a wide selection of axle

ratios, Cruise-O-Matic, Ram Air induction with broad hood scoop, bucket seats, console, tachometer, front disc brakes with power assist, and limited-slip differential. Prices were very attractive: $3164 for the notchback and $3189 for the fastback.

The Cobra lived up to its ready-for-action looks on the dragstrips, where it proved to be the fastest mid-size Ford ever. Its typical quarter-mile time was 14.5 seconds, and the 0-60 mph run took a mere six seconds flat. Fuel economy was appalling—only 8 mpg or so—but who cared when gas cost but 30 cents a gallon? The Cobra gave a much needed boost to Ford's performance reputation among the street-racing crowd. And most professional road testers agreed that of all the '69 supercars it was the tightest, the best built, and the quietest.

Ford enjoyed its last big season in NASCAR stock-car racing this year, and part of the reason was the limited-production Torino Talladega. Named after the new 2.66-mile Alabama superspeedway that opened in 1969, this fastback featured modified bodywork designed to overcome the aerodynamic problems that had plagued the production Torino stockers the previous season. It was also Ford's weapon to counter the still-slippery Mercury Cyclones and Dodge's new long-haul winged warrior, the Daytona. The Talladega's key differences were all at the front. Its nose was longer by about six inches compared to the stock Torino's, and curved down slightly at the front to meet a simple grille (taken from the Cobra) mounted flush with the hood and front fenders. The stock front bumper was swapped for a sectioned Torino rear bumper. These changes, developed with the aid of wind tunnel tests, did indeed lower air drag, so the Talladega ran quicker than a '68 Torino on the supertracks with no more horsepower.

Even so, Ford sought NASCAR approval to run its semi-hemi 429 in the new car, but there was disagreement about how "production" it was. At the time, NASCAR rules didn't specify that an engine had to be sold in the model that was raced, so the 429s being shoehorned into Boss Mustangs counted toward certifying the Talladega

The slick Cobra in action at the Dearborn Proving Grounds

Squire wagon returned as part of the 1969 Torino lineup at $3107. Non-woodie wagons were listed in Fairlane series.

with this engine. The rules also required a minimum of 500 cars, so Ford scrambled. While the 429 wasn't approved until later in the season, Ford had the requisite number of Talladegas built in time for the Daytona 500 in late February.

Altogether, 754 Talladegas, including prototypes, were constructed. Equipment included the regular 428 Cobra Jet engine and Cruise-O-Matic, plus power steering and brakes (with front discs), the competition suspension package, and F70 × 14 tires on six-inch-wide styled steel wheels. All "production" Talladegas left Ford's Atlanta assembly plant with white body paint and flat-black hoods.

The Talladega proved formidable on the high-speed tracks. After a 10-year association with Plymouth, driver Richard Petty was enticed to the Dearborn camp this year, and won with the car his first time out, at the Riverside 500. Lee Roy Yarborough was victorious at the Daytona 500 despite being forced to run the old 427 wedge. David Pearson ended up with the NASCAR crown. In all, Ford won 26 Grand Nationals in 1969—a record never to be equalled . . . at least so far.

Super Cobra toured the auto show circuit in 1969, gave an advance look at styling changes on the '70 mid-size models.

1970

A fresh new compact appears in the midst of another executive shakeup

Ford entered 1970 with a new compact and heavily restyled intermediates. After operating briefly with a troika of presidents following Henry Ford II's dismissal of Bunkie Knudsen in 1969, the company appointed former Ford Division general manager Lee Iacocca as overall president this year. Previously, he had been in charge of Ford's North American operations.

The new compact, called Maverick, actually bowed in April 1969. Billed as "the first car of the '70s at 1960s prices," it was much the same sort of car as Ford's original compact, the 1960 Falcon, and had a similar price: $1995 (the original Falcon 2-door sold for $1912). It also had a similar mission: to counter small import models, sales of which had been creeping steadily upward since the mid-'60s.

Predictably, Maverick was pitched as a roomier, more powerful, more trouble-free import alternative. Like the original Falcon it had resolutely ordinary engineering.

The 103-inch-wheelbase chassis had a typical leaf-spring live rear axle, twin-arm front suspension with coil springs, recirculating-ball steering and all-drum brakes. Under the hood it was 1961 all over again. The standard engine was the same 170-cid cast-iron six (rated at 105 bhp) that had been optional in that year's Falcons. The familiar 200-cid enlargement of this workhorse was extra. Standard gearbox was a "three-on-the-tree" manual, and 3-speed Cruise-O-Matic was optional. Curb weight was in the vicinity of 2500 pounds, making Maverick quite a bit heavier than most of its foreign rivals.

Offered initially only as a 2-door fastback sedan, Maverick was contemporary if a bit overdone in appearance. *Road & Track* magazine noted that "it looks like an American car. That isn't necessarily bad...and the overall impression is detracted from only by the tiny tires [6.00-13s were standard], its fat-hipped look, and the rather unattractive grille...The vogueish blind-rear-quarter routine makes all three rear windows too small from both the visibility and styling standpoint." Inside, trim and equipment were quite basic, necessary to keep the price down. There were no instruments apart from speedometer and fuel gauge, for example, and instead of a glovebox you got a European-style under-dash shelf. However, the plain bench seats were covered in a tartan-

continued on page 273

Maverick was Ford's new 1970 compact. List price was $1995.

1970 Maverick styling was clean if a bit overdone.

Offered initially only as a 2-door sedan, Maverick boasted fastback "SportsRoof" styling. Wheels here are 14-inchers.

Top: Last of the first-generation four-seat Thunderbirds was the 1960 model. The "Squarebird" proved much more popular than the earlier two-seaters, and firmly established the T-Bird as a permanent part of the line. Right: The big news for 1960 was the compact Falcon, Ford's response to the growing late-'50s interest in smaller cars, especially imports. The mechanically simple, clean-lined Falcon scored a solid sales hit, easily besting Chevy's rear-engine Corvair and the Valiant from Chrysler. Bottom: The standard 1960 Fords got smooth new styling (without a wrapped windshield) on a 1-inch longer wheelbase. New to the engine roster was the muscular 390 V-8, a preview of things to come as the decade advanced.

A sample of Ford's wide early-'60s model line. This page: Thunderbird convertible for 1961 (above) and '62 (below) and 1962 Galaxie 500 2-door hardtop (left). Opposite page: The rare tonneau-topped T-Bird Sports Roadster for '62 (top) and '63 (center right), 1963 Fairlane 500 sedan (center left) and Falcon Futura convertible (bottom right), and the "1963½" Galaxie 500 slantback 2-door hardtop.

This page: The burly Galaxie 500/XL convertible, one of Ford's "Total Performance" fleet for '64 (top). The big Fords became quieter and plusher for '65 (Galaxie 500/XL convertible and 2-door hardtop, above left and right), but scored Ford's best-ever year in NASCAR competition. The Shelby GT-350 (1966 shown right) made Mustang the car to beat in road racing.
Opposite page: Mustang was Ford's biggest success of the '60s. Shown are the 1965-model hardtop (above) and 2+2 fastback (below).

Opposite page, top: Only detail refinements were made to Mustang for '66 (hardtop shown). Left: Big-block 428 V-8 was a new Thunderbird option for '66, which also marked the last year for convertibles like this. This page, top: 1966 Fairlane was handsomely restyled, offered 390 V-8 in hot new GT hardtop and convertible (shown). Above: The 1968 version of the Shelby GT-500, with standard 428 V-8.

Opposite page, top: The Original Ponycar was smoothly restyled for 1967 (convertible shown). Center: The new Torino supplemented the Fairlane as Ford's 1968 mid-size entry, and included this racy GT Sportsroof fastback. Bottom: The svelte 1968 Thunderbird Landau sedan. This page, top: The very rare 1969 Mustang Boss 429. Above: The Torino Cobra was Ford's budget muscle car for '69.

Ford's 1970 lineup ran the gamut from economy to luxury to pavement-ripping performance. Representing the first two categories are (clockwise from above) the Maverick 2-door sedan and Thunderbird hardtop; the performance machines included the mean-looking Torino Cobra, plush but potent Torino GT, Mustang Boss 302, and the unreal Mustang Boss 429. Mustang won the Trans Am crown this year, but 1970 would be the end for the true high-performance factory ponycars.

Opposite page: Most Fords grew in the early 1970s. Examples are (clockwise from top left) 1970 Mustang Mach 1, 1972 Gran Torino 2-door hardtop, 1973 Mustang convertible and Thunderbird. New subcompact Pinto (1972 sedan shown) was the exception.

This page: Mustang II (1978 hatchback and King Cobra shown upper left and left) bowed for '74, sold pretty well. Its 1979 successor (Ghia hatchback shown above) had a more European flavor. T-Bird was downsized for '77 and again for 1980 (below).

This page, above: Mustang continued
its winning ways for 1980 with the
Cobra, available with either turbocharged
four or small-block 255 V-8. Right:
The imaginative front-drive EXP
two-seat coupe of 1982. Below:
The front-drive Escort "world car"
quickly became a best-seller. Shown
is the 1982 GLX 5-door sedan. Opposite
page, top: A new smaller LTD with
wind-tunnel tested lines debuted
for 1983. Shown is the Brougham sedan.
Bottom: Ford's first convertible in
a decade appeared for 1983 as this
Mustang GLX model.

Above and below left and right: The 1983 Thunderbird reflects Ford's new emphasis on aerodynamics. Drag coefficient is a slick 0.35. Exciting new Turbo Coupe model features 2.3-liter turbocharged four with port fuel injection, 5-speed manual gearbox, uprated chassis, and special interior with inflatable lumbar support seats. Right: Front-drive Tempo was announced as an early-1984 entry, taking over from the highly successful rear-drive Fairmont in the compact class. Shown is the GLX 2-door.

continued from page 256

plaid cloth, and armrests and full carpeting were standard. Interiors were color-keyed to five whimsically named exterior hues: Anti-Establish Mint, Hulla Blue, Original Cinnamon, Freudian Gilt, and Thanks Vermillion. It was all part of Ford's attempt to promote Maverick as an economical "fun" car for those on a budget—or those who didn't like imports.

Ford liked to compare Maverick to the top-selling import of the day, the VW Beetle. Maverick cost about $500 more in base form, though Ford claimed it was more car. But given its well-known shortcomings the Beetle was, perhaps, too easy a target. And, as *R&T* opined: "If the Ford Motor Company thinks their new Maverick is going to instantly render the imported economy sedan unnecessary for the American driver, they've got to be out of their mind. It isn't a bad car, taken on its own grounds and given all its due, but outside of peppy performance (with the larger optional engine) it has almost none of the virtues that are common to the best of the economy imports..."

With 200-cid six and automatic, the magazine's test car ran the 0-60 mph dash in 14.5 seconds and returned 20.5 mpg on regular gas. But the editors criticized the slow steering, inadequate braking, and uncomfortable driving position. *R&T* concluded that "the Maverick's appeal

must lie in the fact that it is a slightly less big American sedan with an attractive price that may well satisfy those owners who aren't particularly sensitive to the cars they drive...and who want a simple, uncomplicated car that does a job of transportation without fuss or frills."

And in that, Maverick succeeded admirably. Production for the extra-long model year topped 451,000 units, very respectable given the market. Though it would be refined and modified as time went on, Maverick would continue to appeal principally to mainstream buyers and, on that basis, must be considered one of Ford's most successful products ever.

Maverick's arrival signalled the end of Falcon. The '69 models carried into 1970 virtually unchanged, then disappeared after 15,700 had been built. The nameplate would return briefly on stripped versions of the mid-size Fairlane/Torino for "1970½."

All-new styling "shaped by the wind" marked the 1970 mid-size Fords. Wheelbases grew an inch—to 114 on wagons and 117 inches on other body styles. Width spread by two inches, overall length grew by four. Interiors were redone, trim upgraded, and comfort and convenience options proliferated. Basic engineering was untouched. A new top-line Brougham series was added in line with this move upmarket. The GT convertible and "Sportsroof" fastback hardtop and the Cobra fastback remained the hottest members of the clan. The latter con-

Maverick sold strongly in its extra-long debut season.

Only 2262 of the 1970 Falcon Futura 4-doors were built.

1970 Falcon Futura wagon. Production was a mere 1005 units.

Falcon name resurfaced on low-line "1970½" mid-size cars.

1970 Torino GT convertible, again rare at 3939 units

1970 Torino GT SportsRoof with optional hidden headlamps

Styling on mid-size Fords became more sculptured for 1970. Shown is the Torino GT convertible with standard grille.

This 1970 Torino GT SportsRoof wears optional hidden headlamps, Magnum 500 wheels. Model's list price was $3105.

Cobra returned for 1970, but the notchback body style didn't. Base price was $3270, and total production was 7675.

tinued as Ford's budget muscle car, with standard four-barrel 429 V-8 packing 360 bhp. Power options for both GT and Cobra ran to the 370-bhp Cobra Jet 429 with or without Ram Air induction. Cobra appearance was highlighted by NASCAR-style hood lock pins, black-finish hood and grille, and fat glass-belted tires. "Sports slats" backlight louvers *a la* Boss 302 were an option for hardtops. GTs could be dressed up with hidden headlamps, "laser" bodyside stripes, center console, and spoked road wheels.

These mid-size Fords could be blistering street performers. The 300-bhp GT could touch 60 mph from rest in about 8 seconds; the 370-bhp Cobra could do it in a mere 6 seconds. But the new styling proved less aerodynamically efficient in superspeedway racing compared to the 1968-69 Torinos. The concave backlight was said to be one of the problems. Ford had little choice but to run its older models in NASCAR this year, this time without the services of Richard Petty, who returned to the Chrysler camp. Ford took just six big-track events, and by year's

1970 Torino GT looked more slippery than '69, but wasn't.

1970 Torino Brougham 4-door hardtop, a new top-line model

Mid-size 1970 fastbacks like Torino GT had concave backlight.

1970 Torino Squire wagon retailed at $3379.

"Laser" bodyside striping was optional for 1970 Torino GT.

Hidden lamps added aggressive air to 1970 Torino GT.

1970 Cobra with optional "sports slats" backlight louvers

A snail's-eye view of the 1970 Torino GT Sportsroof

351 V-8 was standard for the 1970 Mach 1.

Touted as the "number one" ponycar for 1970, Mustang faced more competition than ever. The beefy new Dodge Challenger and a completely redone Plymouth Barracuda companion appeared to do battle, followed at mid-season by the handsome second-generation Chevrolet Camaro and Pontiac Firebird. Mustang production fell alarmingly—to 190,727 units, down from nearly 300,000 for 1969—despite an exciting model lineup. Though part of the decline reflected the shrinking demand for ponycars in general, part of it had to stem from Mustang's familiarity. Even so, these were the last of the truly nimble, responsive Mustangs in the mold of the '65 original, and as such are worthy collector cars today.

Changes for 1970 were evolutionary. Styling was a tasteful facelift of the new 1969 design, marked by a return to dual headlamps, minor ornamentation shuffling, and recessed taillamps. The seven-model lineup comprising three body styles returned. Powerteams stayed basically the same, and mechanical changes were few. The hot Boss 302 remained a limited-production Trans-Am special: output was just 6318 units for the model year. The high-performance Mach 1 got its own grille with built-in driving lamps and standard rear stabilizer bar. New appearance options included backlight louvers, adjustable rear spoiler, and distinctive C-stripe tape treatment, all for fastbacks only. Optional Hurst shift linkage was new to Ford Division this year. The base Mach 1 engine was

end would abandon the Grand National and most of its other racing programs, including the Trans-Am and international endurance events.

1970 Mustang Mach 1 carried a higher $3271 base price.

Only 505 of the 1970 Mustang Boss 429s were built.

The high-winding Boss 302 regained the Trans-Am championship for Mustang in 1970. Production was low: 6318 cars.

Mach 1 remained the high-performance 1970 regular Mustang.

Like all Mustangs, Mach 1 reverted to dual headlamps for '70.

Mach 1 rear view reveals flat tail panel of 1970 models.

Boss 302 was priced at $3720 basic for 1970.

Boss 429 remained less "obvious" than Boss 302 for 1970.

Mammoth 375-bhp V-8 continued on the 1970 Boss 429.

The 1970 Mustang Grande trunk. Space was still limited.

1970 Mustang dash design was basically a carryover from '69.

277

Landau vinyl top was standard for 1970 Mustang Grande.

At 2926, the 1970 Grande cost about $80 more than the '69.

1970 Thunderbird Landau 4-door failed to crack 8500 sales.

The 1970 Thunderbird hardtop. Base list price was $4961.

Thunderbirds reverted to exposed quad headlamps for 1970.

High-angle shot emphasizes 1970 Bird's large "beak."

A heavy outer skin restyle rejuvenated Thunderbird's looks for 1970. Sales ran fractionally ahead of 1969 levels.

now a 250-bhp two-barrel 351 V-8. Power options ran up to the big Cobra Jet 428, rated at 335 bhp. At the top of the line was the incredible Boss 429, equipped with the 375-bhp crescent-head engine from the Torino Cobra. It's a rare car today: only 505 were built, all before the end of December 1970.

Thunderbird came in for some heavy sheetmetal surgery this year, but its basic 1967 body and chassis engineering was left substantially the same. New frontal styling reflected the influence of the now-departed Knudsen/Shinoda regime, marked by a longer hood terminating in a prominent, forward-thrusting snout, vee'd in the center. The effect was strikingly similar to the 1969

Pontiac Grand Prix, which must have confused buyers. Headlamps were exposed for the first time since 1966, and 2-door hardtop rooflines got a "faster" slope. The 360-bhp 429 V-8 remained the standard and only engine. Production ran marginally ahead of '69 levels, but the 4-door Landau sedan faded, scoring only about half as many sales.

The big Fords had been completely revamped for 1969 on a 121-inch wheelbase that would be retained through 1978. As is Detroit custom, few changes were ordained for the second year of the new design. Appearance was altered by means of different grille inserts and new rear bumpers with integrated horizontal taillamps. The model

The 1970 Thunderbird cockpit with optional bucket seats

The posh 1970 LTD Brougham 4-door hardtop: $3579

429 V-8 remained standard and only T-Bird engine for '70.

Lesser 1970 big Fords wore exposed headlamps, simpler grille.

Full-size Ford appearance changed little for 1970. Pictured is the Galaxie 500 SportsRoof fastback, priced at $3043.

1971

Ford horses aroung with a bigger Mustang and a new little pony

Just 6348 of the final big XL convertibles were built.

Revised grille marked the 1970 LTD Brougham 4-door hardtop.

1970 Galaxie 500 SportsRoof. Big fastbacks vanished after '70.

Cockpit-style dash was billed as the big Ford's "front room."

An all-new minicar and the largest Mustang in history made 1971 a busy year for Ford. The division was fresh from its best sales performance since 1966, recording over 1.8 million registrations for calendar 1970 against 1.6 million for arch-rival Chevy.

This year the Chevy-versus-Ford fight extended to a new arena: the increasingly important subcompact class. Ford's contender was the Pinto, a chunky-looking 2-door sedan on a 94-inch wheelbase, the smallest car yet seen from Dearborn. It arrived coincidentally with Chevy's Vega, a slightly larger small car with typically GM lines, powered by a 2.3-liter (140-cid) overhead-cam four of unusual construction. Both the new domestic minis resulted from programs launched in the mid-'60s to develop direct rivals to the various foreign economy models. Led by the quirky VW Beetle, import sales had climbed steadily, and accounted for 15 percent of the total U.S. market by 1970. That chunk was too large for Detroit to ignore, and Pinto and Vega intended to win some of that back.

Developed under the code-name Phoenix, the Pinto was the outcome of an earlier program that would have led to something far more radical. According to author Jan Norbye, this G-car, as it was called, "had VW exterior dimensions and [would have been] powered by a transversely positioned in-line four-cylinder water-cooled engine in the rear. The chassis configuration was [ultimately] discarded, but the G-car body was adopted for a new project...using a front engine and live rear axle." Phoenix envisioned use of certain components, mainly engines and transmissions, from Ford's German and British subsidiaries in a package sized to compete head-on with the Beetle. Thus, Pinto emerged as a conventionally engineered "world car." Its standard engine was a cast-iron, 1.6-liter ohv four from the British Ford Cortina, rated at 75 bhp. Optional (at $82 extra) was a 2.0-liter 100-bhp overhead-cam four from the German Ford Taunus. The standard 4-speed manual gearbox and optional 3-speed automatic were both imported, too.

Comparisons between Pinto and Vega were inevitable. *Road & Track* magazine said that while the Chevy is "by far the more interesting design...Pinto happens to be the more pleasant car to drive in everyday use—base model for base model—and carries a price tag some $172 less. To be sure there is 'less car' in the Pinto; where the Vega has disc front brakes it has drums; the Vega coil-and-link rear suspension, the Pinto simple leaf springs; it is somewhat less roomy, and in standard form it's not as quick as a standard Vega. But, thanks to a quieter and smoother engine, a superior gearbox, somewhat greater comfort for the driver and better finish throughout, it is subjectively the nicer car." Even so, Pinto lagged behind

line was augmented with a new Brougham series of 2- and 4-door hardtops and 4-door sedan. The XL convertible and "tunnel-roof" fastback hardtop, the last of the full-size cars with sporting overtones, made their farewell appearance this year. Big-Ford sales were strong (though not as much as Chevrolet's), with the Galaxie 500s and standard LTDs the most popular.

Vega and many imports in several key areas. *R&T*'s initial 1.6-liter test car needed 20 seconds to reach 60 mph, compared to 16.5 seconds for the Chevy and a brisk 13 seconds for the lighter Datsun 510. The editors also criticized Pinto's sparse instrumentation, lack of back seat and trunk space, the long stopping distances and poor directional control of the all-drum brakes, and the tendency of the lightly loaded back end to hop around. But it wasn't all bad: "Pinto is maneuverable and handles pretty well. Its rack-and-pinion steering...is not very quick...but it's a far cry from the wheel-twirling of the Maverick. Out on the road we found good cornering adhe-

sion, at least in the dry (with the optional A78-13 tires on 5-in. rims), and steering characteristics close to neutral...Mind you, it's no sports car, but for the economy-car class the handling can't be faulted." And economy was pretty good: 22 mpg in the *R&T* test versus 18.6 for the 4-speed Vega, though both trailed the sprightlier, 25.3-mpg Datsun.

R&T later sampled a 2.0-liter Pinto with the $32 front disc brake option, and liked the new small Ford even more. The engine, they said, "makes it a proper car," being "smooth and quiet, much better than the Vega in these respects." The 0-60 mph performance improved to a

Pinto styling was bulbous, but sporty in its way.

The 1971 Pinto 2-door sedan with optional roof rack

Pinto was the smallest domestically built Ford yet seen.

Hatchback Runabout was added to Pinto stable at mid-1971.

Pinto's distinctive shape wouldn't change much over a long, 10-year production run. Basic 2-door had tiny trunk.

Pinto engineering was conventional, but original concept envisioned a VW Beetle-like engine and chassis layout.

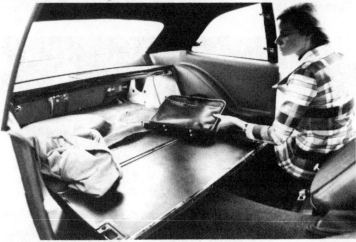

A view inside the 1971½ Pinto Runabout. Even with fold-down back seat, cargo space was hardly vast.

more reasonable 11.4 seconds, and there was no mileage penalty, the larger-engine Pinto actually proving .5 mpg thriftier than the 1600 model. As for braking: "The Pinto with disc brakes stopped in less distance from 80 mph than the drum-brake Pinto did from 70!" Fade resistance was 50 percent better and the car vastly better behaved. Summing up, *R&T* said "The larger engine and the improved brakes make the Pinto good value among the economy cars. It isn't as much fun to drive as most of the imports or as luxurious as the Toyota [Corona], but if your motto is Buy American, the 2-liter Pinto with disc brakes begins to look awfully good."

A lot of buyers agreed: Ford retailed over 350,000 Pintos for the model year. This was achieved despite a re-

call to fix carburetors on all early-production cars because of a rash of underhood fires, and short supplies of the 1.6-liter engine due to a strike in Britain. At mid-model year, Ford brought out an identically styled 3-door hatchback version of the sedan, with standard fold-down back seat and cargo area carpeting. Called the Runabout, it answered at least one Pinto failing, poor trunk space.

Pinto would go on to have a long 10-year production run, remaining a consistent best-seller despite emission controls, weighty safety equipment and, later, a fuel tank design proven unsafe. And, through it all, it would always outsell Vega. Pinto wasn't enough by itself to stem the import tide, but it did serve Ford well through a difficult decade.

The sole "Boss" Mustang in the 1971 lineup was the new Boss 351, with standard four-barrel 351 Cleveland V-8.

1971 Mustang Boss 351 featured flat-black hood paint.

'71 Boss 351 listed at $4124 basic.

Boss 351 would turn out to be a one-year-only model, which gives it minor status as a collectible today.

Mustang was all-new for '71, fully restyled and as big as Ford's ponycar would ever get. The new dimensions were dictated by Ford's belief that it could reverse the continuing sales slide by giving the car more interior room. This, presumably, was the main reason why compacts were generally outstripping ponycars in sales at the time. Accordingly, Mustang's overall length ballooned eight inches, width by six inches, and curb weight some 600 pounds. The familiar long-hood/short-deck proportions were retained on a one-inch-longer wheelbase, and the car was more heavily styled than ever. The new design reflected the look of Ford's GT Le Mans racers as well as the tastes of Bunkie Knudsen and Larry Shinoda. The most notable features were a sweeping, almost horizontal, roofline for fastbacks, plus a full-width grille and Kamm-style back panel inspired by the Shelby Mustangs. The model lineup stayed the same except for the new Boss 351, replacing the Boss 302 and 429 and powered by a tweaked four-barrel Cleveland 351 V-8 with 330 bhp. For other models the engine roster started with a modest 250-cid six and ran through the base-option 302 V-8, with two- and four-barrel 351s and the 429 Cobra Jet available for leadfoots. Later in the year a 351CJ appeared with 280 horses.

These "fat" Mustangs were not the agile handlers their predecessors had been and, with their greater weight, they needed larger engines just to maintain previous performance levels. *Motor Trend* magazine's Chuck Koch tested a 429 Mach 1 with SelectShift and 3.25:1 final drive. It was undeniably quick: 0-60 mph in 6.5 seconds, a quarter-mile time of 14.5 seconds, top speed of 115 mph. "It is a decent mixture for those who want good performance and some comfort, he wrote. Koch found the new Boss 351 quicker in the quarter than the big-block Mach

Seen at Ford's summer press preview, this 1971 Boss 302 was shelved due to the division's withdrawal from racing.

A production prototype for the 1971 Mustang Mach 1

1971 Mustang convertible saw only 6121 copies.

Like all '71 Mustangs, the Mach 1 sported dramatic new styling, a larger overall package size, reworked interiors.

The full-size Ford convertible shifted from the now-discontinued XL series to become an LTD model for 1971.

1 (13.8 seconds) but slower to 60 mph (10 seconds flat). However, the Boss handled better because of its standard competition suspension: beefier springs and shocks, staggered rear shocks, and stabilizer bars at both ends. The "cooking" 302 V-8 wasn't in the same performance league, but it was no slouch. Typical performance figures with 2.79:1 axle and automatic were 10 seconds to 60 mph, 17.5 seconds in the quarter-mile, but only 86 mph maximum. The 302 also delivered decent gas mileage, up to 17 mpg, making it arguably the best all-around powerplant choice this year.

Though it doesn't seem like such a bad car now, the '71 Mustang got a lot of bad press in its day and didn't prove nearly as popular as earlier models. Production took a nosedive, the total falling below 150,000 units. The ponycar market was fading fast, and greater size, copious options, and fresh looks just weren't enough.

The full-size Fords were restyled inside and out for '71,

1971 LTD Brougham 2-door hardtop

The 1971 Galaxie 500 4-door hardtop. Retail price: $3317.

New 4-door was a practical addition for the 1971 Maverick.

Late-1969 mockup for a stillborn Maverick fastback coupe

The LTD Country Squire wagon for 1971, priced at $4032

Favored by fleet buyers, the '71 Custom 500 4-door sedan

Maverick's other new '71 model was this Grabber 2-door.

Price for the standard '71 Maverick 2-door rose to $2175.

introducing a basic look that would continue for the next seven model years. Basic chassis design and the 121-inch wheelbase stayed as before. Again reflecting the Knudsen influence, there was a massive combination bumper/grille with deeply inset quad headlamps either side of an eggcrate-textured center section. Sharp horizontal crease-lines above elliptical wheel arches marked the bodysides. Rear windows on 4-door hardtops and sedans were slightly curved; 2-door hardtops had bulky sail panels ter-

minating just behind the door glass, where tiny vertical panes filled the gap. Inside was a new instrument panel housing all controls in a large pod jutting far out from the cowl. Model offerings were shuffled. The XL series was discontinued, the convertible moved to the LTD series, and the big "Sportsroof" fastback was dropped. The engine chart remained much the same, but there was a new 400-cid V-8, created by combining the 4.00-inch bore of Ford's small-block 351 with a 4.00-inch stroke. This rela-

The Torino Brougham 2-door hardtop for '71. Price: $3175.

Torino Cobra was downgraded to a standard 351 V-8 for '71.

Appearance on the '71 mid-size Fords was little altered.

Priced at $3295, the 1971 Torino Cobra was in low demand.

Returning as part of the top Brougham series, the 1971 Torino Squire wagon carried a suggested list price of $3560.

tively efficient engine had torque and emission characteristics suitable for family car applications. It would find its way into a variety of Ford products in the years to come.

Maverick gained broader appeal in its sophomore year with a second body style and a sporty version of the 2-door. The latter, modishly called Grabber, had a jazzy two-tone hood with curious fake scoops, extra lamps in the grille and no round emblem, plus dual racing mirrors, bodyside tape stripes, and flat hubcaps and wheel trim rings. Floorshift and high-back bucket seats were new op-

tions for both Grabber and the base 2-door. More practical folk were interested in the new 4-door sedan, built on a longer 109.9-inch wheelbase, making it about the same size as the last of the Falcons. Both Maverick sixes lost 5 bhp to emissions tuning, but a 250-cid unit with 145 bhp was now optional. Other changes included larger 14-inch wheels and tires as standard, extra-cost vinyl roof, and new colors.

After a decade, the Fairlane name was retired from Ford's U.S. lineup as Torino 500 became the middle series in the intermediate line. The mid-size cars weren't

Ultra-wide sail panels returned on '71 Thunderbird 2-doors, and all models wore more conservative front-end styling.

changed much apart from new split grilles and minor trim shuffling. The Cobra lost a lot of its bite, being downgraded in standard power to a four-barrel 285-bhp 351 V-8.

Thunderbird sailed along with few significant changes. Rooflines on 2-doors reverted to the huge, blind C-pillars of 1966-69, and all models displayed more restrained, horizontal-bar fronts. Sales continued at their previous pace, but the 4-door hit a new low of only about 6500. New to the options slate was a Turnpike Convenience Group, combining cruise control, reclining front seat backrest, and Michelin steel-belted radial tires. Highback bench or bucket seats were also available.

1972

Two model lines are redesigned to suit the market to a T

For the second straight year, Ford presented two completely new car lines. Quipped *Motor Trend* magazine: "The Ford Motor Company executive who claimed 'the annual model change is dead' must be joking. Either that or he didn't get a good look at the company's plans...."

The most visibly changed '72 Ford was the Torino, all-new from road to roof except for engines. A major departure was the switch from unit to body-on-frame construction, a first for mid-size Fords. This was in line with the firm's concept of using a rigid body on a flexible frame that, in effect, acted as part of the suspension to isolate road shocks. Accompanying this was a new four-link rear suspension with coil springs instead of the previous semi-elliptic leaf springs. Front disc brakes with new single-piston calipers were now standard, and there was a new steering linkage, integral with the boost mechanism when power steering was ordered. Front suspension remained much as before, with upper control arms and coil springs mounted on lower lateral arms.

Also new were different wheelbase lengths for 2- and 4-door models, now 114 and 118 inches, respectively. Overall width grew by 2.5 inches on 2-doors and 4.6 inches on 4-doors, and front and rear track were also increased. The separate frame plus added sound insulation made the new Torinos heavier. With all this, the mid-size Fords had now become about as large and weighty as the full-size Galaxie of the mid-'60s.

A slimmed-down model platoon comprised base Torino and new Gran Torino and Gran Torino Sport series, the latter replacing the old GT and Cobra. Convertibles were gone, and 4-door hardtops were now "pillared hardtop" sedans. Exclusive to the Sport was a full-fastback Sportsroof hardtop. Remaining offerings consisted of three 2-door hardtops, two sedans, and a trio of 5-door wagons. Styling was dramatically different. Front fender

The all-new Gran Torino Squire wagon for '72: $3342

1972 Gran Torino 4-door "pillared hardtop" cost $2675.

leading edges were pointed, wheel arches bulged, beltlines higher, rear fenderlines humped, and bodysides much more heavily sculptured. Gran Torinos carried a distinctive "mouth" grille flanked by quad headlamps and nestled above a scooped-out bumper. The standard Torinos used a full-width grille. Sport models were adorned with a simulated hood scoop.

A familiar group of powerplants was listed for the '72 Torinos, detuned where necessary to run on regular gas, a sign of the times. A 250-cid six and 302 V-8 were standard depending on model. A brace of 351 V-8s, one 400 and one 429 were the extra-cost choices. Most Torinos rolled out the door with SelectShift Cruise-O-Matic, but a 4-speed manual gearbox was available with the four-barrel 351.

A look at the long options list revealed these new intermediates were clearly intended more for comfort and smooth-riding quietness than enthusiastic driving. The only really exciting option was the Rallye Equipment Group, a $443 package for Sport models only. It provided full instrumentation with tachometer, plus higher-rate springs and shocks, rear stabilizer bar, 14x6-inch wheels mounting G70 wide-oval tires and, with manual transmission, Hurst linkage. The four-barrel 351 V-8 cost $127 extra. The 429 cost only $100 if you ordered it with the Rallye package. But the brochure stressed the new Torino's kinship with the big LTD in matters of ride, lux-

1972 Gran Torino Sport Sportsroof fastback hardtop

1972 Gran Torino 2-door hardtop: mid-size plush for $2705

"Mouth" grille marked '72 Gran Torinos like this Squire

The '72 Gran Torino Sport dash with optional instrumentation

Fixed-pillar 4-doors replaced hardtop sedans in 1972 mid-size lineup. Shown is the $2675 Gran Torino version.

ury, and room, and this year's Sport models would be the last "interesting" mid-size Fords in the spirit of the '60s.

Ford seemed to be right on the money with the new Torinos. Total production was up by some 170,000 over 1971, and the mid-line series accounted for about half the 496,000 units sold. The Sport fastback did well at 60,794 units, making it the third most popular model in the line. Some of this initial success may have been at the expense of the big Ford, which sagged by about 100,000 units this year. And some of it was no doubt due to lack of new competition, especially from GM, whose intermediate designs were now five years old. GM had intended to introduce new mid-size models this year, but delays forced a one-

year postponement. Even so, Torino sales were hardly affected for 1973, and they remained strong through the "energy crisis" 1974 model chase.

The personal-luxury Ford was billed as "More Thunderbird Than Ever" for '72, and for once an ad slogan proved accurate. In fact, the Bird was now a close relative of the new Continental Mark IV, sharing basic body structure, a new perimeter chassis, even one engine. There was also "more" to the price, now almost $5400 basic.

This largest T-Bird yet resulted from a series of decisions made shortly after Lee Iacocca moved into the executive suite at Dearborn. The main ones involved a return to more conservative styling and an increase in size so the

All-new '72 T-Bird was a cousin to Continental Mark IV.

More restrained front end distinguished the '72 T-Bird.

Landau bars, vinyl top were popular '72 Bird options.

1972 Thunderbirds still featured wall-to-wall taillights.

The '72 Thunderbird was offered in only one body style. The 4-doors were gone, as was the 2-door Landau model.

Bird could share components with the Mark IV and thus be sold more profitably. Accordingly, the slow-selling 4-door was dropped, and the mainstay 2-door got a 5.7-

Vinyl top was a $75 extra on the '72 Pinto 2-door.

Base price for the 1972 Pinto 2-door was $1931.

The '72 Pinto Runabout shows off its deeper hatch window.

'72 Pinto Runabout cost $2048. Roof rack was a dealer item.

inch longer wheelbase, now up to 120.4 inches. Overall length stretched out to 216 inches, some four inches less than the Mark IV. Though the center body sections of both the Continental and the new T-Bird were identical, Ford stylists played familiar themes at each end of their car. Up front was a much less prominent "bird beak" and a restrained horizontal-bar grille, plus squared-up front fenders housing the parking lamps. Flared wheel arches were accented by slim, full-length moldings about half-way up the bodysides, and the now-traditional full-width taillight lens brought up the rear. Though the new Bird looked heavier, it actually weighed a bit less than previous models.

Underneath the larger body was a new chassis. All-coil springing was retained, but rear geometry was now by a four-link arrangement. The upper links were mounted outboard and splayed inward, and were made of drawn steel rather than being stamped. A rear sway bar was also fitted. Power front-disc/rear-drum brakes were standard, and there was an interesting optional wrinkle called Sure Track. This was an anti-skid device that acted on the rear wheels to prevent premature lockup in hard stops. Not many buyers ordered it, though it was highly beneficial and much less costly than the Bendix all-wheel electronic system used on the Chrysler Imperial. The standard T-Bird drivetrain was Select-Shift Cruise-O-Matic teamed with the 429 big-block V-8, now rated at 212 bhp by the SAE net method (adopted throughout the industry this year). The lone power option was the 460-cid Lincoln engine, packing 224 bhp (net) and available only with air conditioning.

Buyers responded to the new T-Bird enthusiastically. Richard Langworth, in *Personal Luxury: The Thunderbird Story,* records that model year sales were 60 percent up on 1971, putting the Bird firmly ahead of its nearest rivals, the Buick Riviera and Oldsmobile Toronado. All together, close to 58,000 of the '72s were sold. Road testers found little to be excited about but, as Langworth observes, "the package was good enough to remain in production for five years, the longest of any [Thunderbird] design generation. While the Arab oil embargo of 1973-74 put a dent into sales of all large automobiles, Thunderbird maintained a solid lead against its most similar rivals throughout the life of the seventh generation."

In April 1972 a new wagon version of the little Pinto trotted out. Equipped with the optional 2.0-liter engine as standard, it was identical with the 2- and 3-door sedans ahead of the rear wheels, but had 10 extra inches in body length to provide good cargo space. The wagon could be ordered plain or as the Squire with woody-look sides, the latter earning the nickname "Country Squirt" in some quarters. A string of detail running changes begun in 1971 continued this year for all Pintos. These included an 8-inch deeper rear window for the Runabout hatchback, standard carpeting on the 2-door, and newly optional vinyl roof and Accent exterior moldings. Pinto sales improved by about 130,000 units, topping 480,000 for the model year.

Though the brochure described it as "virtually unchanged," the compact Maverick had a few new items. Notable was first-time availability of the small-block 302

1972 Maverick 4-door listed at $2214 with six, $2375 V-8

Longer Maverick 4-door had easier entry/exit than 2-door.

1972 Maverick 4-door sedan

New 302 V-8 option gave '72 Maverick Grabber good go.

1972 Maverick 2-door sedan: $2158/2318 with six/V-8

V-8. It was an especially good choice for the bestriped Grabber, but you still couldn't get a 4-speed or disc brakes at any price. Arriving in time for spring was a new Luxury Decor Option (LDO), available for both 2-door and 4-door. It included copper-color vinyl top and body-side moldings, matching wheel covers, whitewall tires, and low-back bucket seats with reclining backrests. Maverick sales slipped by about 17,000 for the model year.

Heavily revamped the previous year, the big Fords stayed pretty much the same for '72. Appearance was altered slightly with simpler grilles bisected by a new front

bumper cross-piece, and rear bumpers were extended up to the trunk opening on all models (except wagons, of course). The main new option for the year was an electric sliding sunroof for all models except the convertible, which was in its final season. The "Big Six" and 302 V-8 were scratched, and the base engine became a two-barrel 351 V-8.

There's nothing to do with a one-year-old design in Detroit except live with it, and that's what Ford had to do with the '72 Mustang. The main news concerned power-plants, now down to five with departure of the 429 big-

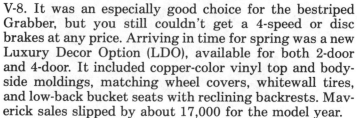

The 1972 LTD Country Squire 8-passenger wagon: $4385

The $3591 Galaxie 500 4-door hardtop for '72.

Front-end styling on full-size '72 Fords was modestly revised. Shown here is the LTD 2-door hardtop, $3853.

Sliding sunroof was a new big-car option for 1972.

1972 LTD Country Squire wagon

The last big Ford convertible was the '72. Price was $4026.

The 1972 Mustang convertible with optional Decor Group.

1972 Mustang hardtop, $2698 with six, $2784 with base V-8

block. Mach 1 was demoted to a standard 302 V-8, but it was still the hottest of the herd as the Boss 351 was also cancelled. On convertibles a power top mechanism was now standard. The disheartening sales trend continued.

Production sank to just under 125,000, a 20-percent decline and the lowest yearly total in Mustang history. Attempting to perk things up, Ford offered two mid-year option packages called Sprint. Both featured white paint

The 1972 Mustang Sportsroof with the optional Sprint package introduced for spring. Note rear fender flag decals.

The 1972 Mustang Grande: $2884/2790 with six/V-8

Mustang Sprint color scheme was red-white-and-blue.

with red accent striping, broad blue hood stripes and rocker panel paint, and stars-and-stripes shields on rear fenders. A complimentary color scheme was used inside. The better Sprint group included Magnum 500 road wheels carrying 60-series raised-white-letter tires.

1973

Dearborn turns to meeting "fed regs" in a mostly quiet model year

Aside from new lower body sheetmetal on full-size cars, the 1973 model year was a quiet one for Ford. Most of the engineering effort went into meeting another round of federal requirements, the most visible of which was heavier, bulkier front bumpers needed to meet the 5-mph impact protection rule that took effect this year. This also meant recalibrating suspensions throughout the line to compensate for the greater bumper weight—not to mention hard work by stylists trying to make the things look acceptable. Ford Division had a so-so sales year. Though it recorded some 80,000 more registrations for the calendar year, the division dropped below 19 per-

cent in market share for the first time in recent memory.

A below-the-belt reskinning made the big Fords appear more substantial and "important." All models wore deeper-section front bumpers and new grilles. The protruding nose was retained in a flatter, more muted form. LTDs had three-element grilles filled with little rectangles, while Galaxie and Custom 500s had a full-width grille. Along the sides the former creaselines were toned down and wheel arches took on a rounder form. Rear ends were redone, with taillamps now set above the bumper and the trunklid curved down in the center. The bigger front bumpers increased overall length by about three inches. And, although not immediately apparent, sedans and wagons got new greenhouse styling with deeper windows. Subtracting the LTD convertible and base Custom sedan and wagon left the model count at 16. The engine lineup stayed the same except for addition of the four-barrel 460-cid V-8 from Lincoln-Mercury as the top option. Inside, the "front room" curved instrument panel, a big-Ford feature since 1969, was abandoned for a more conventional dash that put both radio and climate controls on the driver's right. New options included a factory-fitted alarm system, power "mini-vent" front windows on 4-doors, and steel-belted radial tires. In a year when rival makes had little new, the big Fords picked up about 40,000 additional sales, reaching close to 858,000.

Thunderbird was facelifted for '73 with a busier egg-

New 5-mph federal bumpers changed the look of the '73 full-size Fords. Shown is the new LTD Brougham 4-door hardtop.

1973 LTD Brougham 4-door hardtop retailed at $4157.

1973 Galaxie 500s wore this simpler, full-width grille.

Now called a "pillared hardtop," the '73 Galaxie 500 sedan

The impressive-looking 1973 LTD 2-door hardtop: $3950.

crate grille flanked by headlamps in square chrome nacelles. Small parallelogram-shaped "opera" windows were a new option (at $80) for the rear roof pillars (vinyl top was required), and did wonders for over-the-shoulder visibility. Buyers responded to this more glittery package in record numbers. Production soared to over 87,000, the second highest total in T-Bird history after the record 1964 season. Base prices jumped substantially—to a bit more than $6400—and it didn't take many options to run that up to $7500 or more.

Only minor changes marked the last of the "fat" Mustangs. Slightly less than 10,000 additional cars were sold this year compared to 1972. Convertible sales scored the largest percentage increase—up 100 percent to nearly 12,000 units—but this was partly because Ford had announced in advance that the ragtop would be discontinued the following year. This would be Ford's last convertible of any kind for the next 10 years. A mildly revised grille with vertical instead of horizontal parking lamps marked the front, along with a nicely integrated

New the previous year, Thunderbird received a more sparkling front end for '73. Opera windows were newly optional.

1973 Thunderbird production totalled some 87,000 units.

1973 Thunderbird with optional vinyl roof, wide body moldings

Heavy and softly sprung, the '73 Bird was hardly a handler.

Mustang Mach 1 was far more agile. Price was $3088 basic.

safety bumper. An optional body-color polyurethane cover, previously used on the '72 Mach 1, was available for an even cleaner appearance. Mechanically, Mustang remained about the same. There were fewer axle ratio choices now, mainly due to the high cost of certifying each engine/transmission/ratio combination for emissions compliance under the Environmental Protection Agency's mandatory 50,000-mile durability test. Radial tires were a new option, as was a "dual ram induction system," a special hood with twin air scoops, black or argent

paint, decals, and twist-type hood locks, available with the two-barrel 351 V-8 option. A two-tone hood with the locks and non-functional scoops was also offered. Prices, which had been cut in 1972 to spark sales, remained fairly stable. The Mach 1 sold for $3088, the V-8 convertible for $3189, and the base six-cylinder hardtop for $2760.

Pinto sauntered on with beefier front bumpers as prescribed by Washington, plus a reinforced front structure to better absorb impact loads. These revisions added only about 1.5 inches in length and 40 extra pounds. Standard

1973 Mustang Mach 1, still a "flatback" Sportsroof

1973 Mustang Mach 1, shown with forged aluminum wheels

The 1973 models would be the last of the "big" Mustangs.

Long-lead car shows Boss-type spoiler not offered for '73.

Mustang tail styling stayed the same as 1971-72.

The '73 Mustang convertible with optional "tutone" hood

tires were upgraded to A78-13s, and air-conditioned cars got an extra pair of dash vents. New options included AM/FM stereo radio, forged aluminum road wheels, and a handling package. Model year production breezed past the half-million mark as Pinto continued to outsell the rival Chevy Vega by a comfortable margin. The wagon accounted for nearly 40 percent of the total.

Maverick's main improvement was 35 percent greater lining area for the all-drum brakes, which had been roundly criticized for their lack of stopping power. The 170-cid six was replaced as the base engine by the 200-cid unit, which was switched from four to seven main bearings for smoother running and gained 6 extra horsepower. All models now wore the richer-looking grille from the

Forged aluminum wheels were also a new Pinto option for '73.

Pinto Runabout hatchback carried a $2120 price tag for '73.

The popular 1973 Pinto wagon with optional Squire package

Squire trim was a $237 extra for the '73 Pinto wagon.

1973 Maverick 4-door sedan with extra-cost LDO package

1973 Gran Torino Sport 2-door fastback, priced at $3154.

With standard six, the '73 Maverick 4-door sold at $2297.

Rear-end styling was little changed on '73 Torinos.

Grabber and LDO, and wheelarch and greenhouse moldings became standard along with full carpeting and nicer interior trim. New options were "halo" vinyl roof for 2-doors, AM/FM stereo, and forged aluminum wheels. Overall length increased by 4 inches, all of it in the front bumper.

One of the less successful bumper grafts appeared on the mildly revised 1973 Torino. The change brought wider grilles on upper-line models, while the standard cars retained a full-width treatment. A new Brougham hardtop and sedan arrived at the top of the line, with cloth and "leatherlike" vinyl upholstery, pseudo-wood interior appliques, electric clock, and other amenities. Engines were detuned, but availability was unchanged.

The Ranchero car/pickup for '73 remained a Torino variant.

'73 Gran Torino Sport got shallower grille, deeper bumper.

1974

As the Arabs turn off the oil tap, Ford redefines the ponycar concept

With one major exception, Ford marked time for 1974. The year was marred by the Arab oil embargo, which began in late 1973 and quickly led to panic fuel buying and long lines at gas pumps, plus a big drop in demand for big cars. New federal mandates affecting all cars this year were rear bumpers able to withstand 5-

mph shunts, and the starter interlock. The latter prevented the engine from being started unless the driver's seatbelt was fastened, and it proved so irksome to so many people that it was soon written out of the lawbooks.

Ford's main product news this year was the smaller, lighter Mustang II, a redefinition of the ponycar concept. It arrived almost simultaneously with the energy crisis, though it had been in the works long before that. However, this fortuitous bit of timing undoubtedly contributed to the new car's strong sales—close to 386,000 for the model year, a figure within 10 percent of the original Mustang's 12-month production record of nearly 419,000.

The original Mustang's "father" was the driving force behind the Mustang II. But while Lee Iacocca had only guessed at the market the first time he knew *in advance* that there would be strong demand for Mustang II. Said

First proposals leading to Mustang II were based on the old 108-inch wheelbase. Note extreme windshield rake.

A further development of the mid-1969 study above was this "Mach 1" with rear fender skirts and high "breadvan" tail.

A more conventional approach was this June 1970 mockup.

1970 Mustang work still envisioned keeping the 1971-73 size.

Ford's president: "When I look at the foreign car market and see that one in five is a sporty car, I know something's happening." By 1972, sales of cars like Ford's European Capri, GM's Opel Manta from Germany, and the Japanese-built Toyota Celica were running at 300,000 units; projections for 1974 put sales at over 400,000. Mustang II was assigned to capture a big slice of this "mini-ponycar" pie.

Once again, Dearborn's army of stylists and engineers worked from an idea clearly defined by Iacocca: sporty appearance, a wheelbase of 96-100 inches, standard 4-speed gearbox, four-cylinder or small six-cylinder engine. Most important, "it must be luxurious—upholstered in quality materials and carefully built." Iacocca wanted it to be a "little jewel." What he got was a mini-Mustang, with the popular long-hood/short-deck

Another 1970 mockup, this time with an extreme backlight.

A mid-1970 fastback proposal, probably for Mach 1

Front fenders on this notchback are similar to the 1971-73 design.   Note different greenhouse treatments.

Through the end of 1970, all proposals for the new-generation Mustang were big and bulky. Ford then started over.

A much smaller package was tried and approved in 1971. "Anaheim" notchback by Don DeLaRossa set the design tone.

Ghia of Italy submitted this shapely two-seater for review.

L. David Ash's unusually complete Mustang II interior buck

Getting closer: a fastback mockup from September 1971

A Mustang II-based Mercury Capri was briefly considered.

proportions reinterpreted on a reduced scale—smaller than even the original. Against the 1973 Mustang, the new car was 20 inches shorter, four inches narrower, an inch lower, 400-500 pounds lighter, and nearly 15 inches shorter in wheelbase.

Mustang II styling was a collection of ideas taken from several proposals developed independently by the Ford and Lincoln-Mercury studios and the Italian coachbuilding house of Ghia, which had then recently come under Dearborn's control. The final decision came down to a choice of five clay models, one notchback and four fastbacks. The one selected as the basis for production styling—and surprisingly little altered—was a fastback from the Lincoln-Mercury group.

Iacocca had decided "the convertible is dead and can be forgotten," but hardtop and fastback body styles were developed. There were plain and fancy versions of each, the latter being the Ghia notchback (replacing Grande as the luxury offering) and the Mach 1 fastback, which gained a lift-up rear hatch "door" for the first time.

Interior design was the work of L. David Ash, who took the unusual step of having his mockup fitted with exterior sheetmetal and four wheels so it would be more realistic. "It was a time-consuming thing to build," he recalled, "but it served its purpose very well. We didn't have to go through an elaborate series of meetings...It was all approved right here. We were on a crash basis to get it done, and it was very enthusiastically received...We put everything in that we could conceive of that connotes restrained elegance plus the get-up-and-go that says Mustang..." The final interior package included a neatly styled dash with standard tachometer, plus plush

Mustang II's standard instrumentation included a tach.

The production Mustang II notchback in luxury Ghia guise

pleated cloth, vinyl, or optional leather upholstery. Rear seat room was limited, mainly because the car was seen as being used primarily by one or two adults, who would sit in front. Sadly, front seatback rake adjustment was missing, but the seats themselves were definitely more comfortable than those of previous Mustangs.

For the first time, a new Mustang was designed with no thought of a V-8. In line with Iacocca's instructions, engineering was planned around a 2.3-liter (140-cid) overhead-cam inline four to be built at a new plant in Lima, Ohio. The only option would be a 2.8-liter (171-cid) ohv V-6, es-

sentially a larger version of the German Ford 2.6-liter (155-cid) unit already being used in the U.S. Capri. The "Lima" four was the first American-built engine using metric-measure components, no surprise because it was actually a bored and stroked derivative of the European 2.0-liter engine first seen in the Pinto. The standard four-speed gearbox was a strengthened rendition of the British-built Pinto transmission. The standard vacuum-assisted brake system consisted of 9.3-inch discs in front and 9 x 1.75-inch drums at the rear.

The degree of component sharing between Mustang II

Ford president Lee A. Iacocca poses with his new "little jewel" and the 1965 original in this Mustang press photo.

Henry Ford II gets a consumer's reaction to the Mustang II

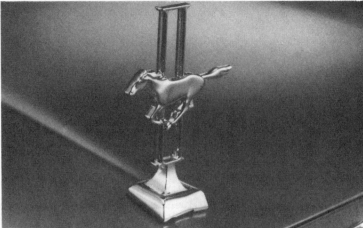

Mustang logo became more trotter than runner for the "II".

The prototype Mustang II Ghia. Car bears "Grande" script.

New 2.3-liter ohc four was standard Mustang II powerplant.

A prototype Mustang II on the proving grounds cobblestones

and Pinto and an identical 94.2-inch wheelbase led some observers to suggest Mustang II was really just a rebodied Pinto. Although the two cars did share a lot, the Pinto was actually upgraded for '74 to take advantage of some parts and features designed for Mustang II. Both had unit construction, and both used the same front suspension: independent with unequal-length upper and lower arms and coil springs. For the Mustang, however, the lower arm was attached to a rubber-mounted subframe; on the Pinto it was bolted directly to the main structure. The Mustang subframe carried the rear of the engine/transmission assembly, and was designed to provide more precise steering and a smoother ride than Pinto. Isolating the rear engine mount also reduced drivetrain vibration in the passenger compartment. Because

Mustang II was intended to sell for more than a Pinto, company cost accountants approved this more expensive mounting arrangement. Both cars also had rack-and-pinion steering, but the Mustang's steering gear was mounted differently, again to minimize shock. Also, the Mustang could be ordered with power steering, but not Pinto. At the rear, the Mustang's leaf springs were two inches longer than Pinto's, and its shock absorbers were staggered as in the earlier high-performance Mustangs. Spring rates were calculated by computer to match equipment, weight, and body style of each individual car. The Ghia notchback, for example, came with very soft settings, while the optional competition suspension had the stiffest rates, along with a thicker front sway bar, a rear sway bar, and Gabriel adjustable shock absorbers.

Mach 1 designation was continued for the sportiest Mustang II.   German-built 2.8-liter V-6 engine was standard power.

The traditional Mustang fastback acquired a lift-up rear hatch with the new design, retained the "2+2" moniker.

Mustang II Mach 1 carried a $3518 base price for 1974. White-letter tires and black rocker paint were standard.

Effect of bumper standards showed up clearly on '74 Pinto.

'74 Pinto had standard 2.0-liter four.   Runabout cost $2568.

In ride and handling, the "cooking" Mustang IIs and the top-line Ghia were typically American. The Mach 1, with its standard V-6, radial tires, and optional competition suspension, was more capable. No Mustang II had overwhelming acceleration. The car was heavy for its size (curb weight of 2650-2900 pounds), so a V-6 with 4-speed would produce 0-60 mph times only in the 13-14 second range, though top speed was around 100 mph.

Mustang II wouldn't change significantly over what would turn out to be a five-year model run. The four-cylinder and V-6 Ghia as well as the Mach 1 were available throughout, and Ford continued to add options (and, later, more model variants). Aside from air conditioning and a variety of radio and tape players, the '74 list

The LTD Brougham 4-door "pillared hardtop" for '74.   This would be the last year for pillarless big Ford hardtops.

Opera windows were a new extra for '74 Torino hardtops.   Shown here is the Gran Torino Brougham 2-door so equipped.

Gran Torino Elite bowed as a mid-1974 addition to the intermediate line. Note different nose, twin opera panes.

showed vinyl top, sunroof, forged-aluminum wheels, and many other goodies.

Apart from those already mentioned, changes to the subcompact Pinto this year were minor. Stronger roof rails and underbody crossbars were fitted to give the unit body/chassis greater structural strength. This meant more weight which, together with ever-tighter emissions controls, rendered the original 1.6-liter engine too weak to provide decent performance. Accordingly, the 2.0-liter four was made standard equipment.

The big Fords were mainly carryovers this year. LTDs received a new fine-checked grille insert and standup hood ornament, along with standard steel-belted radial tires. Solid-state ignition was now fitted on all optional

Grille rehash distinguished '74 Gran Torino Brougham sedan.

Little-changed 1974 T-Bird now had 460 V-8 as standard.

This Gran Torino wagon sold at $3767 for 1974.

Thunderbird's taillamps were separate, segmented for '74.

Thunderbird's face was little altered for '74. Price was now $6799 base and included vinyl roof and opera windows.

V-8s, but the big 429-cid engine was no longer listed.

Deeper rear bumpers also showed up on the mid-size Torino for '74. Gran Torino models got new vertical grille bars, with the parking lights at the outboard ends of the opening. Rear fender skirts were a new option for Gran Torinos, and 2-door hardtop models could be ordered with Thunderbird-style rear opera windows.

Thunderbird was also little altered this year. The one styling fillip was segmented taillamps in the back panel. The assembly incorporated a large, central backup lamp decorated with a stylized Bird emblem. The 460 V-8, now with solid-state ignition and rated at 220 bhp net, was made standard, along with vinyl roof, opera windows, manual air conditioning, power windows, and tinted glass. Two of this year's new options would later show up

on less expensive Fords. One was called "Autolamp." This device used a photocell receptive to changes in ambient light levels to switch the headlamps on or off as needed. It also incorporated a delay timer that would switch the lights off a few seconds after switching off the ignition, thus lighting the way for occupants from car to doorstep. Also new was the "moonroof," a tinted glass panel that could be retracted via an electric motor, and very much a descendant of the "bubbletop" Skyliner idea of the '50s. The fuel shortage put a crimp in sales, T-Bird production crumbling to about 58,500 for the model year.

The compact Maverick benefited from the gas scare, production rising by about 10,000 units. The '74 models were substantially the same as the '73s, identifiable only from the rear by their deep-section bumpers.

Maverick sales improved slightly from the previous year, reflecting the gas crunch. Shown is the standard 4-door.

1975

T-Bird turns 20, and a new model bows with a European accent

Grille treatment on the new Granada mimicked Mercedes-Benz.

A new kind of Ford bowed for 1975, the model year in which Thunderbird marked its 20th birthday. The division also introduced a new intermediate—a kind of junior T-Bird and a forecast of things to come—and made a spate of lesser changes in its other model lines. The U.S. auto industry was still in a sales slump following the Arab oil embargo. Ford's market share reflected this, dropping more than two points for the calendar year to slightly below 18 percent—this despite the broadest range of sizes, prices, and types since the mid-'60s.

In recent years, buyers had shown increasing preference for better-equipped, more luxurious smaller cars, and the "gas panic" of 1973-74 only accelerated the trend. Ford's response was the new Granada, boldly proclaimed as the "car designed for the times." Actually, it had been designed to replace the Maverick. The original plan called for a plusher, slightly larger car of more formal appearance using essentially the same chassis and run-

ning gear. However, Maverick sales had been consistently strong, and in the wake of the energy crisis Ford felt it couldn't afford to drop the older compact. So, the plan was changed: Maverick would continue, while its intended successor would be an addition to the line, occupying a size and price niche halfway between Maverick and the mid-size cars.

Granada's 109.9-inch wheelbase was shared with the Maverick 4-door, but the new car was 10 inches longer overall, an inch wider, and several hundred pounds heavier. Suspension design was also shared and very typi-

Four-square Granada styling was marred somewhat on the 2-door by use of faddish opera windows. Price was $3698.

Granada styling fared better in the 4-door sedan. This is the standard version with a base price of $3756.

The 1975 Granada Ghia 4-door sedan, priced at $4283

Standard Granada engine was Ford's familiar 200-cid six.

cally Detroit. However, Granada was blessed with standard front disc brakes. And engineers made more extensive use of rubber bushings and softened up springs and shocks to achieve more of a "big car" ride. There were no surprises in the powertrain department: the base engine was the familiar 200-cid six, also standard for Maverick, and there were the same 250-cid six and 302

V-8 options. Granada was also offered with a two-barrel 351. A 3-speed manual transmission was standard, 3-speed automatic optional, and floorshift available for both.

Like Maverick, there were 2-door and 4-door body styles for Granada, but that's where the similarity ended. Where Maverick looked American, the Granada strug-

Here's the Granada Ghia 2-door, which listed at $4225.

Granada interiors were plush, instrumentation minimal.

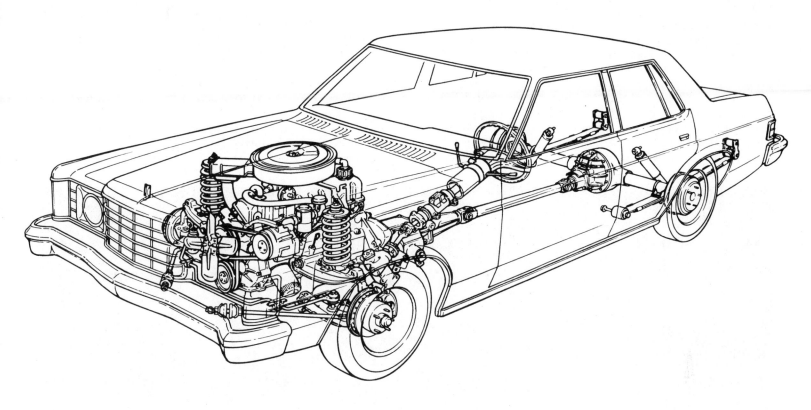

Factory line drawing reveals new Granada's conventional chassis engineering. Both 302 and 351 V-8s were optional.

gled to be European. Styling, supervised by Ford's long-time design vice-president Eugene Bordinat, was an unabashed attempt to capture the look of certain upper-class import sedans. Mercedes-Benz, in particular, had every reason to be flattered by the imitation, and Ford advertising hammered away at the size and styling similarities between Granada and the "New Generation" M-B sedans. (Remember all those TV commercials where passers-by mistook the Ford for the Mercedes?) Of Granada's two body styles, the 4-door was unquestionably more handsome. The 2-door was afflicted with "opera" windows, quite popular at the time but also a mismatch for the rectangular Mercedes-like grille and similarly

boxy body lines. The interior could have come from Lincoln. While there were a few European touches available on the costlier Ghia models—individual front seats with reclining backrests, grab handles, map pockets, and the like, instrumentation was next to nil and the dash was slathered with "test tube" wood.

In handling and performance the Granada was something of a disappointment, at least to enthusiasts. *Road & Track* magazine reported that "the car doesn't handle badly; it corners quite flat, the Firestone radials of the test car gripped well in the wet and on the skidpad it got around only slightly slower than the vaunted Brand M...But Ford's power steering still has little road

This vinyl-topped Mustang II fastback bears "Sport" script, Ghia badges, probably for '75. Idea didn't make production.

feel...and we found ourselves too concerned with just staying on course...The live axle, not particularly well controlled since it's on simple leaf springs, is quite susceptible to bumps and loses traction easily." With 302 V-8, automatic, and 3.00:1 axle ratio, the *R&T* test Granada ran 0-60 mph in a respectable 12 seconds flat and returned a not-so-respectable 12.5 mpg in normal driving. But the editors praised the car's brakes, driving position, and quietness, as well as its more intelligent design. Summing up, *R&T* said: "If we had expected it to be a surrogate Mercedes...we'd be disappointed. But if we look at the moderate price tag [around $3700] and think of the Granada as a reasonable-size interpretation of the traditional American car with a little inspiration from Europe, there's no problem liking it."

A good many buyers liked the Granada, too. For the model year nearly 303,000 were sold, a total that outnumbered Maverick's by nearly 2 to 1. Again, Ford had read the market correctly, and Granada's strong initial acceptance showed clearly that the way to future sales success was upmarket, not down.

Changes to Ford's other '75 models were relatively

Slimmer quarter windows were used on '75 Mustang II Ghia. Car pictured has this year's new Silver Luxury Group option.

"Sport" was probably proposed as Ghia notchback companion.

Wider grille eggcrates marked 302 V-8 on '75 Mustang IIs.

Sliding steel sunroof was a new option for 1975 Mustang II notchbacks. Standard models retained the 1974 quarter glass.

mild. At mid-year, special "MPG" versions of Pinto and Mustang II were issued, equipped with that new emissions cleanup device, the catalytic converter. By obviating the need for much of the add-on emissions control hardware of past years, the converter allowed engines to be retuned for greater efficiency, thus boosting fuel economy—which hadn't been that spectacular of late in Ford's smallest cars—and performance. The 2.3-liter "Lima" four became the standard Pinto engine this year. The 302 V-8 (available with automatic transmission only) was added as a new option for Mustang II, thus answering cries for more go-power. Also for Mustang II was a new Silver Luxury Group option for the Ghia hardtop, with cranberry-color crushed velour upholstery and silver paint and vinyl top. Another new extra was a power moonroof at $454. Pinto and Maverick acquired steel-belted radial tires and solid-state ignition as new no-cost extras. On Mavericks, the letters F-O-R-D appeared on trunklid and the leading edge of the hood, and on Grabber or cars with the Luxury Decor Option you got a covered glove compartment instead of the open under-dash shelf. A heavy-duty suspension option was new for Grabber.

2.3-liter "Lima" four now powered little-changed '75 Pinto.

1975 Maverick 2-door sedan

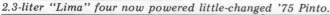

Now simply called Elite, Ford's most luxurious mid-size returned for '75 with few changes. Sales continued strong.

1975 Gran Torino Brougham 4-door pillared hardtop: $4837

The Torino-based '75 Ranchero, here with Squire side trim

Two new color-keyed luxury package options were issued to mark Thunderbird's 20th birthday. Base retail was $7701.

1975 big Fords were facelifted. Shown is the LTD sedan.

Coach windows filled B-posts on full-size '75 2-doors.

Further up the line, the mid-size Torino was left virtually untouched, but there was a mid-year addition to the line, the Gran Torino Elite. This "Thunderbird-inspired" coupe shared the beefier chassis developed for the Mercury Cougar XR-7, and was Ford's counterpart to that model in the intermediate class. Body structure, dimensions, and interior appointments were basically as for Torino. The Elite was distinguished by an aggressive egg-crate grille, dual (instead of quad) headlamps set in square nacelles molded into the hood, wide body moldings, and two tiny opera windows per side. The ubiquitous two-barrel 351 V-8 was standard, and engine options were the same as Torino's. The Elite captured over 123,000 sales in its short debut season, making it the most popular mid-size Ford by far.

The big Fords were given a modest restyle this year. Grilles became more rectangular and flat, rear decks were raised and planed off, and slim vertical windows appeared in the B-pillars of 2-door "hardtop" models. The series hierarchy changed, with the new LTD Landau (identified by hidden headlamps) at the top, followed by LTD Brougham and LTD.

Marking 20 years of Thunderbirds were two new luxury option packages for the otherwise unchanged cruiser. One was done in silver, the other copper, and both were color-keyed to a fare-thee-well. Though not many people knew about it, four-wheel disc brakes had been optional for T-Bird since 1972, and were now included with the extra-cost Sure-Track anti-lock system. Sales sank to 43,000 this year, down about 16,000 from 1974.

1976

Struggling to maintain sales with a renewed emphasis on sport

The 1976 Pinto Runabout with new Stallion trim package

The 1976 model year was hardly a memorable one for Ford fans. Significant product developments were few, and Ford's market share dropped yet again. Despite recent attention, the big Fords would run 4th in sales this year, trailing the full-size Chevrolet as well as comparable Oldsmobile and Buick models. But there were bright spots. Mustang II, for instance, placed 2nd among domestic subcompacts, bested only by Chevy's new-for-'76 Chevette—and then by less than 400 units. And Pinto, despite its now five-year-old design, was still hanging in there, a solid 4th. Granada quickly captured top spot among compacts, leading both Chevy's redesigned Nova and Plymouth's new Volaré by very comfortable margins.

Most of this year's changes involved the smaller Fords.

In further pursuit of sport—or what was left of it—a new package option called Stallion was offered on Pinto, Maverick, and Mustang II. It was strictly for show, consisting primarily of silver body paint set off with lots of black on hoods, grilles, and greenhouse moldings. Bold decals emblazoned with a fiery steed adorned front fenders. More functional—and, in a way, outrageous—was the new

Hidden headlamps marked the full-size LTD Landau, returning at the top of the line.   This 2-door sold for $5748.

The Maverick version of the Stallion package was available only on the 2-door, and added $329 to its list price.

Here's the Stallion treatment applied to the Mustang II fastback. Forged aluminum wheels were a separate extra.

The Pinto version of the Stallion package cost $283, and made a good match with the optional V-6 engine.

Cobra II trim option for the Mustang II hatchback. Intended to evoke memories of the great Shelby GT 350 and 500 of the '60s, it had the requisite rocker panel racing stripes, plus black grille, styled steel wheels with trim rings, flip-out rear quarter windows with louvered covers, a front air dam, ducktail rear spoiler, and simulated hood scoop. You also got radial tires. Inside were a sports steering wheel, dual remote control door mirrors, brushed-aluminum dash and door panel trim, and Cobra II emblems. Initially the package was available only with

white exterior; other color combinations would be added the following year.

Pinto got a minor freshening courtesy of a new close-checked grille housing square parking lamps. To compete more effectively against the imports at the low end of the price spectrum Ford added a no-frills 2-door called Pony. The options sheet got longer as a half-vinyl roof for sedans and "Squire" bodyside appliqués for the Runabout were offered for the first time. The aging but game Maverick also got a new grille, this time a split, horizontal-bar

Mustang II styling was again little changed for '76. This notchback wears the $169 Exterior Accent Group package.

New-for-'76 Cobra II package cost $599. It was a far cry from the original Shelby Mustangs it tried to resemble.

The spiffy interior of the '76 Cobra II package

The 1976 Mustang II Ghia with the $177 Ghia Luxury Group

affair, and front disc brakes at last became standard equipment. The highly successful Granada continued with no appearance changes. A new Luxury Decor Option for the Ghia 4-door offered two-tone black/tan exterior and lacy-spoke aluminum wheels plus color-keyed tan interior with crushed velour upholstery. The standard 2-door could be dressed up with new "Sports Sedan"

equipment consisting of special paint, color-keyed road wheels and pinstripes, floor shift, and leather-rim steering wheel. Other new options included a power moonroof and, interestingly, all-disc power brakes. Headlamp dimmer switches were combined with the turn signal stalk on both Granada and Mustang II.

Ford's mid-size Torino and Elite were practically un-

Squire siding was a new option for the '76 Pinto Runabout.

The Maverick 4-door for '76. LDO package here cost $508.

Sports Sedan package was $482 option on base Granada 2-door.

The '76 Granada Ghia 4-door with $642 Luxury Decor Option

This creme-and-gold trim package was one of three color-keyed option groups for the carryover '76 Thunderbird.

changed. The Gran Torino Sport 2-door hardtop disappeared, but Elite filled the gap by offering bucket seats and console with floorshift as a new option. There were no appreciable changes to the big LTDs, but optional four-wheel power disc brakes showed up here, too, along with a new half-vinyl top for 2-doors. Thunderbird's only alteration this season was a new group of trim and paint

packages—Creme and Gold, Bordeaux (as in wine), and Lipstick (a bright red). Besides the coordinated color scheme each offered a half-vinyl top, thicker carpeting, special upholstery, and body accent stripes. Sales recovered somewhat to nearly 53,000 for the model year, thus ringing down the curtain on the big seventh-generation Bird.

The $5748 list price on this 1976 LTD Landau 2-door hardtop (with Landau Luxury Group) doesn't seem high today.

The 4-door LTD Landau cost less than 2-door: $5694 list.

1976 Gran Torino Brougham 2-door hardtop: $4557 retail

1976 Gran Torino Brougham 4-door pillared hardtop: $4591

Like Torinos, the Elite would vanish after '76. $4978.

1977

Mid-size machinations: a second LTD and a smaller, less expensive Bird

1977 LTD 4-door pillared hardtop sold at $4870 list.

Attempting to shore up a relatively weak position in the mid-size field, Ford made a significant model realignment for 1977. Taking over for Torino as its volume intermediate was the LTD II, styled much in the manner of the Elite but with crisper front and rear sheetmetal. The Elite was cancelled, its place as the "premium" mid-size offering filled by a new smaller and much less expensive Thunderbird. Despite all the name switching and appearance alterations, these new cars were essentially the old cars underneath, retaining body-on-frame construction, the same suspension design, and most running gear.

Described as "a sporty new trim-size line in the LTD tradition," the LTD II sported an Elite-type nose with checked grille and stacked quad rectangular headlamps. Overall appearance was straighter and starchier than Torino's, but the marked similarity in the greenhouse area was there for all to see. Thunderbird got its own egg-

crate grille flanked by flip-up doors concealing the headlamps. The roof featured a "basket handle" effect through the use of wrapover chrome moldings defining body-color B-posts. There were tiny "coach" windows in these pillars, with large rear quarter windows and slim C-pillars aft.

LTD II retained the nine-model Torino lineup of wagons and pillared hardtops and sedans, arrayed in base (called "S"), standard, and Brougham series. There was only one

LTD II replaced Torino in Ford's 1977 catalog, was styled somewhat like the Elite. Shown is the $4785 2-door hardtop.

Price on this 1977 LTD II Brougham 2-door hardtop was $5121.

The 1977 Thunderbird carried a lower base price: $5063.

T-Bird model initially, but in January the Town Landau name was resurrected for a second version sporting an arm-long list of comfort and convenience equipment. The standard engine for federal versions of both LTD II and T-Bird was Ford's 302 V-8, with the optional 351 standard in California. SelectShift Cruise-O-Matic was the only available transmission, and the largest available engine was Ford's 400-cid V-8 in either two- or four-barrel form.

This reorganization produced some interesting sales results. The LTD II failed to match Torino's performance, slipping from 6th to 7th among intermediates. The new T-Bird, however, captured 5th, and outsold the entire LTD II line by some 80,000 units. Part of this was doubtless due to the magic of the Thunderbird name, but much of it stemmed from dramatically lower prices, now just over $5000, down some $2700 for the base version compared with its 1976 counterpart. This sales picture would

Downsized and with a drastic cut in price, the 1977 Thunderbird set a production record for the make: 318,140 units.

Still around in 1977 was the Ranchero car/pickup, as before based on Ford's intermediate platform. GT is shown.

hold until another shakeup was decreed for 1980.

Granada was basically unchanged in its third season, but several new options were now offered. These included a 4-speed overdrive manual transmission, basically the old 3-speed with a high-geared ratio tacked on, plus four-way manual driver's seat (up/down as well as fore/aft), leather upholstery for the Ghia 4-door, and big-car features like illuminated entry system, thermostat control

for heating/air conditioning, and front cornering lamps. Meanwhile, the old-soldier Maverick returned one last time with fewer options and no styling or mechanical changes.

Pinto got another front-end redo for '77, plus larger tail-lamps for sedans. The sloped-back "soft" nose had taller headlamp buckets and a narrower chrome grille flanked by twin vertical parking lamps. A new option for the Run-

Outwardly little changed in its third year, Granada offered more big-car extras. Here, the $4440 Ghia 2-door.

Maverick bowed out after 1977, so final version bore few changes. Shown: the $3322 2-door with Exterior Decor Group.

about was a frameless, all-glass hatch, providing a different look outside and a better view inside. Other new extras this year: 2.8-liter V-6 engine from the Mustang II, bronze-tint flip-up sunroof, four-way manual driver's seat, and a Sports Rallye Package consisting of tachometer, extra engine gauges, sport steering wheel, and front anti-roll bar. Also new was the Cruising Wagon, a youth-oriented version of the regular Pinto wagon with front spoiler, styled wheels, and blanked-off rear quarters containing glass portholes. The Cruising Wagon had all the Sports Rallye features plus a fully carpeted rear deck and interior side walls, the latter a gesture to the "van set." All Pintos now wore front bumpers made of aluminum instead of steel. This and a lighter energy absorbing system reduced total car weight by about 80 pounds. Pinto's popularity waned this year. Sales fell by over 50,000 units,

The 1977 Pinto Runabout displays new grille, lighter bumpers.

1977 Granada 2-door with $511 Sports Coupe package

All-glass hatch was new option for '77 Pinto Runabout.

Appearance Decor Group was $96 on '77 Mustang II 2+2.

Cobra II package was continued for the 1977 Mustang 2+2 at a reduced $535 price. Note prominent snake decals.

This 1977 Mustang sports the optional Cobra II package and this year's newly available T-bar roof.

1977 Mustang II 2+2 with Appearance Decor Group

1977 Mustang II with optional Cobra II equipment package

Mustang II's optional Cobra II package was offered in colors other than white beginning with the 1977 models.

Landau was now the upper of two series in the full-size LTD line for '77. This 4-door "pillared hardtop" cost $5742.

but the smallest Ford remained 4th in its class.

Despite some 34,000 fewer sales, Mustang II moved to the head of the subcompact list, and handily outpaced the less sporting, less expensive Chevrolet Chevette by nearly 20,000 units. Much of this came on the strength of new options. Some of these were: T-bar roof for hatchbacks, with lift-off glass panels; a flip-up/removable glass sunroof for hardtops; new Rallye Appearance Package, replacing the Stallion option; two-tone paint; and a color-keyed Sports Appearance Group for the Ghia. Late in the season, tri-color tape striping and black side window and backlight louvers were added to the Cobra II package. Engine outputs fluctuated a good deal on most cars of the '70s, and Mustang II was not immune. This year's standard four was rated at 92 bhp, the extra-cost 2.8-liter V-6 at only 93, and the 302 V-8 at 139, all in SAE net horsepower.

This was the year GM introduced its first downsized cars, smaller renditions of its full-size models. Ford advertising was quick to seize on this, and the mostly unchanged LTD was promoted as "the full-size car that kept its size." Obviously, the appeal was to those buyers who didn't think the idea of smaller big cars was such a good one. To a degree, it worked: LTD sales moved up by about 24,000. But all big cars scored increases in 1977 as memories of the energy crisis dimmed, and Chevrolet, Buick and Oldsmobile scored healthy gains with their trimmer new models to remain ahead of Ford.

Here's a press photo that's unusual in showing the plain LTD wagon, not the Squire. This '77 sold at $5415 basic.

1978

Facing the future with "Fox" in a milestone anniversary year

Past, present, and future seemed to coalesce in Ford Division's 1978 model line. A nod to the past was the limited-edition Diamond Jubilee Thunderbird, issued to commemorate Ford Motor Company's 75th anniversary. For the present, all Detroit was obligated to meet the government's Corporate Average Fuel Economy (CAFE) requirements that took effect this year. Under CAFE, the fuel economy of all cars sold by a given manufacturer had to average at least 18 mpg on a "sales-weighted" basis; the target figure would then rise in steps to 27.5 mpg for the 1985 model year. Part of the division's response was a

new compact advertised as "The Ford in your future," a twist on an old slogan. The words were prophetic: in its engineering and much of its hardware, Fairmont would be the literal foundation for a whole new generation of Fords.

The genesis of Fairmont (and its near-identical Mercury Zephyr companion) was in the "Fox" program, initiated in the early '70s to develop an eventual replacement for the Ford Maverick and Mercury Comet. Significantly, it had been started at about the time of the Arab oil embargo, which dramatically highlighted the need for smaller, lighter, more economical cars. Efficiency was the project's overriding concern: "The initial objective was an overall body design that would enhance performance and fuel economy through minimized weight [plus] aerodynamic refinements. Once these goals were achieved, the challenge was to design an efficient interior package that would make optimum use of available space." Though certain existing components like engines, transmissions, and suspension pieces would be used, the plan

Show-stopper: This 1978 show car, dubbed Megastar II, was designed by Ghia on the British Ford Cortina chassis.

In size and design, Ford's new '78 Fairmont compact was quite close to mid-range European models like Audi, Volvo.

was to combine "the economy and maneuverability of a compact with the interior roominess and comfort of a mid-sized car."

Ford broke fresh engineering ground with Fox in several areas. For example, this was the first Ford designed with the aid of computers as well as three-dimensional scale models and full-size prototypes. Through the use of mathematical models like the so-called "finite analysis" technique, engineers could "pinpoint where the car's structure may require additional strength, or where it can

The 1978 Fairmont 4-door sedan, shown with optional vinyl roof, wire wheel covers, flow-through ventilation louvers

Fairmont 2-door had a $3589 base price for 1978. Optional ventilation louvers (on car at right) cost just $33.

The handsome, practical 1978 Fairmont Squire wagon. The Squire option added $369 to the wagon's $4031 sticker.

The 1978 Fairmont Squire wagon

The 1978 Fairmont 2-door with ESO (European Sport Option)

Stylish Futura coupe was a late-season addition to the Fairmont line. Roofline was similar to Thunderbird's.

Mid-size LTD II was little changed except for fewer model and engine choices. This Brougham 2-door sold at $5405.

be lightened without decreasing strength or durability." Computer-assisted design, as it is now called, would prove a great time- and money-saver and beginning with Fairmont, all future Fords would be developed this way. Fairmont also made more extensive use than any previous Ford of lightweight materials such as aluminum, high-strength steel and reinforced plastics, again to save weight in the interest of good fuel economy. And despite its conservative, boxy appearance, it was the first Ford styled with an eye to aerodynamics, the aim being to reduce fuel-wasting air drag as much as possible. Both ⅜-scale and, later, full-size prototypes spent more than 320 hours in wind-tunnel testing to refine body lines proposed by the stylists. Ford noted that "although almost imperceptible, these minor refinements were responsible for an approximate 13 percent reduction in drag from the first clay models to the finished vehicle."

The end product was thoroughly modern and a definite advance on Maverick. There were now three body styles instead of two, 2- and 4-door sedans and, something Maverick had sorely needed, a practical 5-door wagon. All Fairmonts rode a 105.5-inch wheelbase, 4.5 inches shorter than the 4-door Maverick's, yet interiors were roomier in every dimension. Space-saving features like thinner front seatbacks and thinner doors helped. So, too, did the pleasingly simple styling. The Fairmont's lower beltline, higher roof, and much greater glass area all contributed to improved outward vision and a feeling of greater interior spaciousness. Trunk space was improved on sedans by a healthy 3 cubic feet. Fairmont also boasted a logi-

The GT version of the largely unchanged 1978 Ranchero GT car/pickup. Note "Starsky and Hutch" striping on cab.

Available in either 2- or 4-door form was a new ESS (European Sports Sedan) edition of the Granada for 1978.

Granada ESS items included console and sports steering wheel.

1978 Granada Ghia 2-door sedan. Suggested price: $4649.

1978 Granada 2-doors like this Ghia gained "twindows."

$3451 was the list price for the 1978 Pinto 3-door Runabout.

cally organized full-width dashboard and European-style steering column stalk controls for headlamp dimmer and windshield wipers and washer. In its overall appearance and packaging, the Fairmont was "close to European middleweights," as Ford put it—cars like the Audi 100LS and Volvo 240. And, in fact, *Car and Driver* magazine called it "an American Volvo."

The Fairmont chassis was, again, conventional but con-

temporary. Up front was a modified MacPherson-strut suspension with coil springs mounted on lower A-arms instead of concentrically around the struts. This, said Ford, meant less noise and harshness, and also saved some body weight. Steering was by the more precise rack-and-pinion mechanism instead of recirculating ball as in the Maverick. At the rear, Ford abandoned antiquated leaf springs for coils, and provided four links to tie down the

The 1978 Pinto Runabout, shown here with newly optional exterior striping and white-painted spoked road wheels.

Enterprising economy. This Pinto Panel Delivery, based on the wagon, was introduced during 1978 for small businesses.

The 1978 Mustang II Ghia hardtop: $3972 suggested list

1978 Mustang II hardtop with Fashion Accessory Package

live axle more securely. The two lower links and the springs were mounted outboard and behind the axle, which Ford said minimized axle tramp and side-to-side shake and also improved ride control.

Because of its light but strong construction, Fairmont tipped the scales up to 300 pounds lighter than a '77 Maverick. This allowed the use of smaller engines for better fuel economy. Thus, the standard power unit was the 2.3-liter ohc "Lima" four from the Pinto/Mustang II, the first four ever seen in a domestic Ford compact. Optional were the company's familiar 3.3-liter/200-cid cast-iron six and small-block 302 V-8. The latter required 3-speed automatic transmission, as did the six in California and high-altitude areas. Otherwise you got a 4-speed manual gearbox with floorshift.

Fairmont was greeted with almost unqualified praise.

1978

Writing in *Auto Test 1978*, CONSUMER GUIDE® magazine's staff declared it "stands head and shoulders above the General Motors and Chrysler compacts. It is efficient...has more room for passengers than any of its competitors, just as smooth a ride, superior handling, and the look of a more modern car. The improvement over the Maverick...is substantial." Our six-cylinder/automatic test car returned an average 21 mpg (versus the 19 city/

26 highway EPA ratings), and we lauded most every aspect of it save the awkward, stalk-mounted horn button and unsupportive seats. Nevertheless, we rated it the Best Buy in its class. So did a good many buyers. Fairmont easily captured the top spot in compact sales, scoring over 312,000 deliveries, easily surpassing all competitors. And as a final "vote of confidence," readers of *Car and Driver*, mainly enthusiasts not inclined to take

The flashy $1277 King Cobra package for the '78 Mustang II included big snake hood decal and 5.0-liter/302-cid V-8.

Other King Cobra goodies included front spoiler, raised-letter tires. T-bar roof was a separate option at $666.

much notice of unpretentious family models, voted Fairmont the most significant new car of the year in the magazine's annual poll.

Overshadowed by Fairmont and its great success were Ford's other 1978 models. There was a reason for this: not much changed. The mid-size LTD II was left alone except for cancellation of wagons. The full-size LTD was also basically unchanged, mainly because a downsized succes-

sor was on the way. Granada was updated with new grilles and dual rectangular headlamps, the latter a first for Ford and shared with Fairmont. Granada's base engine was upgraded to the 250-cid six, and the optional 351 V-8 was deleted. New to the options list were CB and AM/FM/cassette stereo radios along with an ESS (European Sports Sedan) package for base models. The latter included black exterior trim, hood and rear deck paint

Graphics on Cobra II package for Mustang II were changed at mid-1977, continued for '78. Option cost was now $730.

1978 Mustang II 2+2 with optional Cobra II package

1978 Mustang II 2+2 with extra-cost T-bar roof

Another new '78 option for Mustang II 3-doors was this Rallye Appearance Package, priced at $166.

Besides the T-roof shown here, the '78 Thunderbird could be ordered with two-piece vinyl covering or power moonroof.

1978 Thunderbird hardtop with optional Sports Decor Group

The 1978 Thunderbird Town Landau, priced at $8420 basic

stripes, color-keyed racing mirrors, bucket-seat interior with deluxe trim, and heavy-duty suspension, among other items. On 2-doors, the "opera" windows got a vertical chrome rib, transforming them into "twindows." The little Pinto also carried on with few changes, the most notable being standard "bucket-look" rear seat cushion and newly optional variable-ratio power steering.

Mustang II was in its final season, and Ford said farewell with some new options for the '78s. Packing every racy styling touch a kid could want, the new King Cobra package offered a huge snake decal for the hood, front air dam, tape stripes and name decals everywhere, plus snazzy cockpit trim. Unlike the Cobra II, however, this group also had some functional features, like the 302 V-8, power steering, "Rallye" handling package, and Goodrich 70-series tires. Though hardly a muscle car, the King Cobra could run the quarter-mile in about 17 seconds, not bad performance for the times. An appeal to women buyers was the Fashion Accessory Package, an option

group for the standard hardtop consisting of door pockets, striped-cloth upholstery, lighted vanity mirror, and four-way manual driver's seat. Variable-ratio power steering was available on all models.

T-Bird was mechanically untouched for '78, but Ford pushed luxury opulence to new heights with the special Diamond Jubilee Edition, priced at close to $10,000. This got you a whole slew of otherwise extra-cost equipment plus, as a personal touch, your very own initials monogrammed in pinstripes on each door and a 22-carat gold nameplate for the dash. Lesser Birds were offered with something called a Sports Decor Group. This consisted of light tan vinyl roof and spoked road wheels plus matching imitation "luggage straps" for the rear deck, a tacky throwback to the genuine article of the '30s. Thunderbird continued to sell well, moving up two notches to 3rd place in the mid-size class, trailing only Oldsmobile's Cutlass and the Chevrolet Malibu, both newly downsized for this year.

1979

Smaller big cars and a new breed of Mustang before the market falls

A new-generation Mustang and a downsized, thoroughly redesigned LTD were the big news at Ford for 1979. Shortly after the division showed off its new models to reporters, a big shakeup took place at the company's "Glass House" world headquarters. In a surprise move, president Lee Iacocca was abruptly fired by chairman Henry Ford II in what most observers said was a clash of personalities. Iacocca was succeeded by Philip Caldwell, and would go on to become president and, eventually, chairman of a moribund Chrysler Corporation. This would be the last year of "business as usual" in Detroit. Total industry production went up by more than a half-million cars, a figure topped only by the record 1973 model year. Sales, though off slightly from 1978 levels, remained strong. Unfortunately, a big drop was just around the corner.

For the second time in only five years Ford fielded a new Mustang, this time minus the Roman numeral II. The design brief was handed down in 1976 and specified using the basic suspension and floorpan of the just-completed Ford Fairmont/Mercury Zephyr compacts. This platform was eventually shortened by 5.1 inches, all of it in wheelbase. Mustang II power units—"Lima" four, 2.8-liter V-6 and 302 V-8—would be retained. As with the original Mustang, curb weight was pegged at a comparatively low 2700 pounds. The interior package size was planned to accommodate two adults comfortably, four in a pinch.

As with its predecessors, the new Mustang's styling was selected from a variety of proposals. Several teams within Ford Motor Company were given the same parameters, from which they developed sketches, clay models, and fiberglass mockups. Quarter-scale clays were subjected to 136 hours of wind tunnel testing, mainly because aerodynamics was becoming increasingly recognized as an important tool in obtaining good fuel economy. The proposal ultimately selected was created by a team headed by Jack Telnack, then executive director of Ford North American light truck and car design. This group had created the prototype for what went on to become the front-drive Ford Fiesta. Like the original Mustang but unlike the II, a notchback body style was designed first and a fastback developed from it. Per Mustang tradition, several trim/model permutations were planned.

The shape evolved by Telnack's group was a sort of notchback wedge, very slim in front, with the hood tapered from a rather high cowl. The Mustang cowl was actually an inch higher than that of the Fairmont/Zephyr. Telnack said this was to "get a faster sloping hood...to

Early wood mockup from late '74 for 1979 Mustang program

A more formal, mini-Thunderbird theme emerged in early '75.

A very curvy Mustang proposal from September, 1975

Nose workout on this late '75 study is close to final.

Another September, 1975 proposal: resolutely rectilinear

A stable of Mustang and replacement-Pinto proposals line up with then-current production models in October, 1975.

A move toward the '79 Mustang's wedge nose from early '76

Midsection on this proposal is close to production '79's.

Stylists entertained wrapped backlight (also shown above).

From March, 1976, a rather glittery, sharp-edged notchback

pivot the hood over the air cleaner." The shape dictated special inner front fender aprons and radiator supports instead of Fairmont/Zephyr pieces, but everyone agreed this extra expense was warranted. Increased fuel economy was one reward. The front bumper with integrated spoiler and the slight lip on the decklid were also dictated by aerodynamic considerations. Both body styles were given black-finish slats behind the rear side windows, rather like those of the Mercedes 450SLC. They were too wide for optimum visibility, though, one of the new design's less functional styling features.

Telnack described the project to the press in June 1978: "One of the basic themes for this car was 'form follows function'...and we wanted to be as aerodynamically correct as possible before getting into the wind tunnel. In the past we have designed cars and then gone into the tunnel mainly for tuning the major surfaces that have been approved...With the Mustang the designers were thinking about aerodynamics in the initial sketch stages, which made the tuning job in the tunnel much easier. Consequently, we wound up with the most slippery car ever done in the Ford Motor Company: a drag coefficient of

The production '79 Mustang 2-door carried a $4071 price.

Ford design director Jack Telnack and the '79 Mustang Cobra

Full instrumentation was standard '79 Mustang equipment.

1979 Mustang scale model in a wind tunnel smoke test

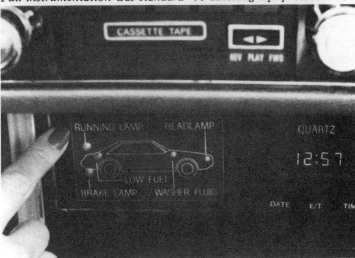

Aerodynamic artistry: Ford's Probe 1 show car from 1979

Graphic warning lights, digital clock were new '79 extras.

0.44 for the three-door fastback, 0.46 for the two-door notchback. [Aerodynamics is] probably the most cost-effective way to improve corporate average fuel economy. We know that a 10 percent improvement in drag can result in a five percent improvement in fuel economy at a steady-state 50 mph . . . That's really worthwhile stuff for us to go after."

Body engineering envisioned use of lightweight materials wherever possible, and plastics, high-strength/low-alloy (HSLA) steel, and aluminum figured heavily. The most significant use of plastics was for the reaction-injection-molded [RIM] soft urethane bumper covers. The number-three frame crossmember and the rear suspension arms were made of HSLA steel. Aluminum was found in the drivetrain and in the bumpers of some models. More weight was saved with thin but strong glass and by thinner door design. The 1979 Mustang thus tipped the scales about 200 pounds lighter on the average than the Mustang II, though the new car was slightly larger in every dimension. In an age of downsizing, this bigger-but-lighter car was a notable achievement.

Telnack's quoted drag figure of .44 sounded good in

As with the original Mustang, the '79 notchback was styled first and the fastback spun off from it.

Here's the up-trim Ghia version of the new-generation '79 Mustang notchback.   List price was $4642 sans options.

1979 Mustang 2-door with TRX package and 5.0-liter V-8

TRX suspension, turbo engine came with 1979 Cobra option

Mustang still offered a wide choice of luxury, performance, or both for '79. Shown are the Ghia 2-door and Cobra 3-door.

1978, but today it seems mediocre. Ford's 1983 Thunderbird, on the other hand, cuts through the wind at an altogether more impressive .35. While that may not appear to be a dramatic reduction, keep in mind that it represents an improvement of over 20 percent and demonstrates how radically standards have changed in just a few years.

Equally careful attention was paid to interior design. More efficient use of available space made the '79 far more roomy, comfortable, and convenient than the Mustang II, and sizable gains were made in several key areas. Rear legroom, for example, was increased by over five inches. Overall interior volume was up by 14 cubic feet on the two-door notchback and by 16 cubic feet on the hatchback. Thinner door construction yielded 3.6 inches more shoulder room and 2.0 inches more hiproom in front. In the rear, the gains were 5.0 and 6.0 inches, respectively. Cargo volume was likewise enlarged. The '79 notchback offered two more cubic feet of trunk space and the hatchback an additional four cubic feet compared to the Mustang II.

Some aspects of the '79 interior must have been inspired by European practice. Luxury-trim models were given higher-quality materials, and the '79 Ghia was less flashy than its '78 counterpart. Full instrumentation (speedometer, trip odometer, tachometer, temperature gauge, oil pressure gauge, ammeter and fuel gauge) was standard across the board. Two fingertip stalks mounted on the left of the steering column controlled turn signals, headlight dimmer, horn, and windshield wiper/washer. A third lever was added on the right for the optional tilt steering wheel. Practical convenience options were intermittent wipers, cruise control, and a console complete with a graphic display for "vehicle systems monitoring." This showed an outline of the car in side view on which warning lights were appropriately placed to indicate low fuel, low windshield washer fluid, and failed headlights, taillights, or brake lights. The display could be tested by a pushbutton. The console also housed a quartz-crystal digital chronometer that showed time, date, or elapsed time at the touch of a button.

As with past Mustangs, this new one was intended to have broad market appeal. From the suspension standpoint, therefore, several levels of capability were deemed necessary. The modified MacPherson strut front suspension and four-link rear geometry with coil springs all around were borrowed from the Fairmont/Zephyr, as was the rack-and-pinion steering. V-8 models would have a standard rear anti-roll bar, though it would serve more for lateral location than sway control. Since it effectively lowered the car's roll center, rear spring rates could be commensurately softer, thus benefiting ride. Product planners decided to offer three suspension setups: standard, "handling" and "special," each tuned for and issued with specific tires. The standard suspension came with conventional bias-plys. The "handling" suspension could be ordered only with 14-inch radials. Compared to the standard chassis, it was tuned for improved handling with higher spring rates, different shock valving, and stiffer bushings. A rear stabilizer bar was also provided when the 2.8-liter V-6 was specified with this package.

The "special" suspension included Michelin's recently

1979 Mustang 3-door coupe with standard suspension

1979 Mustang Cobra 3-door coupe. Note handsome TRX wheels.

Cobra package was potent but pricey: $1173 for 1979.

Mid-'79 Mustang Indy Pace Car replica. About 6000 were built.

1979 Mustang Cobra 3-door demonstrates its deep rear hatch.

Full-size LTD shrank for '79, emerged roomier, more roadable than previous models. Shown is the Landau 2-door.

Standard '79 LTDs (2-door shown) had dual, not quad, lamps.

The 1979 LTD Landau 4-door sedan. Price was $6474.

The evergreen Country Squire wagon in its new downsized 1979 form. List price for the woody-look hauler was $6615.

developed TRX radials with an unusual 390mm (15.35-inch) diameter that required specially sized metric wheels. According to Ford, the special suspension was designed "to extract maximum performance from this tire/wheel combination." It featured its own shock absorber valving, high rear spring rates, a 1.12-inch front stabilizer bar, and a rear stabilizer bar. Power assist was still optional for the steering, and the variable-ratio rack from 1978 was retained.

In addition to the Mustang II's engine offerings, an intriguing new powerplant was offered for '79—a turbocharged version of the standard four. This gave claimed

0-55 mph acceleration of 8.3 seconds with four-speed gearbox, plus fuel economy in the mid-20s. Turbocharging may have been new for Mustang, but the idea had been used for a number of years as a way of improving engine efficiency.

Other mechanical highlights for '79 included revisions for the 302 V-8. It was now fitted with a low-restriction exhaust system, used more lightweight components, and featured a ribbed V-belt for the accessory drive. Since the V-6 was in short supply, it was replaced late in the model year by the old 200-cid inline six. There was also a new optional four-speed gearbox developed for the six and V-8.

In effect, it was a three-speed manual transmission with an overdrive fourth gear tacked on. Third gear had the direct 1:1 ratio, while fourth had an overdrive ratio of 0.70:1. Final drive ratios were 3.08:1 for automatics, four-speed V-6, and unblown four-cylinder engine, and 3.45:1 for all other drivetrain combinations.

As with previous Mustangs, the performance of any particular '79 naturally depended on the engine/transmission chosen. The V-8 was a drag race engine by late-'70s standards: 0-60 mph clocked out at about nine seconds. The V-6's time was in the 13-14 second range, while the turbocharged four took about 12-12.5 seconds with four-speed. Press reaction to the various power-trains was mixed. Some writers thought the V-8 was over-powered and out of step for the fuel-short times. The 2.3-liter turbo got the most attention. As John Dinkel of *Road & Track* put it, "The TRX turbo would seem to be an enthusiast's delight. I just hope that the design compromises dictated by costs and the fact that Ford couldn't start with a completely clean sheet of paper don't wreck that dream...There's no doubt the new Mustang has the potential to be the best sport coupe Ford has ever built, but in some respects [it] is as enigmatic as its predecessor."

This "whole new breed" of Mustang quickly found buyer favor. In the compact class, where it now competed by dint of its larger interior, it was the second bestseller, after Fairmont. Overall model year sales were well over 300,000, making it the seventh most popular car in the land, and a big improvement over Mustang II's 22nd-place ranking among 1978 models.

Ford's new downsized LTD for '79 was less successful in its field, and in some ways this was curious. In size and design it was fully a match for GM's smaller full-size cars, which had enjoyed great success since their 1977 model year launch. Despite a 7-inch shorter wheelbase, down to 114.4 inches, the new LTD offered more claimed passenger and trunk space than previous big Fords, plus better visibility, better fuel economy, and a more competent ride. Styling was up to date—boxier but much cleaner than the 1975-78 cars—and there was a new all-coil suspension system with short-arm/long-arm front geometry and four-bar-link arrangement at the rear with the shocks mounted ahead of the axle. With all this, sales for the "new American road car" should have been better. Yet, deliveries fell by some 80,000 units for the model year, down to nearly 246,000, barely enough to beat out the full-size Oldsmobile and far behind the pace of Chevy's Caprice/Impala line. Two factors seemed to be at work here. One was that GM had a two-year head start. The other was a sudden downturn in the national economy beginning in the spring of '79, with inflation, rising interest rates, and another rise in gasoline prices putting the crimp in U.S. car sales generally. The big Ford would enjoy a sales resurgence, but not before the U.S. auto industry passed through three of its bleakest years in history.

The popular Fairmont returned basically unchanged for '79, but boasted several new options. Among these were tilt steering wheel, speed control, more comprehensive "performance instrumentation," and remote decklid release. Continuing from mid-1978 was a fourth body style,

1979 Fairmont 2-door sedan with $329 European Sedan option.

The 1979 Fairmont 4-door sedan. Price was $3810 basic.

Little changed for '79, Fairmont continued to sell well.

Fairmont-based Futura coupe returned for '79 at $4071.

the distinctive Futura coupe. It was mechanically identical with other models, but had its own unique greenhouse treatment featuring wide, tapering B-posts and T-Bird-style rear quarter windows. A 4-speed overdrive manual transmission replaced the former 3-speed unit as standard on all Fairmonts with the base four or optional six-cylinder engine, and was also available with the top 302 V-8, which was previously restricted to automatic. All top-trim models now wore the badge of Ford's Italian styling house, Ghia. Fairmont remained the nation's top compact, though model year sales were off by some 63,000 units.

Pinto got what would be its final facelift for '79, with a more coherent, horizontal-bar grille and rectangular

Rallye appearance package was one of several new option groups for the '79 Pinto. Note vestigial rear spoiler.

Practical Pinto Runabout carried a $3744 price for 1979.

1979 Pinto wagon with the colorful $566 Cruising Package

ESS option cost $261 on the 1979 Pinto Runabout.

The $4343 Pinto Squire wagon shows off new '79 facelift.

headlamps. Standard equipment was upgraded to encompass power front disc brakes, electric rear window defroster, tinted glass, and AM radio. A new ESS appearance package with black grille and exterior moldings was offered, and the Cruising Package was extended to the 3-door Runabout sedan. By now, the unsafe fuel tank and filler neck on pre-1977 Pintos had been highly

publicized, and Ford would be forced to defend itself in court in a series of class-action product liability suits arising from several horrendous collision-related Pinto fires. Yet this didn't seem to affect new Pinto sales, which remained at about the 187,000-unit level for the second straight year.

Granada, now promoted as "An American Classic," sol-

The 1979 Granada ESS 4-door sedan. List price was $4990.

The Granada Ghia 4-door sedan for '79: $4830

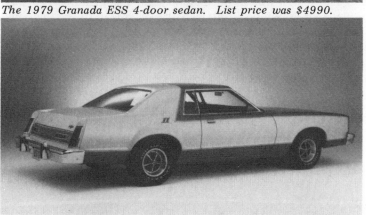

1979 LTD II 2-door hardtop with Sports Touring Package

The 1979 LTD II Brougham 2-door hardtop sold at $5780.

In profile, the '79 Thunderbird displayed minimal styling changes. Shown is the Town Landau model, priced at $8866.

T-Bird taillamps were again divided for '79, split by a backup lamp.   This base model has the optional T-bar roof.

diered on with the same styling and only minor interior revisions. The 4-speed overdrive manual gearbox was made available with the 5.0-liter/302-cid V-8, and the extra-cost all-disc brakes disappeared for lack of interest.

LTD II was in its final year, and continued to languish on the sales charts. The optional 400 V-8 was discontinued, and front bumper systems were lightened in a futile attempt to improve mileage. Highlighting the comparatively poor fuel economy of these mid-size Fords was a new option, a larger 27.5-gallon fuel tank.

Only minor revisions were made to Thunderbird as the 1977 design was in its final season. The grille was revised with an "open bar" latticework set ahead of thin vertical bars, and the full-width taillamps gave way to dual units separated by a central backup lamp. T-Bird remained a twin to the LTD II, so it also lost the 400 V-8 option. Replacing 1978's Diamond Jubilee Edition model at the top of the line was the new Heritage. Like its predecessor, it featured blanked-off rear roof quarters and full-house luxury trim and equipment. Sales dropped by nearly 80,000 units, yet Thunderbird continued to far outpace LTD II, and ended up in 12th spot on the overall industry roster.

Heritage replaced 1978's Diamond Jubilee Edition as the top-line '79 Thunderbird, but equipment was much the same.

1980

The importance of "Fox" is revealed as a new decade brings new problems

A s the '80s dawned, all Detroit was concerned with two major problems. One was meeting the government's Corporate Average Fuel Economy target: failure to comply could mean literally millions of dollars. The 1980 CAFE target was 20 mpg, up 1 mpg from '79, and it would rise to 22 mpg for 1981. The other problem was stemming the rising number of import car sales—or at least holding them at bay. Back in 1974, imports had captured some 1.4 million sales in a total market of about 8.7 million. By 1979, the number had grown to over 2.3 million in a U.S. market that had peaked in 1978 and was declining to similar volume. At Ford, these conditions prompted a model realignment for 1980, one that revealed the significance of the sensible "Fox" platform in the company's near-term product plans.

Pride of the 1980 fleet was the 25th edition of the Thunderbird, an all-new car built on what was essentially an enlongated Fairmont chassis. Compared to the eighth-generation 1977-79 models, the new Bird was nearly 16

Hidden headlamps were early part of '80 T-Bird concept.

Another early sketch exhibits strong wedge profile.

inches shorter overall on a 4.5-inch shorter wheelbase and was slimmer by more than 4 inches. Unit construction returned for the first time since 1966, and chassis specifications—modified MacPherson-strut front suspension, four-bar-link rear suspension, coil springs all

An interesting mockup from August 1975 shows designers toyed briefly with a Mustang II-size Thunderbird package.

Design team for 1980 Thunderbird initially leaned heavily toward radical wedgy shapes. Note dropped beltline here.

Another, less extreme approach bears definite T-Bird hallmarks, especially the aft greenhouse treatment.

around, rack-and-pinion steering—all looked suspiciously like Fairmont's. Weight was reduced dramatically—more than 700 pounds from 1977-79 levels, according to Ford—just the ticket for boosting the Bird's mileage as a proportion of Ford's overall fleet-average fuel economy.

Smaller engines and higher gearing also played a part. There was a new base engine now, a debored derivative of the Ford small-block displacing 4.2 liters or 255 cid. It would also be offered as an option for this year's Mustang and Fairmont. The only power option was the 302 itself, which could be teamed with a new 4-speed overdrive automatic transmission featuring a tall 0.67:1 top gear for economical low-rpm highway cruising. Axle ratios were numerically lower, again to promote good mileage.

This full-scale fiberglass workout from September 1975 bears T-Bird nose emblem, "Royale" fender script.

Design studio manager for the 1980 T-Bird project was Toshie Saito, who contributed many sketches like this one.

Another Saito rendering, still heavily wedge-shaped. Slim front is more a forecast of the '83 than the 1980 T-Bird.

Work on the new T-Bird had begun in 1976. As Richard Langworth notes in *Personal Luxury: The Thunderbird Story:* "There's a lot of tradition riding behind the ninth generation, perhaps because so many talented people connected with the Thunderbird since its inception were still making the decisions." From the first, he records, "the effort was to produce a four-seater of sporty shape and contemporary size, carrying such Thunderbird hallmarks as wraparound parking lights, prominent B-pillar and sculptured bodyside character lines. Aerodynamics... were prominent in the Design Center's thinking...Over 400 hours of wind tunnel testing reduced the coefficient of drag from 0.58 on the first clay model to 0.48 on the final fiberglass model—compared to 0.55 on the production

1979 Thunderbird." Even so, the styling was more throwback than predictive, and it wasn't very favorably received. Rich Ceppos of *Car and Driver* magazine probably summed up many buyers' reaction by saying the new Bird "at first seems to carry less clout than the old one. It's just not as big as New Jersey anymore, and there's only a hint of the old car's screaming baroque architec-

Another view of the square-cut compact model from 1975.

Manager Saito checks rear details on production mockup.

Here's the end result: the 1980 Thunderbird in its mid-range Town Landau form. Coach lamps, half-vinyl top were standard.

ture in its styling." Of course, Ford no doubt felt it crucial to preserve traditional T-Bird appearance "cues" in the new model. Trouble was, they just didn't seem to fit the smaller package.

The main benefits of downsizing showed up in the 1980 Bird's cabin, which remained as luxurious as ever, and its better handling. Said Ceppos: "If the truth be known, the new car does an infinitely better job of carrying four [adults] than the old one did. According to Ford, no interior room was lost up front...though rear hiproom is down about five inches. But more important is the increase of 2.8 inches in rear knee clearance...The Thunderbird still floats along as if it were in dreamland. The [overdrive automatic] shifts as smoothly as any con-

Another view of the 1980 Thunderbird Town Landau. Styling and proportions of this latest Bird drew mixed reactions.

The leather-lined interior of the 1980 T-Bird Town Landau

New electronic instrument cluster was a $275/$313 option.

ventional automatic. And little if any of the T-Bird's bank-vault quietness was lost in the downsizing process. About the only changes in the T-Bird's unenthusiastic road manners are positive ones: a welcome increase in steering effort and precision, and a touch of nimbleness that the engineers couldn't filter out . . . An optional handling package—recalibrated shocks, alloy rims, and the

largest Michelin TRX tires to date, 220/55R-390s—works small wonders.''

Despite its better mileage and handier size, the 1980 Thunderbird failed to make the kind of impression Ford marketing types had expected. Model year sales were down by over 40 percent, and T-Bird slipped from 12th to 19th place in the rankings among domestic models. The

1980 Thunderbird Town Landau retailed at $10,036.

The 1980 Thunderbird Town Landau hardtop

The base 1980 T-Bird hardtop with $359 Exterior Decor Group

The 1980 T-Bird with Exterior Decor Group, two-tone paint

Christened Mustang RSX, this 1980 Ford concept car was designed with an eye to aerodynamics by Ghia of Italy.

grand total, a bit more than 156,000 units, was split among base, Town Landau, and mid-year Silver Anniversary offerings.

An interesting footnote to the 1980 story was unearthed by Richard Langworth: "Just for the fun of it, for the sake of fond memories, Ford designers ran off a two-passenger 1980 Bird after the four-passenger car was locked up for production. In appearance it was a 1980 Thunderbird from the cowl forward and the rear window back. The difference was in between. Cut out of the wheel-base was 8.4 inches; the front seat was met by a carpeted package shelf which extended back to a not-too-distant rear window. The rear roof quarter contained genuine 1957-style portholes...Frosted into the porthole glass was the legend 'Collector's Edition' and '1/2000.' " It would have been an interesting revival but, as Langworth correctly observed, "Costs, and the perils of the present North American market, prevented the model from evolving further."

Mustang evolved for 1980 with only detail styling re-

Mustang's 1980 Cobra package was restyled along the lines of the mid-'79 Indy Pace Car replica. Package cost $1482.

Black lower bodyside paint, "Cobra" lettering on quarter windows marked Mustang's performance package for 1980.

Carriage roof was a $625 extra for 1980 Mustang notchbacks.

Turbo-four could be had without Cobra option on '80 Mustang.

1980 Mustang Cobra sported three-slat grille, big hood bulge.

Here's the basic Mustang 2-door for 1980. Price: $4884.

finements and an expanded options list. Ford's ponycar had been chosen for pace car duty at the 1979 Indianapolis 500, so it was natural a pace car replica would appear as a mid-year addition to the line. It did, and about 6000 were sold. Its main styling features—horizontal-bar grille, front and rear spoilers, integral front fog lamps, hood bulge—plus special TRX suspension were retained

for this year's edition of the Cobra package, giving it some added distinction. The driveline chart now listed the 255-cid V-8 as the largest available engine, and a 4-speed overdrive manual gearbox was a new extra on six-cylinder cars. New to the options slate this year were genuine Recaro front bucket seats, roof-mounted luggage carrier and, for hardtops, a Carriage Roof vinyl top that

The 1980 Granada 2-door sedan, here finished with the optional "tu-tone" paint treatment, which cost $180.

Granada ESS 4-door sedan for 1980 sold at $5598.

1980 Granada Ghia 4-door sedan carried a $5509 price tag.

Pinto Squire wagon returned to the 1980 lineup at $4937.

Rallye package was a $369 extra on the 1980 Pinto Runabout.

simulated the look of a true convertible. Standard equipment and interior trim were mildly revised, and all Mustangs acquired more effective halogen headlamps. Ford's ponycar retained 7th spot in the domestic sales race but, as with most other U.S. cars this year, scored much lower volume. The year-end total was about 75,000 cars short of the previous year's.

A number of minor changes marked Ford's other 1980 models, none of which changed appreciably. Granada was now the division's sole representative in the mid-size field with the demise of the LTD II, and continued to trail both the Chevrolet Malibu/Monte Carlo and Oldsmobile's Cutlass/Cutlass Supreme. The subcompact Pinto, now in its final year, fell two spots on the sales chart and lost its

1980 Pinto Runabout with Rallye package option

The $4662 Pinto wagon for '80 with the $600 Cruising package

1980 Fairmont 2-door with ostensibly optional turbo-four

1980 Fairmont Squire wagon now retailed at $5179.

Ford issued several press photos of turbocharged Fairmonts this year (Futura shown), but option never made production.

The newly named 1980 Crown Victoria 2-door, priced at $7070, poses with the Country Squire wagon, listed at $7426.

previously optional 2.8-liter V-6. Fairmont moved up from 5th to 3rd place in sales despite few changes. The 255-cid V-8 took over from the 302 as the top power offering. Ford also ostensibly offered the Mustang's turbocharged 2.3-liter four as a Fairmont option beginning this year, but few if any cars were so equipped owing to persistent mechanical bugs with this engine. At mid-year, a Futura 4-door wearing the coupe's cross-hatch grille and spiffier interior joined the line, and the Ghia models disappeared. The full-size LTD was again compared with Rolls-Royce for ride and quietness in 1980 advertising. The only mechanical change of significance was availability in most areas of the new 4-speed overdrive automatic with either the standard 302 or optional 351 V-8s. A low-priced "S" sedan and wagon were added to the lineup, and the top series, previously called LTD Landau, was rechristened LTD Crown Victoria, reviving a name from the mid-'50s. Sales as a whole were not great. The big Ford sank to 16th place among domestic nameplates, and unit sales were down by more than 100,000 cars.

Top-line Crown Victoria models like this $7201 4-door sedan boasted wrapover roof trim, half-vinyl roof, coach lamps.

The "world car" debuts: a symbolic small Ford, a solid sales success

Auto industry observers watched Ford expectantly for 1981. The reason was Escort, the all-new replacement for the subcompact Pinto and boldly proclaimed the "world car." In design, it was a complete departure for a domestic Ford product: front-wheel drive, all-independent suspension, an overhead-cam four-cylinder engine of advanced specification, a truly international package size. As Ford's first direct challenger to a hoarde of small import models—especially those from Japan—Escort was commercially very important for the company. It was also something of a symbol: a measure of the U.S. auto industry's ability to compete effectively on its own home ground in the face of the strongest threat yet from overseas.

Escort bowed at a time when Ford Motor Company's financial outlook was decidedly cloudy. The deep recession that had begun in 1979 continued to put a damper on car sales generally and U.S. car sales in particular. With inflation pushing car prices ever higher and interest rates soaring to unbelievable levels, a good many would-be buyers simply could no longer afford to buy a new car—or at least to buy one as often as they used to.

Ford's share of this shrinking market was itself shrinking, hitting an all-time low of 16.5 percent for the entire company—not just Ford Division—by the end of 1980. Worse, the economic slump came at a time when the firm could least afford it. Ford was already well into a multibillion-dollar program to redesign its entire product line top to bottom, and the sudden sales drop only accelerated the drain on the company's capital reserves. Some pundits began wondering aloud whether Ford would survive to its 100th birthday. At this writing, the company has yet to recover fully from this situation, though prospects are brighter now that Ford will not only survive but thrive in the years ahead. But as the 1981 model year opened, some old hands around Dearborn may have had dark thoughts about similar tough times in the late '20s and late '40s.

The Escort (and a companion Mercury line called Lynx) was developed under the code-name "Erika," a project that originated as far back as 1972. At that time, a powertrain development team within the Engineering and Research Staff at Dearborn started exploring engine designs intended for the much smaller cars planned for the '80s. Meanwhile, Ford of Europe had embarked on a new front-wheel-drive car to replace rear-drive designs in the British and German lineups. This became the Fiesta, which bowed in the fall of 1976 and was also sold in America through 1980. The Fiesta proved such a success that European executives decided to offer a slightly larger car of similar design as the next step up the range. This idea dovetailed neatly with U.S. plans to produce a new smaller model to replace the Pinto. By mid-1977, the two efforts had been brought together, and the "world car" was born.

A sneak preview of the European Ford Sierra and 1984 Tempo was this 1981 concept vehicle, the slippery Probe III.

The 250,000th Escort came off the Wayne, Michigan line May 13, 1981. That's sales vice-president Phil Benton on the right.

The plot for Erika was complicated but sensible. The project goal was a basic package suitable for production in both the U.S. and Europe but able to be tailored to suit the differing buyer preferences in each market. Designed for high-volume production in order to realize costs savings through "economies of scale," the new car would utilize components produced locally or imported from various points around the world, whichever was cheaper. Early on, it was decided that the Erika engine would be developed and engineered by the Europeans but would be built on both sides of the Atlantic, while manual transmissions and running gear would come from Ford's Japanese affiliate, Toyo Kogyo, makers of the Mazda. The automatic transmission to be offered optionally would be developed in Dearborn. Body design would be a joint effort facilitated by transatlantic computer hookups and frequent in-person consultation.

The heart of Erika was a brand-new four-cylinder overhead-cam engine. It was dubbed "CVH" for Compound Valve Hemispherical, a reference to its valve and

1981 Escort GLX 3-door sedan. Note tiny "bustle" rear deck.

1981 Escort GL 3-door sedan was priced at $5838.

head arrangement. Ford engineers had determined that, for a variety of reasons, a hemispherical combustion chamber shape was the best choice for both efficiency and performance, and that the spark plug should be positioned as close to the middle of the chamber as possible. To allow this, valve stems were slanted at 45 degrees, which in turn allowed relatively larger valve faces plus separate cam lobes for both intakes and exhausts and crossflow breathing. Two displacements were planned, 1.3 and 1.6 liters, but only the latter was ultimately built in the U.S. The CVH engine also featured a machined aluminum cylinder head and a block made of reliable cast iron.

To save space up front, the compact engine was mounted transversely, as was becoming common small-car design practice. The standard 4-speed manual trans-axle was a wide-ratio unit with a slightly overdriven top gear. The new automatic transaxle (ATX) featured what Ford termed a "splitter" gearset within the torque converter that divided torque between the converter and a direct mechanical connection to the driveshafts. The benefit was less frictional loss to converter rotation and thus better fuel efficiency.

Dimensionally, the Erika was planned to match the size of the rear-drive Escort, next-to-smallest model in the European Ford line, but would be narrower and shorter than the domestic Pinto. A 3-door hatchback sedan would be offered everywhere. Americans would also get a 5-door wagon, while European customers could choose from a 5-door sedan and 3-door wagon as well. Styling on each version was a separate, though coordinated, effort. Partly because of U.S. safety requirements, the American Escort ended up looking duller and boxier compared to its overseas cousins. However, Dearborn claimed good aerodynamics for its styling, quoting a 0.40 drag coefficient for the sedan—quite good for a short, boxy car all things considered. One aerodynamic aid common to both U.S. and European hatchback models was a tiny bustle "deck" (Ford called it a "decklid kicker"), which helped lower drag and rear-end lift by minimizing air turbulence at the back of the car.

By coincidence, the U.S. Escort/Lynx emerged riding a

The 1981 Escort GLX wagon with the $243 Squire trim option

SS models were sportiest '81 Escorts. The 3-door is shown.

94.2-inch wheelbase, the same as that of the old Pinto and Mercury Bobcat. Rack-and-pinion steering was also common to all, but from there the Escort chassis differed markedly. Its front suspension was by MacPherson struts—instead of the Pinto's A-arms—with lower control arms, an anti-roll bar and, of course, coil springs. At the rear was a fully independent setup, much more modern than the Pinto's leaf-sprung live axle. It consisted of one-

Price of the '81 Escort GLX 3-door was $6476 suggested retail.

'81 Escort GL wagon carried a suggested $6178 sticker price.

piece forged spindles mounted laterally, pivoted inboard on the rear frame crossmember, and acting on vertical shock absorber struts. Coil springs were positioned between these arms and longitudinal chassis beams above. A tie rod ran from the hub carrier on each lateral arm to a forward mounting point. In all, it was an elegant, low-cost irs arrangement, and just right for an inexpensive small car. It gave Ford a class exclusive among domestics, not to mention many imports. As in the later Pintos the Escort's front brakes were discs; drums were used at the rear. Power assist was available at extra cost for both brakes and steering.

Despite being three inches narrower outside, the "world cars" were much roomier inside than the old Pinto/Bobcat. Thinner, space-saving doors as well as the compact front-wheel drivetrain were major contributors

to the gains. In overall length, the Escort 3-door was some seven inches shorter than the Pinto Runabout, the Escort wagon a full 15 inches trimmer than the Pinto wagon. The new cars were also several hundred pounds lighter. Glass area was greatly increased, seats were higher, cargo space vastly enlarged. All of a sudden, Ford had itself not only a genuine import-fighter but the most up-to-date domestic subcompact on the market.

Escort was greeted with enthusiasm—but not always the highest praise—by the automotive press. CONSUMER GUIDE® magazine's initial test car recorded a 0-60 mph time of 15.4 seconds with the standard 4-speed transaxle—nothing to get excited about—and returned a creditable 25.5 mpg in a very demanding round of city/suburban driving. Though we thought it a great advance over Pinto, we concluded that, compared to its foreign ri-

Phantom view of the '81 Escort reveals compact front-drive power package and independent rear suspension system.

The standard Escort dash (right) contrasts with that of a more fully equipped model with extra instruments (left).

vals, the Escort "sadly lags behind in ride and handling control, interior design, and workmanship. Still, Ford's billion-dollar baby has a lot of potential. All it needs is detail refinement to stand up fully to the best in its class. Then, it would be a 'world car' in the true sense of the word." Evidently, Ford took such comments seriously, because running changes were instituted almost as soon as the Escort went on sale. By the end of the model year it had become a more pleasant, better-riding, smoother-running car. And such "fine tuning" would continue; in fact, Escort is still being progressively refined at this writing.

Considering the gloomy national economy and the depressed car market, Escort sold exceedingly well in its debut season. Over 60,000 units were retailed between October and the end of December 1980. Total for the model year was over 320,000, making it the second most popular car in the country (after the Chevrolet Chevette). Escort would go on to capture the number-one spot in '82.

Pushed out of the limelight by Escort was a new Granada. Actually, the '81 version of Ford's erstwhile intermediate was less new than it appeared, for it was essentially a restyled Fairmont with softer chassis settings and plusher interior trim. Still, a reconstituted Fairmont wasn't a bad thing to be. The new Granada weighed some 350-400 pounds less than the 1975-80 models, offered more room inside, a better control layout, more precise steering, greater maneuverability, and somewhat better ride control. Fuel economy was also improved even if performance wasn't. While this bit of "badge engineering" made a certain amount of economic sense for Ford, the Fairmont remained a better buy in the opinion of CONSUMER GUIDE® magazine's editors.

During 1980, Ford had given every indication that it was about to get its performance act back together and put it on the road. And Mustang would definitely be the star of the show. A tantalizing "concept car," the Mustang IMSA, toured the auto show circuit that season. Powered by Ford's turbocharged four, it sat astride massive Pirelli P7 tires nestled under outlandishly flared fenders. It featured a deep front air dam, a loop rear spoiler, and pop-riveted plastic covers for side windows, taillight panel, and headlamps. In name and appearance, it hinted strongly that Ford was more than just thinking about a return to competition—and about the International Motor Sports Association GT series in particular.

Then in September, Ford announced formation of a Special Vehicle Operations department. Significantly, it was headed by Michael Kranefuss, newly arrived in Dearborn from his post as competition director for Ford of Europe. The purpose of SVO was to "develop a series of limited-production performance cars and develop their image through motorsport." It quickly got down to business with a turbo Mustang to be driven in selected 1981 IMSA GT events by former Porsche pilot Klaus Ludwig. Other Mustangs receiving similar direct factory help were a Trans-Am car for Dennis Mecham and an IMSA Kelly American Challenge racer for Lyn St. James.

As if to signal its return to the track, Ford debuted the McLaren Mustang in late 1980. The work of designers Todd Gerstenberger and Harry Wykes, it was a heavily

Only 250 of the 1981 McLaren Mustangs were constructed.

Bold 1980 Mustang IMSA show car hinted at a return to racing.

Bulging fender flares, loop spoiler marked Mustang IMSA.

modified Mustang with enough built-in potential to make it easily adaptable for race duty. In appearance, the McLaren was quite close to the IMSA show car. It sported a grille-less nose above a low-riding skirt spoiler, functional hood scoops, tweaked suspension (mostly a mixture of heavy-duty off-the-shelf components), bulging fender flares, and delicate-looking BBS alloy wheels shod with broad-shouldered 225/55R-15 Firestone HPR radial tires. Again, the turbocharged four was used, but it was fitted with a new variable-rate boost control. This provided a maximum boost range of 5 to 11 psi, as opposed to the stock engine's fixed 5-psi pressure. At 10 psi, output was rated at 175 bhp at 2500 rpm, a considerable jump over the stock mill's, which was usually pegged at around 131 bhp (Ford never released official ratings for

1981 Mustang press photo highlights new T-roof option.

Price of the Mustang's Cobra package rose to $1586 for '81.

'81 Mustang Cobra option still included turbocharged four.

its turbo-four). Price for the McLaren Mustang was $25,000 a copy, and only 250 (including the prototype) were built.

All this muscle flexing came too late to affect the 1981 Mustang, however, which was little changed visually or mechanically. Reclining backrests were now standard for the factory bucket seats, and interior trim was upgraded in appearance and completeness. Power side windows and a T-bar roof with twin lift off glass panels were added to the options slate.

A 5-speed overdrive manual gearbox had been an-

nounced as an option for both Mustang fours in mid-1980, and this became more widely available for '81. The new gearbox pulled a shorter 3.45:1 final drive (versus the normal 3.08:1 cog) for better off-the-line snap. The overdrive fifth was geared at 0.82:1 for economical highway cruising. It was just what the base Mustang needed, except for one thing: in adding the extra gear, Ford goofed. As CONSUMER GUIDE® magazine's automotive staff noted in its 1980 test, "Our biggest objections to the 5-speed are its linkage—stiff, yet vague—and its shift pattern. As with the 4-speed unit, 1st through 4th are ar-

A Futura wagon was added to the Fairmont stable at mid-1980. Shown here is the carryover '81 model with the Squire option.

$6151 was the price tag on the '81 Fairmont 4-door sedan.

The Fairmont-based '81 Granada GL 2-door sedan: $6875.

The Fairmont Futura 4-door sedan reprised for '81 at $6361.

The base L version of the '81 Granada 4-door sedan: $6633

ranged in the usual 4-speed pattern. But 5th is awkwardly located at the bottom of the dogleg to the right of and opposite 4th, instead of up and to the right...Why Ford did it this way is a mystery, but it makes getting into or out of 5th real work. Our guess is that the engineers wanted to prevent inexperienced drivers from accidentally engaging overdrive and needlessly lugging the engine, as well as to prevent confusion with the often-used 3rd. If so, they've succeeded admirably.'' Apparently, Ford felt most drivers would want to downshift from 5th directly to third, bypassing fourth. At least that's what one transmission engineer said. A more logical reason was that putting fifth over and up would have entailed excessively long arm reach. The factory's ''official'' explanation was that the U-shaped shift motion would better emphasize the economy benefits of the overdrive fifth gear. Whatever the reason, the idea just didn't work.

Debored 4.2-liter small-block V-8 was standard big Ford power unit for '81. Shown is the LTD Crown Victoria 4-door sedan.

The LTD 4-door sedan for 1981, priced at $7718

1981 LTD Country Squire wagon: $8640 suggested retail price

The LTD Crown Victoria 2-door listed at $8251 for 1981.

The Thunderbird Town Landau for '81 retailed at $8689.

Heritage replaced 1980's Silver Anniversary model as the top-line 1981 Thunderbird. Suggested list price was $11,355.

Elsewhere in the 1981 Ford lineup were few changes, apart from engine availability. The 4.2-liter/255-cid V-8 took over as the new standard engine in the full-size LTD, with the 302 moving to the options column. The 351 Windsor V-8, now in its last year, returned as the top power option, rated at 145 bhp. The previous 3-speed automatic transmission was phased out as standard equipment in favor of the 4-speed overdrive unit introduced as

an option the previous year. There were almost no alterations to appearance or equipment availability. The compact Fairmont soldiered on with no styling modifications. However, the lineup expanded by one with addition of a Futura station wagon, joining the existing 4-door sedan and 2-door coupe. The 4.2-liter V-8 replaced the 5.0-liter engine at the top of the chart, and the turbocharged 2.3-liter four was now officially cancelled. New options included a diagnostic graphic warning light system and digital clock with console from the Mustang, plus Michelin TRX radial tires and specially sized wheels, and an illuminated entry system *a la* Thunderbird and the full-size Fords.

Thunderbird also continued with little change. Ford had made history midway through the 1980 model year by making its 3.3-liter/200-cid six a $76 credit option for the Bird, a first for this model. The six was made standard equipment for '81, with the 4.2- and 5.0-liter V-8s as options. External identification was provided by removing the grille trim extension from below the front bumper, and all models now came with the former extra-cost Exterior Luxury Group appearance trim. In a move that paralleled 1978-79, the Silver Anniversary model from 1980 was renamed Heritage this year, but was basically the same package. Its roof treatment was now applied to the middle Town Landau model, with smaller "coach" rear side windows framed by an up-and-over roof trim band, plus rear-half vinyl top, bodyside striping, and nighttime coach lamps. Thunderbird model year production dropped by nearly half.

1982

Performance makes a surprising comeback, and the two-seater returns

T he first performance Mustang in nearly a decade plus an interesting new 2-seat sporty coupe were the highlights of an otherwise forgettable 1982 model year at Ford. The U.S. auto industry, still reeling from the effects of a nationwide recession, suffered its worst sales season in 20 years. Ford was not immune, and the company's market share remained at its previous dismal level of just under 16.5 percent. There were bright spots, though. The brightest was Escort, which had been voted "Most Significant New Domestic Car" for '81 in the annual *Car and Driver* magazine readers' poll. The front-drive Ford quickly rose to the top of the '82 sales charts, ousting Chevrolet's antiquated Chevette as the country's best-seller by close to 75,000 units. Among compacts, Mustang remained a solid fourth, and Fairmont was right behind in 5th place, despite its now five-year-old design. Unfortunately, Granada was well down among mid-size cars, Thunderbird was even further behind, and the full-size Ford continued to trail the big Oldsmobile, Chevrolet, and Buick models.

If there's one 1982 development enthusiasts will want to remember it would have to be the return of the performance Mustang. This appeared in the form of a newly fortified version of the venerable 302-cid small-block V-8 as an option for all models. Ford left no doubt about the new engine or its mission in life by labelling it "high out-

GT 3-door was the sportiest '82 Mustang, cost $8308 basic.

'82 Mustang GT retained front end from previous Cobra model.

put." Specific changes included a special camshaft adapted from a marine version of the small-block, along with a larger two-barrel carb, bigger and smoother exhaust system, and low-restriction twin-snorkel air cleaner. Offered only with the wide-ratio 4-speed overdrive manual gearbox, the revived 302 was capable of pushing the Mustang to 60 mph in less than eight seconds—actually closer to seven by most magazine accounts. Trumpeted Ford ads: "The Boss is back!" Output was a muscular 157 bhp at 4200 rpm, with peak torque of 240 lbs/ft at 2400 rpm.

Apart from this heartening news there was little about the '82 Mustang to stir the blood. The turbo-four was discontinued after compiling a poor reliability record, though the engine would return in a considerably altered state in about a year. Model nomenclature was revised with L, GL, GLX, and GT is ascending order of price and sportiness. The GT took over for the SS, briefly marketed

With the optional 5.0-liter H.O. V-8 and 157 bhp, the 1982 Mustang GT was the hottest of Detroit's born-again muscle cars.

in 1981, as the sports model of the line. A larger gas tank (up to 15.4 gallons) was adopted for longer cruising range, wider wheels and tires were fitted as standard, and a remote-control lefthand door mirror became a no-cost extra. Aside from the H.O. V-8, other drivetrains continued as before, but the optional 4.2-liter V-8 got a lockup torque converter, effective in all forward gears, for its "mandatory option" 3-speed Select Shift automatic. The new GT kept the low-slung front air dam, integral fog lights, and rear lip spoiler from the previous Cobra and SS, but the "hey, look at me!" decals were now a thing of the past. GTs rode a beefed-up chassis featuring stiffer front and rear anti-roll bars, wider 185-section radial tires, and specially calibrated springs, bushings, and shocks.

The Mustang GT signalled a performance revival in De-

Revived Mustang convertible was scheduled for late-1982 release. This press photo was issued, but model was delayed to '83.

troit after a dull decade in which all U.S. automakers had learned to cope with government safety, emissions, and fuel economy mandates. But Ford was not alone in the swing back to excitement, and at mid-year GM trotted out its totally restyled third-generation Chevrolet Camaro and Pontiac Firebird.

With their 5.0-liter V-8s, tuned chassis, and race-inspired styling touches, the Mustang GT, Camaro Z28, and Firebird Trans Am were quickly matched up in car magazine comparison tests. While the GM cars won points for their superior handling and arguably more modern styling, the Mustang was conceded to be more practical for everyday use—and discernably quicker. *Car and Driver* magazine recorded 8.1 seconds in the 0-60 mph test with its GT against 8.6 seconds for the injected V-8 Camaro with automatic and a comparatively sluggish 10.6 seconds for the carbureted V-8 Trans Am with 4-speed. Writing in the August 1982 issue, *C/D's* technical editor, Don Sherman, noted that "...in terms of sheer visceral appeal, [the Mustang] is right up there with the Porsche [928]."

Not all was sweetness and light, however. In testing the Mustang GT's sister ship, the Mercury Capri RS, CONSUMER GUIDE® magazine's staff found the power-assisted rack-and-pinion steering irritatingly vague, overly light, and severely lacking in feel. Wet-weather traction was also a problem because of the V-8's ample torque, 240 pounds-feet developed at a very low 2400 rpm. We weren't able to evaluate handling fully because our test car was delivered during one of the coldest weeks in Chicago history, and test conditions were hardly ideal. Even so, we found it possible to light the back tires easily in a brisk take-off from a stoplight, accompanied at times by rear-end jitter that made us wonder what would happen in hard cornering on bumpy surfaces. *C/D's* Sherman echoed our concerns: "In left-hand sweepers, the gas pedal acts as a power-oversteer switch...That smooth two-step unfortunately turns into a jitterbug in right-hand bends, where power hop conspires to make life difficult."

Despite such faults, Ford's latterday muscle car had much to recommend it. We found its interior roomier and more practical than the Camaro/Firebird's. Though both are hatchback designs, Ford somehow managed to provide a good deal more usable luggage space in its hot rods than GM. We also found the Mustang/Capri 4-speed manual gearbox had a much lighter shift action [and a more comfortably placed shifter] than the truck-like Camaro/Firebird linkage. Our staff was divided on driving position, some preferring the more confined, low-slung stance of the GM cars to the more upright "vintage" feel of the Ford products. Yet most agreed the Mustang/Capri was a far better compromise for those who have to contend with the daily drudgery of stop-and-go traffic, where the manual-shift Camaro/Firebird would prove tiring to drive for any length of time. There was still work to do, but our overall view was that Ford had injected a much-needed dose of pizzazz into its ponycars with the revived 302 V-8.

Pizzazz of a different sort arrived this year in Ford's first production two-seater since the 1957 Thunderbird. In the tradition of two best-selling Fords of the past—

1982 EXP was Ford's first production two-seater since '57.

Based on Escort chassis, running gear, '82 EXP cost $7387.

Notchback roof set EXP apart from "bubbleback" Mercury LN7.

Maverick and the original Mustang—the new EXP and its Mercury LN7 companion were announced about six months ahead of the model year, in early 1981. Essentially, they were sporty coupes derived from the front-drive Escort/Lynx sedans, planned around a more rakish body with a reworked set of interior dimensions. In other words, they were to the "world cars" what the original Mustang had been to the early-'60s Falcon.

The new coupes shared the 94.2-inch Escort/Lynx wheelbase, plus basic suspension design and running

Two-seat EXP bowed as an early-1982 entry in the spring of 1981. Compared to its "world car" parent, it was longer, lower, and slightly narrower. Lackluster performance and controversial styling were likely factors limiting sales.

gear, even the subcompacts' instrument panel and control layout. Dimensionally, the coupes were about 6.5 inches longer overall, nearly 3 inches narrower and more than 2 inches lower overall. Styling was distinctive, but drew very sharply divided love/hate reactions. Like Escort/Lynx, the coupes offered the convenience of a lift-up hatchback door. The Ford version was styled as a more conservative notchback while the Mercury wore a radical "bubbleback" rear window, a large wraparound affair. Both models featured large wrapped taillamps, prominent lipped wheelarches, and wide bodyside moldings about a third of the way up from the rocker panels. The windshield had a "faster" angle than the sedans', which meant a correspondingly lower roofline and a somewhat "bathtub" seating position. The coupes' "face" was dominated by single rectangular headlamps recessed in prominent nacelles faired into the hood and front fenders. These flanked a sloped center section running down to a "grille" composed of two wide air-intake slots on EXP or 10 small slots on LN7. Overall, the EXP/LN7 certainly looked different, but there were those who said the styling vaguely recalled an Escort with adenoid trouble.

Underneath their sportier bodies, the new coupes used the basic Escort/Lynx chassis but with stiffer springs and shock valving for flatter cornering response. Initially offered for the coupes and later extended to the sportier sedan models was an optional setup designed around Michelin's premium TRX tires in a new-to-America P165/70R-365 size. This comprised harder pivot bushings for front and rear lateral control arms, harder rear tie-rod bushings, even stiffer shock valving all-around, higher-rate front springs, larger-diameter front anti-roll bar, and variable-rate instead of constant-rate rear springs. With either suspension, power steering on the coupes came with higher-effort valving than on the Escort/Lynx for more precise steering control and better road feel.

The coupes also carried a longer list of standard equipment than the sedans in keeping with their higher list prices—$7387 for the basic EXP against $5518 for the least expensive Escort. The list ran to such items as power brakes, electric rear window defroster, full carpeting, tachometer and extra engine gauges, electric hatchback release, digital clock, and a handy roller-blind shade to hide cargo from prying eyes.

Early road tests found a lot to like in Ford's new little sportsters—except performance. There was a reason for this: the coupes used the same 70-bhp CVH four found in the sedans, yet carried about 200 pounds more weight. Additional sound insulation and the extra comfort and convenience features accounted for some of the difference, but a big penalty must have been the weight of the extra body bracing needed to support the heavy hatchback—especially on the glassy LN7.

Ford recognized the problem and, as an interim step, made a shorter 4.05:1 final drive ratio a no-cost option with manual gearbox at the start of the formal 1982 model year. Testing an LN7 so equipped (the Mercury got more press play than the EXP, probably because of its more radical shape), *Road & Track* magazine recorded 15.0 seconds in the 0-60 mph dash, about a second off the pace of the lighter sedan. In CONSUMER GUIDE® magazine's test the time was 15.8 seconds, downright lackluster for a car with sporting pretensions. And the automatic EXP we tested shortly afterwards proved even slower, needing nearly 18 seconds to reach the benchmark speed.

Ford wasn't about to take such reports lying down. Next the division made available a close-ratio gearset with 3.59:1 final drive, which accomplished much the same thing as the old wide-ratio gearbox with the 4.05 gearing. Then, in March 1982, came a high-output version of the CVH four, producing 80 bhp at 5800 rpm—a 14 percent increase. The extra horses were found by boosting compression (from 8.7:1 to 9.0:1), enlarging the air cleaner intake, fitting a free-flowing muffler and twin-branch exhaust manifold, plus higher-lift camshaft and larger carburetor venturis. All this helped knock about a second off the acceleration times—but it also magnified the noisy gruffness inherent in some versions of the "world car" engine.

As for roadability, most reviewers found that the EXP/LN7 could be very capable indeed, provided you had the TRX package. Quantitatively, *R&T* ranked it right along with such nimble handlers as the VW Scirocco. Qualitatively, the story was different. Nobody it seemed liked the power steering—too insensitive and too overassisted—or the ride—an unhappy combination of overly stiff springs and overly soft shocks. CONSUMER GUIDE® magazine's critics found the ride harsh, choppy, and irritating, especially over sharp disturbances like tar strips. However, we praised the handling and maneuverability, and found the car fun to drive on twisty roads—if they were smooth. And offsetting the milquetoast performance was very good mileage: an overall average of 28 mpg in our test versus the government's 27-mpg city estimate.

Ford has often been accused of overdoing its market research when planning new products, and this may have been the biggest problem with the EXP/LN7. These cars were presumably aimed at a new sort of buyer: young, mainly single people with an active lifestyle, the idealized happy-go-lucky professional looking for something sporty, personal, and fun for around-town errand-running or the occasional cross-country trip with a favored companion. What these people got was an Escort coupe with no back seat and somewhat dubious styling (Ford's promise of an optional rear jump seat for occasional use never materialized). To date, neither of these cars has been a sales winner. Despite an extra-long model year, EXP failed to crack 95,000 units—hardly impressive even allowing for the poor market conditions. The LN7 did even

New-for-'82 Escort 5-door sedan in GLX trim: $7302

worse despite its more eye-catching styling. At this writing, perhaps the best we can say of these "sports coupes" is that Ford is still gamely trying to make them into something enthusiasts can relate to, as our final section reveals.

Elsewhere at Ford Division the 1982 story was mainly one of refinements to improve fuel economy. A new engine was part of the plan, Ford's first-ever V-6. At 3.8 liters or 232 cubic inches, it was about the same size as the successful Buick V-6, which by this time had become a workhorse throughout GM. However, the Ford unit was engineered to be far lighter and actually tipped the scales only four pounds heavier than the 2.3-liter/140-cid "Lima" four thanks to use of aluminum for cylinder head,

New 5-door sedan gave Escort three body styles for '82. Pictured (left to right): GL 3-door and 5-door, Squire wagon.

1982 Escorts like this GL 5-door wore Ford oval grille badge.

The 1982 Fairmont Futura coupe, here with two-tone paint

front cover/accessory drive, and intake manifold. Bore and stroke dimensions were 3.87x3.44 inches, and initial power output was 112 at 4000 rpm, with peak torque of 175 lbs/ft produced at 2600 rpm. This would be an important new powerplant in Ford's future. It was initially offered in this year's Granada as the top power option and as the step-up engine for the '82 Thunderbird.

As most observers predicted, a 5-door hatchback sedan appeared this year as a new body style for Escort, which was mostly unchanged. The quickest way of spotting the

new models was by the blue oval emblems bearing the famous "Ford" script front and rear. This was the first time in years the familiar insignia had been used on the exteriors of Ford cars, and it was adopted throughout the 1982 lineup. The five-series Escort line returned minus the base and SS wagons, but the new 5-door in intermediate L, GL, and GLX trim brought the model count to 11. Standard equipment changes included wider radial tires for all models, power front disc brakes for wagons, a larger-diameter exhaust system and, with air condition-

Fairmont wagon was transferred to the upscale Granada line for 1982. Shown here is the lower-price L version, $7983.

"Hatch" tailgate window was optional on '82 Granada wagon.

1982 Granada GL wagon cost $8399. Squire option added $282.

ing, a switch built into the accelerator that disconnected the AC drive momentarily whenever peak (full-throttle) performance was required.

Ford's middleweights changed little this year. All Fairmonts were now called Futura as the 2-door sedan was dropped and the 5-door wagon was restyled as a Granada. Fuel tanks in Fairmonts and Granada sedans were reshaped, which permitted the center trunk floor to be dropped slightly for extra cargo space. Gas caps with plastic tethers to prevent loss during fillups were a fea-

ture new to these models as well as other '82 Fords. Fairmont's most powerful engine was now the sturdy 200-cid six, still in production after some two decades. A new option for the ex-Fairmont wagon was a rear window that could be flipped up for loading or unloading small items without having to open the full tailgate. The new corporate 3.8-liter V-6 took over from the 4.2-liter V-8 as the top Granada engine.

In the quest for better fuel economy, Ford began fitting lockup torque converter clutches to its 3-speed Select-

Like other '82 Fords, this year's Granada bore blue Ford oval emblems. Shown is the GL 4-door with half-vinyl top.

1983

The shape of Fords in our future and more Dearborn dynamite

Alternative Fuel Vehicle (AFV): a driveable '82 experimental

Tomorrow's wagon? Aerovan concept vehicle points the way.

Shift automatic with the six-cylinder engines in Fairmont, Granada, and Thunderbird. Unlike GM's lockup system, however, the Ford design was effective in all forward ratios, not just top gear. The lockup clutch provides direct mechanical drive from crankshaft to propshaft, thus eliminating the "slip" inherent in torque-converter automatics that eats up fuel. It was one of many subtle extremes Detroit engineers turned to in the face of the government's increasingly tight corporate average fuel economy targets. This year's requirement was 24 mpg.

A practical demonstration of Ford's work in automotive electronics appeared this year in a new option for Thunderbird and LTD, which were otherwise virtual reruns. A digital instrument cluster had been offered for the '81 Thunderbird, with digital speedometer and bargraph "gauges" for fuel level and coolant temperature, all in a brilliant blue-green vacuum-florescent display. This year's new "Tripminder" was the next logical step. Basically, it was a sophisticated quartz clock combined with a trip odometer. It kept tabs on fuel flow, vehicle speed, and real or elapsed time. From this primary data, it could then calculate and display such information as instantaneous or average miles per gallon, fuel used, average trip speed, trip mileage, and journey time in either English or metric measure, all at the touch of the appropriate buttons. It wasn't exactly a fuel economy aid, though you could use it as such.

Suddenly, it seemed "Total Performance" was staging a comeback. The 1983 Ford lineup was one of the most exciting in years, with an unusual number of new or heavily revised models, plus a new emphasis on fun combined with practical high technology. Nowhere was there a better expression of Detroit's new way of doing business—or of its determination to survive in the face of both unprecedented foreign competition and an economic crisis of historic proportions. The entire U.S. auto industry had been through some very rough times of late—and they weren't over yet despite faint signs of a general economic recovery as the model year opened. Some critics suggested that the events of the early '80s, the result of a complex set of forces, had changed forever the way American cars are designed and manufactured. And if that was true—and it most certainly was—then Ford was surely in the vanguard of what amounted to nothing less than an industry-wide "renaissance."

A perfect example of the new order was the dramatically restyled 1983 Thunderbird. Though mechanically and structurally similar to the 1980-82 cars, this 10th-generation design signalled a complete turnaround in Dearborn's styling philosophy. Familiar fripperies once used to imply "luxury" and "status" were part of Ford's styling past—things like half-vinyl tops, standup grilles, opera windows, and all the rest. From now on, aerodynamic considerations would shape the Fords in our future. They would be "functional" and "organic" in appearance, a new kind of aesthetic that relies on form for attractiveness instead of tacked-on glitz.

Why this sharp break with tradition? As Jack Telnack, the company's executive vice-president for design, put it: "Efficient aerodynamic design is one of the best ways we know of to cost-effectively increase the fuel economy of our products. Our goal at Ford is to lead the industry in the applications of aerodynamics." The last part of his statement is crucial. Ford probably hadn't been a style-setter since the original Mustang of the '60s. In fact, its cars had acquired a downright stodgy image in recent years. As young Edsel Ford, a product planner and great-grandson of the company founder, told *Time* magazine: "People thought we built boring cars." Now as we all know, most people don't buy cars that look boring, all other things being equal. And Ford Motor Company's steady decline in market share between 1978 and 1982 must have started some executives wondering whether the firm's "baroque" styling might not be at least partly responsible. On the other hand, "aerodynamics" sounds like science, even if it's also partly an art, and an association with "high tech" certainly wouldn't do any harm to Ford's corporate image. At this writing, it's too early to

A very late rendering for the 1983 Thunderbird program. Production car did not have such a pronounced wedge profile.

tell whether the firm's "new look" will be widely enough accepted to have a big impact on sales. But it is encouraging to note that Ford has again charted a design course of its own after years of mostly aping GM.

Design development for the '83 Thunderbird and the companion Mercury Cougar involved more than 500 hours of wind tunnel tests using 3/8-scale and full-size clay models. This work, begun in early 1979, eventually led to more than 850 individual body changes. The end result was sleek, even daring: far more distinctive than the square-cut Chrysler Cordoba/Dodge Mirada and more contemporary than GM's mid-size coupes like the Olds Cutlass Supreme and Buick Regal, which had been given an "aerodynamic" facelift a couple years earlier.

Both Thunderbird and Cougar shared roughly the same styling below the beltline, with rounded contours and a minimum of trim and sculpturing. In plan view, the nose on both cars was tapered markedly toward the front to reduce frontal area, a key factor in reducing air drag. A "fast" 60-degree windshield angle was adopted for the same reason, the steepest slope ever used on a production Ford. However, there was a big difference at the rear. Cougar went with a "formal" roof treatment featuring a near-vertical backlight and a curiously upswept rear side window line that seemed to clash with its lower body. The Thunderbird's roof had a more rounded backlight and a smoother window-to-deck transition that made the whole car look more integrated to many critics. Interestingly, early sales figures indicated Cougar's approach was preferred in the more conservative midwest, while T-Bird's was favored on both coasts. Wind tunnel results definitely favored the Ford, which recorded an impressively low 0.35 coefficient of drag (Cd) as measured at the Lockheed facility in Georgia. By comparison, the Mercury's 0.40 Cd didn't look so hot, and was undoubtedly a penalty of its roof styling. But that didn't matter to the product planners. Let Cougar appeal to traditional mid-size coupe buyers; Thunderbird would be aimed at trendier, more *avant-garde* types.

Underneath the sleek new body, much was familiar. Thunderbird continued to employ unit construction for what Ford now called its "S-shell," one of several body/ chassis derivatives of the original rear-drive "Fox" platform introduced with the 1978 Fairmont/Zephyr. However, the '83 was detectably smaller. Notable were a 4.4-inch cut in wheelbase (to 104.0 inches), a 2.8-inch chop in overall length (now 197.6 inches), and 3.0 inches less width (to 71.1 overall). Overall proportions were much as before, but rear overhang was reduced, which meant about three cubic feet less trunk space. The tradeoff was a slight improvement in turning diameter. Despite the exterior shrinkage, the '83 T-Bird had about the same

'83 T-Bird shape was refined in 500 wind tunnel test hours.

The top-line Thunderbird Heritage for 1983. Price: $12,228.

Sensational new Thunderbird Turbo Coupe went on sale in early 1983 as the first four-cylinder T-Bird in history.

The editors' test Thunderbird was equipped with 5.0-liter V-8.

T-Bird Turbo Coupe's initial base price was $11,790.

amount of interior space as its 1980-82 predecessor, except for 1.2 inches less rear legroom.

Chassis design also remained familiar. There was the expected modified MacPherson-strut arrangement in front with coil springs and anti-roll bar, four-link/coil-spring rear suspension with live axle, standard power-assisted rack-and-pinion steering, and power front-disc/rear-drum brake system. One new wrinkle was introduction of standard nitrogen-pressurized shock absorbers of the sort first used by Ford on the "bustleback" 1982 Lincoln Continental sedan. These were claimed to improve handling response with no penalty in ride comfort.

There were a couple of surprises on the 1983 Thunderbird's model and engine charts. The previous Town Landau was dropped in favor of an equally well-equipped base model. The Heritage returned as the most expensive offering, with such standard amenities as power windows, tinted glass, electronic instrumentation, plush velour upholstery, and illuminated keyless entry system. The standard powertrain for this pair was the 3.8-liter "Essex" V-6 with 3-speed Select-Shift transmission. Optional was a new version of Ford's venerable small-block 302 V-8, now with "central" or throttle-body-type electronic fuel

injection. The V-8 was available only with the corporate 4-speed overdrive automatic, which was an extra-cost item for V-6 customers. But the real surprise was the new Turbo Coupe, which went on sale at mid-model year. This sportiest T-Bird since the last of the two-seaters was also the first ever powered by a four-cylinder engine. With its specially uprated chassis, mandatory 5-speed manual transmission, and multi-adjustable bucket seats, the Turbo Coupe made even jaded car enthusiasts sit up and take notice.

The Turbo Coupe engine was actually a reengineered version of the blown 2.3-liter ohc four last offered for '81 in the Mustang and Mercury Capri, and was also available as an option for those cars this year. Major mechanical changes involved junking the carburetor in favor of Bosch electronic port fuel injection and repositioning the turbocharger upstream of the induction system to "blow through" it rather than "draw down" from it. Ford's latest electronic engine control system, EEC-IV, took care of many functions, including injector timing, idle speed, wastegate operation, supplementary fuel enrichment, engine idle, and emissions control. Other engine changes included forged-aluminum pistons, valves made of a special temperature-resistant alloy, lighter-weight flywheel, die-cast aluminum rocker cover, and an engine-mounted oil cooler. As customary with turbocharged engines, compression ratio was knocked down from the unblown four's 9.0:1 to 8.0:1, and premium unleaded fuel was recommended for best performance. The result of all this was a healthy 145 bhp at 4600 rpm—better than the magic "1 horsepower per cubic inch" ideal. Peak torque of 180 lbs/ft was produced at a relatively low 3600 rpm.

For the kind of road manners enthusiasts would demand, Ford developed a Special Handling Package for the Turbo Coupe. Also available optionally on other models, it consisted of P205/70HR-14 Goodyear Eagle HR performance radials on distinctive aluminum wheels, plus firmer springs and shocks all-round. Unique to the Turbo Coupe was an extra pair of shock-absorber-like dampers for the rear suspension, mounted horizontally to resist axle patter on bumps and axle tramp in hard acceleration. Traction-Lok limited-slip differential pulling a 3.45:1 final drive was also standard. External Turbo Coupe identification was provided by black-finish headlamp surrounds and greenhouse moldings and a pair of fog lamps recessed into the under-bumper front valence panel. Inside were comfortable Lear-Siegler bucket seats with sphygmomanometer-type inflatable lumbar support, adjustable thigh support and side bolsters, reclining backrests, and open-mesh head restraints. Unfortunately, the Turbo Coupe instrument panel was more like that of lesser Birds and not ideal for an enthusiast's machine, though a tachometer and turbocharger "on-boost" and "overboost" warning lights were provided.

Announced at a base price of slightly under $12,000, the Turbo Coupe was roundly applauded by the "buff books." *Road & Track* magazine's review was typical: The Turbo Coupe has excellent road manners...you could close your eyes and think you're in Germany—in a German car...To say this is the best Thunderbird in years is a dramatic understatement. The Turbo Coupe's handling and responsiveness are right up there with the best of its class." David E. Davis, publisher of *Car and Driver,* chimed in: "I love cars that let you feel the tires working, and the Thunderbird Turbo Coupe is exactly that kind of car. The feeling you get as you bend it into a fast corner is absolutely delicious. It is the best Thunderbird in that nameplate's quarter-century of ups and downs..."

Though less inclined to concur with rave reviews, CONSUMER GUIDE® magazine's critics also liked the Turbo Coupe, though we did find a few faults. The main ones were undue engine harshness at high rpm, an irritatingly narrow power band, an ill-placed shifter, power steering with excessive boost for this sort of machine, and that unhappily incomplete instrumentation. In fairness, many of our colleagues echoed our criticisms. We also wondered about the turbo engine's long-term reliability—especially in the hands of a hard-charging owner—and doubted the car's sales prospects when similar performance was available in the proven V-8 (albeit at the price of extra front-end weight that upset handling agility). Still, there was no doubting the Turbo Coupe's performance: 0-60 mph in just 9.6 seconds in our test. And, we scored an honest 23.3 mpg in very demanding city/suburban driving. For a

large, posh, emissions-controlled coupe weighing almost 1.5 tons, this sporty new Bird had to rate as an amazingly good balance between performance and economy.

In an age when many Americans think only the Japanese make durable goods, it's nice to report that the '83 Thunderbird proves them wrong. One of the more pleasant aspects of the several cars sampled so far by CONSUMER GUIDE® magazine's test team has been uniformly excellent quality control. Bodies are tight and rattle-free, panels are properly aligned, interior assembly is neat and tidy and with good-looking, apparently sturdy materials. Even paint finish, once a nightmare of many Detroit cars, stands comparison with the best in the world. We know. By chance, our test Turbo Coupe arrived at about the time we were evaluating a Mercedes-Benz 380SL—and there wasn't that much difference in exterior finish. Considering the Turbo Coupe sells for about a fourth what the SL does, this has to be heartening news. Evidently, Ford is serious when it says "Quality is Job 1."

Of course, there was more to the '83 line than the impressive new Thunderbird. The sporty Mustang was treated to its first major appearance change since 1979, and a convertible body style returned to the fold after a 10-year absence. All models now wore a sloped, slightly vee'd horizontal-bar grille bearing the proud Ford oval, and taillights were restyled. The new nose was good for a 2.5 percent reduction in aerodynamic drag—not much, but every little bit helps. The 4.2-liter V-8 was dropped from the engine roster, and Ford's 3.8-liter lightweight V-6 replaced the 200-cid straight six as the step-up power option. The standard powerplant remained the 2.3-liter

Ragtop Mustang emerged for '83 in GLX trim. Price: $12,467.

The hot 1983 Mustang GT 3-door with four-barrel H.O. V-8

four, now with a new one-barrel carburetor instead of a two-barrel, plus long-reach spark plugs for fast-burn combustion, a move aimed at reducing emissions while improving warmup and part-throttle engine response. Standard on manual-shift models was a new Volkswagen-like upshift indicator light. This signalled the driver when to shift to the next higher gear for economy, based on the fact that an engine is most efficient running at relatively low revs on wide throttle openings. Other changes included revised seat and door trims, a standard roller-blind cargo area cover for hatchbacks, easier-to-read gauge graphics, and less interior brightwork. A new extra-cost sport seat with mesh-insert headrests replaced the previously optional Recaro buckets, which hadn't sold well. Again reflecting Ford's emphasis on aerodynamics, the liftgate louvers and rear window wiper for hatchbacks and the Carriage Roof for notchbacks were all scratched from the options sheet.

During 1982, Mustang had been overshadowed—both in the press and on the street—by the third-generation Chevrolet Camaro and Pontiac Firebird. Though the GM cars couldn't outperform the H.O. V-8 Mustang, they could outcorner it, and their sexy styling simply wowed the public. Of course, Mustang was at something of a disadvantage in such showdowns. It was an older design and based on a humble family-car chassis to boot, while Camaro/Firebird was brand-new and shared little with other GM cars. Even so, Ford wasn't making excuses, and instituted a raft of refinements to give the '83 Mustang better cornering power and more go-power.

First, the handling suspension, standard on the top-line GT variant, was revised from the tires up as a new 220mm Michelin TRX with broad 55-percent aspect ratio was offered optionally. Also, there was a slightly thicker rear anti-roll bar, softer rear spring rates, stiffer bushings for the front control arms, and revised shock valving, plus higher-effort power steering. Next came even more horsepower for the H.O. 5.0-liter V-8, up from 157 bhp to a full 175 bhp at 4000 rpm. The main change was substitution of a four-barrel carb for the previous two-barrel, but Ford also tossed in an aluminum intake manifold, high-flow air cleaner, enlarged exhaust passages, and a modified valvetrain. To answer complaints about the wide gap between 2nd and 3rd on the '82 car's wide-ratio 4-speed transmission, Borg-Warner's new T-5 close-ratio 5-speed gearbox, the same one used in the T-Bird Turbo Coupe, was made available at extra-cost. And for good measure, Ford specified a shorter 3.27:1 final drive for the 5-speed versus the 4-speed's 3.08:1 gearing. The *coup de gras* was one GM couldn't match. Of course, it was the revitalized 2.3-liter turbo-four, returning as a late-season option. It was tuned as for the Turbo Coupe, and came only with 5-speed. Unfortunately, the blown engine couldn't be combined with air conditioning in the Mustang.

Undoubtedly, the most glamorous '83 Mustang was the new convertible, offered only in top-line GLX trim. Since the late '70s, a number of small companies had been doing good business snipping the tops from Mustang notchbacks (and other cars) to satisfy a small but steady demand for top-down motoring. Ford apparently decided it was time to get in on the action, too.

The little-changed '83 Escort GL wagon. Price was now $6779.

Escort GT was upgraded for '83 with fuel injection, 5-speed.

Offered only as a 3-door, 1983 Escort GT listed at $7339.

Unlike the Buick Riviera and Chrysler LeBaron ragtops announced at about the same time, the Mustang was a regular assembly line model, the first factory-built convertible from Dearborn since the last soft-top Mustang of 1973. Interior trim and top installation was carried out by a contractor, Cars & Concepts of Brighton, Michigan, but Ford built the rest of it. Unlike the aftermarket conversions, the '83 Mustang convertible featured roll-down rear side windows and a rear window made of tempered glass. It was available with any drivetrain (except the base four-cylinder and automatic combination), including the four-barrel H.O. V-8. It added another dash of excitement to an already impressive Mustang lineup.

The mid-size Granada gained new aero-look sheetmetal and was renamed LTD for '83. Shown is the Brougham 4-door sedan.

1983 LTD wagon carried a suggested retail price of $8577

1983 LTD 4-door featured higher "bustle" tail, sloped front.

EXP coupe was available with new 5-speed and fuel-injected four from the '83 Escort. Standard power was the H.O. 1.6.

This year's Escort and its EXP coupe cousin also gained an extra dash of excitement. The sporty GT version of the Escort 3-door was revised to more closely approximate the handling, performance, and appearance of the European XR3 model. Changes included a newly developed port fuel injection system with electronic control for the 1.6-liter "CVH" four, teamed with a new 5-speed overdrive manual transaxle pulling a shorter 3.73:1 final drive for faster pickup. Appearance was slicked up with front and rear spoilers, under-bumper fog lamps, a different taillight design, and "spats" around the wheel openings. The chassis was also tweaked, the GT receiving its own specifically tuned suspension with Michelin TRX radial tires. Inside were standard full instrumentation with special graphics, floor console, and new sport bucket seats with cloth upholstery and mesh-type headrests. It was quite a zippy little package, and attractively priced at $7339. The new 5-speed and electronic fuel injection were optional for other Escorts as well as EXP. The EFI engine packed 88 horsepower at 5400 rpm, compared to 80 bhp for the high-output four (still available) and only 72 for the standard-tune engine.

Other changes to Ford's front-drivers were mostly minor ones. The base Escort series was dropped, leaving L models as the low-end offerings. As with Mustang, an upshift indicator light was made standard on all cars with manual transmission, alerting the driver when to change gears for greater fuel economy. Larger fuel tanks and all-

Full-size 1983 Ford line was trimmed to just one series. Here is the 4-door Crown Victoria. Note new eggcrate grille.

season radial tires were adopted across the board, and heater fans got a fourth speed. A locking fuel filler flap with inside release was a new standard item for all but L models.

Escort would lose its rank as the nation's best-seller this year, mainly due to a steady decline in gasoline prices that led many buyers back to intermediates and full-size cars. However, it continued to do well, remaining the most popular of the domestic small cars. EXP, though, continued to languish on the sales charts.

As it had done once before in the '70s, Ford applied the LTD nameplate to a second model line for '83. This was essentially a Fairmont reskinned from the waist down in Ford's new aero-look sheetmetal. It took over for the similarly derived Granada as Ford's mid-size contender.

There were no major mechanical changes to this latest version of the sturdy "Fox" platform except for gas-pressurized front struts and rear shock absorbers, as on the 1983 Thunderbird. Body style offerings comprised 4-door sedan and 5-door wagon, both with more sloped hoods and slightly raked grilles. Engine choices comprised standard 2.3-liter "Lima" four, with the venerable 200-cid six and 3.8-liter "Essex" V-6 optional. Also new and available on a limited basis was a propane-fuel version of the four, intended mainly for high-mileage fleet users. New to the compact/mid-size line was availability of the corporate 4-speed overdrive automatic.

The full-size Fords were little changed this year. To distinguish them from the new "downsized" LTD, sedans were renamed LTD Crown Victoria and the wagon be-

Fairmont was a virtual carryover for '83, was dropped at mid-year. Shown: Futura coupe (left) and sedan (right).

came LTD Country Squire. This also eliminated the previous "S" and standard models. Except for a more open eggcrate grille, there were no appearance changes. The one drivetrain now offered was the new fuel-injected 5.0-liter V-8 teamed with 4-speed overdrive automatic.

And what of the trusty Fairmont? It was a carryover in most respects and for a very good reason: Ford was ready to introduce a smaller front-drive replacement in early 1983. This was the new Tempo, designated an '84 model (and described in the next section). Though it would be gone quickly, Fairmont would not be quickly forgotten, and much of its basic engineering continues.

1984

Turbos, Tempo, and SVO: America watches the newest Fords go by

Once again, Ford jumped the gun on a new model year by announcing the first of its '84s in May 1983. This was the new front-wheel-drive Tempo, successor to the aging rear-drive Fairmont. It was an important product for the division—its first front-drive entry in the high-volume family-compact market then dominated by GM's X-car quartet (such as Buick Skylark and Chevrolet Citation) and Chrysler's popular K-car twins (Dodge Aries and Plymouth Reliant). The mission for Tempo was simple if difficult: win back sales lost to these competitors while further polishing Ford's new image as a builder of modern, high-technology cars with advanced "aerodynamic" styling.

Tempo emerged as one of the few recent American cars that honestly deserved the label "all new." Indeed, Ford went to great pains to impress on auto writers the fact that this was *not* simply a puffed-up Escort. Work on the new compact was initiated in late 1979 as the "Topaz" project (unusually, that name survived for Mercury's version of the car). The goal was to develop a larger running mate for Escort, incorporating some of that car's design principles but not necessarily its hardware. Unlike the Erika program that produced the transatlantic Escort design, Topaz was strictly an American effort. The idea was to utilize the packaging benefits of front-wheel drive to preserve the Fairmont's interior space within a smaller, lighter, more economical car. This meant the new model would have to have its own purpose-designed engine as it would likely be underpowered with the 1.6-liter Escort unit. And, it must embody all Ford had learned about aerodynamic styling, not only for distinctive appearance but also for enhanced fuel economy and reduced wind noise. Of course, the division would hedge its marketing bets by effectively continuing the Fairmont in its plusher, restyled LTD form introduced for '83.

Once again, Ford designers went to the wind tunnel, spending more than 450 hours testing scale and full-size clay models, which led to more than 950 separate design changes. Interestingly, the aerodynamic work was started a full year before Topaz got management's formal go-ahead, and continued until quite late in the game, March 1981. Another round of tests was conducted with production-approved prototypes during 1982. Only two body styles were planned, 2- and 4-door sedans. Both would be notchbacks to clearly separate the newcomers from the hatchback Escort. A wagon was deemed unnecessary, which is strange considering the popularity of the K-car wagons, the only such models among the domestic compacts. Ford product planners evidently felt the Escort and LTD wagons catered adequately to those buyers looking for a smaller hauler.

Tempo's styling was definitely from the new Ford mold: chunky and rounded, with a shortish, sloped nose and an abbreviated bustle tail. The look was fresh, contemporary, and pleasingly different from the boxy lines of GM and Chrysler compacts. Its most eye-catching elements were a three-slat horizontal-bar grille done in body-color plastic, large wraparound parking lights that formed the front fender leading edges, a 60-degree windshield angle (as on the latest T-Bird), and a bodyside character line running just below belt level and slightly upswept at the rear. Rooflines differed markedly. The 4-door featured the "six-light" greenhouse so favored in Europe, with rounded-off window corners and thick, sturdy-looking door frames. Small vertical panes in the C-pillars eliminated a potential blind spot. The 2-door also had rather heavy A- and C-posts, but long rear side windows gave it an altogether lighter, sportier air, more coupe than sedan. Both bodies sported "aircraft" door openings cut up into the roof slightly. This made for easier entry/exit, and also provided a way to conceal the roof drip rails to smooth airflow over the body.

Ford's wind tunnel work paid off handsomely. The Tempo's Cd (coefficient of drag) figures worked out to just 0.36 for the 2-door and 0.37 for the 4-door. By comparison, the slick new T-Bird came in at 0.35, and the vaunted Mercedes-Benz 380SEL claimed only 0.36. Since achieving low Cd is much more difficult on a shorter car like Tempo, its aerodynamic efficiency is even more impressive than the bald numbers suggest.

Dimensionally, Tempo fell about halfway between Escort and the old Fairmont. Its 99.9-inch wheelbase and 176.2-inch overall length were 5.5 and a whopping 20 inches under Fairmont's. The new car also weighed in a significant 400 pounds lighter. With this size and weight, Tempo was very close to Chrysler's 99.6-inch-wheelbase K-car models. Compared to GM's X-body cars, Tempo offered similar interior space despite its 4-inch shorter wheelbase.

The Tempo chassis was bang up to date. Front suspension was by MacPherson struts, with the coil springs concentric with the struts as on Escort instead of mounted on a separate lower arm as on Fairmont. An anti-roll bar was standard, and steering was by the Escort's basic rack-and-pinion mechanism. Unlike its competitors, which used a beam rear axle, Tempo's rear suspension was fully independent. Called "Quadrilink," its geometry was similar to Escort's, but instead of a single lower lateral arm pivoted at the center, there were twin thin rods

Front-drive Tempo appeared in May 1983 as Ford's first '84s. Pictured are the GLX 4-door (foreground) and 2-door sedans.

The editors' Tempo GL 4-door test car. Prices on both Tempo body styles were identical. GL models cost $6256 basic.

mounted laterally either side of each hub carrier. The carriers, in turn, were acted on by vertical shock/strut units with concentric coil springs, and were connected to tie-rods running forward to the chassis rails. Thus, Tempo followed certain Hondas and Datsuns by having Mac-Pherson struts at all four corners. Brakes were front discs and rear drums with standard power assist. Tires were a new all-season radial design in a P175/80R-13 size.

Under the Tempo hood was an interesting new four-cylinder engine, the first of what Ford said was a whole family of "fast burn" powerplants. Though its displacement was roughly the same as that of the overhead-cam 2.3-liter "Lima" four, this new engine was quite different. It was, in fact, a heavily reengineered version of the firm's familiar overhead-valve 200-cid six, with the same 3.68-inch bore, a longer 3.30-inch stroke, and two fewer cylinders. Called the 2300 HSC (for High Swirl Combustion), it featured a redesigned cylinder head with wedge-shaped combustion chambers and shrouds around the intake valves designed to speed up or "swirl" the incoming air/fuel mixture for faster, more complete burning. Ford claimed this promoted lower emissions levels and provided more torque at low rpm. The latter was a key consideration

in handling the optional automatic transmission that Ford expected most Tempo buyers to order. Engine auxiliary components were carefully placed to keep the entire drivetrain as compact as possible, and the intake manifold, water pump, and front cover were all made of aluminum to hold down weight. On a fairly high 9.0:1 compression ratio, the two-barrel HSC produced 85 bhp at 4400 rpm and 125 lbs/ft of torque at a low 2400 rpm.

Initially, the standard Tempo drivetrain comprised the 2300 HSC teamed with either a wide-ratio 4-speed overdrive manual or a closer-ratio 5-speed overdrive transaxle. The former was part of a special Fuel Saver package of the sort offered on Escort, but it was not available with air conditioning, so most manual-shift cars had the 5-speed. As with Escort, both manual transaxles were supplied by Toyo Kogyo (Mazda) of Japan. Optional at extra-cost was an American-made 3-speed automatic (ATX) similar in principle to Escort's.

At the start of the formal model year, a 2.0-liter four-cylinder diesel, also built by TK, became optionally available for Tempo, but only with 5-speed. Ford stressed this power unit had been designed as a diesel, and was not simply a converted gas engine. Features included a belt-driven overhead camshaft, aluminum cylinder head, altitude-compensated fuel injection pump, and swirl-type combustion chambers. Bore and stroke dimensions were exactly square (3.39 × 3.39). Besides the by-now customary quick-start glow plugs, this diesel also had what was termed an "after glow" feature. This kept the plugs lit even after the engine was running to burn off excess hydrocarbons and particulates visible as "white smoke."

Ford had long since mastered the art of merchandising-with-options but, except for the basic L versions, Tempo was quite well-equipped. The upper GL and GLX models boasted such standards as full carpeting, padded door panels with armrests, intermittent windshield wipers, luxury wheel covers, sound insulation package, and individual front seats with reclining backrests. Of course, if you wanted more, Ford was ready to accommodate you: electronic radios, extra gauges, fingertip Speed Control, air conditioning, power windows, a longer center console, and tilt steering wheel.

With its handy size, rakish looks, and 5-speed gearbox, the Tempo 2-door would have made a dandy sports coupe. Ford lent credence to the idea by offering a special TR Handling Package for all models, replete with the special Michelin tires, metric-size cast-aluminum wheels, and uprated steering and suspension pieces. But though this did wonders for the car's transient response, Tempo just wasn't cut out to be an enthusiast's car. Even with 5-speed, CONSUMER GUIDE® magazine's test 2-door needed about 14 seconds in 0-60 mph acceleration—adequate but hardly exciting. Also, you couldn't get a tachometer at any price, the shift linkage was problematic at times, and the suspension remained a bit soft even with the TR treatment or the optional heavy-duty setup. But perhaps we're being premature in our criticism. Ford may yet offer Tempo with the sort of equipment that would make it a serious driver's car.

Until then, we'll have to content ourselves with what it is: a competent, well-made family compact. Our test staff especially liked the Tempo's roomy interior, its comfortable seats both front and rear, the low noise levels, the ease of getting in or out (you don't need to be a contortionist even in the 2-door), and the exceptionally well-laid-out engine installation. Workmanship also earned high marks: rattle-free body construction, lustrous paint, high-grade interior finish and materials. In fact, about the only thing that might hamper the Tempo's success is buyer resistance to its unusual new styling. At this writing, the jury has yet to render a verdict on that, but we think that the more people become accustomed to this look the more they'll like it. Certainly, more and more automakers will be moving to aerodynamically shaped design in the years ahead, as the slick new Audi 5000 so graphically predicts. Ford fans can take pride in the fact that Dearborn is helping to blaze this new trail.

Tempo may not have been intended to delight enthusiasts but several other 1984 Fords definitely were. The most striking of this year's performance models was the long-rumored Mustang SVO, a new limited edition based on the turbocharged four-cylinder Mustang hatchback. Developed by (and named for) Ford's Special Vehicle Operations section, it incorporated a lengthy list of modifications that read like a hop-up artist's wishbook. The most notable were addition of an air-to-air intercooler to the production 2.3-liter turbo-four plus the first-ever use of electronic control to vary the amount of boost delivered, which can range up to 14 psi, the highest on any production turbo engine. These and other changes result in a claimed 20 percent gain in horsepower and a 10 percent increase in maximum torque. Though exact ratings were not available at this writing, we'd estimate the SVO's engine output in the region of 174 bhp and close to 200 lbs/ft of torque. Other mechanical features included a cockpit fuel selector switch that "tuned" the engine's electronic control system to the grade of fuel being used and the use of special engine dampers to resist drivetrain rocking in hard power applications.

Putting the power to the ground was handled by a 5-speed manual gearbox with special Hurst linkage and standard Traction-Lok limited-slip differential with 3.45:1 final drive ratio.

Chassis revisions were equally thorough. In place of the stock 9.0-inch rear drum brakes, the SVO had beefy 11.25-inch-diameter discs working in concert with front discs enlarged from 10.06 to 10.92 inches. Standard tires were European-made Goodyear NCT high-speed (V-rated) radials on fat 16 × 7-inch cast-aluminum wheels. (Later production cars were slated to wear P225/50VR-16 Goodyear Eagle GT50s with "directional" or "gatorback" tread as specified for the 1984 Corvette.) Spring rates and bushings were stiffened at all corners, and Koni adjustable shocks replaced the stock dampers. Front anti-roll bar thickness was increased from .94 to 1.20 inches, and the SVO also got a rear bar, plus an extra inch of vertical front wheel travel. The Mustang's power rack-and-pinion steering was retained, but with a quicker constant ratio instead of variable-ratio and less power assist for better road feel.

Setting the SVO apart from lesser Mustangs were its distinctive "bi-plane" rear spoiler, made of polycarbonate plastic, special "grilleless" nose styled in manner of the European Ford Sierra XR4i, and a large, functional hood scoop feeding the turbo intercooler. Larger dual square headlamps were used in place of the normal Mustang's smaller quads. A wide air intake slot sat above the front bumper, and the deep front air dam incorporated standard foglamps. Small "spats" or fairings were fitted at the leading edges of the rear wheel openings to smooth airflow around the fatter tires.

Inside, the SVO sported such driver-oriented accoutrements as a rest for the clutch foot, repositioned brake and accelerator pedals for easier heel-and-toe shifting, 8000-rpm tachometer, turbo boost gauge, plus multi-adjustable performance seats similar to those of the T-Bird Turbo Coupe. Several Mustang extras were standard for the new premium model: rear-window defroster, tinted glass, AM/FM stereo radio with speaker/amplifier system, leather-wrapped steering wheel with tilt-adjustable column, and center console with graphic warning light display. Only six major options were listed: air conditioning, power windows, cassette player, flip-up glass sunroof panel, and leather upholstery.

This formidable new Mustang is perhaps the closest

Grilleless nose, large hood duct marked 1984 Mustang SVO.

"Bi-plane" spoiler identified Mustang SVO's rear aspect.

1984 Mustang SVO packed around 175 bhp from 140-cid four.

Mustang SVO's deep air dam, rear wheel spats are seen here.

thing yet seen from America to a true high-performance grand touring machine in the European tradition. During brief drives around the handling course at Ford's Dearborn Proving Grounds, we found the SVO the best-balanced Mustang ever, with near-neutral cornering response under almost any conditions, and very quick reflexes. The SVO's steering has much better feel than that of recent Mustang GTs we've tried, and demands effort more appropriate to a high-speed flyer than any Ford power system in recent memory. Cornering is flat and undramatic—as indeed is braking behavior—and the fat NCTs grip the pavement with assurance. Engine performance is satisfying. Although we weren't able to make timed runs, the two prototype SVOs we drove felt slightly faster than the '83 T-Bird Turbo Coupe—which is as it should be for this lighter, smaller car. Ford claims a 0-60 mph time of less than 7.5 seconds, the quarter-mile in 15.3 seconds at 90 mph, and a top speed of 134 mph—all of which we think quite realistic. Despite amazing power and torque output for its size, the intercooler-equipped turbo-four isn't unduly peaky, and it exhibits good low-rpm flexibility for those times when you want to cool it on the loud pedal to conserve gas. Speaking of which, the SVO's projected fuel economy ratings are the kind we used to associate only with the most sedate compacts: 21 mpg city and 32 mpg highway. Combine all this with the Mustang hatchback's practicality and price expected to be well under $15,000 and you've got a potential world-beater from the heart of the good ol' U.S.A. We predict enthusiasts will quickly use the SVO initials to signify "Simply Vanquishes Opponents."

Another hot tip for '84 was a new turbocharged edition of the 1.6-liter "CVH" four as an option for Ford's smaller front-drive cars. Like its 2.3-liter brother, this unit featured a blow-through turbocharger system and electronic fuel injection with separate squirters for each cylinder. The high-lift cam from the H.O. version of the 1.6 was used, along with Ford's EEC-IV electronic engine controls to govern injector and spark timing, exhaust-gas recirculation, and the throttle-actuated shut-off switch for the air conditioning compressor, among many functions. The turbo wastegate was integral with a new split or bifurcated low-restriction exhaust manifold, and a high-flow air cleaner was fitted to satisfy the turbo's greater oxygen demands. With maximum boost of 8 psi, the new little blower engine delivered up to 35 percent more peak power than its normally aspirated counterparts—or about 1.2 bhp per cubic inch.

This engine formed the heart of a new turbo package option for the 2-seat EXP, and would also be offered at mid-year for the 3-door Escort/Lynx as the Turbo GT/RS. On EXP, the turbo engine was matched to an uprated suspension with standard Koni shock absorbers and higher-rated front springs. Front ride height was lowered by .75-inch to reduce half-shaft angles as a means to counter-act torque-steer tendencies. The package also included P185/65R-365 Michelin TRX tires on newly styled cast-aluminum wheels, 5-speed manual transaxle (automatic was *verboten*), front air dam, "teatray" rear spoiler, and black lower bodyside paint with bold "turbo" lettering.

All EXPs now adopted the taillamps and distinctive

"bubbleback" hatch of the now-discontinued Mercury LN7, and the base engine was now the normally aspirated H.O. unit, available with standard 5-speed manual or optional 3-speed automatic. Other changes included a redesigned instrument panel, standard roof-mounted console with map lights and digital electronic clock/stopwatch, and fold-down center armrest. A new interlock system was adopted so that the engine couldn't be started without first depressing the clutch—thus eliminating a potential source of embarrassment. New EXP options included all-electronic radios, graphic equalizer, and tilt steering wheel.

Several laps around the Dearborn Proving Grounds handling course revealed that the turbo engine is exactly what the EXP needed. In fact, Ford admitted as much in its press kit, saying the car had evolved "from a mild-mannered, fun-to-drive two-seater to a bona fide, high-performance car." We're not that sure about the "high-performance" part, mainly because time and circumstance prevented us from clocking the car. Still, the EXP Turbo has plenty of snap, the kind of power a skillful driver can use—but never had before—to exploit the handling potential of the chassis. Now Ford's two-seater is a *much* more entertaining machine. The pressurized CVH is a bit on the peaky side, but its power delivery is smooth and there's just enough of that rewarding "shove in the back" as the turbo comes on to let you know something energetic is going on up front. In short, the turbo engine simply transforms the character of what used to be an "all brag and no action" car.

Some things remain to be done, though: the assisted steering is still too light for our tastes, exhaust noise is as high—and irritating—as ever, and we'd still prefer a less "bathtub" driving position. Nevertheless, the turbo-powered EXP represents real progress for Ford's little sportster, which should gain a new lease on life from its newfound muscle.

Besides the all-new Tempo, Mustang SVO, and Turbo EXP, Ford had other noteworthy developments for 1984. Let's begin with the popular Escort. All models received the basic redesigned instrument panel of this year's EXP, plus many of that car's new options (including, as mentioned, the turbocharged engine). Also newly available was the Tempo's 2.0-liter diesel engine, again only with 5-speed manual. Replacing the three top-line GLX models were a new LX 5-door sedan and wagon, with standard fuel-injected engine, 5-speed transaxle, TR suspension package, and blackout exterior trim. Inside were luxury cloth upholstery, floor console, overhead console with digital clock/stopwatch, and full instrumentation including tachometer. The rear seatbacks on all Escorts got a redesigned two-stage folding mechanism to replace the simple flop-down arrangement previously used, so the resulting cargo deck would be flatter. Another change was adoption of a split rear seat backrest as standard for all except the basic L models. Power door locks, tilt steering wheel, and electronically tuned radios joined the options list for the first time.

Compared to the new SVO model, changes for other '84 Mustangs were minor. A base-trim hatchback joined the existing 2-door at the bottom of the heap, the former GL

Little changed outside, 1984 Escort GT boasted new interior.

Big news for the '84 EXP was availability of turbo engine.

EXP Turbo package also included special suspension and trim.

and GLX offerings were combined into a new LX series, and the fun-loving convertible was now available with GT equipment as well as the new LX trim, bringing the ragtop total to three. Interior changes for all models included red instrument lighting, longer (7.1 inches) front seat tracks, new steering wheels, horn buttons relocated from a steering column stalk to the wheel hub, standard cloth upholstery, and split-back rear seat for all 3-doors except the base version. Automatic transmission was extended to the H.O. 5.0-liter V-8 for the first time, in which case you also got electronic fuel injection. Ford's "central" or throttle-body EFI was also applied to the mid-

Aerodynamics showcase: Probe IV boasted ultra-low 0.15 drag coefficient. Front wheel skirts flex for turning.

range 3.8-liter "Essex" V-6 option, now available only with Select Shift. GT models with the port-injected turbo-four were appropriately renamed Turbo GT. And as with the EXP and Escort, a clutch/starter interlock was now standard with manual transmission.

Thunderbird was brand-new for '83, but there were a few embellishments for the encore '84 edition. These included a self-propping counterbalanced hood, a Tempo-style "A-frame" steering wheel with hub-mounted horn hooter (except on Turbo Coupe), and amber instead of clear lenses for the parking lamps. Powerteam revisions comprised electronic fuel injection for the base "Essex" V-6 (thus eliminating carbureted T-Birds), availability of 3-speed automatic with that engine nationwide, and optional availability of 3-speed automatic for the Turbo Coupe. The Heritage name was discarded for the top-trim offering in favor of elan (Ford's spelling). A new "designer" model was the Fila, named after the Italian sportswear manufacturer. It was distinguished by two-tone pastel charcoal/dark charcoal paint, red and blue pinstripes, and grey, suede-like cloth upholstery. New for the Turbo Coupe only were viscous-clutch drive for radiator fan and an oil-temperature warning switch.

The full-size Crown Victoria and Country Squire continued virtually without change except for addition of a wagon without the Squire's woody-look side trim. Big-car sales were enjoying what would probably be a temporary resurgence, as buyers took advantage of the then-current drop in fuel prices to enjoy what they feared would be the last full-size cars from Detroit. By now, of course, Ford had long since written off the tooling costs for its big models, and as long as they continued to sell there was no reason to change them. Every one out the door represented almost pure profit—and a handsome one at that, which delighted cash-starved dealers no end.

The mid-size LTD had enjoyed a good reception in its debut year, and predictably there was more of the same

for '84. After more than 20 years, the faithful 200-cid six was retired. This left the standard 2.3-liter "Lima" four or optional 3.8-liter V-6 in its new fuel-injected form as the only engine choices. Also, manual transmission was deleted with the base four. The interesting propane-fuel engine also returned, still on a limited basis. All models wore amber parking light lenses instead of clear ones and received standard power steering. Horn buttons were relocated to the steering wheel hub as on most other '84 Fords. A return to the old styling days was a new standard cloth roof covering for the upscale Brougham sedan, with blind sail panels and a smaller "frenched" rear window. To get the Brougham model without the fancy top you had to order the base sedan with the Interior Luxury Group option, also available for the wagon. With the growing popularity of "talking cars," it was hardly a surprise when Ford introduced its new Voice Alert System as an LTD option this year. As with other similar devices, this one "spoke" to the driver in a synthesized voice to warn that "the key is in the ignition," "the headlights are on" and "the door is ajar".

With the 1984 model year we reach the end of the Ford story—at least for now. Of course, the story is still being written, and should continue to be for many years. As with other automakers, events of the recent past have not been kind to Ford. As *Time* magazine summed it up in July 1983: "Only two years ago, Ford seemed to be racing Chrysler to the bankruptcy courts . . . Suddenly, things are looking up, way up." They seem to be as we close this book, though the improvements in the national economy and Ford Motor Company's financial picture are small ones to be sure. While no one can predict the future with certainty, let us leave you with one thought: if the 1984 models are a forecast of things to come, we'll all be able to "watch the Fords go by" well past the company's centennial in 2003. And we can't think of anything nicer to look forward to than that.

Index

Index

Index